ALFRED P. SMYTH

Celtic Leinster

ALFRED P. SMYTH

Celtic Leinster

TOWARDS
AN HISTORICAL GEOGRAPHY
OF
EARLY IRISH CIVILIZATION
A.D. 500 – 1600

IRISH·ACADEMIC·PRESS

This book was designed by Jarlath Hayes
and printed in the Republic of Ireland
by Mount Salus Press Limited
for Irish Academic Press Limited,
Kill Lane, Blackrock, County Dublin.

The publication of this book has been made possible
by generous subventions from the following

The British Academy
Jesus College Oxford
The American Irish Foundation
Mr. Sean Galvin
The Bank of Ireland Ltd.

The maps in the Historical Atlas are based on maps of
the Ordnance Survey of Ireland with permission issued
under permit by the Ordnance Survey.

Contents

Page

Lists of illustrations   vi
Abbreviations   xvi
Preface   xiii
Introduction   1

I   History and Landscape: the Formation of
      the Leinster Kingdom   7
II   Geography and Tribal Genealogy   13
III   Reconstruction of the Dark Age Landscape   21
IV   Tribes and Dynasties of the Northern Region   41
V   Tribes and Dynasties of the North-Eastern Region   50
VI   Tribes and Dynasties of the Central and
      Southern Regions   59
VII   Tribes and Dynasties of the North-Western Region   68
VIII Geography and Inter-tribal Marriage   78
IX   Midland Ecology in a Golden Age   84
X   Lords of the Wilderness   101

      Appendix   118
      Notes   127
      Historical Atlas   139
          List of Map Plates in Historical Atlas   140
      Indexes   159
          Index to Historical Atlas: English-Irish   161
          Index to Historical Atlas: Irish-English   172
          General Index   183

List of illustrations

Colour Plates   *Page*

Frontispiece: Map of Leix and Offaly, *c.*
A.D. 1563 (British Library)   *viii-ix*
A. Map of the Barony of Idrone, Co. Carlow,
    c. A.D. 1662 (Trinity College Dublin)
    following page 67
B. Map of the Barony of Scarawalsh Co. Wexford,
    A.D. 1657 (P.R.O. Dublin) preceding page 68
C. The Festival of St Kevin at the Seven Churches,
    Glendalough, by Joseph Peacock, 1817
    (Ulster Museum) following page 69

Figure Plates

1   Dinn Ríg, Iron Age fortress, Co. Carlow
(author's drawing based on Hall's, *Ireland*, i, p. 413) 7
2   St Anne's, Bohernabreena, Co. Dublin
(author's drawing based on O'Hanlon, *Lives*,
v, p. 141)   11
3. Beginning of *Testament of Cahair Mór* in the
Book of Ballymote (author's drawing)   13
4   Detail of map of Leix and Offaly *c.* A.D.
1563 (author's drawing)   21
5   Map of the Barrow Valley in Co. Carlow
(Taylor and Skinner, p. 134)   24
6   Map of east Wicklow (Taylor and Skinner,
p. 141)   24
7   Fragments of High Cross at Old Kilcullen
(Ledwich, *Antiquities*, facing p. 385)   27
8   Clonmacnoise, Co. Offaly (O'Hanlon, *Lives*,
vi, p. 657)   29
9   Terryglass, Co. Tipperary (O'Hanlon, *Lives*,
v, p. 559)   33
10 Lorrha, Co. Tipperary (O'Hanlon, *Lives*,
iv, p. 151)   33
11 Map of Monaincha, Co. Tipperary (Ledwich,
Antiquities, facing p. 69)   37
12 Ruins at Monaincha, Co. Tipperary, (Ledwich,
Antiquities, facing p. 74)   37
13 Map of Tullamore and Daingean region in
Offaly (Taylor and Skinner, p. 85)   39
14 Round Tower and Castle, Kildare (*Dublin
Penny Journal*, 1834, p. 297)   41
15 Clondalkin Round Tower, Co. Dublin
(O'Hanlon, *Lives*, viii, p. 100)   43
16 Penannular brooches
    a. Co. Kildare (Coffey, *Guide to Celtic
    Antiquities*, p. 30)   43
    b. Kilmainham, Dublin (ibid., p. 28)   43
17 Cloncurry, Co. Kildare (O'Hanlon, *Lives*, ix,
p. 399)   45
18 Laraghbryan, Co. Kildare (O'Hanlon, *Lives*.
ix, p. 32)   45
19 Moone, Co. Kildare (O'Hanlon, *Lives*, vi,
p. 333)   47

20 Castledermot, Co. Kildare (O'Hanlon, *Lives*,
vi, p. 762)   47
21 Kileencormac, Co. Kildare (Shearman, *Loca
Patriciana*, 1879, frontispiece)   47
22 Old Kilcullen, Co. Kildare (*Dublin Penny
Journal*, 1836, p. 228)   48
23 Glendalough, Co. Wicklow (O'Hanlon, *Lives*,
ii, p. 452)   50
24 Reefert Church, Glendalough (Hall's *Ireland*,
ii, p. 228)   53
25 Stone lamp from Co. Wicklow (Coffey, *Guide
to Celtic Antiquities*, p. 76)   53
26 Inscription on a cross-slab at Glendalough
(Macalister, *Corpus*, ii, p. 85)   53
27 Powerscourt Waterfall, Co. Wicklow (*Dublin
Penny Journal*, 1834, p. 236)   55
28. Great Sugar Loaf Mountain, Co. Wicklow
(*Dublin Penny Journal*, 1835, p. 361)   56
29 Ullard, Co. Kilkenny (O'Hanlon, *Lives*,
v, p. 66)   60
30 Killeshin, Co. Leix (O'Hanlon, *Lives*, i,
p. 460)   60
31 Old Leighlin, Co. Carlow (O'Hanlon, *Lives*,
ii, p. 682)   61
32 St Mullins, Co. Carlow (O'Hanlon, *Lives*,
vi, p. 696)   62
33 St Mullins monastic ruins, Co. Carlow
(O'Hanlon, *Lives*, vi, p. 711)   62
34 Ferns, Co. Wexford (O'Hanlon, *Lives*, vii,
p. 401)   64
35 Figures from the Shrine of St Máedóc
    a. (Coffey, *Guide to Celtic Antiquities*,
    p. 50)   64
    b. (Stokes, *Christian Art in Ireland*,
    p. 107)   64
36 Croghan Hill, Co. Offaly (O'Hanlon, *Lives*,
iv, p. 488)   68
37 Clonfertmulloe (Kyle), Co. Leix (author's
drawing based on O'Hanlon, *Lives*, i, p. 179)   73
38 Coolbanagher, Co. Leix (O'Hanlon, *Lives*,
viii, p. 329)   73
39 Bronze figures from the Shrine of St Manchán
(Joyce, *Social History*, ii, p. 204)   76
40 Clonenagh, Co. Leix (O'Hanlon, *Lives*, ii,
frontispiece)   84
41 Antiquities from the Bogland Zone
    a. (*Dublin Penny Journal*, 1833, p. 328)   87
    b. (Joyce, *Social History*, ii, 217, fig. 248) 87
    c. (Coffey, *Guide to Celtic Antiquities*,
    p. 73)   87
41 The Roscrea Brooch (Stokes, *Christian Art
in Ireland*, p. 80)   88
43 Portraits of Evangelists from Leinster
illuminated Gospels (author's drawing)   90

44 Book-shrine of the Stowe Missal (Stokes, *Christian Art in Ireland*, p. 95) 95

45 Leather satchel of the Shrine of St Máedóc (Coffey, *Guide to Celtic Antiquities*, p. 52) 95

46 Monk illuminating the lost Book of Kildare (Joyce, *Social History,* i, p. 481) 98

47 High Cross at Durrow, Co. Offaly (O'Hanlon, *Lives,* vi, p. 307) 99

48 Book of Durrow (Stokes, *Christian Art in Ireland*, p. 19) 99

48a *The Marriage of Strongbow and Eva* by Daniel MacLise, 1854 (National Gallery of Ireland) following page 99

49 Rock of Dunamase, Co. Leix (Ledwich, *Antiquities*, facing p. 200 101

50 Noghaval (Oughaval), Co. Leix (O'Hanlon, *Lives,* i, p.331) 102

51 *a.* Grave-slab of Suibne of Clonmacnoise (Macalister, *Clonmacnois*, p. 97) 104

b. Crozier of the Abbots of Clonmacnoise (Stokes, *Christian Art in Ireland*, p. 105) 104

52 Meeting between Art MacMurrough Kavanagh king of Leinster, and the Earl of Gloucester in 1399 (Webb, 'Deposition of Richard the Second', *Archaeologia*, xx, facing p. 40) 107

53 The relief of Richard II's army on the Wicklow coast, 1399 (Webb, 'Deposition of Richard the Second', *Archaeologia*, xx, facing p. 36) 110

54 Holy Wells at Killeigh, Co. Offaly (O'Hanlon, *Lives,* vi, p. 788) 112

55 Detail of map of Leix and Offaly, *c.* A.D. 1563 (author's drawing) 115

Genealogical Charts

1 Schematized inter-tribal genealogy 14

2 Inter-tribal Genealogy of the Leinstermen 15

3 Inter-tribal Marriage and Circulating Kingship in Leinster, A.D. 550-700 57

4 The Irish Highkingship *c.* A.D. 800-1000 80

5 Rotational kingship in Leinster, A.D. 700-1050 123

Photographs

(i) Knockaulin Hillfort, Co. Kildare 124
(ii) Knockaulin (detail) 124
(iii) Killeigh, Co. Offaly 125
(iv) Lorrha, Co. Tipperary 125

These (aerial) photographs are © D. L. Swan, Archaeological Air Survey.

Maps in the Historical Atlas

I The Natural regions of ancient Leinster 141
II Mountains and river basins 142
III Soils and settlement 143
IV Geology 144
V Migration of peoples A.D. 300-550 145
VI Medieval diocese 146
VII Baronies 147
VIII Tribes A.D. 800 148
IX Irish dynasties A.D. 1150 149
X Anglo-Norman conquest in Leinster and Meath *c.* A.D. 1200 150
Key to Plates XI-XVI 151
XI Northern and North-Eastern Regions: Political 152
XII Northern and North-Eastern Regions: Topographical 153
XIII North-Western Region: Political 154
XIV North-Western Region: Topgraphical 155
XV Southern Region: Political 156
XVI Southern Region: Topographical 157

ELY o Carols coantrey

Sleabloume M.

OSSERIE
The baron of Osseries or McGill fatricks
countrey

Balachaffan

peach Black Water

Gortenoble

Neure f.

Comlan M.

Keilinein

Keildaragh

RAVN RE

Gouly f.

Dirtayle

Keleune

chloenkin

Rofent talp

GLANDIBVI

Balafin

chloen ingaun

Neure f.

Shanchog

Killine

Kutebram

Truno

Moenta
Chloenengah

Kringloton

Caymoyt

chlone

FRANAMANACH

TOVAYOVI

orlone

clonadagie

Tho White boge

Neire

Moennon

Greg f.

TOVACHLOV

L E I

Colt

chloekine

FERANODOVLIN

Roskonil

Iybegini

Brafeligue

Balaochiflii

Marktoran

Baliffteaffe

Telbur

Dopar

chlon Iadodora

ftoan

Palfen
cochi

Protectour

Enochoegin

ENE

GALIN

Balacha
fian

Cnocha Dogaun

Ieudlo

M coulinogh

FRRANO
IAVLER

Kilcolman

Baiencgan

Difert

Streabe
o Deluer

Shiart

E

TOVMOLO
GAN

Muxet

Greg f.

Difere lin

FERANOPRIOR

Timochon

croche
Doure

Carigin
ban

Copigot

Dunamaft

Frugh
more

Culuanche

steonachiare M.

tho Grange

CLA

EDOVGH.
My L. of Ormound.

Aginte brid

Nuiadi

Muriady

Stronagre M.

fote

Tvage
closanogh

Timoge

Balladoi
gue Kilmory

Stradbeg

Praenoch caffe

ochonal

ERHIR

Garynia da

Kilgourno

KEILDOVNAN
enotor
Iohnacen

corghe

Cnala
ohile

FERANOKEL

LEI

Slewto

Derribuck

Moenf

The great wood

FERAINCLAN

EVGH

Black
ford

Balachalun

Kilbery

DIMEDOH

Baliada

Balitybnil

Boherd

cno

Roue
Roue

Roerinogh

Pochiche
towne

FASAGHREBAN

Baro

Tireflon

MERG

Ares
th

Baldinga

Meien

Woodfheky

Kiluarugh

KILIHIDE

Tulhog f.

Kiliban

Tankendon

Shongan

Dumeore
nin

Athee

SLEA

oldarig

Carlogh

Graugrs
managh

FERANCLANDIDONIL

Louetston Baro f. Ardre

Cloghgrynan

Caffe nay
guigne

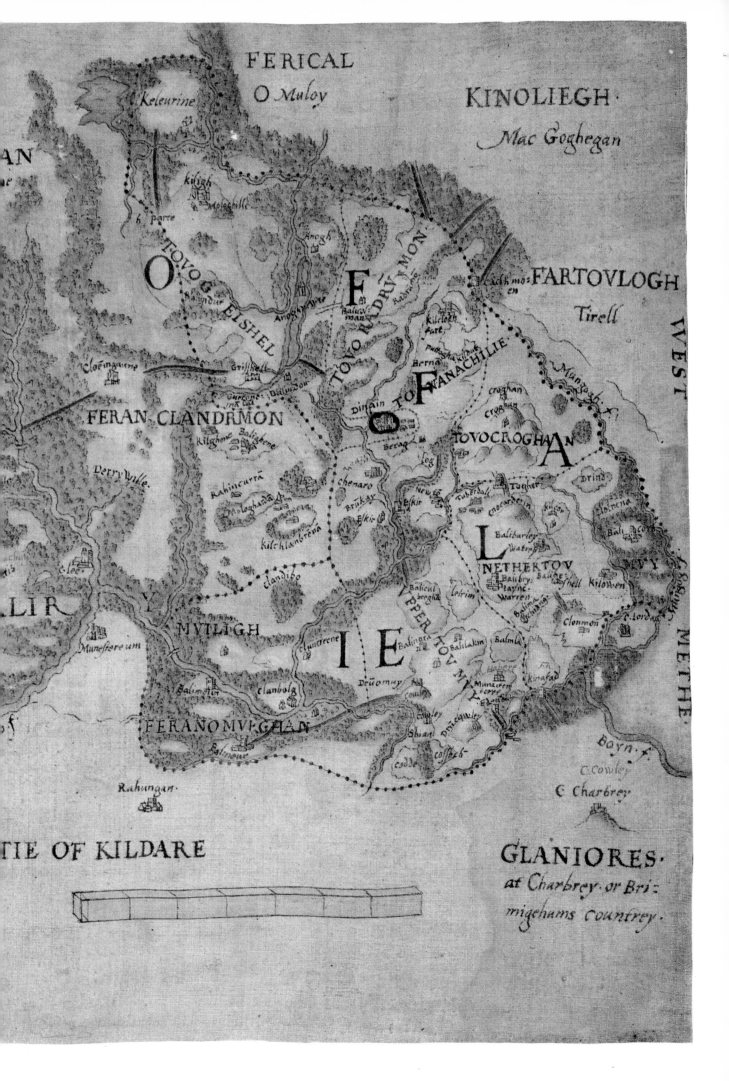

FERICAL
O Muloy

KINOLIEGH·

Mac Goghegan

Keleurine

kilagh

Molaghille

h Parre

Anogh

Radnile

cadh mo: en

FARTOVLOGH

Tirell

WEST

O

TOVOG ELSHEL

Rahindur

Anoghmdira

BALLOWran

Kilcloth Fart

putt Shane. dilte

Berna

Mangagh

Cloémgaune

Griffhell

Gurgore

Balmydou

TOVO KI DRVMON.

Dinain

TO FANACHILIE

croghan

croghan

FERAN CLANDRMON

Kilghous

Balighene

Berag

teg

TOVOCROGHAN

Drin.

Derrywille.

Rahincurra

Mologhadad

chenaro

Brikay

News

Elkir

Elkir

Tugher

Cnocarderin

kilcor

Balibry.

Balrne

Bali Acore

Balibarley Watre

kilchianbrena

Tuherdal

L NETHERTOV

Playne

Bali:

Cofhell Kilowen

VY

Clee-

clandibo

Baliry

Warren

Clonmon

C. lordag

METHE

Balima

Bchania

LLIR

VY

MVILIGH

Muneggrene

Balicul: bregha

letrim

kinafad

Munefereum

I E

Balinora

Balflakin

Balnia

Halane

Munaneen

feret Ed

Clanbolg

Drúomay

couflan

FERANOMVIGHAN

Balinoue

cowley

Dn: cawley

Sbian

cosfhich

cadde

Boyn. f.

C. Cowley

C Charbrey

Rahungan

TIE OF KILDARE

GLANIORES·
at Charbrey. or Bri=
migehams Countrey.

FRONTISPIECE Map of Leix and Offaly, c. *1563 (British Library, Cotton: Augustus, I, ii. 40).* Tudor administrations availed of new and improved cartographical methods in their efforts to subdue the Gaelic territories of Ireland. This map is remarkable for the detail which it offers on the two kingdoms of Loígis and Uí Failge. It was meant to accompany a survey of those territories, with a view to conquest and confiscation. The map is on its side, with the top facing west rather than north, while true north faces right. Despite its relative accuracy and detail, this is a picture map rather than a modern survey, for although the surveyor took the river Barrow as his base line, from Carlow (bottom left), to Athy and Monasterevin (bottom centre), the survey seems to be based on itineraries from the Barrow rather than on triangulation methods. The picture becomes more and more vague and distorted the further west we move across the Great Forest of Offaly towards the foothills of the Slieve Bloom (top centre). Nevertheless, this map provides a unique picture of an ancient Celtic region still under the control of its native kings and it provides us with a panoramic view of an essentially medieval Celtic ecology which had changed little since the Dark Ages.

END PAPERS Based on a Map of Ireland *by Batista Boazio,* fl. *1585-1603 (Trinity College Dublin, Hardiman Atlas no. 83).* This fine map shows, for Leinster, extensive tracts of forest surviving in Wicklow, North Wexford, Central Carlow and in Offaly.

for
MARGARET

Mo bheannacht leat, a scríbhinn,
go hinis aoibhinn Ealga.

Geoffrey Keating, *c.* 1610

Preface

A childhood spent within walking distance of the Hill of Tara and fortunate access to a collection of annals and Victorian histories meant that I have been fascinated by the Irish landscape and its antiquities for as long as I can remember. The Meath countryside is capable in itself of exercising the most powerful influence on the historical imagination but the happy chance of Professor Séan Ó Riordáin beginning his epoch-making archaeological excavations on Tara in 1952 meant that I grew up accepting archaeology as a normal part of educational experience. It meant in more immediate terms that I was fired to undertake excavations of my own which resulted in the discovery by the age of eleven, of a flat axe of the Early Bronze Age in the grounds of my home—an object now deposited in the National Museum in Dublin. The finding of this and other antiquities helped to focus the mind, in a childlike but powerful way, on the relationship between transient communities of the remote past and the relatively immutable landscape which they inhabited. Yet, in Meath prehistoric men of the Neolithic had succeeded in projecting their own fleeting days into the immortality of the landscape by building megalithic tombs of cyclopean proportions which were to dominate the countryside from Newgrange, Tara and Lough Crew forever. A rich Celtic folklore relating to these monuments, some of it backed by a medieval manuscript tradition, survived into modern times and lent substance to the conviction that every field and hollow had been hallowed by its association in the *senchus* (or traditional lore) with warriors and holy men of a prehistoric and heroic past. That was a belief shared by the Cork scholar, Fr Donncha Ó Floinn at Maynooth, and in a less romantic way by Ruaidhri de Valera, under whose guidance I read archaeology at University College Dublin. A pre-occupation with topography and with the relationship of archaeology to history led me to research under the supervision of Professor Francis J. Byrne who gave me a professional training in those sources I had first encountered as a boy. This book owes much to his great knowledge of Early Irish History and to the tradition of Ryan, McNeill and O'Curry from whom he inherited his chair. Professor Conn Ó Cléirigh, Dr Próinsias Ní Catháin, Dr Donncha Ó hAodha, and the late Fr Francis Shaw devoted countless hours in specially arranged seminars at University College Dublin, in an unselfish effort to impart their wisdom in Old and Middle Irish to an eager student. My debt to them is incalculable. Other scholars who helped me significantly with my work in Dublin were Professor Dudley Edwards, Professor Françoise Henry, Professor Ludwig Bieler, Mr. A. T. Lucas, Professor F. X. Martin, Mr. Liam de Paor, Professor James Carney, Professor Michael Herity, Dr. Seamus Caulfield, Professor Donncha Ó Corráin, Mr David Sweetman, and the late Myles Dillon and Seamus Delargy. I have benefitted immensely from the advice and published researches of Professor J. Otway-Ruthven and Professor J. Lydon of Trinity College Dublin, and I am particularly indebted to Dr. J. H. Andrews, also of Trinity College, for devoting so much of his time in explaining the complexities of Early Modern Irish cartography.

Early Irish manuscript materials were written up and preserved by a professional body of *seanchaidhthe* or antiquaries working outside what we might call the European historical tradition. Theirs was a world where history, genealogy, saga and court poetry were not rigidly distinguished from each other but merged together to form the traditional lore of a barbarian nation. It is essential therefore, if we are to succeed in a proper evaluation of this unique

Gaelic record that those who study it are conversant with the whole ethos of the *senchus* while at the same time being trained in the methodological and critical approach of the modern schools. A deeper knowledge of Anglo-Saxon and Scandinavian sources has helped me to set the wealth of Irish material into a better prespective, and has led to a new appreciation of the amazing output of medieval Irish writers; the wealth of their monastic and secular culture; and the unique nature of the environment in which it all flourished. It is with the ecological basis of that literary culture that this book is concerned, and I have tried to compose a text which constantly focusses on the maps in the Historical Atlas. These maps are intended to introduce the specialist and non-specialist alike to early Irish civilization by way of the landscape which fostered it. I have prepared them over many years in the hope of providing an obscure and daunting corner of European history with 'a local habitation and a name'. The collection of line drawings throughout the text, by Wakeman, O'Hanlon, Margaret Stokes and others, enables the reader to assess in a general way the condition of the ruined monasteries of Leinster in the late eighteenth and early nineteenth centuries before many of them were either completely destroyed, or transformed by restoring architects in the Ministry of Ancient Monuments. I record my sincere gratitude to those scholars who have laboured with dedication in the field of Irish topography and genealogy in the distant and more recent past: John O'Donovan, Eugene O'Curry, Francis Shearman, Patrick Woulfe, Edmund Hogan, Edmund Curtis, Paul Walsh, Margaret Dobbs, Liam Price, Toirdhealbhach Ó Raithbheartaigh, Eileen McCracken, and Michael O'Brien — all of these scholars have laid the secure foundations upon which this study is based.

This book has been written in a difficult economic climate when the publication of specialist work has become virtually impossible and when a subject such as this is forced to retreat more and more into the pages of learned journals and so out of reach of the layman and very often of the non-Irish specialist as well. My greatest debt, therefore, is to those who have helped with the problems of publication, and my acknowledgement of the following scholars and friends has a special significance since many of them are either not immediately involved in Irish learning or are working outside Ireland. These include Professor Ellis Evans, Jesus Professor of Celtic, Oxford University; Sir John Habbakuk, Principal of Jesus College Oxford; Professor J.M. Wallace-Hadrill, my former teacher at All Souls; Professor R.H.C. Davis, University of Birmingham; Mr W. Shannon, United States Ambassador to Ireland; Mr Sean Galvin, Fitzwilliam Square, Dublin; Mr Cornelius Ryan, Houston, Texas, U.S.A.; Mr J.F.M. Rudd, Secretary, Bank of Ireland Ltd.; Professor Patrick Collinson, University of Kent; Professor F.S.L. Lyons, The Provost, Trinity College Dublin; Mr P.W.H. Brown, Deputy Secretary, The British Academy; Dr John Hatcher, Corpus Christi College, Cambridge; Professor Michael Herity and Mr Denis Bethell, University College Dublin; Mr Pádraig Ó Tailliúir, Muckross Avenue, Dublin; Mr Séamus Breathnach, Thorncliffe Park, Dublin; Fr Conor McGreevy, Kilskyre, Co. Meath, who has done so much to promote topographical studies among county antiquarian societies in the Irish Midlands; and finally, my friend Pat Holland of Fuengirola in Spain who once made it possible for me to visit so many of the ancient places of Leinster and who died before this book was published.

My colleague Mr Richard Eales has advised me on the preparation of the map on the Anglo-Norman Conquest (Plate X); Dr Graham Anderson has helped with medieval Latin texts; and Dr J. Eades has helped me with problems in demography. Professor Bernard Wailes of the University of Pennsylvania has been most helpful in providing me with material on his important archaeological excavations at Knockaulin Hill-fort; Mr. Leo Swan has kindly assisted with matters of aerial photography, and Mrs Vera Schove of St. David's College Beckenham, has most generously offered her help with the General Index. My friends and colleagues in universities in Great Britain have provided me with ideas and information over many years for which I am extremely grateful. Professor Peter Sawyer of Leeds, and Mr. David Dumville of Cambridge, have kindly read the text, and while they may dissent from it in many places, I am indebted to them for the great care they have taken. Mr. Patrick Wormald of Glasgow, and Dr. Wendy Davies of University College London, have frequently offered help and advice from their expert knowledge of Dark Age British History. To all these scholars, I apologize for any errors and inconsistencies which inevitably remain in a work of this scope, and for which I alone must take responsibility.

I am grateful to the following officers and their institutions for the courtesy of providing me with access to books and manuscripts, and for permission to reproduce some of this material photographically as acknowledged elsewhere in the book; Miss A. Oakley, the Chapter Library, Canterbury Cathedral; Mr William O'Sullivan, Keeper of Manuscripts, Trinity College Dublin; Mr B. Mac Giolla Choille, Deputy Keeper, Public Records Office, Dublin; Mr Ken Hannigan, Public Records Office, Dublin; Miss Eileen Black, Ulster Museum; The National Maritime Museum, Greenwich; The British Library; The National Gallery of Ireland, and Mr John Kennedy of the Green Studios, Harcourt Street, Dublin. The Ordnance Survey of Ireland issued a permit allowing many of the maps in the Historical Atlas to be based in part on various maps of its Survey. The maps of the Historical Atlas have been prepared for publication by Mr Christopher Panton, St Peter's Place, Canterbury. Mr Panton has shown a dedicated interest in his treatment of a landscape so far removed in place and time, and he has spent countless hours consulting me on how best to present, within strict financial constraints, a multitude of detail to the reader. Mr Michael Adams has shown a genuine enthusiasm for the publication of this work from an early stage, and he has taken a personal interest in seeing it through his press. Finally, the book is dedicated to my wife, Margaret, for her help with this study over the years and for her abiding interest in the Irish landscape which inspired it.

Canterbury, 1981   A.P.S.

Abbreviations

Ann. Ulst.
Annala Uladh: Annals of Ulster; otherwise Annala Senait Annals of Senat; a Chronicle of Irish Affairs from A.D. 431 to A.D. 1540, ed. W.M. Hennessy and B. MacCarthy, 4 vols. (Dublin, 1887-1901)

B.B.
Book of Ballymote. Page, column, and line references as found in *C.G.H.* (*q.v.*)

Bethada Náem, ed. Plummer
Bethada Náem nÉrenn: Lives of Irish Saints, ed. C. Plummer, 2 vols. (Oxford, 1922).

C.G.H.
Corpus Genealogiarum Hiberniae, i, ed. M.A. O'Brien (Dublin, 1962)

Coffey, Guide to Celtic Antiquities
G. Coffey, *Royal Irish Academy Collection: Guide to the Celtic Antiquities of the Christian Period preserved in the National Museum Dublin* (Dublin and London, 1909)

Cogadh Gaedhel, ed. Todd
Cogadh Gaedhel re Gallaibh: The War of the Gaedhil with the Gaill, or the Invasions of Ireland by the Danes and other Norsemen, ed. J.H. Todd (London, Rolls ser., 1867)

EIHM
T.F. O'Rahilly, *Early Irish History and Mythology* (Dublin, reprint, 1964)

Essays to Eoin MacNeill, Ed. Ryan
Féil-sgríbhinn Eóin Mhic Néill: Essays and Studies presented to Professor Eoin MacNeill, ed. J. Ryan (Dublin, 1940)

Four Masters, ed. O'Donovan
Annala Rioghachta Eireann: Annals of the Kingdom of Ireland by the Four Masters, from the earliest period to the year 1616, ed. J. O'Donovan, 5 vols. (1st edn., Dublin, 1848-51)

Giraldus, Topographia, ed. Dimlock
Topographia Hiberniae by Giraldus Cambrensis in: *Giraldi Cambrensis Opera,* ed. J.F. Dimlock (Rolls Ser., 1867),v.

Hall's Ireland
Mr and Mrs S.C. Hall, *Ireland, its Scenery, Character, etc.,* 3 vols (London, 1843)

Irish Eccl. Rec.
Irish Ecclesiastical Record.

Joyce, Social History
P.W. Joyce, *A Social History of Ancient Ireland,* 2 vols (2nd edn., Dublin 1913)

Kenney, Sources
The 'Sources for the Early History of Ireland, ed. J.F. Kenney (New York, 1923)

Ledwich, Antiquities
E. Ledwich, *Antiquities of Ireland* (Dublin, 1790)

L.L.
The Book of Leinster: formerly Leabar na Núachongbála, ed. R.I. Best, O. Bergin and M.A. O'Brien (Dublin, 1954), Vol. i only cited. Other references to *L.L.* are cited from *C.G.H.i, (q.v.).*

Loca Patriciana, J.F. Shearman
Loca Patriciana: an identification of localities, chiefly in Leinster, visited by Saint Patrick and his assistant missionaries (Dublin, 1879)

Macalister, Clonmacnois
R.A.S. Macalister, *The Memorial Slabs of Clonmacnois, King's County* (Roy. Soc. Antiq. Irel. Extra Volume; Dublin, 1909)

Macalister, Corpus
Corpus Inscriptionum Insularum Celticarum, ed. R.A.S. Macalister, 2 vols (Irish Manuscripts Commission, Dublin, 1949)

Onomasticon, ed. Hogan
Onomasticon Goedelicum locorum et tribuum Hiberniae et Scotiae, ed. E. Hogan (Dublin, 1910)

Rawl. B. 502
Manuscript *Rawlinson B 502* in Bodleian Library, Oxford

Roy. Irish Acad. Proc.
Royal Irish Academy Proceedings

Roy. Soc. Antiq. Irel. Jrnl.
Royal Society of Antiquaries of Ireland, Journal

Stokes, Christian Art in Ireland
M. Stokes, *Early Christian Art in Ireland* (London, 1894)

Taylor and Skinner
Maps of the Roads of Ireland, Surveyed 1777 by G. Taylor and A. Skinner (London and Dublin, 1778)

Three Fragments, ed. O'Donovan
Annals of Ireland: Three Fragments copied ... by Dubhaltach Mac Firbisigh, ed. J. O'Donovan (Dublin, 1860)

Tripartite Life, ed. Stokes
The Tripartite Life of Patrick, with other Documents relating to that Saint, ed. W. Stokes (London, Rolls Ser., 1887)

V.S.H. ed. Plummer
Vitae Sanctorum Hiberniae, ed. C. Plummer, 2 vols. (Oxford, 1910)

V.S.H. ex codice Salmanticensis, ed. Heist
Vitae Sanctorum Hiberniae ex codice Salmanticensis, ed. W.W. Heist (Studia Hagiographica, 28, Brussels, 1965)

Introduction

'Ireland, separated from the rest of the known world, and in some sort to be distinguished as another world, not only by its situation, but by the objects out of the ordinary course of nature contained in it, seems to be nature's especial repository, where she stores up her most remarkable and precious treasures.'

Giraldus Cambrensis, *Topographia Hiberniae*, ii.

The British Government founded the Ordnance Survey of Ireland in 1824, and under its first director, Colonel Thomas Colby, assisted by Lieutenant Thomas Larcom, the study of early Irish historical geography may be said to have begun. A team of historical researchers worked in the field alongside the Victorian sappers, attempting to correlate topographical evidence from the ancient manuscript records with the precise findings of modern cartography. The official efforts of the Anglo-Irish Ordnance Survey went hand in hand with a renewed interest in the Celtic past, and here the field was led not only by professional academics but by gentlemen scholars such as the painter George Petrie and the Queen's Surgeon in Ireland, Sir William Wilde (father of Oscar Wilde). These writers had the good sense to harness the labours of two of the greatest nineteenth-century masters of the native Gaelic tradition. The first of these was Eugene O'Curry, who later became professor of archaeology at Newman's university in Dublin, and the second was John O'Donovan, who began his working life as a topographer for the Ordnance Survey and who ended his career as professor of Celtic Studies at the Queen's University, Belfast. While the field-work of O'Donovan and O'Curry has remained largely in manuscript form in field-books and letters of the Irish Ordnance Survey, nevertheless, both scholars made extensive use, later on in their careers, of their topographical researches undertaken for the Survey. O'Donovan's edition of the *Annals of the Four Masters* which first appeared in 1848 contained a vast store of geographical information on settlement in its footnotes, which O'Donovan must have compiled during his earlier years with the Ordnance Survey. Publications such as this still form the starting-point for all serious studies in early Irish historical geography.

The output of these scholars was staggering and their handling of the ancient texts was characterized, above all, by complete and lucid translation together with extensive commentaries on ancient topography. It was inevitable that scholars with a liberal nineteenth-century education would turn to historical geography as holding the key to understanding early Irish sources. It becomes immediately clear from reading any major work in Early Irish, whether it be a saga or a saint's *Life*, that the corner-stone of ancient Irish antiquarian learning rested on the importance of the association with place. This preoccupation with focusing on placenames to evoke historical associations in Celtic literature is not found to the same extent in the writings of any other people apart, perhaps, from the Hebrews and Icelanders. Indeed, it is no coincidence that all of these peoples built up civilizations in a geographical wilderness and their isolation, each in their separate and distinct environments, promoted a literature characterized by a great sensitivity and feeling for landscape.

1

What scholars in the Anglo-Irish tradition grasped was that unless we understand the topographical illusions in medieval Irish manuscript sources, and unless we understand the subtle relationship between one place and another, the entire essence of ancient Irish antiquarian lore is lost. For scholars today the abundance of topographical information on ancient Ireland must mean much more. Not only does it allow us gain a greater insight into the workings of early Irish writers, but the sheer profusion of this material enables us to reconstruct the ecology of a lost world from the Dark Ages, at a level of detail which is quite impossible for any other region in Europe. The topographical information can now be used in its own right or in conjunction with the genealogies and annals, and from it we can reconstruct the geography and settlement-pattern of a tribal nation barricaded behind a wilderness of forest and bog, divided into hundreds of tribal *tuatha* or petty kingdoms, each with its own royal forts and monasteries and mythological sites of timeless association. In time, too, with the development of aerial photography and cartographical studies, we may hope to study the lay-out of individual settlements and the precise density of population.

The impetus given to geographical studies by early nineteenth-century scholars was not to last. Already by the closing decades of the century the emphasis in Germanic scholarship on the importance of philology in the study of a nation's past combined with the rise of nationalism within Ireland itself to push the broader and more liberal Anglo-Irish tradition to one side. Whatever liberalism had remained within the Gaelic League in its emphasis on the appreciation of literature, was replaced by a rigorous professionalism in Irish scholarship, combined with a heavy and stultifying emphasis on philology. Dead now was the interest in historical geography, and gone, too, were the elegant translations. Occasionally, historians such as Mac Neill and Ryan, who contributed so ably to the political history of Early Medieval Ireland, ventured into the field of 'identification of placenames', but, by and large, philology and the study of language reigned supreme. Nothing on the study of placenames was produced for early Ireland, for instance, to match the achievement of the English Place-name Society, nor was there anything produced in the land, where so much history is by its nature local, to rival the formidable output of the *Victoria County Histories*. The historian who wishes to work on the historical geography of ancient Ireland is faced with a daunting task. He is confronted with a lack of suitable modern translations in English and very often of suitable textual editions; lack of detailed and comprehensive studies on placenames; and above all by the almost complete lack of a tradition in the study of historical geography since the nineteenth century. It is a rare thing to have to return to where scholars such as Petrie and O'Donovan left off over a century ago.

The objectives I have set myself in this book are limited. I have confined myself to Leinster, in the belief that significant progress can only be made in early Irish historical studies by examining the country kingdom by kingdom. As we shall see, the physical shape of each kingdom was determined by natural features in the landscape, and each region developed in isolation from its neighbour. Since the manuscript materials show an obsession with topographical lore it makes sense to study these on a regional basis. Geographers may be disappointed that I have not devoted more space to the problem of settlement in relation to the lay-out of individual communities. I have avoided this subject partly because I have approached the study as an historian and partly because so much field-work still remains to be done that any conclusions must be by nature speculative. On the other hand, I have tried by means of the maps and commentary in this volume to establish for the first time the overall picture of tribal settlement in south-eastern Ireland and some definite conclusions have emerged from this. It is now possible to establish that the Celtic population in the period A.D. 500-1200 favoured more or less the

same type of land for settlement as the population of today, with the qualification that in modern times improved drainage techniques have made settlement possible in areas which were formerly waterlogged for much of the year. Thus in Celtic Leinster, the vast majority of the population lived in the Liffey Plain in Co. Kildare (Mag Life), further south in the Barrow valley in Carlow (Mag Ailbe) and in more confined areas along the Slaney valley in Wexford. There was also a scatter of settlements along the gravel ridges and fertile clearings in the Bog of Allen, but these were significant less for their size than for the remarkable cultural achievements which they attained within the security of the peat bogs. Similarly to the north, in the kingdoms of Brega and Mide, the majority of the population lived in the valleys of the Boyne and Blackwater, and in Westmeath the greatest density lay in the south and centre of the county in the region between Mullingar and Kilbeggan.

The distribution of monastic sites, which has been studied in detail, shows that few of these —and certainly none of any importance—were located higher than the 500-foot contour, while many lay not far below it. This is a powerful indication that settlement avoided the high ground and gives the lie to the popular misconception—often backed by political ideologies—that everything Celtic and best in ancient Ireland was by its nature either 'mountainous' or 'western'. The ancient Irish could recognize good land as well as any modern farmer, and the Curragh of Kildare and Plains of Meath formed the heartland of early Irish civilization as they form the backbone of the agricultural economy of today. More surprisingly, perhaps, we find that the eastern Leinster seaboard shared the same fate as the barren mountains in its rôle as a demographic and cultural backwater. The land from Dublin to Arklow was on the whole fertile, but it was poorly drained in medieval times; cut off from the Liffey and Barrow valleys by high mountains; and traversed by rivers flowing from west to east thereby impeding the natural trend of communication from north to south. Apart from Glendalough which was approached from the west, there were no important monasteries on the eastern seaboard and the tribal inhabitants were all in a permanent state of political exile and decline.

This overall picture contrasts with earlier Bronze Age settlement which, in spite of our poor understanding of it, suggests that the higher slopes of the Wicklow and Dublin mountains were favoured for Bronze Age agriculture. Archaeological remains from the Early and Middle Bronze Age at Ballyedmonduff or Mount Seskin in south Co. Dublin, for instance, show that where the blanket bog has now taken over the upper slopes of the mountain foot-hills, prehistoric communities once found land accessible for ritual if not for agriculture. Similarly, there are Bronze Age stone circles and other monuments on the western foot-hills of the Wicklow mountains on the fringes of the Kildare Plain, such as those at Castleruddery or Athgreany, which suggest a concentration of settlement there. This area was indeed settled in the Celtic period, but its soils of indifferent quality supported the Uí Máil, a people who occupied a position about half-way down the political pecking order of Leinster tribes. The Bronze Age population had also thoroughly penetrated the Midland Bog Zone, as is demonstrated by Early Bronze Age cist burials found along the esker gravel ridges. The impressive Late Bronze Age hoard discovered at Dowris, Co. Offaly, in 1825 and the La Tène Iron Age torc from Clonmacnoise are but two of the numerous examples of archaeological material which testify to the sustained interest of prehistoric traders and communities in the remote recesses of the Midland Bogs.

It may be that a deteriorating climate with increased rainfall towards the end of the Late Bronze Age saw a rapid spread in peat cover which drove the population from the upper and middle slopes of the Wicklow mountains and restricted settlement in the Midlands to the better-drained gravel ridges. On the other hand, if we look again at Uí Máil country on the western slopes of the Wicklow Granite Massif, we are faced with the problem of Iron Age hillforts such as Rathcoran, which nestles on the summit of Baltinglass Hill, 1200 feet above the

Slaney valley. Another fort at Rathnagree lies less than half a mile away. Rathcoran and other forts lie shrouded in the mists of the Wicklow summits, far above the line of later Celtic settlement in the Early Christian period, and in a region of poor land even further down the valleys which was occupied by weaker tribes in the historical period. The conclusion is inescapable that a fortress such as Rathcoran was constructed not by conquering invaders but by a declining indigenous political group driven off the Kildare Plains, yet still strong enough to fortify their lines in the remoter countryside of west Wicklow. The Uí Máil were just such a people in the historical period, but the hill-fort era must go back to the earliest centuries of the Christian era, if not to the closing centuries B.C.

Not all hill-forts were perched on the Wicklow summits. The prestige site at Knockaulin (Dún Ailinne) near the Liffey in Kildare dominated the heart of the Leinster lowlands and was remembered in Leinster manuscript tradition as an ancient royal capital in prehistoric times. There are hints that Knockaulin, like Tara in Co. Meath and Emain Macha in Co. Armagh, was not abandoned until the fifth or sixth centuries. It may be, however, that since all three of these sites were associated with sacral pagan kingship they survived as ritual centres in pre-Christian Ireland long after other hill-fort sites had been abandoned. It is certainly significant that Tara and Emain Macha declined with the coming of Christianity, and Leinster tradition, too, saw St Brigit and her cult triumphing over ancient kingship and its cult-centres in Leinster (Fig.4, p.21 below). We are still faced with the problem, however, of what the Iron Age hill-forts were used for—whether for defence or as assembly places—and why they were abandoned. The abandonment of hill-forts in favour of more compact and cellular ring-forts has parallels with a similar transition in western and northern Britain in the later Roman period and this must clearly have implications for the social organization of the population, but so far its significance for pre-Christian Ireland has eluded us.

It is possible that in Ireland hill-forts served as quasi-urban centres which enjoyed periodic use only as tribal assembly points for the holding of an *óenach* which included not only legal and ritual ceremonies but also commercial activity involving traders from outside the region. The rôle of these quasi-urban centres involving markets and trade was very definitely taken over by the more important monastic centres from the sixth century onwards. We know that early Irish as well as Anglo-Saxon monastic complexes afforded permanent security and patronage to craftsmen and traders alike, and these communities must have provided the essentially rural society of Ireland with its first experience of urban life. In the face of this wide-scale development combined with the rapid secularization of the monasteries, the old secular assemblies must have found themselves unable to compete at the commercial level at least. This may help to account for the eclipse of some hill-forts, if indeed they had not been abandoned long before.

One problem from the historical period which I have deliberately avoided is the question of population, simply because there are no sources to guide us. The early Irish, like their Anglo-Saxon neighbours, felt no need to count either households or heads. It was only the obsessional interest which Norman and Angevin administrations took in the raising of revenue and armies which led to the *Domesday* survey of 1086 or the *Cartae Baronum* of 1166 for England. We have nothing like this for Ireland and it is extremely difficult to deduce figures of a relative nature for that island based on analogies with the *Domesday* survey. England was not only four times larger than Ireland, but it had far less mountain and rocky terrain, and lacked the extensive basin peat of lowland Ireland. Furthermore, we shall see that Ireland was an under-populated country in the Celtic period with much good farmland still under forest or lying waste. This helps to account for the survival for centuries of entire dispossessed dynastic groups or 'nations' alongside the Anglo-Norman invading population. Accepting the popu-

4

lation of eleventh-century England on current estimates as being nearer two million than the one million of earlier estimates, we may still have to think of as little as 250,000 for the whole of Ireland in the Dark Ages. Bearing in mind that Celtic Leinster did not include the rich farmland of the modern counties of Meath, North Dublin, Kilkenny and Westmeath, and that it lacked much of Offaly and Leix, we may have to think in terms of less than 40,000 for the entire Leinster population. Round figures such as these can only be speculative. A detailed knowledge of the Leinster landscape, however, combined with an accurate assessment of the relative political and military strength of its tribal territories, does enable us to make some firmer statements about the density of the overall population. We can safely assume that more than half the entire population lived in the lowland parts of the Liffey and upper and middle Barrow basins, while as little as five per cent may have lived along the Wicklow seaboard and south Wexford. The Uí Failge, as we shall see, owed their economic and political importance to the fact that they enjoyed a share in rich land on the western fringes of the Kildare Plain, but the population of Loígis and western Uí Failge territories in the Bog of Allen can scarcely have accounted for more than ten per cent of the whole. It may be rash to transpose these percentages into round figures, but a detailed study of the extensive genealogies of the Leinstermen combined with a study of land usage suggests that some of the more obscure and territorially restricted Leinster tribes such as Uí Crimthainn Áin of Leix or the Fotharta, for instance, may not have numbered more than about 500 or 700 people in the pre-Viking Age. We move from these figures up to perhaps somewhere in the region of 12,000 people living under the rule of the powerful Uí Dúnlainge confederacy on the Liffey Plain. Such round figures are merely conjectural. Not only is it impossible to be certain of overall numbers, but we must also bear in mind that we have no precise knowledge of nutritional and fertility levels for this period.

Assuming that the population of Dark Age Ireland experienced the same problems as a Third World population in the modern period, and bearing in mind that as in the case of many Third World societies the Irish had a warrior society where warfare was endemic, then we must consider the possibility that fifty per cent of the population were infants under two years old, while few adults survived beyond forty. The three per cent or so who survived beyond fifty would have consisted largely of matrons and clerics who had been sheltered from the horrors of Dark Age warfare. If we were to apply these statistics to the Uí Dúnlainge, for instance, who were divided into three major dynastic groups, we would conclude that any one group such as the Uí Fáeláin could command the resources of about 700 men who were capable on age grounds of taking part in warfare. Of these, however, a significant number would be clerics or monastic tenants, while others would be prevented by physical disability or by their debased social status from taking part. Similarly, a minor tribe such as the Dál Messin Corb of east Wicklow might be capable of sending as few as 200 warriors or less into battle if we think of their entire tribal population in terms of 1000 people. Clearly, these figures are all too capable of being dismissed out of hand, particularly in a field which has been dominated by pedantry for so long. I offer them merely as part of a working model with a view to promoting an awareness of the great gaps in our knowledge of Dark Age societies. We are dealing with some Leinster tribes whose territories covered a few modern parishes, with land under peat and forest, and it would be naïve to think of them—as medieval writers did—in terms of great tribal 'nations'. Significantly, while Leinster annalists record a relentless inter-tribal slaughter over seven centuries, in spite of extravagant language used to describe these battles, the catalogue of slain aristocrats rarely runs beyond four or five persons in each case. But we still have little knowledge as to who was eligible to take part in warfare, and who was definitely obliged to take part, much less how many people fought in individual battles.

The maps in the Historical Atlas (Plates I-XVI) form the centre-piece in this study and it is hoped that they will provide a basis for future research not only on the Celtic period but for students of the later medieval Anglo-Norman age. The Irish landscape, unlike that of England for instance, presents stark contrasts both in physical features and in the quality of soil over quite short distances. In the case of Leinster the countryside is even more dramatically divided up than elsewhere by the presence of impassable and sterile granite mountain masses, together with the presence of extensive basin peat dividing up areas of the fertile lowlands. This variety of terrain has conspired to demarcate one tribal grouping from another and indeed it may be said to have consolidated tribal feeling within Celtic Ireland and to have promoted a strong sense of regionalism which has survived into the modern period not only in Ulster but throughout the island. This cannot be appreciated by consulting conventional physical maps including standard Ordnance Survey quarter- and half-inch sheets. Unless the bog cover is added to these maps by abstracting it from geological surveys, the true physical nature of the Irish landscape will forever elude geographer and historian alike. The Atlas, then, attempts to set the political and major ecclesiastical settlements against the natural background of mountain, bog and re-constructed forest, as well as tracing the evolution of tribes, dynasties and their political boundaries over seven centuries.

The numerous line-drawings throughout the text are not intended as decorative illustrations. They and their captions have been deliberately chosen to constitute a parallel theme within the book—namely, the essentially unified and indivisible nature of early Irish civilization. In other words, we cannot hope to understand the geographical picture of settlement within the Mid-land Bogs, for instance, without understanding the function of the monasteries, and without knowing something of their literary and artistic output as reflected in the material which still survives in libraries and museums all over Europe. This inter-disciplinary approach will not always satisfy the specialist; on the other hand, it does have the advantage of attempting to present an early civilization in its entirety by integrating a study of the manuscript and material remains into the all-important ecological setting.

CHAPTER I

History and Landscape:
the Formation of the Leinster Kingdom

Dinn Ríg, a platform hill-fort on the banks of the Barrow near Leighlinbridge in Co. Carlow, as it appeared about 1840 (Hall's Ireland). It was here, according to Leinster saga, that Labraid Loingsech, ancestor-god and king of the Leinstermen, overcame his rival, Cobthach king of Brega (Co. Meath), by burning him and his followers in an iron hall. This origin tale of the Leinstermen (The Destruction of Dinn Ríg) may relate to a Gaulish invasion of the Barrow valley in the third or fourth century B.C.

1

Dinn Ríg, strong Túaim Tenba, thirty nobles died there in anguish
Labraid the fierce champion crushed and burned them
The warrior of Ireland, grandson of Lóegaire Lorc.
Old Irish poem from the Scél Senchas Laigen;
translation by Myles Dillon

The early Irish disliked reality, and they disliked it as much in their politics as they did in their art. Just as their artists shunned the forms of nature and chose to draw the unreal twists and turns in the bodies of fantastic animals, so, too, their geographers and politicians preferred to see Ireland divided into five provincial kingdoms or Fifths (*Cóic cóiceda*) instead of the real and infinitely more complex situation which prevailed all through the Dark Ages and into the later medieval period. In addition to the five provinces recognised from antiquity—Leinster, Munster, Connaught, Ulster and perhaps Mide—at least three other regions had for all practical purposes the status of provinces in their own right—Ossory (Osraige) in the south, Airgialla in the north, and Brega in the east. Within these larger spheres of political influences there were usually two, and sometimes more, major power centres, which were frequently hostile towards each other and which were usually autonomous in respect of each other. We might cite Mide and Brega within the Southern Uí Néill alliance if 7 we choose to take that as a unity rather than two provinces; the Cenél Conaill and Cenél Eógain among the Northern Uí Néill; the Uí Maine and Uí Briúin in Connaught; or the Eóganacht Locha Léin and the Eóganacht Chaisil in Munster. Within this complex web of greater kingdoms or provinces and their major internal divisions, there existed a multitude of ancient tribal areas or *tuatha* which might still be ruled and occupied by their old tribal population-groups or by subdivisions of the ruling dynasties within each province. Ireland may have had as many as eighty or more tribal kings as late as the ninth century. The precise number is impossible to determine, because if the numerous septs represented by the subdivisions within our extant genealogies were ruled by magnates with the status of king or *rí*, then the total number of kings may have run into hundreds, before the decline of tribal kingship in the Scandinavian period.

To medieval Irish writers, however, the overall framework of the island was seen in terms of the Fifths and while there may well have been five major divisions in the prehistoric period, such a situation did not conform to the reality of things in the Christian era. Early Irish writers were even capable of ignoring the presence of the *Gaill* or Scandinavian Foreigners who came in the ninth century to Dublin and many other coastal areas—and who came to stay. The *Book of Invasions* (*Lebor Gabála*), listing the various people who had come to colonize the island in antiquity, was re-edited from century to century, but a place was never found in it for either the Scandinavians or the Anglo-Normans. Clearly, some invaders were more 'foreign' than others, and whatever the real situation, the doctrine that the Goidels (those Celtic Sons of Míl) were the last invaders to 'take' Ireland, could not be abandoned, in spite of the impact of Turgesius, Imhar or even Strongbow. This policy of refusing to recognize political and geographical realities was shared also by the ancient Welsh in regard to their Anglo-Saxon neighbours. The tenth-century Welsh poem, *Armes Prydein*, still saw the English—some five centuries after their conquest—as squatting precariously on old British lands. This poem held out the extravagant hope that, with the assistance of Scandinavian invaders, the English might be driven back to the North Sea and indeed beyond.[1]

Leinster, as an Irish kingdom, occupied a special place in the real and imagined scheme of things in the Middle Ages. Firstly, it was considered to have existed from time immemorial as the ancient Fifth of the Laigin or Leinstermen, and its ruling dynasties had their own impressive origin legend which testified to their identity as a distinct population-group which was alleged to have invaded Ireland through the Barrow valley under the leadership of a mythical ancestor, Labraid Loingsech.[2] Labraid established his people, the Laigin, in Leinster after his destruction of the fortress of Dinn Ríg, whose ramparts still survive overlooking the Barrow in south Co. Carlow (Plate XVI). It is the Leinstermen who have claim to antiquity, however, and not their province, for in the Dark Ages and before, tribal organization would have taken account of the Laigin as a people rather than the territory which they occupied. What little evidence we have, suggests, that originally the Laigin, or their relatives the Fir Domnann and the Gáileóin, once occupied territory as far afield as north-west Connaught.[3] Even in the historical period we can recognize the tribe of Dál Caipre Arad having a Laginian origin although occupying territory far west near the Shannon in Munster.[4] Monasteries near the Shannon, such as Lorrha and Terryglass[5], also had very strong Laginian connections which suggests that their Leinster founders may not have strayed very far from home when they established these monasteries in the sixth century. These houses later became isolated from the Leinster homelands as the power of the Laigin waned and as the borders of the Province receded behind the barrier of the bogs of Offaly. We can be more certain about Leinster domination of the Irish Midlands as far as the Hill of Ushnagh in Westmeath, until the Leinstermen were pushed back into the south-eastern corner of Ireland by the Uí Néill after the battle of Druim Derge in A.D. 516.[6] It is likely, too, that a powerful Leinster confederacy which controlled the southern plains of Mide in Co. Westmeath would also have dominated Tara in Meath. Leinster tradition certainly reiterated that the kings of the Province once ruled from Tara, and it is possible that Tara's occupation as a royal site may have come to an end with the retreat of Laginian warriors before the Uí Néill advance from Connaught into Brega in Co. Meath. Later Uí Néill tradition claimed the ancient kings of Tara for their own, but even the famous Cormac mac Airt, one of the prototypal law-givers of Ireland, may have been a Laginian ruler—if indeed he ever ruled at all.[7]

The Iron Age hill-fort on Tara is of similar construction to that of Knockaulin (Dún Ailinne) in Co. Kildare, another royal site—this time in the heart of Leinster—and one synonomous in Laginian tradition with the antiquity and prestige of Leinster kingship. There are tantalising hints[8] that the Fir Domnann were responsible for the building of the hill-fort on Knockaulin and, if so, it is possible that Ireland's eastern royal hill-forts were constructed by an invading aristocracy which came from western Britain, for the Fir Domnann were clearly related to the Dumnonii of Cornwall and their cousins in northern Britain.[9] Other evidence, too, such as the relationship between the name Laigin and that of the Lleyn peninsula in Wales suggest a West British origin for at least some of the Leinstermen.[10] We may point also to the connection between the placename Mag Nuadat, 'The Plain of Nuadu' (Maynooth, in northern Kildare), and the temple erected to serve the cult of the same Celtic god, Nodens, in Lydney Park in Gloucestershire.[11] Early Leinster sagas and origin tales, including *Orgain Denda Ríg* (*The Destruction of Dinn Ríg*), do allow for connections with Britain, but they also vouch for a Gaulish origin for other sections of the Laigin. But the argument for a West British or 'Welsh' origin for a section of the Leinstermen is supported by analogy with firmer evidence from the early monastic period where, once again, many prominent Leinster ascetics either visited St David's in Pembrokeshire, or actually came from Wales. Máedóc of Ferns, patron saint of the powerful Uí Cheinnselaigh is said to have apprenticed himself to the monastic calling under St David[12] while Molua of Clonfertmulloe in Leix (Plate XIV) was indirectly associated with St David in his *vita*[13]. St Finian of Clonard and Cainnech of Aghaboe in northern Ossory (Plate XIV), were both pupils of the Welsh saint, Cadoc, at Llancarvan in Glamorgan.[14] A number of lesser-known saints had a Welsh or British origin, such as Sanctán who founded his little community in the Dodder valley at St Anne's (Cell episcopi Sanctani) in Bohernabreena.[15] Monastic placenames, too, point to the presence of Britons as an important community in establishing Christianity among the Leinstermen. Unfortunately, writers who have held up the progress of research into the origins of Irish Christianity by squabbling over the details of Patrick's mission, have largely ignored evidence for the independent evangelization of the Leinstermen from fifth-century Britain. Patrician documents point to a mission under Iserninus in the central Barrow valley[16], and strong traditions, later transferred to Patrick, claimed that Palladius made his landfall on the Irish coast at Inber Dee (Arklow).[17] It is very likely that most of these early Leinster missionaries had come from western Britain and from Wales in particular. Placenames survive from the early monastic age in Leinster such as Cell na mBretan, 'Church of the Britons' (Brannixtown, Co. Kildare), and Gailline na mBretan, 'Gallen of the Britons' (Gallen, Co. Offaly), which again testify to a Welsh connection; and individual names in Laginian genealogies such as *Blat*, a ruler of the Uí Bairrche,[18] may show Welsh rather than Irish linguistic forms; while the tribal name *Uí Bairrche* may also have a linguistic relationship with that of the powerful northern British tribe of the Brigantes.[19]

We do not get a detailed picture of the political geography of Leinster until about A.D.800, and by then the heroic age had passed for warriors and monks alike. The heady days of conquests in Connaught and rule at Tara were over, and the initial impact which Christianity had wrought on the Leinstermen was now no more than a dim memory, which at Sleaty on the

Barrow was being worked into St Patrick's saga, where originally it did not belong.[20] Leinster was on the decline and, like the remnants of the ancient Ulstermen in the north, was in full retreat in the face of Uí Néill aggression. The island as a whole was bracing itself for an all-out assault from a wild and heathen people who were pouring out of the Norwegian fjords, hungry for loot and land. The Leinstermen had been living now for three centuries on the defensive against the Uí Néill, and their restricted territory had taken on the appearance of a natural fortress—the Fifth of the Leinstermen, a barricaded land, which ninth-century commentators liked to believe had existed from the beginning of remembered time. Leinster's borders did remain more or less fixed from c. 516 to the Anglo-Norman invasion in 1169, although the twelfth century saw a resurgence of Leinster power in the north which resulted in an expansion into southern Brega (Co. Meath). It is, therefore, possible to speak in very real terms of the political geography of Leinster and to assume that the boundaries of the Province, and many of its internal divisions, had a substantial degree of permanence during a period of six centuries. From frequent references to the location of monastic sites in terms of the tribal regions in which they stood, it is possible—given the great number of these monasteries—to establish the general extent of tribal areas. This information is confirmed in turn by the position of early Anglo-Norman baronial boundaries which were frequently (but not always) based on earlier Celtic tribal units. The extent of the larger political units within Leinster bears some relation at least to the diocesan boundaries established at the synod of Kells in 1152.

Clearly, no people could ever have thought of their territory in terms of lines on a map before the development of modern cartography, and the lines which we attempt to draw for these ancient territories today are invariably a crude reflection of barriers placed by nature which separated one tribe from another. Thus diocesan, baronial and ancient tribal divisions were all predetermined by the presence of mountain, river, forest and impassable bog which to this day fill the Leinster landscape with contrasting beauty. Hemmed in, as they were, in the south-east corner of Ireland, the sea provided protection along two coastlines on the east and south. In the north, the Leinster coast ran as far as the mud-flats of the Liffey estuary at Dublin Bay, and although this was fordable at low tide—hence Áth Cliath, 'The Ford of the Hurdles'—it offered a treacherous entrance or exit to an invading army. In 770, for instance, a Ciannachta army from Brega invaded Leinster and successfully slaughtered the Uí Théig, only to suffer casualties from drowning when caught by the incoming tide on the Liffey at Dublin as the Ciannachta made their way home[21]. The fact that the Norsemen chose to establish their chief fortress in Ireland at Dublin on the Leinster side of the Liffey suggests this was a no man's land between two enemy kingdoms, which was easily approached from the sea by those familiar with the sand bars in Dublin Bay, but which was inaccessible to the Uí Néill and exposed only to Leinster attack from the south. From Dublin the Leinster border ran west along the steep natural terracing of the Liffey valley, and it followed its tributary, the Rye Water, until it joined up with the head-waters of the Boyne. Here, on the borders of counties Meath and Kildare, the Leinster border was most exposed to Uí Néill incursions in the region of Cloncurry (Cluain Conaire Tomain: Plate XII). Apart from Dublin this area seems to have been the only other regular crossing point between Uí Néill territory and that of the Laigin. It was at this border monastery of Cloncurry, for instance, that a royal council or *rígdal* was attended by Fedelmid, king of Munster, and the northern highking, Niall, in 838.[22]

From a few miles west of Cloncurry, the Leinster boundary was defined by the impassable natural barrier of the Bog of Allen, and its extension westwards into Offaly. This boggy waste is seen on the maps (Plates XI-XIV) to sprawl in great irregularly shaped areas across the Midlands, but it is everywhere permeated by 'islands' and sometimes by extensive strips of fertile farmland. The Leinster border with the Uí Néill of Mide to the north and west is seen to hug the line of the bogland in places where it is particularly extensive, along the modern Offaly-Westmeath border. It then turned south across modern Co. Offaly, following diagonal strips of bog until it reached the Slieve Bloom mountains (Plates III and XIII). From the Slieve Bloom the Leinster boundary ran eastward once more along the upper reaches of the Nore basin through forest and bog which offered protection from Ossory until it reached the safety of the Slievemargy hills. These hills protected the Barrow valley in Carlow—the heartlands of Celtic Leinster—from Ossory and Munster to the west. The border next ran due south along these hills to the west of the Barrow, and across the Pass of Gowran (Belach Gabráin) until it joined the river Barrow in the region of St Mullins; and the tidal waters of that river isolated the Leinster kingdom from Munster for some twenty five miles from St Mullins in the north to Hook Head on the coast in the south (Plate XV). We know from the *Life of Moling* that the Barrow could only be crossed by a ferry at his monastery in southern Carlow.[23] The only vulnerable point in nature's defences from the Slievemargy hills to the sea was the Pass of Gowran which provided Leinster's enemies in Munster and Ossory with a natural entry point. Gowran was regarded as a major frontier post of the Leinstermen. In 858 we are told the high-king, Maelsechlainn I, carried off the hostages of Munster 'from the Pass of Gowran to Dursey Island in the West of Ireland'; while in 870 the highking Áed Findliath plundered the Leinstermen 'from Dublin to Gowran'[24] Yet again, in 906, Flann Sinna (the son of Maelsechlainn I) swept across Munster 'from Gowran to Limerick'.[25] Time and time again, invading armies must have marched through or near Gowran, one of the most notable historical occasions being the Munster and Ossory invasion led by Cormac mac Cuilennáin, the bishop-king of Munster, in 908. Cormac's forces were met by the Leinstermen and Uí Néill at Belach Mugna in southern Kildare and in the ensuing battle the Munster bishop lost his life.[26] Muirchertach of the Leather Cloaks led his army from Belach Mugna through the Pass of Gowran on his famous circuit of Ireland in the winter of 941.[27] It was through this forest pass at Gowran that MacMurrough and his Anglo-Norman storm-troopers forced their way, with heavy losses, into Ossory in 1169, and on their return to the Barrow valley they had to force their way across the *fásach* or wilderness of the Slievemargy hills.[28]

The boundary of the kingdom of Leinster was not an arbitrarily defined line of demarcation: it was a boundary imposed on the Leinstermen by nature due to their military weakness, and provided a natural barricade of wilderness, forest and bog which they relied upon in turn to bolster their essentially defensive position. This boundary not only followed the line of more obvious physical features such as rivers and bogs, but it can also be seen (Plate II) to follow with remarkable precision the watersheds of the Barrow and Liffey—the two great rivers of south-east Ireland. The limits of the kingdom were of course nothing more than a physical

2

St Annes, or Kilnasanctan at Bohernabreena in the Dublin mountains, was founded by Sanctán, a Welsh bishop of aristocratic origin who flourished in the early sixth century. Early Irish tradition also held that somewhere nearby in this valley at Bohernabreena was a palace of the Otherworld—the bruiden *or hostel of Da Derga—where the legendary Leinster king, Conaire, was lured to his death.*

shell, which enclosed a remarkably varied landscape settled by a people organized into at least fifteen lesser tribal kingdoms, all of whom lived in a complex political relationship with each other. The territorial extent of the kingdom coincided almost exactly with the drainage basins of the Barrow, Liffey, Slaney and Avonmore (Plate II). The major political axis of Leinster ran from the Slaney valley to the middle and upper Barrow, and across to the Liffey in the north and north-east. These rivers constituted a roughly north-south axis running through the centre of the kingdom with the high ground of Ossory and the Wicklow mountains on either side. The land varied in quality from some of the richest farmland in the whole island in Kildare, to the most desolate heights of exposed granite on the Wicklow hills, and to the wilderness of basin peat in the Bog of Allen (Plates I, III). Clearly, the strong seized and held the rich central lowlands, and the weak were consigned to the mountain and waste on the periphery. Early Irish topographical records allow us to study in unique detail the ecology of this Dark Age kingdom, and it is to the internal political structures and geography of Leinster that we must next turn.

CHAPTER II

Geography and Tribal Genealogy

Book of Ballymote *(127.b.1). Beginning of* Testament of Cathair Mór,
where this ancestor-god of the Leinstermen
addresses his eldest and favourite son, Rus Failge

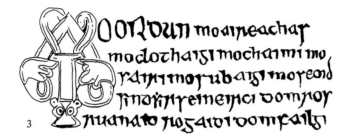

My rank and my lordship
My beauty and my fame
My cherished ancestral possessions
To my chosen champion Rus,
To my noble Failge of the red blade
To my strong and sturdy shelter of good oak

To my charioteer triumphant in battle.
May he be head and king of the Province,
This festive Rus Failge.
The fair-haired radiant ridge-pole
May he be the moon of the Provinces
And the long summer sun.

Based on the translation by Myles Dillon in
Lebor na Cert (*abridged*)

The genealogies of some seventeen Leinster tribes have been preserved by early Irish historians, and while a few of these consist of fairly rudimentary pedigrees, most contain detailed ramifications of the various septs or dynasties within each population-group. The total number of names contained in these records amounts to thousands of individual members of the aristocracy and hundreds of septs spanning seven centuries. In the Uí Failge pedigrees, for instance, the ancestry of over 220 persons is traced prior to the twelfth century, and these belong to any one of a dozen major sub-divisions of the tribe.[1] Some twenty-two other Uí Failge septs are listed but their precise pedigrees are not given. Apart from the Fothairt and Loígis who were universally recognized to be alien peoples among the Leinsterman,[2] the remaining fifteen tribes were considered by the genealogists to be descended from a common ancestor, Sétna Síthbacc,[3] who in turn was regarded as a descendant of Labraid Loingsech, that mythological king who was believed to have led the Leinstermen into Ireland from Gaul. The idea of this common ancestry for all the Laigin had little basis in reality and reflects the tribal nature of early Irish society, but in spite of that, the historian and geographer alike can learn a great deal from studying the precise relationship which the genealogists had worked out for each tribe in relation to another. To begin with, 13 these fifteen allegedly related tribes were not considered to descend according to a simple scheme involving descent from an original group of fifteen brothers thus:

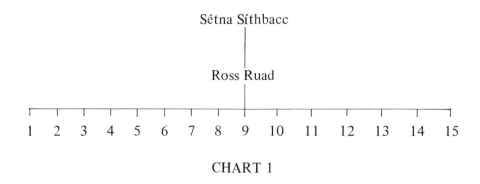

CHART 1

The relationship between tribes was conceived as being much more complex than this, constituting an overall tribal genealogy in its own right (Chart 2), and its intricate structure has much to tell us of the political and geographical status of each group. Unlike the genealogies proper (such as that of the Uí Failge mentioned above) which provide us with accurate information from *c.* A.D. 600 onwards, the overall tribal scheme has probably little historical validity in so far as many of the ancient Irish tribes may not have been related to each other at all. This is particularly true of tribes which were alleged to descend from a common ancestor who was considered to have lived back in the second or third century A.D. The interest of the inter-tribal framework, however, lies in its reflection of the social, political and even geographical position of each tribe within Leinster.

One of the most remarkable things about the tribal genealogy of the Leinstermen is that it consists of various strata—like archaeological or geological layers—which present us with a chronological and geographical progression, based on the principle that the 'youngest' tribes in the Province's genealogy occupied the fertile central axis within Leinster, while the 'oldest' tribes which descended from more remote ancestors occupied a correspondingly remote and unfavourable geographical position within the kingdom, either in the bogs of Offaly or the mountains of Wicklow (cf. Plates I and VIII). Beginning with the 'youngest' population-groups (Chart 2), we find that these consisted of the Uí Dúnlainge and Uí Cheinnselaig who occupied the richest lands in northern and southern Leinster respectively, and who monopolized the kingship of Leinster for more than four centuries before the Anglo-Norman Invasion (Plate VIII). It is no coincidence that the genealogies for these people are the most complex in the entire collection, and that their sub-divisions are presented with the same depth of information as was otherwise reserved for whole tribes in the case of more obscure peoples.[4] The Uí Dúnlainge and Uí Cheinnselaig provided Leinster with the same sort of political polarity as we have noted existed elsewhere among the other major provinces in Ireland— particularly among the Uí Néill. Although often bitter rivals, these two dominant Leinster dynasties conspired between them to dominate the Northern and Southern zones of the Province at the expense of weaker tribes.

When we move one step further out from the central genealogical stem of these two peoples, we find that their immediate 'cousins' occupied a geographical position slightly off the central axis of the kingdom but still close to the richest land and the centres of power. Thus the Uí Briúin Chualann (Chart 2) who were 'first cousins' of the Uí Dúnlainge (descended from Brión the brother of Dúnlaing) lived to the east of Uí Dúnlainge proper in south Co. Dublin (Plates VIII and XI). They were separated from the Uí Dúnchada (part of the mainstream of Uí Dúnlainge who occupied the rich country in the Liffey Plain) by Uí Fergusa who, although

Chart 2

Inter-Tribal Genealogy of the Leinstermen

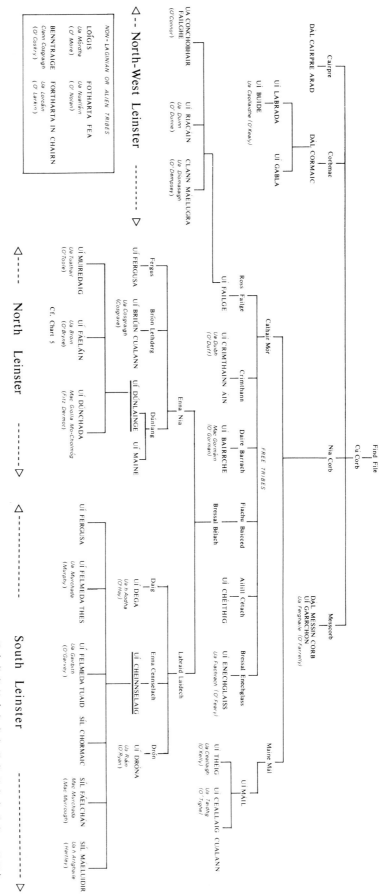

The Leinstermen liked to believe that with few exceptions all their freemen were descended from a remote and common prehistoric ancestor, Cú Corb. This chart shows how the various tribes of the Leinstermen were thought to fit into this common but artificial inter-tribal genealogy. The chart also shows how genuine aristocratic surnames evolved in the tenth and eleventh centuries from equally genuine dynasties of the seventh and eighth centuries. Some Leinster genealogies preserve genuine traditions going back to the sixth century, but the information shown at the top of this chart tells us more about how the Leinstermen liked to view their descent from remote ancestral tribes than about the more elusive prehistoric reality.

This chart may be studied in conjunction with **PLATES VIII** and **IX** of the Historical Atlas where the geographical distribution of tribes and dynasties is shown.

15

descended from Dúnlaing through an obscure son, Fergus, were not of the main stem. Nevertheless, both Uí Fergusa and Uí Briúin Chualann occupied reasonably good agricultural land, except that they were geographically on the periphery of the central axis of the whole kingdom (Plates III, IV and VIII). Similarly, the Uí Cheinnselaig in South Leinster had a cousinly relationship with Uí Dróna and Uí Dega (Plate VIII) and this genealogical relationship was reflected accurately in their peripheral geographical position in relation to Uí Cheinnselaig proper. Uí Dróna lands in Carlow were centred on the southern Barrow valley in a sort of *cul-de-sac*, hemmed in between the Ossory border on the west, and the Blackstairs mountains on the east (Plate XV). The Uí Cheinnselaig, by contrast, controlled the Slaney valley in both Carlow and Wexford, and it was the Slaney, and not the lower reaches of the Barrow, which formed the heart of southern Leinster in Celtic times (Plates I-II). The Uí Dega were also to one side of this central area occupying poorer lands in north Wexford on the foot-hills of the Wicklow mountains. It is likely that neither the *original* Uí Dróna nor Uí Dega were related in any way to the Uí Cheinnselaig. In later centuries their lands were occupied by Uí Cheinnselaig rulers and a genealogical 'explanation' was invented to account for this conquest.[5] It is true that most of the 'younger' septs of Uí Dúnlainge and Uí Cheinnselaig were genuinely related to each other, since these sub-divisions evolved during the historical period, and it may even be true that Uí Dúnlainge and Uí Cheinnselaig were themselves descended from a common ancestor, Bressal Bélach, who was alleged to have reigned as king of Leinster in the early fifth century.[6] What is clear from a map showing all the Leinster tribes (Plate VIII) is that, between them, Uí Dúnlainge and Uí Cheinnselaig controlled the most fertile land available within the kingdom, and the distribution of their lands coincided later with the area most densely occupied by the Anglo-Normans who replaced them in the late twelfth and early thirteenth centuries (Plate X). For Strongbow and Bressal Bélach alike, the valleys of the Liffey, Slaney and Barrow were clearly of crucial importance.

Bressal Bélach, the shadowy ancestor of Uí Dúnlainge and Uí Cheinnselaig, was, according to Leinster tradition,[7] a son of Fiachu Baicced who was in turn one of the children of Cathair Mór, an ancestor-god and father of all free peoples of Leinster. Thus, while the position of Bressal Bélach constitutes a genealogical landmark or stratum in the pedigree as ancestor of Leinster kings from the seventh to the twelfth centuries, so we reach a second stratum with Cathair Mór, who was ancestor not only of kings of the Province but of all tribes who were exempt from paying tribute to those over-kings.[8] These Free Tribes consisted of Uí Failge, Uí Bairrche and Uí Enechglaiss, while lesser tribes such as Uí Chéthig, Uí Chrimthainn Áin and Uí Luascán originally enjoyed that status. Again, remarkably, we find that these Free Tribes occupied a geographical position either further out on the periphery of the Leinster kingdom than those occupied by Uí Cheinnselaig and Uí Dúnlainge or that their lands were appreciably poorer. Uí Failge were forced to occupy the boggy wastes of basin peat and its fertile 'islands' in the north-west; Uí Bairrche lived on the uneasy frontier in north Carlow which separated the rival overlords, Uí Dúnlainge and Uí Cheinnselaig; while Uí Enechglaiss had been forced to leave the central lowlands altogether and crossed over the Wicklow mountains to the Arklow area on the east coast. Uí Chéthig and Uí Chrimthainn Áin occupied an obscure and remote position on the borders of the Province in northern Kildare and Leix respectively. There is evidence, however, to show that Uí Failge in particular had once controlled the Liffey Plain as kings of Leinster in the sixth century, and at one stage they ruled far beyond the historical boundaries of Leinster as far as Ushnagh in Westmeath.[9] The Uí Bairrche, too, once supplied kings to Leinster probably in the fifth century,[10] and it is interesting to find that both peoples still had a small but significant share in a portion of the richest soil of the northern and central regions respectively. The richest area of Uí Failge was located in what is now western Co. Kildare and included Kildare monastery itself. Uí Failge occupation of this region is recalled in the names of the Kildare baronies of Offaly East and Offaly West (Plate VII). This region was lost to Uí Failge at the Norman Invasion, if not before.[11]

Moving further back in the genealogy of tribes (Chart 2), we find that the Uí Máil were considered to descend not from Cathair Mór, but from his brother, Maine Mál. Thus, while they were not free they were regarded as very nearly so, by custodians of Leinster tradition. In spite of this cousinly relationship with the Free Tribes of Leinster they may have had a very different ethnic origin from them, because we know from contemporary sources that the Uí Máil dominated the kingship of Leinster in the seventh century before being ousted eventually by the Uí Dúnlainge.[12] It is remarkable that genealogists could not agree that they were free from tribute in spite of their relatively recent greatness within Leinster. The fall from power of the Uí Máil and their sub-groups (Uí Théig and Uí Cellaig Cualann) was clearly reflected in their later geographical situation which centred on a long strip of territory along the western foothills of the Wicklow mountains, from the Glenn of Imaal (Glenn Ua Máil) in the south to Blessington in the north (Plates VIII and XI).[13] This was the area they occupied from c.A.D. 700 to 1200. The soil of this region was enriched by glacial drift from the Central Plain, but it gave way higher up on the western slopes of the mountains to sterile granite. By occupying these western slopes of the Wicklow mountains, the Uí Máil were living in a region half-way between the central axis of Leinster, dominated by the reigning kings of the Uí Dúnlainge and Uí Cheinnselaig, and the wilderness to the east of the mountains occupied by Uí Enechglaiss and the Dál Messin Corb.

We might almost predict, therefore, that Dál Messin Corb, who lost the kingship of Leinster back in the fifth century, occupied a remoter place in the Leinster tribal pedigree that most other tribes, and this was indeed the case. The third and one of the remotest strata within the tribal pedigree (Chart 2) centres on a legendary king, Cú Corb, who was the father of Niacorb, a direct ancestor of both the Free Tribes and the Uí Máil. But Niacorb had three brothers: Messcorb, ancestor of the Dál Messin Corb; Coirpre, ancestor of the Dál Cairpre Arad; and Corbmac, ancestor of the Dál Chormaic.[14] Kuno Meyer first pointed out that Cú Corb and all four of his sons have the same element corb or 'chariot' in their names, and clearly the tribes incorporating this element represent a distinct layer within the Leinster tribal genealogy.[15] What the genealogists were saying in effect at this point in the pedigree was that Leinster tradition believed that at some remote stage, prior to the ascendancy of the Uí Máil and even the Uí Failge in the sixth century, the Dál Messin Corb and its related tribes once occupied a central and powerful position within Leinster. Equally, the genealogists were recognizing the political weakness of these tribes from the eighth century onwards. We are fortunate to be able to confirm this interpretation in the case of the Dál Messin Corb at least, who can be shown to have ruled as kings of Leinster in the Liffey Plain in the fifth century, before being driven east across the Wicklow mountains to the coast.[16] Their 'cousins' the Dál Cairpre Arad lived outside Leinster altogether as a subject tribe in Limerick and Tipperary in Munster, though no doubt they once ruled in that area when it was part of the greater kingdom of Leinster before its contraction in the fifth century (Plate V). The Uí Buide, a sept of the Dál Chormaic, survived north of the Uí Bairrche as an insignificant people in Leix and southern Kildare (Plate VIII), but there is evidence to suggest that they, too, were once an important people, and perhaps the semi-legendary Cormac mac Airt, a king of Tara, was once part of their tradition before he was taken over by the usurping Uí Néill dynasty which conquered the northern half of Ireland (Leth Cuinn) in the fifth century. O'Rahilly was correct in his view that the name Lifechar, ('Lover of the Plain of Liffey') as applied to Cairpre Lifechar, the alleged son of Cormac mac Airt and king of Tara in the fourth century, indicates a Laginian origin for this king at   17 least.[17] The Dál Chormaic were not always confined to the central frontier zone between Uí Dúnlainge and Uí Cheinnselaig. Their relatives the Uí Gabla were situated further north on the Figile river (on the borders of modern Kildare and Offaly) and yet another group of Uí Gabla held lands in north-east Co. Kildare (Plate XI). It is significant, too that the Cuthraige who were first evangelized by Iserninus and his followers, were a branch of the Dál Chormaic,[18] and it is just this tribal group which we should expect to find flourishing in the fifth century.

Cú Corb and his sons bring us to the limits of the historical period within Leinster, and take us back to the legendary era of Setna Síthbacc and his son Mes Delmann Domnann, and to his grandson, Mac Domnann—those shadowy Dumnonii who invaded Leinster some time before the fourth century and established a ruling dynasty, the last remnants of which lived on as the Dál Messin Corb. A connection between the dynasty of Sétna Sithbacc and his supposed descendant, Cú Corb, with the British tribe of Dumnonii now seems virtually certain, and credit for first recognizing the consequences of this relationship regarding the origin of the Leinstermen is shared by O'Rahilly and Ryan who put forward their views on this subject in the 1940s.[19] Art Mes Delmann was regarded in Leinster tradition[20] as the builder of the ramparts of Dún Ailinne (Knockaulin, Co. Kildare), a hill-fort dominating the centre of the fertile axis of ancient Leinster (Plates III and V) and regarded as the centre of political power in pre-Christian times along with Dinn Ríg and Maistiu (Mullaghmast) further south. Alternatively, Art Mes Delmann's son is named Mes-Domnann in the *Book of Leinster* and the *Book of Ballymote*, a form which bespeaks a Dumnonii connection (Chart 2). Art himself is styled Mes Telmann Domnann ('of the Domnainn') and was believed to have slain the heroes of the world from the top of Knockaulin and to have built a fort on the side of that hill, called the 'seat' of Sétna Sithbacc.[21] Mes Delmann's son was also called Mac Domnann ('Lad of Fir Domnann'), while his brother's name, Nuadu Necht,[22] reminds us of Mag Nuadat (Plain of Nuadu) in north Kildare (Plate XII) and of the connection mentioned earlier with the British god, Nodens. Nuadu was believed to have slain Etarscél Mór, a legendary king of Ireland in Dún Ailinne, while Find File, a great-grandson of Nuadu Necht, and grandfather in turn of Cú Corb, was also associated in the Leinster *senchus* or traditional lore with Knockaulin.[23] Find's brothers, Ailill and Cairpre, ruled from the hill-forts of Cruachu in Connacht and Tara in Meath respectively.[24] The remarkable point about these legends is that they not only establish a British origin for an ancient Irish dynasty, but they connect that dynasty in turn with a series of archaeological monuments which do indeed belong to one class and which date to the late Iron Age—precisely the time we should expect an invasion from western Britain to have taken place.

The earliest invaders who were believed, in the native tradition, to have conquered Leinster were the Fir Domnann, Gáileóin and Laigin.[25] The Fir Domnann, as their Dumnonii connection suggests, must have formed an important contingent. Yet they may have been chronologically earlier than the Laigin since virtually all memory of them was lost to later tradition. A few placenames, such as Inber Domnann (Malahide Bay, Plate V) and Irrus Domnann (Erris, Co. Mayo) testify to the once wide areas of Ireland which they conquered.[26] Ryan saw the Gáileóin as a band of mercenaries from Britain,[27] while O'Rahilly believed they could be identified with the Gailenga Móra and Gailenga Becca who in later centuries ruled in Meath (Brega) and north Co. Dublin (Plate VIII).[28] We do have the lost placenames Dún nGáileóin ('Fortress of the Gáileóin') which cannot now be identified.[29] Significantly, it is stated to have been in Dál Messin Corb territory, and the Dál Messin Corb and their immediate ancestors have the best claims to being identified with the invading Dumnonii, the legendary builders of Knockaulin. The home of the Dál Messin Corb in the historical period was along the Wicklow coast (Plate VIII), but originally they controlled the Kildare Plains (Plate V). We ought not to seek for this lost fort in the wilderness of Wicklow or on its coast, but in the central Kildare region which the Dál Messin Corb (and their relatives the Dál Chormaic) held, up to the end of the fifth century. Finally, Ryan believed that the Laigin or Leinstermen were a sub-group of the invading Dumnonii coming from western Caernarvonshire, south of Anglesey in Wales, from the region of the Lleyn peninsula.[30] The linguistic connection between Laigin and Lleyn is a valid one, but the Laigin may have constituted a more important group of invaders than Ryan supposed. They have, after all, imposed the name of their tribe on the whole of south-east Ireland from their own time to the present. It is likely that the so-called Free Tribes of Leinster (Uí Failge, Uí Bairrche and Uí Enechglaiss, etc.,) constituted the original Laigin who replaced the Fir Domnann.

The British origin of yet another great Leinster people, the Uí Bairrche, seems equally certain, their name being related to that of the Brigantes of northern Britain. O'Rahilly was quite wrong in treating this people as non-Laginian, and he was in error, too, concerning their place in later Leinster history.[31] It seems clear that originally the Uí Bairrche controlled the whole of Laigin Desgabair (south Leinster) from the earliest centuries after Christ, until late in the fifth century. Their power was broken by the Uí Cheinnselaig who drove them out of the Slaney valley (Plate II) and split the once great tribe into two (Plate V). The northern section was henceforth confined to a corner of Leix and north and west Carlow, while the southern section (Uí Bairrche Tíre) was pushed into the area covered by the later barony of Bargy in Wexford (Plates VII and VIII). The Fothairt who, like the Loígis, were certainly not a Leinster people, seem to have been the mercenary troops of Uí Bairrche and Uí Failge. We find a tribe of Fothairt alongside the Uí Bairrche of Carlow (Forth Barony) and yet another branch of the Fothairt in south-east Wexford (Forth Barony, Wexford, Plates VII and VIII), alongside the Uí Bairrche Tíre.

The Uí Bairrche had a close genealogical connection with the Uí Failge and Uí Enechglaiss,[32] as Free Tribes descended from Cathair Mór (Chart 2), and all three peoples were once powerful in Ireland prior to the seventh century. The Uí Failge were the last of the Free Tribes of the Laigin to fall from power, and we can trace their rule as kings of Leinster in the sixth century. It is possible, too, to establish their position as overlords of Mide (the Central Plain about the Hill of Ushnagh) before being driven behind the bogs of Offaly by the Uí Néill in the early sixth century (Plates III and V).[33] The Uí Enechglaiss were probably toppled from a position of strength long before the decline of either the Uí Failge or Uí Bairrche. But we do have evidence to suggest that they once ruled not only to the west of the Wicklow mountains near Kilashee in the Kildare Plain (Uí Enechglaiss Maige, Plate XI), but Professor Ó Corráin has drawn attention to an Ogham inscription near Duleek in Brega (Plate III) which commemorates a ruler, Mac Cáirthinn of Uí Enechglaiss.[34] The Arklow home for the Uí Enechglaiss of later centuries (Plate VIII) was clearly a place in the wilderness for a tribe who had once enjoyed lands beside the Liffey and the Boyne (Plate V).

Finally, there are other indications from the earliest traditions regarding the coming of Christianity to Leinster which show that the Uí Cheinnselaig and Uí Dúnlainge dynasties of later centuries had not always been masters of that Province. To begin with, the tribal origin of some of Leinster's greatest saints conforms to a picture which we have already outlined for the fifth and sixth centuries. St Kevin of Glendalough and Conláed (St Brigit's first bishop of Kildare) were both of the Dál Messin Corb,[35] while Brigit herself was of the Fothairt (Plates III and VIII). Brigit's branch of the Fothairt was associated not with the Uí Bairrche but with Uí Bairrche's 'cousins', the Uí Failge. Colum of Terryglass and the two Sinchells of Killeigh were of the Dál Chormaic[36] (Plates III and VIII), while the Uí Bairrche claimed Fiach (and later also Áed) of Sleaty, and Ethne the mother of Columcille.[37] Neither the Uí Dúnlainge nor the Uí

19

Cheinnselaig could match this gallery of saints, in spite of strenuous efforts on the part of later ecclesiastical writers to connect these dynasties with St Patrick. These findings on the tribal origins of early Leinster saints are all the more significant when it is appreciated that in the Celtic world the founding fathers of the infant Church were usually sprung from the ranks of the ruling aristocracy. This was true in the case of Columba, the founder of Iona, as it was also true in the case of many of the early Welsh saints.[38]

It was inevitable that a place would be found for Patrick in the earliest traditions concerning the evangelization of Leinster, but it is highly unlikely that this famous northern saint ever set foot in the Liffey Plain. Early Christianity came to Leinster perhaps first with the mission of Palladius from Rome in A.D. 432, but more certainly through the labours of men such as Iserninus the Briton who preached in the Barrow valley in northern Carlow and southern Kildare. The first missionaries in fifth-century Leinster found the Province ruled by the Dál Messin Corb in the north, and by the Dál Chormaic and Uí Bairrche in the south. This is the reason why the Uí Bairrche and Dál Messin Corb figure so prominently in the saga of Patrick's 'grand tour' of Leinster. Patrick's involvement may well be fictitious, but the rôle of the Dál Messin Corb, Dál Chormaic and Uí Bairrche as royal patrons of the earliest Christian missionaries from Britain is based on a firmer historical foundation. Such a real and great event as the advent of a new religion made too deep an impression on the tribal memory for all the circumstances surrounding it to have been forgotten.

Thus, in Patrick's saga (the *Tripartite Life of Patrick* and other earlier seventh-century documents), while the Uí Dúnlainge and Uí Cheinnselaig overlords of the ninth century and later, have their ancestors introduced to the saint,[39] nevertheless other more obscure people still enjoy a prominent place in this great story. We are told that Dricriu, the Dál Messin Corb king of Uí Garrchon, refused to invite Patrick to his feast, and we learn also that Dricriu's queen was a daughter of the powerful Uí Néill king of Tara, Lóegaire son of Niall of the Nine Hostages (Noígiallach).[40] The Uí Garrchon would never have been allocated such a prominent place in this story had there not been a strong tradition which testified to their political dominance in the earliest Christian centuries. Patrick is said to have consecrated Fiach (of Sleaty) of the Uí Bairrche as the first bishop of the Leinstermen,[41] and there are obscure references in Patrician documents to the crushing of the Uí Bairrche by the Uí Cheinnselaig.[42] As for the earliest Christian settlements in Leinster, and perhaps even in Ireland as a whole, we must seek for these at places such as Laragh (barony of Shillelagh, Wicklow, Plates XII, XVI), Aghade (Carlow), *Toi Cuile,* and in the region of Clíu in Uí Dróna in Carlow—places not associated with Patrick, but with Iserninus. Further north in Leinster, Mac Táil's monastery at Old Kilcullen (Plate XII) beside Knockaulin hill-fort; Killashee (Cell Auxili); and Kileen Cormac (Cell Fine) with its possible associations with Palladius—all of these sites—take us as close as we can hope to get to those wandering Britons and Gauls who first preached the Christian message to a people ruled by the war-lords of the Fir Domnann, Gáileóin and Laigin.

CHAPTER III

Reconstruction of the Dark Age Landscape

Detail from the map of Leix and Offaly c. A.D. 1563 (see Frontispiece). This section covers the region from Rathangan and Monasterevin (bottom) east of the Barrow, to Clonygowan, shown deep in the forest of Offaly which was connected with Geashill by a tóchar (togher) or ancient causeway through the forest and bog.

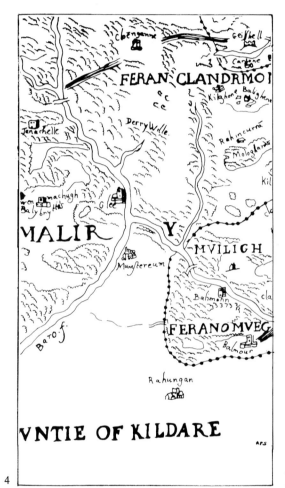

When from its side I gaze upon the fair
    Curragh,
The lot that has befallen every king causes
    awe at each downfall.

The Curragh with its glitter remains
None of the kings remain who ruled thereon.

Of each generation which it reared in turn
Liffey of Lorc has made ashes.

The Curragh of Liffey to the brink of the
    main,
The Curragh of Sétna, a land of peace as far
    as the Sea,
Many is the king, whom the Curragh
Of Cairbre Nia Fer has overthrown.

O Brigit, whose land I behold
Upon which each one in turn has moved
    about,
Thy fame has outshone fame of kings,
Thou art king over all.

Hail Brigit: a poem c.A.D. 900 honouring the patroness of the Leinstermen; translation by Kuno Meyer

The extent of ancient Leinster or Cóiced Laigen consisted in terms of modern counties (Plates VII and X) of all of Wicklow, Wexford and Carlow; the southern half of Dublin; all of Kildare excluding the barony of Carbury in the north-west (Plate VII); the eastern portion of Offaly and Leix; and finally a narrow strip of Kilkenny where it borders on Carlow. This framework of the modern county boundaries provides the most familiar frame of reference to the reader, and is reproduced in most of the accompanying maps. The county boundaries themselves are all of Anglo-Norman or later English origin, but 21

in the chronological order of their shiring they conform to an historical pattern whose roots lie deep in pre-Norman times (Plate X). The first Leinster counties to be marked off for shire ground before the end of the thirteenth century were Dublin, Carlow, Kildare and Wexford,[1] along with adjoining Kilkenny (Osraige) in the west, and Meath (Brega) to the north. These oldest shires covered the most fertile part of Leinster and the Southern Uí Neill kingdoms, and clearly the Anglo-Normans, like the Gaelic war-lords before them, were determined to settle on the most productive agricultural land.

The counties lying on either side of this central axis formed by the drainage basins of the Liffey and the Barrow were not defined until a much later date. In the north-west, the counties Offaly and Leix were constituted as the King's and Queen's County respectively, in 1555, but they were not finally defined until as late as the reign of James I [2] when the ancient non-Leinster territories of Fir Cell, Muinter Tadgáin and parts of Éle and Delbna Ethra were added in the west (Plates VIII-X). On the eastern side of Leinster's central fertile belt, Wicklow was the last county to be shired in the reign of James I.[3] Thus, the last remnant of the Laginian aristocracy survived on the poorer soils on either side of the Anglo-Norman invaders for 400 years in possession of their lands, protected in the west by bog and in the east by high mountain waste (cf. Plates I and X).

This shiring sequence in Anglo-Norman and later centuries emphasizes the status of the North-West and North-East regions (Plate I) as survival areas, for the dynasties which held out in these regions originally had a share in the rich central lowlands. The O'Tooles and O'Byrnes of Wicklow once held the rich Kildare Plains under their older sept names of Uí Muiredaig and Uí Fáeláin respectively (Plates VIII-X), before being pushed into the mountains by the Normans. Thus, the geography of the region conspired to send tribe after tribe on the road to eventual extinction across the Wicklow hills; and history, which had dealt so unkindly with Uí Enechglaiss and Dál Messin Corb in the sixth century, repeated itself in regard to the fate of O'Byrne and O'Toole in the thirteenth. In the north-west, Uí Failge lands extended eastwards into Co. Kildare as far as the Curragh (Plates VIII and XI). After the Norman Invasion the Uí Failge were confined to the boggy portion of their territory behind the Barrow and its tributaries. It was this greatly confined remnant of the lands of Ua Conchobhair Failge that formed the nucleus of King's County in 1555. When the non-Leinster Gaelic territories in the west were added to this county, and the ancient eastern extension was ignored, the area truly became the King's County rather than Uí Failge. The modern restoration of the name Offaly bears little relation to *Offalie* or Uí Failge of Tudor, much less of earlier times. The name Leix restored to Queen's County pays homage to the memory of the Loígis of Leinster, but the old Leinster border divides this county in two; the Loígis occupied its eastern half only, while the western portion (Plates VII and VIII) was held by the kingdom of Ossory and by the sept of Uí Duach in particular.

The study of the geographical background is not merely ancilliary to our research: it provides us with an additional source in its own right. The manuscript sources contain a wealth of references to territorial divisions and to individual sites—secular, ecclesiastical and mythological; these provide us with an intricate settlement pattern, the full significance of which can only be appreciated when examined in relation to the physical geography of the region. In this study, where we are attempting to integrate two very different kinds of information, a rigid policy of selection has to be followed, lest the material from one discipline should become irrelevant to the other. Ó Lochlainn's comment on his efforts to recover the road-systems of pre-Norman Ireland may be repeated with all the greater application here: 'The field is so wide that nothing like finality could be hoped for even if one had no other care in life.'[4]

We are interested not in Leinster of to-day but in reconstructing the landscape and settlement pattern of the pre-Norman kingdom of the Laigin. The pattern of river, mountain and fertile plain has not changed in the centuries that separate us from our subject. The recovery of the picture of bogland and forest on the other hand depends on the availability of documents describing these features in past centuries and upon the rate of change of their natural growth. The rate of bog growth is infinitesimally slower than that of trees, and the continued presence of a bog is as relatively lasting as that of the prevailing climate. Bogland, until the advent of the industrial revolution, was unreclaimable for man, while the forest, from prehistoric times, was an easy prey to his axe and vulnerable also to climatic change. In spite of these sudden and dramatic changes that may alter the extent of woodland, we are fortunate in having documentation describing its extent in Ireland by the beginning of the seventeenth century, while our first reliable and general survey of the more enduring bogland does not occur until the early nineteenth century.

In the case of forests, documentation from State Papers, general descriptions and maps, all began to record evidence before vast tracts of native woodland were exploited for the many English industries hungry for the precious commodity of timber.[5] This documentation— mainly from the seventeenth century—came none too soon, because by 1700 only a fraction of the original forest cover had survived. It is the maps alone of our sources which indicate the actual extent of the woodlands,[6] and an investigation of other manuscript evidence from the sixteenth and seventeenth centuries is outside the scope of this study. Such an enquiry is unlikely to alter greatly the conclusions reached from an examination of the maps in conjunction with McCracken's very valuable researches on Irish forests in the Early Modern period. Most sixteenth and early seventeenth-century map-makers working on Ireland were borrowing from a common source. Their information seems to have been derived from the survey of Robert Lythe, undertaken during his visit to Ireland 1568-1571.[7] Few maps of Lythe have survived, but two important points in connection with them have a bearing on this study. Firstly, since Speed and other contemporary map-makers borrowed heavily on his surveys, the information in their maps derives from as early as the third quarter of the sixteenth century; and secondly, since all these sources are so heavily indebted to Lythe, even an exhaustive study cannot give to any one of them—not even to Speed—the status of an independent authority.

We are fortunate to have three detailed regional maps for the Leinster area. Two of these— the map of Leix and Offaly c.1563[8] (Frontispiece) and the map of the barony of Scarawalsh, Wexford (1657)[9], (Plate B), are independent of Lythe's survey, while the third—covering the Carlow barony of Idrone (1662)[10] —derives from Lythe's work (Plate A). These three valuable surveys not only substantiate the small-scale evidence of the larger and more general maps, but they cover between them three important areas of medieval Leinster. Their larger scale enables us to plot features in detail against the Celtic topography, giving a very convincing picture and adding greatly to our knowledge of the early Leinster landscape. It is important to bear in mind, (as Andrews has shown in the case of Lythe), that all these Early Modern Leinster maps under discussion were drawn up, not for antiquarian or scholarly purposes but to further the English conquest of Ireland. These maps deal either with Gaelic regions marked off for conquest or for plantation and as such they are immensely valuable to the historical geographer interested in the Celtic environment. Ironically, as instruments designed for the destruction of the Gaelic past they now serve to rescue that lost world from oblivion.

If we set 1550 as the earliest date for which we can give an adequate account of Irish forests, it needs stressing that we are still 400 years at least from the kingdom of the Leinstermen. Accepting these limitations, however, and remembering that the forests described were of a natural character and were destroyed not by climate or disease, but to further the Tudor conquest of Ireland and English industries, this sixteenth-century picture is still of use for a study   23

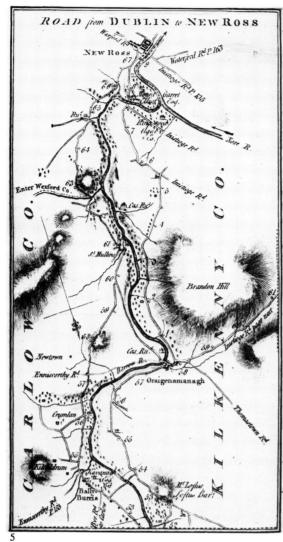

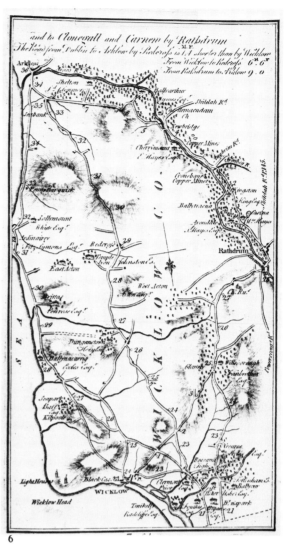

5
Taylor and Skinner's map of roads between Borris in Southern Carlow and New Ross in Wexford, showing extensive forest cover in all this part of the Barrow valley still surviving prior to 1777. The presence of woodland or ros *is preserved in place-names such as Ros mBroc, the old name of St Mullins; and Ros Ua mBerchon, now Rosbercon opposite New Ross (Ros Mhic Thriuin) on the Barrow. The* Life of St Moling *refers to dense forest along the Barrow in southern Carlow, and the Leinster king, Art MacMurrough Kavanagh, had his principal fortress in the wood of nearby Leighlin in the late fourteenth century. The taming of the Gaelic land-*

scape was not achieved in this region until Lord Deputy Sir Edward Bellingham turned the old Carmelite convent at Leighlinbridge into a fortress in 1548, by means of which the Kavanaghs were subdued and the forests cleared.

6
Taylor and Skinner's map of the roads between Wicklow and Arklow surveyed before 1777 showing forest still surviving in the valleys of the Avoca, Avonmore and Avonbeg. There is also extensive woodland shown along the lower reaches of the Vartry and in the valleys surrounding Glenealy.

of the medieval landscape. The extent of the primeval forest was great. While the position of clearings no doubt varied from century to century, the probability of extensive woodlands existing in a particular area in the Middle Ages must be high if that region is shown under forest on Tudor maps.

The extent of the primeval forest in ancient Ireland as shown by sixteenth-century map-makers is confirmed by the writers of saints' *Lives* in the eleventh and earlier centuries. Forests are referred to in the *Lives* of Carthage of Lismore, Fintán of Clonenagh and Munnu of

Taghmon.[11] The *Life* of Moling graphically confirms the presence of 'dense forest in a very rugged valley' near his monastery at St Mullins in southern Carlow (Plates I, III, V, XVI).[12] The exact location most likely refers to Glyn on the eastern side of the Barrow, but it is certain that most of the western bank of that great river from Slievemargy to St Mullins was covered in forest. Similarly, a forest near St Ciarán's monastery at Seirkieran (Plates III, XIV) blocked the path of a Munster army,[13] and we know that an alternative name for the nearby Slieve Bloom mountains was Ros mic Edlicon[14] (Plate XIV), the *ros* or 'forest' being the great wood which clad the foot-hills of Slieve Bloom and which was vividly drawn on the sixteenth-century map of Leix and Offaly (Frontispiece). The forest of Offaly which covered so much of Uí Failge territory survived intact until the sixteenth century where it can be seen stretching on the Tudor map in a panoramic picture from the banks of the Barrow westwards across Loígis and Uí Failge to Fir Cell in Mide, and to the foot-hills of Slieve Bloom. 'The Great Wood' of Leix is specifically named on this map (Frontispiece) and placed north and west of the Barrow at Kilberry, but as early as 1514 the Fitzgeralds of Kildare had cut down a significant portion of this 'Great Wood in O'More's country' (Coill Mór ar Laíghis Uí Mórdha)[15] in an attempt to break the natural defences of that Gaelic kingdom. Individual woodlands set within the great Offaly forest are sometimes named in the early sources, such as Ros Corr (Roscore Wood) south of Rahan, and Fid Elo near Lynally, or Coill an Cláir (Kilclare) mentioned in connection with Lynally monastery in the *Life* of St Colmán.[16]

The high proportion of 'Ros' and 'Derry' (*doire*, 'oakwood') placenames which survive from Uí Failge and Loígis territory also testify to the existence of great stretches of oak and other forest in that region. On the Leinster slopes of the Slieve Bloom, we have Rosenallis (*Ros Finnghlaise*, 'Wood of the Bright Stream'), Camross and Rossnagad; as well as Derrycon, Derrylough, Derry Hills, and Derrylemoge—all in Leix. In Uí Failge territory, in modern Offaly, we have Derryounce, Derryvilla, Derrygarran, Derrylesk, Derryrobinson and Derrygawny in the east; while in western Uí Failge (i.e. central Co. Offaly) we have Derrycoffey, Derrygreenagh, Derrygrogan and Derryclure. Some eight miles west of the Leinster border near Fir Cell in Mide lies Ballinderry Lough on the borders of Offaly and Westmeath. Here two lake-dwellings or *crannóg* sites were excavated by the Harvard Archaeological Expedition in the early 1930s (Plate XIV), and *crannóg* No. 1 proved to be immensely rich in archaeological finds from the tenth century when the *crannóg* was built. The great timbers which formed the raft for this artificial island dwelling were significantly of oak, an appropriate timber for a site called *Baile an Doire*, 'Place or settlement of the Oakwood'. Other timbers used in the construction of the island and its houses were mainly of alder and ash, while numerous wooden vessels and artifacts discovered on the site were made mainly from willow, yew and oak. The layers of brushwood used to stabilize the raft contained branches of silver birch, hazel, holly, poplar, and bracken. *Raithean*, the Irish for 'bracken' has probably given its name to the great monastery of Rahan just a few miles to the south (Plate XIV) while the memory of hollywoods are preserved in the name of the monastery of Drumcullen (Druim Cuilinn) also in Fir Cell, Co. Offaly (Plate XIV).

It is clear from the *Life* of St Kevin of Glendalough that vast areas of the Wicklow mountains were still under natural forest in the pre-Norman period. This north-eastern region of Leinster is referred to as containing *deserta loca* in Kevin's *Life*; and a solitary traveller is described as going through a region in Wicklow of 'deserted forests and mountains' which provided a retreat for wolves, birds of prey, highwaymen and outlaws from Uí Dega in northern Wexford and elsewhere.[17] All of this region from south Co. Dublin to north Wexford must have had dense forest on the mountain foot-hills while the tops of the mountains were covered with bare granite or blanket bog (Plates III, XII). A northern portion of this woodland survived into the later Middle Ages as the royal forest of Clencree,[18] while in the south the forest on the borders of Wicklow and Wexford survived into the seventeenth century. The entire region from Moyacomb (Mag dá Chonn), on the Carlow-Wicklow border, to the sea at Arklow was completely devoid of early Christian monastic sites (Plate XII), nor can we ascribe any Celtic tribe to this region with any certainty (Plate XI). It was obviously an uninhabited wilderness, a combination of forest and marsh in the adjoining valleys of the Derry River and Derry Water. It is significant that both rivers take their names from *Daireach*, 'abounding in oaks', and in this region, too, the barony of Shillelagh (Plate VII) may have given its name to the celebrated Irish walking-stick from the abundance of timber there in more recent times. Apart from the 'Derry' placenames of Wicklow, other names remind us of the great diversity in the make-up of the ancient Wicklow forest. Among these we might note Newrath (*an Iubhrach*, 'abounding in yews'), Oghil (*Eóchaill*, 'yew wood'), Cullenmore (*Cuilleann Mór*, 'great holly'); Glencullen (*Gleann Cuilleann*, 'holly glen') in the mountain foot-hills of south Co. Dublin, and other Wicklow placenames such as Bahana (*beitheánach*, 'abounding in birch') and Farnees (*fearnach*, 'place of alders'). It is perhaps the cultivated apple tree which appears in Aghowle (*Achad Abhall*, 'orchard', Plate XVI) and Ballynowlart (*Baile an abhall ghuirt*, 'settlement of the orchard'), and yet the crab apple was plentiful too, as is demonstrated by the fact that several wooden vessels preserved in Irish bogs were made from that wood. The frequent occurrence of the yew tree as an element in Gaelic placenames reminds us that Giraldus was struck by the abundance of that tree in Irish woodlands.[18a]

Even the more densely inhabited areas still had some uncleared forest in Celtic times such as Fid Cuilind (Feighcullen) under the Hill of Allen in Kildare (Plate XII), or Fid Dorcha, 'The Dark Wood', near the monastery of Lynn (Lann in Fir Tulach), Westmeath (Plate XIV). The Old Irish placename *mag*, 'open plain', also provides us with an indication of which areas had been cleared of forest, confirming our view that Mag Life and Mag Ailbe (Co. Kildare); Mag Breg (valleys of the Boyne and Blackwater in Meath); Mag Asail in Westmeath; and the Barrow and Slaney valleys in south Leinster were the most densely occupied areas. Nevertheless, the reader comes away from the early literature with the decided impression of a greatly under-populated land, and of the island as a whole consisting of a wilderness of timeless beauty, barricaded by bogs, mountains and vast expanses of mixed forest, mostly of oak, hazel and ash, but also with woods of rowan, holly and yew. And in the midst of this primeval splendour were great tribal clearings occupied by population-groups who lived in isolation from each other. Only holy men, courageous traders, wandering poet-scholars or marauding armies dared to brave the wilderness beyond.

We may proceed less cautiously in regard to bogland than with the forest. While bogs have been forming within Ireland since the retreat of the great ice-sheets, it was the onset of wet conditions during the Late Bronze Age which saw the bogland attain its maximum growth.[19] Since that time, throughout the Early Christian period and later, the distribution of boggy tracts in Ireland has remained virtually unchanged until the middle of the nineteenth century. As early as 1810 the *First Report of the Commissioners appointed to enquire into the nature and extent of the several bogs in Ireland, and the practicability of draining and cultivating them* was published by the British Government. It was not, however, until the middle of the century that the first great Arterial Drainage Schemes got under way.[20] Since that time, several million acres of waste have been reclaimed. By the second quarter of the nineteenth century, however, the Ordnance Survey had completed its work of surveying the country systematically and accurately for the first time. This survey has preserved for us the configuration of the bogland before the great drainage operations began, although it had come too late to record smaller and insignificant patches of marsh and bog drained by progressive

26

eighteenth-century landlords.

The bogland and ancient forest have been plotted in detail for the Leinster region on Plates XI-XVI. Against this physical background, including rivers and mountains, the ancient secular and ecclesiastical settlements of the Leinster kingdom have been plotted. Where the state of knowledge allows, pass ways and track ways have been added. These maps give us a picture of Cóiced Laigin, or the 'Fifth of the Leinstermen', c.A.D. 800. With few exceptions, all the monasteries shown were in existence by then, while the secular or royal sites date from earlier in the Christian period and in some cases from the Iron Age or proto-historical period. The fact that many of these royal forts were deserted by 800 does not invalidate their presence on the maps, for these forts, deserted or not, still played an important rôle in the life of the Province. Deserted fortresses, with particularly strong historical associations, were used by the eulogistic court poets as symbols of kingship, or as symbols of Leinster resistance to Uí Neill and later Anglo-Norman aggression, long after they ceased to be occupied.[21]

A notable feature of the detailed map plates (XII, XIV, XVI) is the relative scarcity of secular settlements, contrasting with the abundance of monastic centres. Almost all the ecclesiastical sites were monastic in character, but due to the peculiar nature of Irish monasticism we can take it that these sites served local communities, in the manner of parish churches in medieval England. We may assume, too, as in the case of early Wales, that for every monastic site on the map there was at least one corresponding important secular centre. Detailed field studies on the nature of early Irish settlements are virtually non-existent, but it is very likely that Professor Glanville Jones's findings on settlements in Aberffraw Hundred on the Island of Anglesey, for instance,[22] will prove in time to hold good for Ireland also. Here the settlement pattern tended to gravitate around two focal points—one ecclesiastical and the other royal. As in Wales, too, we can already recognize, in the siting of certain Irish monastic foundations, a close geographical and historical relationship with nearby centres of royal power. Examples of

7

Fragments of a High Cross at Old Kilcullen (Cell Chuilind) near Knockaulin hill-fort, Co. Kildare, from Ledwich's Antiquities of Ireland *(1790). The fragment in the foreground has since been lost, and shows a section of panels with the Twelve Apostles. The scene on the top-left panel of the vertical column shows the abbot of the monastery being slain by a marauder, and this most likely commemorates the sack of Old Kilcullen by King Olaf Gothfrithsson, the Scandinavian ruler of Dublin and York, who led a thousand people captive from this centre on a slave-raid in A.D. 938.*

this occur in the relationship of the church of Slane with the palace of the kings of Northern Brega at Knowth; the church of Trevet with the nearby palace of the kings of Southern Brega at Lagore; the church of Kill with the palace of the kings of north Leinster at Naas; the church of Ferns with the royal palace there in south Leinster; the church of Kilranelagh with the palace of the Uí Máil kings, and so on. The closeness of the geographical relationship in these cases suggests that the monasteries in question served as royal chapels to the local tribal leaders, and in many cases we can show that members of the local aristocracy actually ruled these monastic houses. This relationship was born out of geographical proximity and is a rather different phenomenon than, say, the tight control which the kings of Leinster kept over such great monastic houses as Kildare and Glendalough. These two monasteries had been founded by saints whose cults had spread their fame as miracle-workers far and wide. Such sanctity and fame in turn had caused places like Kildare and Glendalough to build up large *paruchiae* and grow wealthy from the revenues of their dependent houses and tenants. It was inevitable, with the degeneration of Irish monasticism from as early as the seventh century, that such rich and powerful houses would fall under the influence, not of local tribal kings, but of the ruling overlords of the Province. And so Kildare, although in Uí Failge territory—and originally belonging to the Fothairt—fell under the patronage of Uí Dúnlainge overlords. From the seventh century it was ruled by 'royal-abbots' of the Uí Dúnlainge such as Áed Dub (+639) or Muiredach (+965). Similarly, Glendalough, although located in Uí Máil territory in a remote Wicklow valley, was carefully monitored by the Uí Dúnlainge. It was ironic that monasteries founded by genuinely holy men and women, who had fled from the world, became too lucrative an asset to be ignored by the warrior aristocracy. The same was true of course for Anglo-Saxon England, Carolingian Francia and Ottonian Germany.

The precise location of early Irish monasteries has been recorded in the annals and ecclesiastical literature and most of these centres have survived on the ground as places of Christian burial, if not of worship, into the modern period. Given the survival of these monuments in their geographical setting in such remarkable numbers, it is extraordinary that so little fieldwork has been carried out with regard to local geological conditions and to the environment generally. Apart from significant advances in aerial photography undertaken by St Joseph and by Swan, scholars still appear content with rather obvious observations. Thus, many Irish monasteries have been seen to be located near streams, as if a water supply were an exotic facility even for an Irish ascetic. The overall distribution of monasteries on Plates XII, XIV and XVI shows that they were relatively low-lying—avoiding both high ground and also the ill-drained boggy flats—concentrating on well drained soils either on the lower slopes of mountains or on gravel ridges in the bogland territories. With a few obscure exceptions, such as Rathaspik and Kilgory on the Slievemargy hills in Leix (Plate XIV) and others in Wicklow, all monastic sites are below the 500-foot contour line. Many important religious houses occur quite near this line or just below it. Examples of these are Kinnity, Rosenallis and Clonfertmulloe—all on the foot-hills of the Slieve Bloom mountains (Plate XIV); Timahoe and Kileshin, in relation to the Slievemargy hills; and Dysart beneath the Rock of Dunamase (Dún Masc, Plate XIV). Moving from north to south along the foot-hills and deep valleys of the Dublin and Wicklow mountains we have St Anne's, Saggart, Kilteel, Oughterard, Brannixtown, Gilltown, Kileencormac, Timolin, Moone, Clonmore and Aghowle—all near the 500-foot line (Plate XII). In the Barrow valley, Kileshin, Old Leighlin, Shankill and St Mullins (Plate XVI) all lie in the shadow of this contour, and finally in Uí Cheinnselaig we have Templeshanbo (Senboth Sine) in north-west Wexford, on the foot-hills of Mount Leinster (Suidhe Laigen) (Plate XVI). The distribution of Irish monasteries is not unlike that of the early Welsh churches and settlements

28 which tended to avoid the higher ground over 600 feet and concentrated in the coastal low-

lands and river-valleys of north and south Wales.[23] Studies on Welsh settlements such as Llanynys in the Vale of Clwyd, or the Celtic nucleated settlement at Kirkby Overblow (near Harrogate, West Riding, Yorks.), show that early British settlers carefully chose well drained brown earths and favoured ridges located near the 400-foot contour.[24]

Some Irish monasteries began as *disert* or hermitage sites. A classic example of this – and one which can only be appreciated after taking local geological conditions into account – is Clonmacnoise on the Shannon (Plate XIV). This house was surrounded by several square miles of basin peat with a narrow access route over ten miles long, leading along a limestone gravel ridge or esker into Mide. This route became known in later centuries as the Pilgrims' Road. Glendalough, in the heart of the Wicklow mountains (Plate XII), is shown from the *Lives* of St Kevin to have started life as an ascetic retreat and at this monastery, too, a famous trackway (St Kevin's Road) was used by pilgrims of later centuries, who crossed the mountains from the Kildare Plains.[25] The vast majority of monasteries, however, owed their existence to serving local communities. Even Clonmacnoise and Glendalough later became centres of great wealth and political influence, and there is no doubt that this was facilitated by their geographical position. Both monasteries were founded far from the settlements of men, yet both lay near important communication routes that undoubtedly existed before their foundation. Several important monasteries of the Loígis lay on or very near the Slige Dála (Road of Assemblies), a major trackway of pre-historic origin (Plate XIV) joining Roscrea with the Plain of Liffey. These houses included Coolbanagher, Clonenagh, Mountrath, Mondrehid, Clonfertmulloe and Roscrea. Further north in Mide (Plate XIV), Clonfad in Fir Bile and Clonfad in Fir Tulach, along with Rahugh, all lay near the Slige Mór (Great Way) which ran from Brega to Athlone on the Shannon. Rahugh also lay on the only major route from Northern Ireland into Munster which once again passed near several important monasteries – Durrow, Tihilly, Lynally, Drumcullen, Kinnity, Seirkieran, Roscrea and Birr.

Here we are reminded of the researches of Professor Melville Richards who observed[26] that many great early Welsh monasteries were not located in the wilderness as was once believed, but rather on highways of – sometimes even international – importance, as in the case of St David's near the crossing-point to Ireland. Other examples included Bangor on the Menai Straits; St Asaph on the crossing of the River Clwyd, or Llandaff near the crossing of the River Taf and on the borders of Senghennydd and Gwynllŵg.[27] Irish monasteries were also located on borders, as well as trackways and fording places on rivers. Thus, Clonmacnoise on the Shannon lay on the borders of Mide and Connaught; Birr and Roscrea on the borders of Mide and Munster; Clonfertmulloe on the borders of Leinster (Loígis) and Munster (Éle); Clonenagh on the borders of Leinster (Uí Failge) and Mide (Fir Cell); St Mullins on the borders of Leinster

8

Clonmacnoise (Cluain maccu Nois) on the banks of the Shannon in Co. Offaly was the greatest monastery in Celtic Ireland, and a royal church and mausoleum for the highkings of the southern Uí Néill. It was surrounded by a vast expanse of bog, and the only access was either by river or along the Pilgrim's Road, which wound its way along a gravel esker ridge (right) running north-east into Mide. Ballinderry Crannóg, a lake-dwelling rich in archaeological finds from the Viking Age, lay near the continuation of this road which ran from Clonmacnoise to the palace of the highkings among the Westmeath lakes.

(Uí Cheinnselaig) and Ossory. The list is endless and the reader may easily discover more examples from studying the accompanying maps. Clearly, we must alter our view of early Celtic monasticism as a movement which concentrated exclusively on the 'desert'. Even an apparently remote island site such as Lindisfarne was founded by St Aidan just off shore from the great Bernician capital of his Northumbrian royal patron at Bamborough. On the other hand, the original 'desert' idea persisted among reformers at least, and Lindisfarne, Glendalough and Roscrea, for instance, although developing into monastic 'cities', still maintained hermitages nearby for enthusiastic ascetics.[28]

We must abandon, too, the earlier accepted picture of Celtic society as being one of an almost exclusively pastoral nature, as reflected, for instance, in the sagas of cattle-raiding kings. The absence of all mention of agriculture in the extensive list of tributes in the eleventh-century *Book of Rights* seems to reinforce this view as does also, perhaps, the relative scarcity of Celtic domestic pottery. We would expect a predominantly pastoral people, however, to leave much more evidence for ecclesiastical and secular settlement behind them on the Wicklow, Wexford, and Dublin hills, and to prefer the mountain slopes for grazing-land in preference to the Liffey and Barrow valleys. These fertile plains, however, in the wide river basins seem to have been the most densely occupied where there was good natural drainage, and the pattern of early Leinster's rural settlement did not differ significantly from that which exists today. An increasing volume of evidence is going to show that agriculture played an important part in the early Irish economy alongside pastoralism. The monastic system itself no doubt encouraged this, and Caulfield's study of early Irish querns[29] emphasizes the rôle of agriculture in the economy even if the presence of a quern does not actually prove that corn was grown in the vicinity of any particular site. But field-work in Ireland has a long way to progress before we can speak with any confidence about the physical lay-out of settlements, either in regard to buildings and the social status of their occupants or in regard to field management and the location of grain crops. A study of Early Irish law-tracts may well help here, but for the past century these sources have been studied for their linguistic rather than their historical significance.

The distribution of monastic sites and bogs is mutually exclusive, a fact that takes on added interest when it is realised that the many monasteries of the Irish Midlands were confined to narrow fertile stretches, winding through millions of acres of boggy waste (Plates XII and XIV). This cannot be put down to coincidence, and confirms the view that the pattern of bog-cover as gleaned from the one-inch Ordnance Survey geological sheets is substantially the same as it was in the Early Christian period. The evidence presented by this bog-cover shows that the Old Irish *cluain* element in placenames meant 'a fertile clearing surrounded by an expanse of bog'. Thus, Cluain Ednech (Clonenagh), Cluain Ferta Molua (Clonfertmulloe), Cluain Fada Fine Libráin (Clonfad), Cluain Fada Báedháin Abha (Clonfad), Cluain Iraird (Clonard), Cluain Ferta Mughaine (Kilclonfert), and so many other monastic sites, all occupied fertile 'islands' free from bog-cover. A dramatic confirmation of this equation of *cluain* with a fertile 'island' in an expanse of bog is presented by a study of the local geological and soil conditions surrounding the monastery of Clonown. This site is situated near a bend on the Shannon at Long Island in eastern Roscommon, south of Athlone. It is Cluain Emain of early sources,[30] and the ancient church was situated on the southern end of an oval 'island' less than a square mile in area (Plate XIV). The island consists of limestone gravel drift and is entirely surrounded by bog. On the east there is difficult but vital access to the Shannon—to Clonmacnoise and the island monasteries of Lough Ree—but on the west the settlement is cut off from the rest of Roscommon by a 'sea' of bog, ranging from three to ten miles wide. The advantage of studying sealed-off communities such as Clonown or indeed that at nearby Clonmacnoise can scarcely need stressing, since the field-worker is presented with a settlement of great antiquity whose boundaries and focal point are already clearly defined. The centres of these settlements clearly lay beside the medieval churchyards and monastic buildings, while the limits of the monastic estates are still defined by the extent of the surrounding bog. The safety from sudden attack afforded by these 'bog-island' sites must have enhanced their rôle as repositories for monastic treasure during the Viking wars. It is significant that the splendid Derrynaflan treasure, consisting of an Early Christian chalice, paten and wine-strainer, was discovered in 1980 on just such a bog-island in Co. Tipperary.

Lullymore is yet another example of a monastic community sealed off in a bog-island on fertile limestone in north-west Kildare. This was ancient Lilcach on the borders of the Leinstermen and the Uí Néill of Uí Cairpri (Plates XI and XII). A poem, traditionally ascribed to Dubthach Ua Lugair in the *Book of Leinster*, but of a later time, celebrates the achievements of Crimthann son of Énna Cennsalech, a king of southern Leinster who is alleged to have died *c*.A.D. 485. Crimthann's victories over his Uí Néill enemies in Brega are discussed and the poet describes him as 'The destruction of Mide, glorifier of the Leinstermen and the "leap over Lulcach"'.[31] Regarding the last phrase, O'Curry remarked:[32] 'I am at a total loss to know what this is', but if the great nineteenth-century scholar had access to the cartographical knowledge available to linguists today he would have quickly solved the problem. It is clear that *Lulcach* is an error for *Lilcach*, that monastery sitting in a tiny island of limestone drift in the Bog of Allen, while the bog surrounding it separated the Leinstermen from the Uí Néill of Brega and Mide. To describe Crimthann, therefore, as 'the leap over Lilcach' (*léim dar Lilcach*) was a most appropriate compliment to a Leinster king who harassed the Uí Néill and who was alleged to have slain the Uí Néill king, Ailill Molt, in the battle of Ocha in Brega in 484. On the other side of this bog borderland, to the north of Lilcach was Uí Cairpri Laigen. This area had been conquered from the Leinstermen by the Uí Néill in the late fifth century, and at Síd Nechtain (Carbury Hill), only four miles north of Lilcach, the Uí Néill king, Lóegaire son of Niall of the Nine Hostages, met his death at the hands of the Leinstermen *c*. 462.[33] To 'leap over Lilcach', therefore, in the fifth century was a mark of courage for a Leinster king.

In addition to referring to the great expanse of Midland bog in general terms as Móin Almaine (Bog of Allen) or Móin Éle (The Bog of Éle—stretching from Cruachán Brí Éle to Éle on the Munster border with Mide) early sources occasionally mention individual areas of bog. The *Life* of Colmán of Lann in Fir Tulach, for instance, mentions Móin Lainne (Bog of Lann) beside that monastery,[34] and in the placename Móin Inse Cré (Bog-island of Cré)[35] in Tipperary we have an instance of the fertile 'island' being actually described as *inis*, 'island' or 'peninsula', reminding us of similar Welsh placenames such as Llanynys ('church of the island') referred to earlier.[36] Early Celtic communities had a keen eye for the nature of local terrain and for the quality of its soils.

A remarkable example of how only a knowledge of geological conditions can make an early medieval document yield its full meaning is found in the Old Irish Life of St Brigit. Brigit, we are told,[37] went to Croghan Hill (Cruachán Brí Éle) in Uí Failge (Plate XIV) in search of Bishop Mel, but on reaching the church of Croghan she learnt from two local virgins that Bishop Mel was 'in the churches of Mag Tulach' (i.e. in Fir Tulach in Mide). In other words, looking at the map (Plate XIV), Mel could only have crossed the Leinster border into Uí Néill lands by first travelling south to avoid a huge barrier of bog and then he had to go via Kilclonfert (Cluain Ferta Mughaine) into Uí Néill lands of Cenél Fiachach in Mide (Plate XIII). To a saint of Brigit's calibre, however, such detours were not necessary, and to reach Bishop Mel in Fir Tulach, the saintly heroine achieved the impossible by crossing the wilderness of bog to the north of Croghan—a countryside described in the *Life* as 'trackless, with marshes, deserts, 31 bogs and pools'. According to a marginal note in the Franciscan manuscript of the *Book of Hymns*, 'God so brought it about that the bog became a smooth flowering meadow.'[38] The name of this particular stretch of bog is given by the writer of the gloss in the Franciscan manuscript as Móin Faíchnig, and this name is preserved to this day in the form Boughna Bog now applied to an outlying section of the great bog around Brí Éle.[39] But Móin Faíchnig to-day is significantly in Kilbride Parish in Westmeath—a name (*Cell Brígde*, 'Church of Brigit') which commemorates St Brigit's visit to Bishop Mel in Fir Tulach.

Finally, we may observe that early Irish ecclesiastical placenames exhibit the same variation in their combination of ecclesiastical and geographical information as those in early Wales.[40] Some placenames such as Cell Brigde (Kilbride: 'Church of Brigit') or Domnach Sechnaill (Dunshaughlin: 'Church of Secundinus') are strictly ecclesiastical in origin. To this class also belong the *tech* placenames such as Tech Moling (St Mullins: 'Moling's House') which are exactly paralleled by Welsh *tŷ* forms as in Tyddewi. *Tech* elements in Irish monastic placenames spread as far west as Connaught but there can be little doubt that originally they were inspired by Welsh prototypes introduced into Leinster and Brega by Welsh missionaries in the fifth century. In this connection it is significant that, according to *The Additions to Tírechán's Collections*, Iserninus, the fifth-century missionary in the Barrow valley, based himself at Toicuile in Clíu (in Uí Dróna, Plate XVI).[41] We cannot identify Toicuile but clearly the first element *Toi* represents Welsh *tŷ* rather than Old Irish *tech*.

Other Irish monastic placenames are completely geographical in character, such as Cluain Maccu Nois (Clonmacnoise: 'Bog-clearing of the tribe of Nos'); Achad Bó (Aghaboe: 'Cow Pasture' or 'Meadow') or Glenn dá Locha (Glendalough: 'Glen of Two Lakes'). Some placenames combine the geographical element with the name of a saint, and in most cases the purpose may have been to distinguish one monastery from another of similar name. Thus, Cluain Fada Fine Libráin was so called to distinguish Librán's 'Long Bog-clearing' in Fir Tulach from the nearby Cluain Fada Báetáin ('Báetán's Long Bog-clearing') in Fir Bile (Plate XIV). To-day, both monastic sites are in Westmeath and both are referred to simply as Clonfad—a confusing situation for topographers. Similarly, we may cite Cluain Ferta Molua and Cluain Ferta Brénainn as monasteries of the same name (*Cluain Ferta*, Clonfert: 'Bog-clearing of the Graves'), but founded by the different saints, Molua and Brendán, respectively.

It is much more difficult to identify the fortresses of the secular aristocracy than the more permanent church sites. Many of these royal forts were deserted long before the Anglo-Norman Invasion, and all were deserted in the more important areas of settlement as soon as the Invasion occurred. Celtic Ireland lacked what we might call conventional diplomatic sources—charters, writs, surveys, and so on—of the kind which survive from Anglo-Saxon England and the Carolingian empire. Such source-material is of a practical nature, dealing with the all-important business of landed property, and therefore concerned with specifying boundary details and extent in precise terms. The Irish warrior aristocracy were no less interested in land—their only source of wealth—and in acquiring it at the point of the sword if necessary; but they were too far removed from the traditions of Roman and Merovingian administration to put their knowledge of writing to use in the business of administering their estates. Writing was monopolized by the poets, jurists, genealogists and saga-writers, and by their equivalent in the monasteries, who wrote the ecclesiastical sagas or *Lives* of saints. The phenomenon of a writing office, where kings employed clerks to further the process of written government, never developed in Ireland in spite of the high degree of literacy among churchmen and laymen alike. The reason, I believe, is connected yet again with the essentially tribal nature of Irish society. Tribal kings ruled such tiny kingdoms that it was a relatively easy matter for the king and his immediate entourage to supervise personally the running of a territory—collecting tribute and food-rents, supervising services, the administration of justice, and so on. The Provincial kings and highkings of the Uí Néill did exercise a nominal overlordship over wide areas and also, on occasion, would receive tribute from satellite kings. But the authority of an over-king was virtually non-existent as far as the day-to-day running of a subordinate tribal kingdom was concerned, and so the administrative machinery required by a highking was little greater than that needed to organize his own tribal area. In such a society it is little wonder that a writing office was found unnecessary, nor were there great problems concerning the delegation of authority and the consequent need to keep records of important administrative proceedings. The tribal king patrolled his small territory in person, knew all his petty officials by name, and knew exactly the extent of his limited royal demesne. But in spite of this absence of written government, the proliferation of kings and royal courts in Celtic Ireland created a unique situation where artists and craftsmen enjoyed an adundance of patronage out of all proportion to the size and economic resources of the island. When the church, too, adapted to the tribal cellular form of monastic organization, the amount of patronage increased even more, and it is this one single factor which more than any other accounts for the staggering artistic and literary output in Dark Age Ireland. Instead of one king and a bishop ruling the entire Province as was the corresponding situation prevailing in Anglo-Saxon England or on the continent, Leinster could muster no less than forty-seven kings in attendance at the *Óenach* or Assembly of Carman, and it could boast, too, of an equal number of important abbots.

The skills of writing were put to other uses, and instead of noting the boundaries of estates, the literate classes wrote of heroic deeds in a bygone age and gave vent to their obsession with genealogy and topography. Early Irish sagas contain a wealth of information on local topography and prehistoric kings were made to drive their chariots over mountain passes and river-

9

10

Terryglass (Tír dá Glass) (9) and Lorrha (Lothra) (10) were two north Tipperary monasteries near the Shannon, which had very close Leinster connections and may have begun life within an enlarged Leinster kingdom in the early sixth century. Rhodán, the founder of Lorrha, was a close friend of Finian of Clonard, while Colum of Terryglass was an associate of Fintán of Clonenagh in Leix. Clonenagh and Terryglass were united under the rule of the same abbot in the middle of the ninth century, and both Lorrha and Terryglass shared in the cultural and spiritual reform movements which united the bog-land monasteries of Leinster, from the seventh to the ninth centuries, in particular.

The Stowe Missal, *dating from about A.D. 800,*

has connections with Terryglass and was housed at nearby Lorrha in the early eleventh century. Terry-glass, too, was the monastic home of Máeldithruib, a Céli Dé monk who died in 840 and who helped to compile a Reform document called Notes on the Customs of Tallaght. *The central geographical position of Terryglass accounts for why it played host to a 'royal assembly' in 737 which was attended by the king of Munster and by the northern highking, Áed Allan. Little evidence for Ireland's Golden Age remains at either Terryglass or Lorrha today. The monastic ruins at both centres date from the High Middle Ages, but at Lorrha two bases of High Crosses of the Leinster and Ossory type survive from the tenth century.*

33

crossings which were real places in the medieval landscape—many of which we can identify to-day. We can identify, too, a surprising number of royal forts belonging to the great Provincial aristocracies, such as Lagore and Knowth in Brega (Plate III) and Dún na Scíath in Mide (Plate XIV) for the Southern Uí Néill; or Naas, Rathangan, (Plate XII) and Ferns (Plate XVI) for the kings of Leinster. We can locate, too, the fortresses of the prehistoric rulers of the Laigin such as Dinn Ríg, Mullaghmast, Knockaulin and perhaps Lyon's Hill (Liamain) (Plate XII). We know disappointingly little, however, about the royal forts of the tribal kings. We can identify Tullyard as the centre for the kings of Lóegaire Breg (Plate XII) and Carrick near Lough Ennel for the kings of Fir Tulach (Plate XIV). For the Uí Failge we have Rathangan and Geashill (Plates XII and XIV); Kilranelagh for the Uí Máil (Plate XII); Dunamase for Uí Crimthainn Áin, and later for the Loígis (Plate XIV); Rathedan for the kings of Uí Dróna; Rathvilly, Tullow, Ardristan, Ardamine and Ferns for the kings of Uí Cheinnselaig (Plate XVI). We can even identify some forts with individual rulers such as Ráth Branduib in west Wicklow, which was almost certainly occupied by Brandub mac Echach, the Leinster hero-king who died in A.D. 605 (Plate XII). The amount of topographical information is indeed impressive and compares favourably with more developed societies such as those of Rome or Byzantium where systematic records were made and archives maintained. But the number of forts we can identify is small compared with those which will always elude identification. We do not know the whereabouts of royal fortresses of the Uí Bairrche, Fothairt, Benntraige, Uí Enechglaiss, Dál Messin Corb, Dál Cormaic or Uí Briúin Cualann, to name but some prominent Leinster tribes.

A feature of many of the royal sites which we can identify is their association with ritual monuments from Ireland's prehistoric past. The kings of Tara built the ramparts of their hill-fort about a Neolithic and Bronze Age cemetery; while the tenth-century kings of Knowth resided on top of a gigantic Neolithic passage grave, and both Tara and Knowth figured prominently as ritual centres in the pagan mythology embedded in early Irish literature. Similarly in Leinster, Knockaulin and Ardamine seem to have had a pre-Christian ritual existence, while prehistoric standing stones with distinctive vertical grooves are to be found quite near Mullaghmast and Ardristan. Neolithic and Bronze Age monuments on the Curragh of Kildare and in northern Carlow also seem to have been favoured by the Leinstermen for the location of their tribal assemblies such as the Óenach Cholmáin and Óenach Carmain. It seems clear that the rituals associated with pagan Iron Age Celtic kingship had borrowed from the non-Celtic prehistoric past. If we allow for the survival of such rituals as the archaeological evidence suggests, then we may also have to allow for the survival of Bronze Age and even Neolithic population groups, albeit in transmuted form, down into the historical period.

It seems clear that a case can be made for holding that the warriors of the Irish Iron Age deliberately chose to link the rites of Celtic kingship (and particularly of inauguration) with ritual centres from Ireland's indigenous prehistoric past. This much is certain from the monuments that survive at Tara, the inauguration place of the Uí Néill highkings, and at Mag Adair, a similar ritual site chosen as the inauguration place of the O'Brien kings of Dál Cais in Thomond. In addition to their royal fortresses, which symbolised the prestige of Iron Age kingship, the Leinstermen, like their Uí Néill neighbours, held tribal assemblies at regular intervals. The greatest of the Leinster assemblies was the Óenach Carman and while we are not as yet certain of its geographical location, a considerable amount of information has survived as to its function. Óenach Carman was the major triennial assembly of the Leinstermen attended by all their tribal aristocracies and kings, and presided over by the king of the Province. It played a major social and economic rôle in the life of the Province. We know that it included competitions in athletics, poetry and other arts; that it allowed for the standardization of the *senchus* or tribal lore and laws, thereby consolidating inter-tribal relationships; and that it also included three markets—one of food and clothing, one of livestock and horses, and a special market attended by foreign traders.

But the assembly at Carman also had a strong ritual function. The contests, involving not only athletics and horse-racing but also music and poetry, were exactly parallelled by the Isthmian Games held on the Isthmus of Corinth in Classical Greece. The Isthmian Games were funerary in origin and were held in a sacred grove associated with the rituals of the sea deities, Poseidon and Melicertes. The Carman Games also had a funerary aspect (Carman was one of the seven major prehistoric cemeteries of Ireland) and as such the games were held near the tombs of the tribal ancestors of the Leinstermen. Just as the Isthmian Games were held every two years in the first month of Spring, so too the Carman assembly was convened every third year on the festival of the Celtic god, Lug, (at *Lugnasa*) during the first week in August. The Óenach Carman was also associated with tribal fertility kingship and with Irish high-kingship. It was the prerogative of the king of the Leinstermen to preside as over-king of other tribal rulers in the Province at this assembly, and a pecking order existed among tribal kings in attendance reminding us of the hierarchy of tribes which can be discerned in the inter-tribal genealogy of the Leinstermen (Chart 2). At Carman, in later centuries, the king of Uí Failge sat on the left of the king of Leinster acknowledging the memory of former Uí Failge dominance over the Leinstermen, while the Loígis and the Fothairt (mercenary troops of the Uí Failge, Uí Bairrche and Uí Enechglaiss) had a prominent rôle in the assembly. All this suggests that Carman's heyday dated from a time which knew nothing as yet of the Uí Dúnlainge or Uí Cheinnselaig when the Uí Failge and Uí Bairrche, as the original *Laigin*, dominated south-east Ireland. Survivals of such ritual protocol were also apparent at the Isthmian Games, where, for instance, the Corinthians had a traditional presidency and the Elisians were excluded altogether. Fertility aspects of Carman may be implied in the special competitions, sports and assemblies set aside exclusively for women, and by poems on the subject which promised fertility to man and nature if the Óenach were properly held.

Óenach Carman was, above all else, the embodiment of the political integrity and tribal identity of the Leinstermen as an autonomous nation. There, its tribal war-lords sat in ritual assembly presided over by the king of the Province, consciously or unconsciously paying homage to their pagan ancestors and outmoded Celtic gods, while regulating the affairs of their tribes. It was little wonder that Uí Néill and Munster enemies could not resist the temptation from time to time of trying to preside forcefully over these ancient rites, thereby imposing their overlordship on the Leinstermen. Thus in 841, Feidlimid, the bishop-king of Cashel, was forced to withdraw in disgrace from Carman by the Uí Néill highking, Niall Caille, who resented Munster interference in Leinster's affairs; and in 956 the highking, Congalach, was ambushed and slain by the Leinstermen and Vikings for presumptuously presiding over their assembly for three days in the Liffey Plain. An ancient Leinster tribal assembly was held on the Curragh (Cuirrech Life, Plate XII), but whether this was the Óenach Cholmáin or Óenach Carman and whether these were the same or different assemblies is not yet clear. In later centuries it may be that the Óenach Carman was held at different places, but there is an impressive body of evidence to suggest that the original location was at the junction of the river Barrow with its tributary the Burren, at Carlow. This place (Plate XII) in the heartland of Leinster was near to both Dinn Ríg and Mullaghmast, two ancient centres of royal power, and central besides for all the tribes of the Province.

The secular sites which we can identify (for the historical period) are all—as in the case of the monasteries—relatively low-lying. But we must bear in mind that bogland, high mountain and forest were not entirely outside the life of a Dark Age community. The mountains provided summer grazing for cattle and, according to the *Lives* of Kevin, even the Wicklow wilderness might be visited by a wandering chieftain driving his herds to summer pastures.[42] The memory of the *buaile* or 'summer milking place' is enshrined in such Wicklow placenames as Knocknaboley in both Kilcommon and Hollywood parishes; at Ballynultagh in Kilbeg parish; at Bullford near Kilcoole, and at Boleycarrigeen Bronze Age Stone Circle ('the Griddle Stones') in Kilranelagh parish. These shielings or *buaile* sites have not yet been systematically surveyed but other likely examples include such places as Booleyvannanan in the Slievemargy hills and Ballynaboley in Killanane parish, both in Co. Carlow; Boley in the parish of Owenduff, Co. Wexford; and perhaps also Boley, the site of a small Iron Age hill-fort in south-west Leix.[43]

Forest provided excellent foraging ground for swine, as is clear from references in Irish literature and even from the more laconic annalistic sources, which note years which yielded 'an abundance of acorns'. Great crops of nuts and acorns are reported in the *Annals of Ulster* for the years 576, 836, 1066, 1097, 1147 (*Chronicum Scotorum*), and 1421. In 836 and 1066 this harvest was reported to have choked up streams, while either 1066 or 1097 was remembered as the 'Year of Fair Nuts'. Hunting of wild fowl and game in the wilderness must have still played an important rôle in the economy, and the early law-tracts make provisions regulating one's entitlement to the natural resources of waste and commons land, including fish from rivers, wildlife and nuts from the forest as well as nightly firewood, and timber for making some basic implements. The common rights to woodland were confined to forest which was *gen treniugad* or 'without partitions' which suggests that some woodland, while not perhaps literally fenced off, had been appropriated for the use of lay or ecclesiastical lords.[44] The farmlands on the open plains were not systematically fenced off until as late as the eighteenth century although permanent enclosures had been established in the fields surrounding Anglo-Norman towns in the later Middle Ages. It would be rash, on the other hand to view Celtic Ireland as a disorganized patchwork of forest and clearings. Temporary fences must have been used to protect crops from trespassing animals, and in stoney terrain, dry stone walling must have been used for permanent enclosures from prehistoric times. Such field systems, subsequently buried under blanket bog in north-west Mayo, have been discovered by Herity at Carrownaglogh and by Caulfield at Belderg Beg and have been dated to the Early Bronze Age.[45] A writer in *Leabor na hUidre* (*c*.A.D. 1100) clearly acknowledges the existence of permanent enclosures in pre-Norman Ireland but also testifies to the memory of an earlier age when the countryside was truly open:[46] 'There was neither mound nor hedge nor stone walls round land in Ireland then [nothing] but unbroken plains, until the time of the sons of Áed Sláne [i.e. A.D. 600-50].'

Giraldus Cambrensis speaks of Ireland in terms of a politically backward nation, but basically he viewed it as a superb wilderness and a veritable storehouse of nature's treasures. He speaks of rivers abounding in salmon, trout and eels; and of bird life—eagles as numerous as kites in other countries, and an abundance of hawks and falcons[47](which continued to delight the aristocracy into the Elizabethan Age).This information is probably quite accurate since these birds of prey flourished in deciduous woodland. The prehistoric and medieval Irish Midlands must have provided one of the most important breeding grounds for marsh feeders in Atlantic Europe due to the great expanse there of bog and swamp. Giraldus reports seeing flocks of crane up to a hundred strong; thousands of barnacle geese; and an abundance of swans, snipe, quails and capercailzie.[48] Some of his other observations are clearly culled from Irish hagiographical tradition, such as the tale of the tame falcon at Kildare, or that of the ravens at Glendalough. Yet even these stories must be based on the common experience of the time, and early annalists although not primarily concerned with these matters occasionally allude to contemporary wildlife as when the Four Masters, for instance, record the destruction by lightening in A.D. 962 'of swans and barnacle geese in the Plain of Eastern Liffey (Airther Life, Co. Kildare, Plate XII).'[49] The *Lives* of Irish saints abound with anecdotes of birds and animals. We might

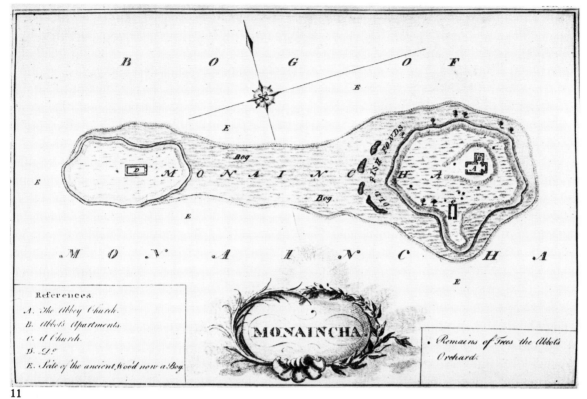

11

12

Monaincha (Móin Inse Cré), Co. Tipperary, in Led-wich's Antiquities of Ireland *(1790), is a good example of a 'bog-island' (móin inse) which in this case began life as an ascetic retreat for the monks of nearby Roscrea (Ros Cré). In 923 Limerick Vikings raided this monastery and carried off Flaithbertach, ex-king of Munster, whom they held for ransom. The top engraving (11) shows the monastic settlement still surrounded by the lake or boggy morass, which covered 100 acres before being drained in 1799. This was Loch Cré of Dark Age sources and was surrounded by 4500 acres of bog proper. The monastic complex is sited on a gravel ridge. The ecclesiastical ruins (bottom: 12) show the remains of the twelfth-century Romanesque abbey in 1790.*

37

cite the tame partridge of Molua; the stag of Cronan; the tame fox of Moling, or the swans who befriended both Colum of Terryglass and Colman of Lynally (Lann Elo).[50] Giraldus speaks of vast herds of a small variety of wild pig more numerous than anywhere else he had experienced; he mentions martins, badgers, stoats and hares as common Irish mammals (but excluded beavers and moles) and he relates apochryphal tales of wolves, treating those animals as a commonplace of the Irish forest. Wolves and wild pig figure prominently in Irish saints' *Lives*—both species, for instance, being assumed to frequent the hinterland of Glendalough in the *Lives* of St Kevin.[51] It was not just anti-clerical villains or shepherds and their flocks who might fall victim to the wolf in medieval Irish tradition. Even prominent holy men from among the founding fathers of the Irish Church in the sixth century were rightly or wrongly believed to have been vulnerable to the ravages of this predator. Cormac Ua Liatháin, a friend of Columba's and a monk of Durrow, and Bishop Conláed of Kildare were both believed to have been devoured by wolves.[52] Conláed was said to have met his fate on the side of Liamain or Lyon's Hill, in the Liffey Plain, and while that tradition may well be apocryphal, it shows that, say, tenth-century writers considered it plausible that travellers might be attacked by wolves even in the populuous part of north Leinster in Mag Laigen.

In contrast to identifying individual monasteries or forts, the more difficult task of defining the extent of tribal territories within the kingdom of the Leinstermen *c*.A.D. 900 can only be attempted with partial success. This time has been chosen because it provides us with a representative picture of the whole period. By the ninth century we have, for the first time, a sufficient amount of source-material for a detailed picture. The more obscure earlier period was one of greater political upheaval, and the growth of Christianity within the Province effected sweeping topographical and political changes. The eleventh and twelfth centuries on the other hand, although better known for the larger political groups, saw the eclipse of the smaller tribes, and being much simpler in their political make-up are less representative than earlier periods. The ninth century was chosen by Mac Neill and others as the most suitable for their more limited topographical studies, and the choice to a great extent was inevitable. This is so, because the sources themselves all seem to have preserved a ninth-century picture of Ireland, even if these compilations belong to a later period. The Viking catastrophe triggered off a cultural rescue operation which involved the gathering of genealogies and *senchus*, as if there were a real danger of the ancient records being completely destroyed. Our earliest and most reliable genealogical compilation,—that of the Oxford MS Rawlinson B 502, dates to the early twelfth century. This and most later genealogical works provide the basic information on the distribution of tribal areas. The Rawlinson manuscript, although dating to *c*.1100, gives us a picture of Leinster *c*.700-900. A detailed study of the structure of the Leinster genealogies[53] shows that a compilation date of *c*.800 is embedded in this work, and this earlier period of compilation provided the basis for later additions. Similarly, the numerous notes and topographical data added to the *Félire Óengusso* in the eleventh century seem to derive from an early ninth- or tenth-century work. Since, therefore, most of the topographical works themselves rely on a ninth-century framework, it is inevitable that modern research should also centre on this period.

* * * *

Before going on to examine the precise extent of the tribal kingdoms of the Leinstermen, it may be useful to establish, formally, the major geographical divisions within the Province as a whole, since these natural regions correspond to major spheres of political influence. The Leinster landscape is so dramatically divided between bog, mountain and fertile plain, that there is little danger of forming artificial environments which have or had no basis in reality. We associate Uí Failge lands with the Bog of Allen, for instance, just as we associate the Dál

Messin Corb with the remote eastern slopes of the Wicklow hills (Plates I and VIII). The two territories are as different as the tribes which occupied them, and the following outline of Leinster's natural regions confirms the picture of tribal adaptation to the local environment.

The Northern Region

This region covers the fertile plains of the Liffey and the continuum which it forms with the upper and eastern region of the Barrow (Plates I and II). The soil of this area (Plate III) is rich with limestone and other elements in its glacial drift, and comprises some of the richest land in the whole island. It is no coincidence that this flat, fertile area was dominated from the middle of the seventh to the eleventh century by the Uí Dúnlainge—the most powerful dynasty in the whole Province (Plates V and VIII). On the west it is bordered by the bogs of western Kildare, Leix, and Offaly. On the east this fertile basin is bounded by the high masses of the Wicklow mountains. Topographically this region comprised Mag Life and Mag Ailbe (Plates II and XII)—the Plain of Liffey and the north-eastern plain of the Barrow. Since no high watershed divides these two plains, the area was a geographical as well as a historical unit.

The Central Region

This area corresponds roughly with Co. Carlow. Geographically and geologically in its northern half, it is a continuation of the drainage basin of the Barrow from the Northern Region. The

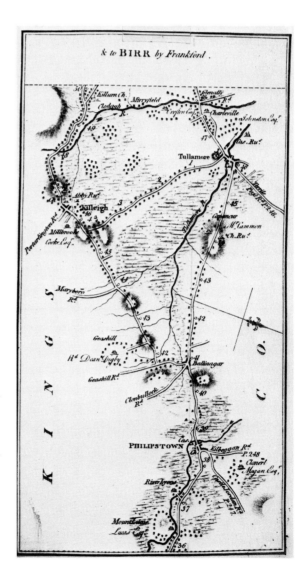

13

Map of roads between Killeigh, Tullamore and Daingean (formerly Philipstown), surveyed by Taylor and Skinner prior to 1777, showing extensive peat-bogs with some forest still on the fringes. Note how the surveyors recognized the existence of pass ways joining settlements which are confined to well-drained clearings and gravel ridges or eskers. The high proportion of 'Derry' placenames in this part of Offaly testifies to the former abundance of oak forest on the fringes of the bog. The building of Fort Governor on the site of the O'Connor stronghold at Daingean (Philipstown) by Lord Deputy Bellingham in 1547 marked the beginning of English influence on the wooded Celtic landscape and on the politics of this region.

Barrow basin in this region (Plate II) however, is noticeably more contracted than in its upper reaches, being tightly confined by the Blackstairs mountains on the east and by the Slievemargy hills and the Kilkenny hills of Brandon and Ballinvarry in the west. This region is of some geological interest (Plate IV). The fertile limestone drift covers the northern half, and then quite dramatically, in the centre, forsakes the Barrow valley and the Province of Leinster, turning abruptly into Ossory. Topographically this fertile pass from Carlow into Kilkenny corresponds to the ancient Belach Gabráin—the gateway from ancient Leinster into the lands of the Osraige (Plates IV and V). The soil of the southern part of the region (Plate III) is poor for agricultural purposes, consisting largely of a granite base, and compared with the northern half we shall see that the poorness of the soil here reflects the status of the tribes which occupied it. While this region combines the geographical and geological features of the adjoining regions, historically also it lay between the two major dynasties of Leinster—the Uí Dúnlainge of the north and the Uí Cheinnselaig of the south (Plates V and VIII). The tribes of Uí Bairrche and the Fotharta who occupied this central area seem to have acted as buffer states in Leinster politics, and in studying the origins of the major Leinster dynasties this region will be seen to be truly central and of prime importance.

The Southern Region

This region is hemmed in by the Wicklow mountains in the north, and is separated from the Central Region by the Blackstairs mountains on the west (Plate I). Geographically it coincides with the basin of the Slaney (Plate II) and historically this area has a very real existence as a unit—being dominated by the Uí Cheinnselaig (Plate VIII). The soil (Plate III) is fertile in the central area but belts of poor soils exist along the east and south coasts. To the north the region was heavily wooded and never supported a great population. The remarkable feature of this Southern Region is the fact that it is completely separated from the north of the Province by the high granite masses of the Wicklow and Blackstairs mountains.

The North-Eastern Region

This region consists of the mountains of Wicklow and north Wexford (Plate I) and was the most sterile of any within the Province. The mountain masses consist of the bare granite covered in many places by blanket bog. The lowland area adjoining this region has an acidic quality in its soils. Historically the region was occupied by tribes who played little part in the life of the Province, and from the tenth century onwards this region was referred to as the territory of the Fortuatha (not to be confused with Fothairt or Fotharta) or alien (and therefore non-privileged) tribes. The eastern lowland coastal strip is in places fertile, but there must have been difficulties with communication due to the great number of small mountain streams (Plate II) running transversely to the sea. This entire area was heavily wooded and difficult of access from the fertile Northern Region, while its lowland coastal soils were for the most part badly drained and under forest.

The North-Western Region

This region differs from the fertile northern area in its great expanse of bogland (Plates I and III). Historically it was dominated by the Uí Failge, with the alien tribe of the Loígis in its southern portion. Geographically (Plate II) the region coincides with the meeting place of many river-basins, a fact connected with the presence of so much marsh and bog.

* * * *

Having sketched, then, the character of the ancient Leinster landscape, and having isolated these five regions of ancient Leinster on the basis of environmental studies, we shall now take each area in turn and discuss it in relation to the tribes which occupied it c.A.D. 900.

Tribes and Dynasties of the Northern Region

14

The Round Tower and Castle of Kildare (Dublin Penny Journal, *1834*). *Although Kildare lay on the fringes of Uí Failge territory in the North-Western Region, its association with the Curragh and its domination by the Uí Dúnlainge kings of Leinster from the seventh to the twelfth centuries, made it one of the most important centres in northern Leinster. After the Anglo-Norman invasion, it was here, almost certainly, that Strongbow established his headquarters. Kildare began life in the prehistoric Celtic past as a cult centre of the godess Brigit, beside a sacred oak, which in the sixth century was taken over by a Christian virgin and her community of nuns— hence Cell Dara (Cell of the Oak Tree). The ritual fires which were kept continuously burning here into the thirteenth century testify to the origin of Kildare as a pagan sanctuary (Giraldus,* Topographia, *ed. Dimlock, v. 120-1). It soon fell a prey to the ambitions of the kings of Leinster and its first royal abbot, Áed Dub (died A.D. 638), was the brother of King Fáelán of Leinster. In the following poem, Áed Dub (Áed the Black), addresses his other brother, Áed Find (Áed the Fair), trying to dissuade him from seizing the kingship of Leinster:*

Brother . . .
Are your drinking horns, horns of the wild ox?
And is your ale, ale of Cualu?
And is the Curragh of Liffey part of your land?

Are you a descendant of fifty highkings?
Is Kildare your church?
And is your companionship with Christ?
Book of Leinster, 316.a.26; translation by Kuno Meyer

The Leinstermen recognized that their Province consisted of two major divisions, North Leinster, or 'Leinster north of Gabair' (Laigin Tuathgabair), and south Leinster, or 'Leinster south of Gabair' (Laigin Desgabair). The area of Gabair which marked the boundary between these two zones has been variously identified with the watershed between the Liffey and the Slaney, or even more implausibly with 'the diocesan boundaries between Dublin, Glendalough and Kildare in the north . . . and Leighlin and Ferns in the south'.[1] Neither of these two identifications have much to recommend them. The Slaney-Liffey   41 watershed, as will appear on Plate II, runs across the no man's land of the Wicklow mountains, dividing Uí Máil territory in half, all of which belonged to North Leinster, while the Slaney's eastern watershed runs north-south, and borders that of the Barrow not the Liffey. The region of Gabair, on the other hand, clearly must have had an east-west orientation if it divided North Leinster from South Leinster. Diocesan boundaries are equally unhelpful. The Leighlin-Kildare boundary (Plate VI) assigns Loígis territory to South Leinster, where it never belonged prior to the twelfth century, but the Leighlin-Glendalough boundary, where it coincided with the later county boundary between Carlow and Kildare (Plate VI) did run through the ancient border-land of Gabair. Gabair Laigen, as we whall see, was that region where the central lowland zone narrows noticeably as in a great funnel, hemmed in by the Wicklow mountains on the east and the Slievemargy hills in the west (Plates I, II and V). It was the area also where the courses of the Slaney and Barrow run closest together in northern Carlow (Plates II and XII). In short, it was the natural meeting place between North Leinster, dominated by the Kildare Plains, and South Leinster, consisting of the lowlands to the south of the Wicklow mountains. Laigin Tuathgabair, then, consisted of those regions described as Northern, North-Western and North-Eastern, while Laigin Desgabair comprised the Central and Southern Regions.

The lowland area of the Northern Region stretched from Dublin, or Áth Cliath, west and south into the heart of Leinster between the Midland bogs and the Wicklow mountains, and it was dominated by the Uí Dúnlainge. This dynasty branched out, at the end of the first quarter of the eighth century, into three powerful septs of Uí Muiredaig, Uí Dúnchada, and Uí Fáeláin (Chart 2), whose territories adjoined on the Kildare Plains. The Uí Muiredaig in the south of Kildare were traditionally associated with Mullaghmast (Maistiu), an ancient hill-top site, and they occupied the later baronies (Plate VII) of Kilkea-and-Moone, Narragh-and-Reban and parts of Connell. They have left their name on the deanery of Omorthy which was coextensive with their territory in the twelfth century. The boundary between the Uí Muiredaig and their cousins the Uí Fáeláin to the north is not at all clear. The nature of this flat, fertile country is such that there are few physical features to guide us, and in the case of these particular dyn-asties it is rash to seek for too rigid a definition of their borders. The extent of their terri-tory was continuously increasing from their origins in Patrician times down to the eleventh century. The object of their conquest was this level expanse of Mag Life and we can never hope for absolute certainty in relation to borders here. The Uí Muiredaig may have extended as far north as the Curragh of Kildare (Cuirrech Life) to meet the lands of Uí Failge and their own relatives the Uí Fáeláin in a triangle near Knockaulin hill-fort (Dún Ailinne, Plate XI).

We can securely locate the Uí Fáeláin in 'Eastern Liffey' (Airthir Life) about the fort of Naas (Nás) in Co. Kildare—a fort which was also associated with their Uí Dúnlainge ancestors (Plates V, XI and XII). Hogan[2] assigned to Uí Fáeláin the baronies of North and South Salt, Clane, Ikeathy and Outhterany (Plate VII), in addition to the barony of North Naas. This would seem to represent Uí Fáeláin lands at a period of maximum expansion. The adjoining baronies of North Naas and South Salt (Plate VII) were confined on the north and extreme west by the course of the Liffey, and we would expect that the baronies to the north of this river came directly under Uí Fáeláin control last of all, since, as we shall see, the expansion was from south to north. The combined baronies of Ikeathy and Outherany to the north of the Liffey preserve the older tribal names of Uí Chéithig and Uachtar Fine respectively (Plates VIII and XI). However, by the middle of the ninth century the territory from 'Western Liffey' (Íarthar Life) to the Brega border (Plate XI) at Cloncurry (Cluain Conaire Tomain) seems to have already fallen to the Uí Fáeláin. The barony of South Naas (Plate VII) was never alloc-ated to any Leinster tribe by modern topographers such as O'Donovan or Walsh. Since the

42 Liffey, on its course from the Wicklow hills, divides this barony in two, its northern half has

no natural boundaries between it and the barony of North Naas. It is logical to conclude that the Uí Fáeláin occupied this barony as far south as the Liffey, to meet their Uí Muiredaig cousins at Knockaulin (Plate XI).

The third Uí Dúnlainge sept—the Uí Dúnchada (Chart 2)—controlled the most northerly part of this region. The dynasty was centred on Lyon's Hill (Liamain) on the Dublin-Kildare border (Plates XI and XII). This hill commands a view of the whole of the flat country across the Liffey over Mag Nuadat (Maynooth), to the Brega border. There is no evidence for a Dark Age fortification on top of this hill, but a systematic survey ought to yield some evidence for a fort nearby. Uí Dúnchada were overlords of south Co. Dublin between the Liffey and the Dodder (Dothra) rivers prior to the Viking wars. Hogan implied[3] that by the Anglo-Norman Invasion, they had extended their influence around the Dublin hills as far east as Delgany (Dergne) in north Wicklow (Plate XII). The position of Liamain, however, suggests that this dynasty, like the rest of the Uí Dúnlainge, probably originated further south in the Barrow basin. The sites of Maistiu, Nás and Liamain provide us with stepping stones in this advance from Mag Ailbe in the heart of the region of Gabair Laigen to the sea at Dublin. The final extension of Uí Dúnchada territory into the coastal region of north-east Wicklow may not be an indication of their strength, but rather of decline. The Uí Dúnchada found themselves in a very difficult position in the Viking Age, particularly after the foundation of Dublin as the headquarters of the Norwegian kingdom in 841. Places such as Carn Uí Dúnchadha (Dolphin's Barn) lay within sight of the Scandinavian stronghold. Uí Dúnchadha power did not collapse at once, but it is significant that the last king of the Leinstermen from this section of the Uí Dúnlainge was Donnchad son of Domnall Clóen, who was taken prisoner by Sitric Silkenbeard of Dublin in 999.[4] After Donnchad's day the kingship passed to Uí Fáeláin and Uí Muiredaig until the

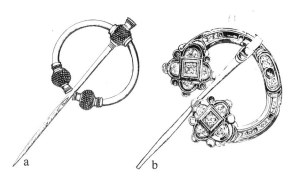

here as an outpost of Scandinavian Dublin. This same Olaf also ruled a Norwegian realm and is very probably the king who was buried in the Gokstad ship south of Oslo.

16

These two Irish penannular brooches date from the tenth century. The specimen on the left (a) is a thistle brooch from Co. Kildare and belongs to a type of silver brooch found in Ireland and also in the Viking colonies in western Scotland and northern England. This type was also worn by the Irish as is clear from the fact that Christ is shown wearing such a brooch on the Cross of Muiredach at Monasterboice in Louth (c. A.D. 920). The brooch on the right (b) was found at Kilmainham just west of the medieval city of Dublin.

15

The monastery of Clondalkin first appears in contemporary annalistic records in A.D. 781, although the church was probably founded by its patron, St Mo Chua, in the early years of Irish Christianity. Its ninth-century round tower was built to withstand Viking attacks from Dublin, which lies only five miles to the east. In the 860s the centre was captured by King Olaf the White who built a fortress

43

middle of the eleventh century when Murchad, the last Uí Muiredaig king, was slain by Donnchad Mac Gilla Pátraic of Ossory in 1042.[5] The second half of the eleventh century saw Leinster politics dominated by the dynasties of the south—the Osraige and Uí Cheinnselaig—and eventually, of course, by Strongbow. What is significant here is that the Uí Dúnchada dropped out of the royal race for control of all Leinster by the end of the tenth century—half a century before the collapse of Uí Dúnlainge as a whole—and clearly the great power of their Scandinavian neighbours in Dublin at that time must account for their decline.

The Uí Dunchada were one of the few Irish dynasties to do a deal with the Anglo-Normans and to survive. The family name of the dynasty at the time of the Invasion was Mac Gilla Mo-Cholmóg and the estates which they were allowed to keep under their new masters centred on Lyons Hill and Rathdown, south of Bray in north-east Wicklow.[6] It seems as though the Uí Dúnchada had been forced out of their richer and older lands between Lyon's Hill and the Dodder, and they had moved in on lands once occupied by their relatives the Uí Briúin Chualann. There is reason to believe that this migration had taken place before the Anglo-Norman invasion, and that it had been forced on the Uí Dúnchada by the Hiberno-Norse kings of Dublin. The Norseman in turn had taken over the Uí Dúnchada homelands about Lyon's Hill, while the Uí Dúnchada had passed into a tributary position *vis-à-vis* Norse Dublin. Thus, with the coming of the Anglo-Normans, the Uí Dúnchada exchanged one foreign overlord for another, serving Strongbow as they had served the Ostmen, and surviving as an Irish aristocracy under their new Anglo-Irish name of Fitz Dermot.

It seems that the Uí Dúnchada were either expelled from Liamain by the Norsemen or held it as a Norse stronghold for their Dublin masters, and that the place was temporarily restored to them by the Anglo-Normans until 1209. This hypothesis is supported by evidence from the eleventh-century *Book of Rights.* The stipend or ritual gift of the king of Cashel, when he was highking, to the 'warriors of Liamain' is specified at thirty ships—a prize more appropriate for a Scandinavian people than for the Uí Dúnchada.[7] Elsewhere in the *Book of Rights* the Foreigners of Dublin are referred to twice as being 'from Liamain' or associated with it—a clear indication that the erstwhile stronghold of Uí Dúnchada had fallen into Scandinavian hands by the eleventh century.[8]

The Mac Torcaill dynasty controlled Dublin in the twelfth century. A Raghnall Mac Torcaill is described by the *Four Masters* as *mórmaor* or high-steward of Dublin in 1146,[9] and the last king of Dublin, beheaded by the Anglo-Normans in his own hall, was Ascall mac Torcaill.[10] *Thorcall* was a Hibernicization of the Norse name *Thorkettle,* and it survives in at least two Irish placenames: the first, Rath Turtle (Ráth Torcaill), is situated north of Blessington in north-west Wicklow (Plates IX and XII), and the other, Curtlestown (Baile mhic Thorcaill), is near Powerscourt in north-east Wicklow[11]. The location of Ráth Thorcaill provides an indication of the extent of Norse territory south of Lyon's Hill along the Wicklow foot-hills; and Curtlestown occurs in an area where Price has shown evidence for other Norse placenames.[12] The territory of Ascaill Gall ('the Angle of the Foreigners') in eleventh-century Ireland was of much greater extent than historians have hitherto believed possible. Further placename evidence from east Wicklow, together with the presence of strongholds at Wicklow and Arklow, show that Dublin controlled the coastal zone from the Liffey south to Glais in Ascaill—the Glassgorman river in north Wexford (Plates XII, XVI), which was also the boundary between the medieval dioceses of Dublin-and-Glendalough and that of Ferns.[13] The name of the stream, Glais in Ascaill, seems to be related to Ascaill Gall, the territory of the Foreigners. North of the Liffey, the Norsemen controlled Fine Gall, which extended from the Liffey to the north of Skerries (Plate IX).

At the time of the Anglo-Norman Invasion the Angevin king chose to keep for his demesne lands all of north and south Dublin and the littoral as far as Arklow (Plate X).[14] In effect, Henry II retained for himself the old kingdom of the Dublin Ostmen. At that time the Ostmen's territory does not seem to have extended south or west of Newcastle Lyons as is suggested by the boundaries of the shires of Kildare and Dublin. But other evidence suggests that prior to the late twelfth century the Norsemen did directly control land in the Kildare Plains—or that, at the very least, they ruled part of this area through their subject-kings of Uí Dúnchada. How else could the medieval diocese of Dublin possibly include the barony of North Salt in Kildare (Plates VI and VII) if the Scandinavians did not exercise control there? So, while the Dublin Norsemen may have declined in international importance in the twelfth century, nevertheless they had become masters of a territorial kingdom of considerable size within Ireland.

The old Leinster border with Brega and Mide ran along the north of the Province. In the east this was sufficiently defined by the Liffey which is wide and deep at this point, and whose valley, for instance in the Chapelizod area, is particularly steep. The border ran west along the Ryewater (Ríge, a tributary of the Liffey) to Kilcock (Cell Choc, Plate XI). The Ryewater does not seem to offer sufficient natural protection along a border that saw some of the most bitter warfare in pre-Norman Ireland, although in places the river has cut out long and deep channels, as in its course north of Maynooth. Boazio's map of Ireland from the Elizabethan period shows a belt of forest running south of, and parallel to, the course of the Ryewater. In spite of charges of inaccuracy levelled against Boazio, there are reasons to accept his indication of forest here. Firstly, as we shall see,[15] Boazio's indications of forest in Co. Wexford can be independently supported by a detailed map of that region; secondly, in placing woods at this point so near Dublin, the matter would have been easily verified or contradicted in his own time. Finally, an extensive forest in this area must have fed the Sarney ironworks as located by Mc Cracken.[16] The site of Sarney is north-east of Maynooth and about four miles north of the Ryewater.

The Ryewater or Ríge was recognized to be the major boundary between the Uí Néill and **the Leins**termen in pre-Norman times. According to Keating, the legendary Uí Néill king,

17

18

Cloncurry (Cluain Conaire Tomain) (17) and Laragh-bryan (Lathrach Briúin) (18) are both located in north Kildare and both Leinster houses lay just inside the sensitive border with the hostile Uí Néill kingdom of Brega in Meath. Cloncurry lay at one of the few crossing points between the Leinster and Uí Néill kingdoms which accounts for its choice for the 'great royal assembly' of 838 attended by kings from northern and southern Ireland. A similar royal parley was held at nearby Rathcore in Meath in 804. Irish annals differ from most other Dark Age chronicles in Anglo-Saxon England and Europe by paying

attention to local details such as freak weather conditions or remarkable local happenings. In Laragh-bryan, in 657, for instance, a cow astonished the chronicler of the Annals of Ulster *by giving birth to four calves! In the eleventh and twelfth centuries, when the blood-feuding and anarchy of the Irish aristocracy reduced the whole island to 'a trembling sod', border monasteries such as Laraghbryan fell on evil times. This Leinster house, which had survived the Viking wars, although so near to Dublin, was devastated in 1036 and again in 1040, not by Vikings but by the Irish of Brega in Meath.* 45

Tuathal Techtmar, set the Ríge as the frontier between the Laigin and Uí Néill, and much earlier sources refer to the Ríge Laigen in a similar context.[17] In 781 the Uí Néill of Brega met and defeated an invading Leinster army 'on the banks of the Ryewater' (*for bru Righi*).[18] The Leinster war-party, which included Cucongalt, king of Uí Garchon at Arklow, and an obscure tribal king of Cenél nUcha, was defeated on 1 November; so the attack which was designed to coincide with *Samain*, the great autumn festival, was met and repulsed by the men of Brega on their own border with Leinster. Fergal mac Ailella, *tighearna Ceniuil Uchae*, is mentioned only by the *Four Masters*.[19] There is no doubt that in an eighth-century context Fergal's true title was that of *ríg* or 'king' rather than *tigerna* or 'lord'. The *Four Masters* describe the Uí Garrchon ruler also as *tigherna*, although he is called 'king' by the *Annals of Ulster*. This particular record, then, not only emphasizes the position of the Ryewater as the Leinster boundary, but it shows us that an obscure people such as Cenél nUcha were still ruled by their own tribal leaders in the late eighth century, and had not yet been completely absorbed by the Uí Fáeláin. Other evidence for more primitive tribal survival in this area may be lurking behind a reference in the annals to the slaying of Mac Assida, king of Uí Gobla, by the people of Southern Brega (Descert Breg) in 1072.[20] This may refer to a branch of the Uí Gabla (a sub-division of Dál Chormaic: Chart 2), who occupied a corner of North Salt in Kildare on the border with Southern Brega.

Before joining the extensive belt of bog which formed the frontier between the Leinster Uí Failge and the tribes of Mide, the border of the Province passed from Kilcock (Plates XI and XII) through an area of bog north of Cloncurry to the upper reaches of the Boyne. The itinerary of St Patrick as described in the *Vita Tripartita* (*c*.A.D. 900) indicates the presence of a crossing point from Brega into Leinster near Cloncurry, and we have seen how this monastery was the scene of a council between the kings of the northern and southern halves of Ireland in 838.[21] A short distance north-west of Cloncurry, lay Rathcore (Dún Cuair) on the Brega side of the Leinster border (Plate XII). Here the abbot of Armagh presided over a synod in 804 in which the clergy were exempted from military service.[22] The synod was attended by the high-king, Áed Oirdnide, who led an expedition into nearby Leinster in this same year. At this point the Leinster border can be studied with greater certainty, due to the presence of bogland. It ran south and west along the bog which separated Uí Cairpri Laigen from the Province of Leinster (Plate XI). The very name of this territory, and the fact that it was later included within the twelfth-century Leinster diocese of Kildare (Plate VI), suggest that it may have traditionally belonged to Leinster.

It is clear from Plates III and XI that Carbury was separated from the rest of Kildare by an extensive belt of bog, and that the region forms a continuum with the Plains of Meath (Brega) rather than with Leinster. Consequently, if the area ever belonged to the Leinstermen in the early period, they must have lost it to Brega at about the same time as they lost adjoining lands in the Mide region. The tribal name, Uí Cairpri, from Cairpre son of Niall of the Nine Hostages, the founder of the Uí Néill dynasty (to the north of Leinster), supports this theory. This Cairpre of the Uí Néill played a large part in traditions relating to the end of the fifth century in the *Annals of Ulster*, where he is said to have engaged in numerous battles against the Leinstermen.[23] It was either Cairpre or his sons who conquered Carbury from Leinster in the opening years of the sixth century (Plate V). Earlier in this Uí Néill war, Cairpre's brother, Lóegaire, met his death fighting the Leinstermen at Carbury Hill (Síd Nechtain) *c*.462.[24] Significantly, the territory of Lóegaire's descendants (Lóegaire Breg) lay immediately north of Carbury, based on a power-centre at Tullyard (Telach Árd) just north of Trim in Co. Meath (Plate XII). The fact that Carbury later formed part of the Leinster diocese of Kildare reflects the state of affairs in the twelfth century, when the Leinster Uí Cheinnselaig were expanding

Mag Ailbe in southern Kildare was particularly rich in important monasteries, and the archaeological remains that survive in this region testify to a rich past. Moone (Móin Coluimb) was a Columban house attached to the paruchia of Iona, and a splendid high Cross survives here from the tenth century.

19

Castledermot, (Dísert Diarmata) the 'desert' retreat of Diarmait, still preserves a tenth-century high cross and round tower. It was here in 908 that the Munstermen buried the decapitated body of their bishop-king, Cormac mac Cuilennáin, who was slain by the Leinstermen in the battle of Ballaghmoon.

20

Kileencormac (Cell Fine Cormaic), near the Wicklow border in southern Kildare, is one of the most interesting Early Christian sites in Ireland. The Christian cemetery and its church (now destroyed) perch on top of a prehistoric tumulus and a number of Ogham stones also survive there. This centre has the best claims to being Cell Fine, one of the churches associated with Palladius, that mysterious missionary who was sent by Pope Celestine in A.D. 431 to take care of those Irish who already believed in Christ.

21

once more over the Uí Néill border against a weakened enemy. The reconquest of Uí Cairpri by the Leinstermen from the Uí Néill in the twelfth century also explains why this territory formed part of Strongbow's lordship of Leinster and not part of de Lacy's lordship in Meath (Plates IX and X). The name and extent of Uí Cairpri territory was preserved in the Kildare barony of Carbury (Plate VII). The Anglo-Norman baronial boundary — as indeed the earlier Celtic tribal boundary—was determined by the configuration of the bogs, and when we compare Plate III with Plates VII and VIII we see how environmental considerations greatly clarify and explain a picture which relies on later civil divisions alone.

The Bog of Allen, that great expanse of basin peat which covers the North-Western Region, takes its name from the Hill of Allen (Almu), a hill which figured prominently in mythical Irish tradition and which is situated on the border of the Northern Region. This hill is almost completely enclosed by a ring of bogland, and the area is in fact marked on printed maps of the eighteenth and nineteenth centuries as 'The Isle of Allen.'[25] It is no coincidence that Almu in early Irish tradition was considered the principal fortress of Finn mac Cumail, legendary

22

Old Kilcullen, Co. Kildare, with the Iron Age hillfort of Knockaulin (Dún Ailinne) in the background (Dublin Penny Journal 1836). Cell Cuilind was one of the first churches founded in Leinster in the late fifth century. Its siting beside the ancient Leinster capital at Knockaulin indicates its importance, and its founder, the mysterious Mac Táil, brought Christianity to the Kildare Plains.

The earliest Leinster tradition asserted that Knockaulin had been built by the Fir Domnann— a people identified with the Dumnonii, a Celtic tribe who occupied Devon and Cornwall, and south of the Firth of Clyde in Scotland.

A prince has gone to the meadow-lands of the Dead,
·The noble son of Sétna.
He ravaged the ranks of the Formorians over worlds of men.
From the height of Knockaulin he slew the mighty ones of the Earth,
A powerful tribune of many nations, Mes Delmann of the Domnainn.

(Seventh-century Old Irish poem
MS Rawlinson B 502; translation by Kuno Meyer)

48

leader of the *fiana* or hunting bands, whose exploits took place in the remote wilderness. This cycle of literature associated with Finn is generally agreed to be later than that of the heroic sagas proper, and to have enjoyed popular rather than an aristocratic patronage.[26] Whether or not we accept Kuno Meyer's claim[27] that already in the seventh century the Finn legend had sufficient popularity to justify the invention of a pedigree for its hero—connecting him with the royal line of Leinster—there is little doubt that Leinster was the home of this literary cycle. O'Rahilly saw a whole section of this literature connected with a Leinster rather than with a national Finn.[28] The strict meaning of the word *fian*, and perhaps the original one, was that of a band of roving warriors waging war on their own account.[29] These bands often consisted of men expelled (*éclaind*) from their own *tuatha* or tribes, and men without land (*dithir*). Under Old Irish Law, such men living outside the community of the *tuath* had few rights, and consequently we should expect to find them in the bogs and dense woodland such as cover vast areas of the north-west of ancient Leinster. The literature on the legendary Finn abounds in references to the wilderness and wood,[30] and it comes as little surprise to find Almu as the centre of Finn's activities, surrounded as it was by bog and wood stretching westwards for miles across the Irish Midlands.

Before leaving the Northern Region it should be stressed that is *was* Leinster. With the exception of the Central Region we could take away from the ancient Province all its other regions and still preserve the identity of Cóiced Laigen from this Northern area alone. Its kings, the Uí Dúnlainge, were for centuries not only kings of North Leinster, but kings of the Province. The kingship of Leinster was, in bardic literature, symbolically tied up with key sites in this region, which were held up as status symbols to the Leinstermen and seen to be representative of their Province on the national scene. Thus Maistiu, Dún Ailinne, Nás and Liamain were thought of in somewhat the same way as the House of Windsor in England to-day. The hill-fort of Knockaulin (Dún Ailinne) overlooking the Curragh, although deserted by the historical period, continued to symbolize the ancient glories of the Leinstermen, taking its place on the national scene beside Tara, Cruachain, Ailech and Emain Macha. The importance of the symbolism and ancient associations of these sites as preserved in the *senchus* or traditions of the Leinstermen, cannot be overestimated. As late as the sixteenth and seventeenth centuries the court-poets of the O'Toole's and O'Byrne's, whose works are preserved in the *Leabhar Branach* (*Book of the O'Byrnes*), were constantly referring in their eulogies to the ancient glories of the rich Central Plain, which their lords had lost to the Anglo-Normans four centuries before. References to Maistiu, Nás Life, Almhu and the like, recur regularly,[31] either signifying Leinster as a whole, or as a vehicle for comparison with the valour and beauty of one of the O'Byrne or O'Toole families. All this, in spite of the fact that for centuries (Plate X) the O'Byrnes and O'Tooles had been consigned by the Normans to the wilderness of the Wicklow hills. We are reminded of the tenth-century Welsh poet in *Armes Prydein* who still dreamt of chasing the Anglo-Saxons out of Sandwich! Memories of the Dark Age and medieval past in Ireland were kept green, not only on account of the conservative and tribal nature of society, but also on account of the continuity which existed between Elizabethan society and that of the Dark Ages. In spite of centuries of political and military turmoil, the O'Byrnes and O'Tooles who ruled in the Wicklow hills in the sixteenth century were the descendants of the Uí Fáeláin and Uí Muiredaig respectively, who held the Kildare Plains in the pre-Norman era. Similar claims could be made by other great sixteenth-century families in other parts of Leinster, such as O'Conor, O'Dempsey, O'More or O'Dunn (cf. Plates IX and X).

CHAPTER V

Tribes and Dynasties of the North-Eastern Region

23

Glendalough, Co. Wicklow,
The conical top on the Round Tower today is a nineteenth-century restoration.

Kevin searched through a great part of Erin,
In the company of an angel,
To find a retreat for prayer.
He did not rest till he found it.

Kevin crossed the summits
With the angel — they were swift —
He built a monastery in the glens.
The Heavenly Father blessed it from above.

High above every church is the seat of Kevin,

The bond of alliance between the Leinster-
men and the men of Northern Ireland.
A place triumphant with its cemeteries, wild,
Lofty, compact with its harbours and woods.

There will come a time at the end of the
world,
Though to me it will be a sorry trespass,
When my beloved church will be ravaged,
And will be deserted under its fill of
treachery.'

Late Medieval Metrical *Life of Kevin*; translation, Plummer, *Bethada Náem,* ii

The North-Eastern Region was undoubtedly the poorest in all the Province from the point of view of land value, and historically the Wicklow area was occupied by the weaker tribes. It is significant that the *Book of Leinster* (fols: 39b-40d)[1] preserves three king-lists which cover every region in Leinster but this. For the Northern Region we have the Ríg Lagen (Kings of the Leinstermen) whose Uí Dúnlainge kingship can be taken as synonymous with that of the whole Province. For the North-Western Region we have Ríg Hua Falge (Kings of Uí Failge), and for the Central and Southern Regions we have Ríg Hua

Cendselaig (Kings of Uí Cheinnselaig). No king-list has been preserved for any of the tribes which occupied the north-east, such as the Uí Máil, Dál Messin Corb or Uí Enechglaiss, and the surviving genealogies of these tribes, when taken as a group, are the least detailed in the Leinster collection.

Annals and other sources deal sparingly with the Wicklow area and there are many questions which must remain unanswered for topographers. The location of Inber Dee, for instance, a key site in Patrician sources, and crucial for the precise location of Uí Enechglaiss, has been disputed by several authorities. We know it was a harbour somewhere on the Wicklow coast, but it has been located by scholars at places as far apart as Bray, Wicklow Town and Arklow.[2] Hogan's location of Inber Dee (Plate XII) at Arklow is correct.[3] This being so, then we can locate the Uí Enechglaiss about the mouth of the Avoca river. This tribe, although never very powerful and later to be eclipsed in the tenth century by Viking settlements on the Wicklow coast, were regarded by the genealogists as a free people in the same company as Uí Failge and Uí Bairrche. It is almost certain that earlier in the historical period the Uí Enechglaiss were located on the Kildare side of the mountains and even further north, in Brega. A branch of this people was situated on the western side of the mountains, south of Naas in Kildare (Plate XI), and this may indicate the homeland area of the tribe. It is interesting that Kilroe singled out the area about Arklow as being particularly fertile, with its soils of shell and Wexford marls which are admirably suited for agriculture. In the Anglo-Norman period the manor and barony of Arklow was closely associated, administratively, with Kildare.[4]

The other tribe which occupied this east coast region to the north about Wicklow Town was the Dál Messin Corb. This tribe had also been forced to cross the mountains from the Kildare Plains, in the seventh century at the latest. Although this people (Chart 2) represented an older genealogical stratum than most other Leinster tribes, there is good evidence to show[5] that they held the kingship of the whole Province in the later years of the fifth century, at which time they must have held considerable lands in the fertile Northern Region. A branch of Uí Garrchon, which was the chief sept of the Dál Messin Corb, was beleived in the eighth century to have been centred on the Kileencormac (Cell Fine) area in southern Kildare (Plates XI and XII).[6] Kevin, the founder of Glendalough, was of this people, and his *Lives*, which preserve traditions from as early as the eighth century, show this saint to have been born at Tipperkevin in the Kildare Plains (Plate XII) near Naas, and to have crossed from there to found the monastery of Glendalough on the eastern side of the mountains.[7]

O'Rahilly, who paid little attention to Irish topography generally, based much of his theories on the Leinster region on the correct observation that the Wicklow mountains acted as a survival area for tribes dispossessed by stronger peoples on the Kildare Plains. Price convincingly traced the line of three major passes across the mountains connecting the east coast with the Northern and Central Regions.[8]. One of these passes connected the Uí Enechglaiss, in the valleys of the Avoca and Avonmore (Plate XI), with lands across the mountains (via Glenmalure) in the Glen of Imaal. The placename Glenmalure (Glenn Maoil 'oraidh) has an uncertain derivation[9], but Glen of Imaal (Glenn Ua Máil) preserves the name of the Uí Máil. This tribe (Chart 2), with their sub-septs of the Uí Théig and Uí Chellaig Chualann, seem to have held all the fertile western foot-hills of the Wicklow mountains along the border with Co. Kildare and to have extended east to Glendalough. Genealogically, we have seen (Chart 2) they were assigned a position by ancient compilers between older tribes such as the Dál Messin Corb and the later descendants of Cathair Mór, such as Uí Enechglaiss. This intermediate position is reflected historically in their holding the kingship of Leinster in the seventh and opening years of the eighth centuries, and topographically by the fact that they occupied lands half-way between the rich Kildare Plains and the road to extinction on the east of the barren 51 mountains.

There is evidence to show that the Uí Théig branch of Uí Máil had crossed the mountains and settled along the eastern side of the Vartry river where they left their name in the district of Othee by early Anglo-Norman times.[10] How early before the Norman Invasion this extension of their territory was effected, it is impossible to say. Their migration would have been easily accomplished by way of the pass through the Sally Gap (Plates XI and XII) which connected Eastern Liffey (Airthir Life) with the upper reaches of the Vartry and the Avonmore.

Uí Máil power, however, seems to have centred on the Glen of Imaal. Price examined the placenames of this area in particular detail and identified the fort on Brusselstown Ring with Dún Bolg, and the ancient site of Kilranelagh with Dún Buchat—two sites which figured prominently in Leinster saga in the early historical period.[11] Price was certainly correct in locating these sites in the Imaal area. The eighth-century saga of *Fingal Rónáin* centres also on this region, and it can be shown that this saga has members of the Uí Máil dynasty for its main characters and not, as Professor Green stated,[12] kings of the Uí Dúnlainge.

The Uí Máil tribes occupied the countryside extending from the Dublin mountains to southern Kildare, which was traversed by the ancient road known as Slige Chualann (The Cualu Road). The course of this road as plotted on Plate XII is based on the findings of Ó Lochlainn, who correctly located it on the western, and not, as was formerly held, on the eastern side of the Wicklow hills.[13] Confusion in finding the line of this road by early topographers centred on the whereabouts of the region of Cualu. This name applied to all the North-East Region from Arklow in the south-east to Eastern Liffey (Airthir Life) in Kildare in the north-west, but O'Rahilly correctly observed that the name was applied with special frequency to the foot-hills of the Dublin rather than the Wicklow mountains.[14]

St Kevin's road ran through the most important pass across the Wicklow mountains (Plate XII). This road connected the lands about the Curragh (Cuirrech Life) and Knockaulin hill-fort in the Kildare Plains with the monastery of Glendalough, and ultimately with Arklow via the Avonmore valley. Glendalough monastery was founded by St Kevin, a member of the Dál Messin Corb, and we gather from the *Félire Óengusso* and the *Martyrology of O'Gorman* that Glendalough was in Uí Máil.[15] In spite of these connections, however, the monastery was controlled from the middle of the seventh century by the Uí Dúnlainge dynasty of the lowlands to the west in the Northern Region.[16] This control was clearly facilitated by Glendalough's position on one of the three great passes which lead across the Wicklow hills from west to east. We may assume, too, that all of the tribes occupying the Wicklow hills (with the exception of Uí Enechglaiss) paid regular tribute to the Uí Dúnlainge kings in the pre-Viking era.

The boundaries between individual tribes on the east coast are virtually impossible to determine, and from the location of monastic sites these boundaries do not appear to have been constant, reminding us of the futility of seeking too rigid a definition of some tribal areas. The land, for instance, between Arklow and Wicklow Town, with its extensive acidic and poorly drained soil, could only have supported a few scattered communities. Movement north and south along the coast here was impeded by the numerous streams flowing eastwards to the sea and also by a great *sescenn* or swamp in the coastal area stretching five miles from Kilcoole to the south of Newcastle. Discussions, therefore, on the precise dividing line between Uí Enechglaiss and Dál Messin Corb in this mainly uninhabited region are pointless.[17] The coastal strip from Kilcoole to Dublin was of a more fertile nature, a fact which is reflected in the greater number of monastic sites in this region (Plate XII). In the north, this area was inhabited by the Uí Briúin Chualann (Plate XI), a people related to the powerful Uí Dúnlainge and not to be confused with the Uí Máil sept of Uí Chellaig Chualann (Chart 2). Both septs, as their names

24   25

26

24
The Reefert church in Glendalough as it appeared about 1840 before restoration by the Commissioners of Public Works. This was the most hallowed spot in the entire monastic complex which by the twelfth century had spread over most of the valley bottom. The Reefert with its surrounding clocháns, *or beehive cells, was St Kevin's earliest monastic centre and he is almost certainly buried in the graveyard here. Here, too, lie the bones of Leinster kings of the Uí Máil and Dál Messin Corb, including heroes of Leinster sagas such as Máelodrán, the seventh-century champion. It is these royal occupants in the ground here who gave the place its name* Rígfert, *'Cemetery of the Kings'.*

25
Stone lamp from Co. Wicklow in twelfth-century Romanesque style

26
Inscription on a cross-slab at Glendalough
In spite of its size and importance as evidenced by its extensive architectural remains, Glendalough has yielded very few inscribed crosses or slabs. This is largely due to the intractable nature of the local stone. An inscription on a slab once preserved at the Reefert church (Fig. 24) was read by Petrie in the 1820s. This asked for prayers for Cairpre mac Cathail identified with Cairpre the Generous, an anchorite of Glendalough who died in A.D. 1013. The inscription illustrated here is from a drawing by Macalister (Corpus inscriptionum, ii, 85), *based in turn on a moulding from a slab in Glendalough Cathedral in 1873. If we accept Macalister's reading, the text asks for a prayer for* Muircher(tac)h U Chathal(ain) .i. do thigerna U Fog(artaig), *and we must then accept that this refers to Muirchertach Ua Cathaláin, lord of Uí Fogartaig, who fell in the battle of Móin Mór in 1151. But there are difficulties with this interpretation. The Uí Fogartaig were a sept from Éle in Munster. This inscription must refer to a Leinsterman and most probably to a member of the Uí Máil or the Uí Dúnlainge.*

imply, occupied the region of Cualu. The Uí Briúin Chualann extended as far south in the coastal lowlands of Wicklow as Kilcoole, but they were separated from the Dál Messin Corb and Uí Théig, further south, by a swampy wilderness some five miles deep. This Newcastle area was the boundary between the medieval dioceses of Dublin and Glendalough, so that Dublin diocese ran south along the coast to the southern borders of Uí Briúin Chualann—a people from the Northern Region who had migrated from south Dublin into this isolated coastal area. The Uí Briúin Chualann had penetrated from the north as far as the swampy coastlands of Kilcoole, while to the south and west of this swamp the Uí Théig and Dál Messin Corb had reached the coast by crossing Wicklow Gap and Sally Gap. A small and obscure branch of Dál Messin Corb—the Uí Bráen Deilgni[18]—had, as their name implies, managed to push northwards past the lowland marshes and settle around Delgany (Plates XI and XII).

Apart from the vast tracts of mountain and blanket bog shown on Plates III and XII, the North-Eastern Region was noted in Tudor times for its great forests. Speed, Boazio and the T.C.D. copy of a sixteenth-century map of Ireland[19] enable us to reconstruct the woodland in the valleys of the Dodder, Dargle, Vartry and Avonmore rivers. The forest in the Dargle basin, due to its proximity to Dublin, was marked off in Anglo-Norman times as the royal forest of Glencree. Holinshed and Spencer confirm the evidence of the maps in stating that the sides of the Wicklow glens were clothed in great forests,[20] while the *Lives* of Kevin confirm the fact that in the eighth century the valleys east and west of the mountains on either side of the Wicklow Gap were covered in dense forest.[21] These *Lives* even imply that the bare granite heights of the mountains were free of woodland (see pp. 25-6 above).

It was along this isolated and wild coastline of Wicklow that the Vikings established their strongholds at Wicklow and Arklow in the tenth century. Before this time, the coastal area had played little or no part in the life of Leinster. We can point to no incident of any importance in the annals involving this area in the pre-Norse era. It was once thought, even by Ryan, that Kilcoole was the scene of the assassination of the Leinster king, Bran Ardcenn and his queen Eithne, in A.D. 795,[22] but this event took place in Cell Chúile Dumai in Loígis territory in Co. Leix (Plate XIV). The first time we can prove that a Leinster king bothered to visit this remote corner of the Province was in 1021 when, significantly, King Ugaire mac Dúnlainge defeated Sitric Silkenbeard of Norse Dublin in a battle at Delgany (Plate XII).[23] By this time, however, the coastal region which had once been a backwater of no interest to the Leinstermen had now been taken over by the Norsemen who had easy access to it from the sea, and who were protected from the more powerful Leinster tribes by the mountains and forests of Wicklow.

The two Irish tribes which must have borne the brunt of the Norse invasion and settlement along the Wicklow coast were the Uí Enechglaiss and Dál Messin Corb. In the pre-Norse era the Uí Enechglaiss, who held the more fertile lands about Arklow, were regarded by the genealogists as a Free Tribe and, therefore, superior to the Dál Messin Corb. But it was the Uí Enechglaiss who lost most from the Viking occupation of Arklow and its hinterland, and we find that in the later Celtic period the Dál Messin Corb re-emerged as the dominant tribe in the Wicklow hills. From the ninth century onwards the tribes of the North-Eastern Region were referred to collectively as Fortuatha (not to be confused with Fothairt) or Alien Tribes, and individual groups within this community were rarely mentioned by name. It seems as though the separate tribal groupings on the east coast had suffered so badly from the Viking onslaught that they were reduced to the level of one amorphous tribe inhabiting the wilderness—at least in the eyes of chroniclers in Kildare and Clonard. Yet, remarkably, both Uí Enechglaiss and Dál Messin Corb did preserve something of their individual identities until the coming of Strongbow. As late as 1170 we have the record of Murchad Ua Ferghaile, a king or lord (*tigerna*) of Fortuatha being slain by Ua Fiachrach, a chieftain of Uí Enechglaiss.[24] We can show from the genealogy of the Dál Messin Corb in the *Book of Leinster* and the *Book of Ballymote* that not only did this tribe survive into the twelfth century, but that its kings were also 'kings of the Alien Tribes' (*rí na Fortuath*).[25] Their dynastic name, Ua Ferghaile (O'Farrell or O'Farrelly), can be traced through the annals right back into the early eleventh century. Domnall Dub Ua Ferghaile, king of the Fortuatha of Leinster, died of the great plague in 1095, while his royal predecessor, Gilla Pátraic Ua Ferghaile, was slain by the Uí Néill in the battle of Odba in distant Brega along with his Leinster over-king, Diarmait mac Maoil na mBó, in 1072.[26] Yet another and earlier Domnall Ua Ferghaile, king of the Fortuatha, was assassinated by his own people in Termonn Cóemgin (Trooperstown) beside Glendalough in 1043.[27] Glendalough was tightly controlled by the Uí Dúnlainge of Kildare, and later by their descendants, Ua Tuathail (O'Toole) (Plates IX and X). With pressure from Vikings along the coast, it was obvious that the eastern tribes of

27

With the notable exception of Glendalough, there were no important monastic sites in the mountainous North-Eastern Region, which supported only a tiny population. There were, however, small churches and monastic cells all over the region, few of which may have seen continuous worship throughout the Celtic period. The church at Stigonnell in Powers-court demesne, near Enniskerry, is of interest in that its name most likely derives from the Old Norwegian Gunnhilds Stadir *(The homestead of* [the lady] *Gunnhild)*. All of the Wicklow seaboard, and even the glens further inland, were more thoroughly colonized by the Scandinavians than we have hitherto realized. About a mile from Stigonnell is Curtlestown, which takes its name from Baile mac Thorcaill *(The place of Thorkell's sons)*, and was part of the royal lands of the Mac Thorcaill kings of Scandinavian Dublin in the twelfth century. The present church at Stigonnell owes its origins to Richard Wingfield's patronage in the early seventeenth century. The medieval foundation at Churchtown was already a pile of rubble by 1838.

Not far from Stigonnell church, and also within Powerscourt demesne, is Powerscourt Waterfall (27), as sketched here in R. Lovett's, Irish Pictures *in 1888. Protected in the twentieth century behind the walls of a great private estate, this natural treasure has escaped the ravages of modern 'planners' and has lost nothing of its primeval beauty. Beside this waterfall in the Dark Ages was the tiny cell of Cell Cornáin and the whole valley was known as* Glenn Esa *('Glen of the Waterfall'). The place is mentioned in a poem celebrating the exploits of Felim son of Fiach Mac Hugh O'Byrne who ruled over the Wicklow Hills from 1597 to 1606. During the time of Felim, – referred to in this poem as 'the raven of Leinster and the prince of Barrow's hills', – these valleys about Enniskerry were in the hands of the O'Tooles. Felim O'Toole's lands at Powerscourt were confiscated in 1589 and granted to Richard Wingfield in 1603.*

Wicklow would fall back into the mountains, and so inevitably they clashed with the powerful dynasty of Uí Dúnlainge who creamed off revenue from St Kevin's monastery at Glendalough deep in the Wicklow hills. We find, for instance, that the Fortuatha slew an Ua Tuathail abbot of Glendalough in 1127 and Domnall of the Dál Messin Corb, who was assassinated at the *termonn* or boundary of Glendalough in 1043, had earlier himself slain a king of the Uí Dúnlainge sept of Uí Fáeláin (Domnall mac Donnchada) in 1039.[28] We may note, too, that an Uí Enechglaiss king was slain by the king of Ua Tuathail in 1154.[29] Translated into more general terms, this detailed record of inter-tribal feuding tells us that the Viking occupation of coastal Wicklow increased competition for the control of Glendalough between Wicklow tribes engaged in the desperate struggle for survival, and the richer kings of the Province who lived in the Liffey and Barrow basins but who took tribute from the Wicklow area by right of their overlordship.

The Viking Age had opened ominously for the Dál Messin Corb, whose king, Conall son of Cuchongalt, fell in a Viking slaughter of the Leinstermen's war-camp in 827.[30] Cináed, the king of Uí Enechglaiss, was slain by the famous Norse king, Sitric, grandson of Ívarr, in the battle of Cenn Fuait in Carlow, in 917.[31] But it may be that the Dál Messin Corb survived by coming to terms with the Foreigners. In 984, for instance, Domnall Clóen, king of Leinster, and father of Donnchad, the last Uí Dúnchada king of the Province, was slain by Fiachra king of the Fortuatha.[32] Did the Dál Messin Corb assist the Norsemen, directly or indirectly, in 55 weakening the power of Uí Dúnchada in south Dublin? We find Domnall mac Ferghaile, king of the Fortuatha, fighting on the side of Sigurd of the Orkneys at the battle of Clontarf in 1014.[33] It is difficult to decide whether he fought with the Vikings out of choice, or simply because he was told to do so by his Leinster over-kings who also joined the Viking cause.

The question of the survival of the early Celtic tribes in the Wicklow hills during four centuries of attack, both from Vikings on the coast and from their more powerful Irish neighbours inland, is an important one for the understanding of early Irish demography. Thus, the Dál Messin Corb and Uí Enechglaiss survived until the Anglo-Norman Invasion as Ua Ferghaile (O'Farrelly) and Ua Fiachrach (O'Fieghraie or Feary) respectively (Plates IX and X). Further north, along the eastern foot-hills of the mountains behind Newcastle, Uí Briúin Chualann held out under pressure from both Norsemen and the Uí Dúnchada, as Ua Finnacáin (or Ua Cuinneacháin) and re-emerged in the fourteenth century as O'Kindghan (or O'Cnigon). The Uí Máil survived in west Wicklow under the dynastic name of Ua Taidhg (O'Teige or Tighe), while their Uí Théig cousins further north, below Blessington, survived as Ua Ceallaigh (O'Kelly). The remarkable point about this sequence of survival is that it did not end with the Anglo-Norman Invasion. After the Invasion the North-Eastern wilderness continued to absorb dynasties such as the Uí Muiredaig and Uí Fáeláin kings of Leinster, as they fled to the hills in the face of Strongbow's ruthless and powerful army in 1170. Here these two dynasties, with their camp followers, were to survive in the wilderness as the O'Tooles and O'Byrnes for another four centuries until the reign of Elizabeth I. While they may have survived in a state of

28

The remarkable cone of the great Sugar Loaf (Dublin Penny Journal, *1835*) *dominates the mountainous wilderness of Wicklow with a presiding presence of timeless beauty. The name Sugar Loaf first appears for this mountain in 1685, and until that time this entire area was Gaelic-speaking and ruled by the O'Tooles and O'Byrnes into the* early seventeenth century. Sugar Loaf has the best claim to being Óe Cualann ('The Ear of Cualu'—Cualu being the name of the Wicklow hills) of ancient Irish documents. This was one of the three 'heights' of Celtic Ireland crowned with a fairy palace or síd of the Dagda, ruler of the Otherworld.

Chart 3

Inter-Tribal Marriage and Circulating Kingship in Leinster
A.D. 550–700

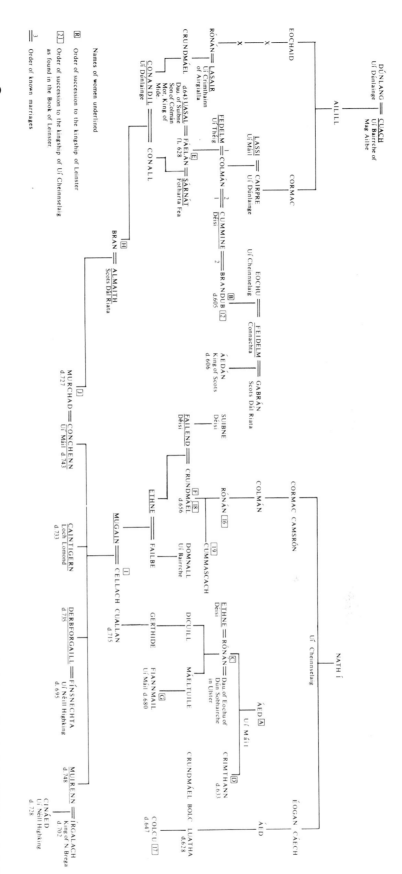

Names of women underlined

[R] Order of succession to the kingship of Leinster

[27] Order of succession to the kingship of Uí Chennselaig as found in the Book of Leinster

═ 1 Order of known marriages

═ Order of known marriages

Royal descent was reckoned through the male line by early Irish genealogists and succession to kingship was agnatic. But women could possess and inherit property on their own account, and some women also had royal blood in their veins. Descent through the female line may have been much more important in *reality* than the genealogists cared to admit in their records. The fact that the Irish compiled a *Ban-Shenchus* ('Lore on Women'), devoted to the descent of women within the agnatic system, suggests that cognatic elements were strong within early kin groups. This chart shows the wealth of information which survives on early Leinster queens and it shows, too, how aristocratic women consolidated relationships between otherwise rival tribes. This society was clearly not matrilinear, but historians may have underestimated the crucial rôle of the Celtic matriarchy in the politics of early Irish overlordship.

57

cultural regression, they nevertheless raised armies which were capable of striking dread into the burghers of Dublin, and resisted all interference from the English administration. The obvious conclusion suggests itself yet again, that Ireland was a greatly under-populated country prior to the Anglo-Norman Invasion, with vast areas still under forest which were capable of being turned into farmland . This is the only adequate explanation for the flourishing of Gaelic dynasties in the Wicklow hills and in Offaly into the Early Modern period.

To this day there are farmsteads on the high plateau of Calary stretching between the remarkable cone of Sugarloaf Mountain and Roundwood village, over 700 feet above sea-level. The soil is not good, and Calary Bog uninviting to farmers, yet at least one ring-fort near the top of the Long Hill bears silent testimony to the presence of a Celtic magnate and his household who made a living there long ago. All around are the heights of Djouce (Digais) and Maulin (Málainn), and to the south the lofty wilderness of Lugnaquillia, second highest mountain in Ireland (3039 feet). These remote mountain peaks of timeless beauty were never occupied by the Celts or their prehistoric forerunners, but tales and legends of how these places got their Celtic names held a fascination for the early Irish mind and they can still be read by the few who are interested in such things in the *Dinn Senchus* of the Leinstermen.[34]

The wind over the Hog's Back moans
It takes the trees and lays them low,
And shivering monks o'er frozen stones
To the twain hours of night-time go.
Old Irish poem on Glendalough (Robin Flower, *The Irish Tradition*)

CHAPTER VI

Tribes and Dynasties of the Central and Southern Regions

The terms Laigin Tuath Gabair (North Leinster) and Laigin Des Gabair (South Leinster) were used in the historical period in a loose political sense to signify the territories ruled by the northern and southern dynasties of the Province. While the Uí Dúnlainge were overlords of the tribal confederacies of the north, the south was dominated by the Uí Cheinnselaig. Laigin Des Gabair became synonymous with Uí Cheinnselaig and comprised geographically the Central and Southern Regions (Plates I and VIII). Individual kings appearing in the king-list of the Uí Cheinnselaig in the *Book of Leinster* are styled kings of Laigin Des Gabair in the annals. In the *Lives* of Kevin, Máedóc, Munnu, Abban, and Moling, on the other hand, the sept name Uí Cheinnselaig is applied to southern Leinster in a territorial sense and is interchangeable with the concept of Des Gabair (Lands south of Gabair).[1] O'Rahilly correctly interpreted this term Des Gabair as political in its later use and noted that Laigin Des Gabair was used to signify the men of Ossory in the twelfth-century *Book of Rights*.[2] This extension of the term to Ossory was encouraged by the political interference of that people in Leinster affairs in the eleventh century, when a fictitious pedigree for the Osraige kings was invented to unite them to the Leinster royal house.

There seems also to have been confusion between *gabair* in Laigin Des Gabair and the word *gabrán* in Belach Gabráin (The Pass of Gowran). Gabrán, as we have seen, was the name of the pass leading from Ossory into Leinster in Co. Carlow (Plates IV, V and XVI), while Gabair was the region between the Burren river and the Slaney in north Carlow (Plate XVI). The confusion between Gabair and Gabrán can be seen in a genealogical text dealing with women of the Uí Dúnlainge dynasty.[3] The *Book of Leinster* text of this tract says that Cuach, a princess of the Uí Bairrche, was presented with three forts, one of which was *Magen Garbáin*,[4] while *The Book of Lecan* has *Maigen Gabair* and T.C.D. MS H.3.17 reads *Daingin Gabra*. The area referred to is undoubtedly the locality of Gabair in north Carlow and it is interesting to find in this reference a connection between it and the Uí Bairrche. This tribe (Plates VII and VIII) was located in the barony of Slievemargy in Leix and in adjoining parts of Carlow.[5] The monasteries of Killeshin and Sleaty in Leix (Plate XVI) were in Uí Bairrche, but the territory at one stage extended much further south to take in the monastery of Lorum (Cell Molapóc) in the barony of Idrone East in Carlow, opposite the Pass of Gowran. Originally, then, Uí Bairrche territory included both Gabair and Gabrán, and in the tract known as the *Testament of Cathair Már*, dating to the eighth century or earlier, the Uí Bairrche are praised for defending North Leinster (Tuath-Laigin) from the *Crícha Tes-Ghabair* ('the borders of South Leinster'), and for raiding south around Gabrán.[6] In the eleventh and twelfth centuries this dynasty ruled under the family name of Mac Gormáin (MacGorman, O'Gorman) and were dispossessed in the earliest years of the Anglo-Norman conquest by de Clahull and other tenants of Strongbow (Plates IX and X).

The lands of the Uí Bairrche are of key interest in determining the political divisions between North and South Leinster. Obviously lands to the south of Uí Bairrche (in Carlow) belonged to Laigin Des Gabair and those to the north belonged to Laigin Tuath Gabair. It is clear from this also that the Loígis (Plate VIII) belonged to the northern tribal confederacy. Another branch of the Uí Bairrche have left their name on the barony of Bargy in south Wexford (Plates VII and VIII) and in the early centuries of the historical period the Uí Bairrche may have occupied most of Carlow and Wexford. O'Rahilly's theory that the Uí Bairrche were outposts of the northern Laigin is correct only for the later centuries.[7] It is interesting to observe that the Fothairt or Fotharta, an alien tribe in Leinster (Plate VIII), who have left their names on the baronies of Forth in Carlow and Forth in south Wexford (Plate VII), bordered on Uí Bairrche lands in both areas; and remnants of Uí Bairrche and Fotharta survived side by side in Eastern Liffey (Airthir Life) in the north of the Province. The origin tales of the Fotharta show them to have been introduced into Leinster as auxiliaries of the Laigin, and the topographical evidence would point to the Uí Bairrche as their immediate overlords. When the Uí Bairrche were fragmented by the power of the Uí Cheinnselaig, their mercenaries, the Fotharta, seem to have suffered the same fate as their masters. It is worth noting that the Fotharta who occupied Mag Fea in Carlow, and the Fotharta in Chairn, of Carnsore Point in south Wexford (Plate VIII), both had a considerable amount of granite in the rock-formations of their territories (Plate IV). This in turn produced poor soils with high levels of acidity and both the Uí Bairrche and Fotharta of south Wexford also had to cope with lands which were poorly drained (Plate III). From the eleventh century the Fotharta of Carlow took the family name Ua Nualláin (O'Nolan), while their Wexford cousins survived alongside the Wexford Norsemen as Ua Lorcáin (O'Larkin). The O'Nolan's of Carlow retreated into the Wicklow forests after Strongbow's arrival (Plates IX and X).

In the ninth century the chief dynasties which controlled all of the Southern and Central Regions were the Uí Cheinnselaig and the related tribes of Uí Dega and Uí Dróna. The sept

29

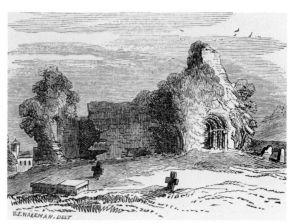

30

The monastery of Ullard (Irarda), although now in Co. Kilkenny, and situated west of the Barrow, was in ancient Leinster territory, and belonged to the Uí Dróna. This Kilkenny region is still within the Leinster diocese of Leighlin. The archaeological remains at Ullard include a Romanesque doorway and a tenth-century high cross.

30
The monastic ruins at Killeshin (Cell Eision) (30) and Sleaty (Sléibte), lie a few miles apart under the shadow of the Slievemargy hills near the Barrow

in south-eastern Leix. The origins of Killeshin are obscure, but Sleaty was a most important centre in the first two Christian centuries in Leinster. This was the monastic home of Fiacc, who in very early Patrician tradition was the first bishop of the Leinstermen. The anchorite, Bishop Áed of Sleaty, who died in A.D. 700, collected much of the early Christian traditions of the Barrow valley and passed these on to Armagh. Sleaty was overshadowed from the eighth century onwards by the rising power of royal monasteries such as Kildare, Glendalough and Ferns.

31

Old Leighlin (Leth Glenn) situated in the Barrow valley in west Carlow not far from the Iron Age hill-fort at Dinn Ríg (Fig. 1) was a relatively late foundation of St Mo-Laise who died in A.D. 639. Mo-Laise was a champion for conformity with Roman church usage, and eventually his foundation became the centre of the diocese of Leighlin in the twelfth century. The Long Book of Leighlin (Lebar Fata Lethglindi) *was an ancient manuscript compil-* *ation, now lost, which testified to this region of the Barrow valley as being a centre for early scholarly activity. The twelfth-century cathedral (above) was restored in the sixteenth century. This area from Killesin in the north to St Mullins in the south constituted yet another Leinster zone of monastic culture similar to, but less important than, the Bogland zone in the north-west.*

name, Uí Dróna, is preserved in the baronies of Idrone East and West in Carlow (Plate VII). The survival of this tribal name in a modern barony is somewhat misleading. Much of Idrone country once belonged to Uí Bairrche as far south in Co. Carlow as Lorum and across the Kilkenny border to Kilmacahill near Gowran (Plate XV). Secondly, we know from the annals and genealogies that the territory of Uí Dróna was ruled from the tenth century at least, not by the Uí Dróna but by a branch of the Uí Cheinnselaig who later took the family name of Ua Riain (O'Ryan). In the Uí Cheinnselaig genealogies in the *Book of Leinster* we find the genealogy of one of the chief Uí Cheinnselaig lines headed: *Genelach Ríg Hua nDróna* ('Genealogy of the Kings of Uí Dróna').[8] There was, of course, a distinct genealogical difference between the Uí Cheinnselaig and the Uí Dróna. The Uí Dróna were made to descend from Drón, a brother of Énna Cennselach,[9] while all the septs of the Uí Cheinnselaig descended from Énna himself. The take-over of Uí Dróna lands by the Uí Cheinnselaig may have been a relatively late phenomenon, but Rián, the progenitor of Ua Riain, was of the tenth century, and there is evidence to show that a similar overshadowing of the Uí Dega took place even earlier than this.

The sept of Uí Dega were genealogically independent of the Uí Cheinnselaig. Their lands, according to Hogan, were centred on Limerick Hill (Luimnech) in north Wexford (Plates VIII and XV).[10] Dondgal son of Laidcnén, however, a member of the main Uí Cheinnselaig line   61 who died as early as A.D. 761 in a battle at Gowran,[11] is described in the *Book of Leinster* as *Dondgal a quo Cellach Bairne .i. taisech Hua nDega* ('Dondgal from whom is descended Cellach Bairne, head of the Uí Dega').[12] Since the genealogy ends with Dondgal we cannot precisely determine the position of this Cellach in time, but genealogies which are discontinued seldom refer forward over many unrecorded generations. Indeed, one of the best indications that the Uí Dega and Uí Dróna faded out early in the face of Uí Cheinnselaig expansion is the fact that little or nothing of their genealogies have survived. The Uí Cheinnselaig, on the other hand, present us with one of the most elaborate and detailed genealogies of any sept in Ireland.

The sources at our disposal for determining the precise distribution of the various Uí Cheinnselaig septs throughout southern Leinster are far from adequate. This is due no doubt to the fact that from the fifth to the ninth centuries, while the Uí Cheinnselaig were extending their sway over all the south, the kingship of the Province was monopolized by the Uí Dúnlainge of the north. This ensured that the material which was supplied to the national collections had a northern bias. It was only in the century before the Norman Invasion that the Uí Cheinnselaig finally emerged as masters of the Province, and while they produced extensive genealogies to bolster their claims, the amount of detailed historical information on their territories remained scant.

The centre of Uí Cheinnselaig power was originally based on Rathvilly (Ráth Bilech) in northern Carlow, as is shown by early traditions in the *Vita Tripartita* of St Patrick (c. A.D. 900) and by earlier documents in the *Book of Armagh*.[13] The *Lives* of Saints Moling and Máedóc show that the monastery of St Mullins (Tech Moling) in southern Carlow had earlier claims to Uí Cheinnselaig patronage than the house of Ferns in Wexford, which did eventually, in the eleventh century, become the overall centre of the dynastic power.[14] St Mullins is surrounded by barren, granite-based soil, but is itself situated on an extensive fertile 'island' of

32

33

St Mullins (Tech Moling) in Co. Carlow with Brandon Hill in Kilkenny, beyond. Moling, the founder of this monastery who died in A.D. 695, was remembered in Leinster tradition as the saint who persuaded the Uí Néill highkings of Tara to remit the hated bórumha, or cattle tribute, imposed on the Leinstermen. St Mullins was founded in the forest of Ros mBroc at a ferry on the Barrow which is tidal at this point. In his own lifetime, Moling seems to have acted as the bishop of the Uí Cheinnselaig dynasty, but in the next century Ferns in Co. Wexford replaced St Mullins as the most important church in south Leinster.

The monastic ruins of St Mullins include several churches, the base of a round tower and remains of a tenth-century high cross. The Book of Moling *in Trinity College Dublin, is an illuminated gospel book of the smaller variety, and was produced at St Mullins about A.D. 800. An historical compilation,* The Yellow Book of Moling (Lebhar Buidhe Moling), *is unfortunately now lost and was probably a twelfth-century work. Moling, like St Columba, had a great reputation as a writer and several works have been, rightly or wrongly, ascribed to him.*

limestone drift,[15] in the same way as so many monasteries in the North-Western Region lay in fertile islands surrounded by basin peat. St Mullins also seems to have been strategically placed near a ferry-point on the Barrow which was tidal at this point. Both the ferry and the tidal waters of the river are mentioned in Moling's *Life*.[16]

Since the Uí Cheinnselaig first appeared as an expanding and hostile political force in the heart of Leinster in the Carlow area, it is reasonable to assume that they invaded the Province, not earlier than the fifth century, through the pass of Gowran from Ossory. This would explain how St Mullins on the Barrow, and near the Ossory border, had early connections with the Uí Cheinnselaig. It would explain, too, how the Uí Cheinnselaig broke the power of Uí Bairrche by seizing the Slaney valley from Rathvilly (Ráth Bilech) to Tullow (Tulach mic Fheilmeda), thereby separating the Uí Bairrche of northern Carlow from those of southern Wexford. The Fothairt, allies of Uí Bairrche, shared the same fate and were separated into two groups—one the Fothairt in Cairn in south-east Wexford, and the other Fothairt of Mag Fea in Carlow.

The expansion of Uí Cheinnselaig from Carlow into Wexford took place by one of two possible routes. The first, and least probable, was by Scullogue Gap (Berna an Scala, Plate XVI), a high mountain pass in the Blackstairs south of Mount Leinster (Suidhe Laigen, Plate XVI) which led into the forests of Bantry and Ross. The second, and more probable route, led from Rathvilly in Carlow down the Slaney valley into Wexford between the Blackstairs and the Wicklow mountains. This pass, which ran somewhere between Clonegall and Bunclody, was the gateway from Mag Ailbe in northern Carlow into Wexford. Here was the ancient Fid Dorcha (Dark Forest), later known as the fastness of Leverocke, which guarded the gateway to southern Uí Cheinnselaig (Plate XVI). It was through this pass that the highking Rory O'Conor forced his way with a Connaught army when he twice defeated Dermot MacMurrough, once in 1166 and again in 1167.[17] On this second campaign the highking approached the pass from Kellistown (Cell Osnaid) in Carlow.[18] A seventeenth-century map of the barony of Scarawalsh preserved in the Dublin Public Records Office[19] (Plate B) shows this pass about the village of Bunclody to coincide with a break in the great forest that followed the line of the Blackstairs and Wicklow mountains. This cordon of forest and mountain completely sealed off Wexford from the rest of Leinster. So vast was the woodland here that as late as 1654 (about the time when the map of Scarawalsh was drawn) there was a rudimentary forestry department for Wicklow and Wexford. It was of these woods in Shillelagh that Chichester reported in 1608 as being sufficient to supply the King's navy for twenty years.[20] The extent of woodland as shown on the seventeenth-century survey of Scarawalsh in north-west Wexford is indicated on Plates XV and XVI, and is confirmed by Boazio's map of Ireland, although that Elizabethan work is on a much smaller scale.

It is clear that this whole area of northern Wexford can never have supported a great population in Celtic times and we see from Plate XVI that there were very few monasteries in this area. The monasteries near the coast no doubt communicated with the rest of the country mainly by river and sea. This is suggested by brief references in Adamnan's *Life of Columba* (*c*.A.D. 700). Fintán travelled to Iona and returned to found Taghmon (Tech Mundu) in Wexford, 'in the coastal region of the Leinstermen', and elsewhere in his *Vita* Adomnán informs us of travellers from Leinster arriving at Iona.[21]

The Uí Felmeda Tuaid branch of Uí Cheinnselaig (Plate XV) remained about the old centres of Rathvilly and Tullow in Carlow, while another section (Uí Felmeda Thes) settled in the barony of Ballaghkeen (Plates VII, VIII and XV). The northern branch of Uí Felmeda were ruled in the twelfth century by Ua Gairbhíth (O'Garvey) and the southern branch by Ua Murchadha (O'Murroughe, later Murphy). These Leinster Murphys ought not to be confused with 63

34

35a / b

The church of Ferns (Ferna Mór) in north Wexford was founded by St Máedóc, a monk who had been trained by St David in Wales, and who died in A.D. 625. By the middle of the eighth century the Uí Cheinnselaig dynasty had expanded from Carlow into Wexford where they took over Ferns as their chief centre and turned its church into a royal monastery. From then on Ferns replaced St Mullins as the principal monastery of South Leinster and an important civitas or township grew up there. Its monastic life had become so degenerate that in 817 the monastic communities of Taghmon and Ferns fought a pitched battle in which 400 were slain. Ferns grew even more powerful in the later Celtic period as its kings graduated to the throne of all Leinster. It withstood attacks from heathen Vikings and the O'Briens of Munster, but its most turbulent period came with the reign of Dermot MacMurrough (Diarmait mac Murchada) who introduced the Anglo-Normans into Ireland. MacMurrough held his court here, and it was in Ferns that he died, as the last king of all Leinster, in 1171. The event was recorded by the hostile chronicler in the Annals of Ulster thus:

> Dermot, King of the Province of Leinster, after destroying many churches and territories, died in Ferns without Extreme Unction, without Communion, without Penance, and without a Will, in reparation to Columcille and Finian and all those saints besides, whose churches he destroyed.

Gilt-bronze figure of a seated harper on the side of the Shrine of St Máedóc of Ferns (Breac Maodhóg). The harp is of a small variety, played with two

hands and rested on the knees. The nearby bird is symbolic of the spirit of inspiration. This panel may be older than the other figures which appear on the side of the shrine and which date from the eleventh century. Two of these male figures illustrated here (35b) have long hair, moustaches and parted beards, and they are clothed in the brat or cloak, and léine or tunic of the early Irish aristocracy and clergy.

The reliquary was kept in the church at Drumlane in Co. Cavan up until the middle of the nineteenth century and was preserved in a leather satchel illustrated in Fig. 45 below.

64

the MacMurroughs of Wexford. The MacMurroughs (Mac Murchadha) descend from Dermot MacMurrough (Diarmait mac Murchada) who first invited Henry II to send Strongbow and his followers to Ireland. Diarmait, who ruled as king of Leinster at the time of the Anglo-Norman Invasion in 1169, was descended from Éogan Cáech son of Nath Í, the founder of Síl Mella and grandson of that Crimthann son of Énna Cennselach who was converted at Rathvilly in the fifth century. But Diarmait's line of descent was not of the main Uí Cheinnselaig House, and his dynasty only came to prominence in the time of his great-grandfather in the middle of the eleventh century. At that time, Diarmait's immediate ancestors usurped the richest land in the Slaney basin, comprising the royal demesne around Ferns, which had previously been held by the Síl Cormaic (Plate XV). The Síl Máeluidir (Plate XV) have left their names on the baronies of Shelmalier in Wexford (Plate VII); and the eastern part of this territory, north of Wexford, was ruled in the twelfth century by Ua hArtghaile (Hartley) of Ferann na Cenél (Plate IX). Hogan connected the Síl Mella with the Idrone area of Carlow near Cell Bicsige, but else-where he located Cell Bicsige in the territory of the Uí Garrchon about Arklow—an identi-fication supported by Price.[22] The Síl Mella occupied north-east Wexford, and it was here that their descendants, Ua Finntighearn (Finneran), ruled on the eve of the Anglo-Norman Invasion (Plates IX and XVI). Their neighbours here, Ua hAodha (O'Hay or Hughes), ruled the old terri-tory of Uí Dega. As for the other branches of Uí Cheinnselaig, such as Uí Fergusa, Clann Fiachu meic Ailella or the Clann Guaire—all of whom yield genealogies in the *Book of Leinster* —we know little of their whereabouts.

The Uí Cheinnselaig set out in the late fifth century to control the Slaney valley and to dominate the regions now covered by Carlow and Wexford (Plate V). Uí Cheinnselaig pene-tration of the lower Slaney may have been relatively slow. In the second half of the sixth cen-tury an Uí Bairrche king, Cormac mac Diarmata, is shown in hagiography as a restless ruler still striving to hold on to the southern Wexford region. The monastery of Taghmon once lay in the lands of Cormac's tributary people, the Fothairt of Carn, and the *Life* of Fintán of Taghmon relates that Cormac of the Uí Bairrche was imprisoned by Colmán son of Cormac Camsrón of Uí Cheinnselaig.[23] The monastery of Camaross (Camros) lay to the north of Uí Bairrche terri-tory in the region later known as Síl Máeluidir (called after an Uí Cheinnselaig sept). In the *Life* of Abbán of Camaross this same Cormac of the Uí Bairrche is shown attacking Abbán's monastery,[24] and the implication is that it once lay within Uí Bairrche territory on the richer soil of central Wexford (Plate III). All this is a reflection of the struggle for power in the Wex-ford region between the Uí Bairrche and Uí Cheinnselaig in the late sixth century. It may not have been until the eighth century was well advanced that Uí Cheinnselaig domination of the lower Slaney was complete, and that Ferns had been established as a new Uí Cheinnselaig head-quarters. We read of a battle at Ferns between two rival Uí Cheinnselaig rulers in A.D. 769. In that year Dubcalgach, the reigning Uí Cheinnselaig king (and sixth in descent from that Colmán who imprisoned the king of Uí Bairrche), was slain by his rival and successor, Cennselach of the southerly Síl Máeluidir.[25] Dubcalgach's dynasty had established itself in the north and west of Wexford, at least by 722, since his cousin, Colcu, is styled 'king of Árd Ladrann (Ardamine)' in that year (Plate V).[26]

While the origins of the Uí Cheinnselaig in the central Barrow valley and their expansion into Wexford is reasonably clear, the same cannot be said for their opposite numbers, the Uí Dúnlainge, who ruled in later centuries as kings of North Leinster. We must pay close atten-tion to the tribal genealogy of the Leinstermen when studying this problem of Uí Dúnlainge origins, since they emerge as a new people, genealogically, at the opening of the historical period. They differ from the Uí Failge or Uí Bairrche, for instance, in that not only were they free, and descended from Cathair Mór, but both the Uí Dúnlainge and the Uí Cheinnselaig 65 descended from Cathair's grandson, Bressal Bélach, a Leinster king who was alleged to have died in c.A.D. 436. If the relationship between Uí Dúnlainge and Uí Cheinnselaig was in reality so close, and so relatively recent, then there is every reason to believe that the Uí Dúnlainge also began life in the north Carlow area at Gabair alongside the Uí Cheinnselaig, and that while one group pushed south along the Slaney, the other moved northwards across southern Kildare and eventually to their principal stronghold at Naas (Nás) (Plate V). The two dynasties may, or may not, have been closely related. The genealogical relationship may reflect nothing more than that the Uí Cheinnselaig and Uí Dúnlainge invaded Leinster from Ossory in the fifth century and eventually took over the entire Province from older groups such as Uí Bairrche, Uí Failge, Dál Messin Corb, Dál Chormaic and Uí Máil. The important tract known as the *Testament of Cathair Mór* confirms that the Uí Failge and Uí Bairrche, in particular, were eventually ousted from power in Leinster by the Uí Cheinnselaig and Uí Dúnlainge.[27]

It is very difficult to follow the precise lines of Uí Dúnlainge expansion within Leinster, or the particular direction from which it originated. We know that it was not until the death of the Uí Máil king, Cellach Cualann, in A.D. 715 that the Uí Dúnlainge finally succeeded in monopolizing the kingship of North Leinster and became kings of the entire Province.[28] The first historical Uí Dúnlainge king of Leinster was Fáelán mac Cholmáin who ruled c.635. There are many uncertainties regarding the chronology of his reign, and on his death the Leinster kingship oscillated between the Uí Cheinnselaig and the Uí Máil until it was finally secured for Fáelán's descendants on the death of the last Uí Máil king in 715. Already, however, in Fáelán's reign over Leinster, the Uí Dúnlainge were tightening their grip on the northern half of the province. Fáelán's brother Áed Dub, who died in 639, had become bishop of Kildare[29] —one of the wealthiest monasteries in Ireland, but situated within Uí Failge and under the immediate control of the Fothairt, to whose tribe, Brigit, the foundress had belonged (Plates XI and XII). Fáelán's nephew, Óengus, and a certain Brandub, a distant cousin of the same generation as Óengus, were also abbots of Kildare.[30] Clearly, by the second quarter of the seventh century, the Uí Fáeláin were displacing both Uí Failge and the Fothairt at Kildare, and the rich estates round about it. The violent nature of this Uí Dúnlainge expansion is hinted at in a genealogical note attached to the name of Máelumai, a brother of Fáelán, who ruled c.A.D. 635. This note states[31] that Máelumai slew Deichtre mac Findig of Uí Meic Cruaich of the Uí Ercáin in his fortress or *dún* at Cell Rois and seized his wealth. The details of Deichtre's tribal origin hold the key to the meaning of this obscure record. The Uí Ercáin were a branch of the Fothairt of Uí Failge and this branch was settled around Bile maicc Cruaich in Uí Ercáin, the old name of Forrach Pátraic, a low hill at Narraghmore in the Liffey Plain (Plate XII). Bile maicc Cruaich was an ancient inauguration site, as the name *bile* or sacred tribal tree implies, and the fact that the Uí Dúnlainge prince who seized this from the Fothairt was a brother of Fáelán, the first Uí Dúnlainge king of Leinster, is surely significant. Further evidence of the violent suppression of older population-groups within the rich Central Region of Leinster by the Uí Dúnlainge is provided in the case of Cellach mac Cennfáelad. This Uí Dúnlainge prince (*fl. c.*A.D. 720) was three generations later than Fáelán, and descended from Fáelán's brother, Rónán. The genealogists noted that he was defeated on an unidentified battleground at Áth Slabai. But the alliance of his enemies was a Munster and Uí Cheinnselaig coalition, which would suggest that he met an invading army somewhere in north Carlow. The genealogists also tell us that he destroyed the Uí Gabla Roirend and that he was cursed by a holy man called Mo-Chuille Dresna.[32] The Uí Gabla Roirend were a branch of the Dál Chormaic who took their name from Roíriu, now Mullaghreelion (Plate XII), five miles south-east of Athy in south Kildare. Dresan, the home of Mo-Chuille, who was offended by Cellach's suppression of older tribes, seems to have been in Mag Fea, not far to the south of Roíriu, and a plain in the Slaney valley near Tullow in

66

Carlow (Plate XVI). After the suppression of the Dál Chormaic the region was considered part of Uí Muiredaig (a branch of Uí Dúnlainge) by later Irish writers.

The central stronghold of Uí Dúnlainge from the seventh century until the Norman Invasion was at Naas, and the nearby mausoleum of the dynasty was at Cell Náis (Kill, Co. Kildare). In spite of genealogical statements alleging that two aunts of Fáelán–Sodelb and Cumaine, the daughters of Coirpre Mór of Uí Dúnlainge–died as holy virgins in Cell Náis,[33] I believe that these associations of Uí Dúnlainge saints with northern Kildare may be later inventions design-ed to give Uí Dúnlainge ancestors a respectable place in the annals of early Leinster Christian-ity. There are other traditions claiming that two other holy women of the Uí Dúnlainge–Eithne and Dar-carthaind, the daughters of Cormac the great-grandfather of Fáelán–had lived as nuns at Tullow, Co. Carlow (Tulach Meic Fheilmeda).[34] If these ladies ever existed, we might date their *floruit* to c.A.D. 560 and at that time we should expect to find the Uí Dún-lainge in the Carlow region if as the genealogists claimed, they originally derived along with the Uí Cheinnselaig from a common ancestor, Bressal Bélach. It is significant that early genea-logical traditions associated Uí Dúnlainge ladies of the sixth century with Tullow–a place which was otherwise regarded as a palace of the Uí Cheinnselaig and of the Uí Felmeda Tuaid in particular. It may be, therefore, that we should view the north Carlow or Gabair region as a dispersal area from which expanding political groups emerged (Plate V). It was in this region, yet again, that the Osraige invaded Leinster in the eleventh and twelfth centuries in an effort to take over the entire Province, and we recall, too, that Leinster proto-history began at Dinn Ríg, on the banks of the Barrow near Leighlin, when in the distant past Labraid Loingsech stormed that fortress with his warriors from Gaul and Britain.

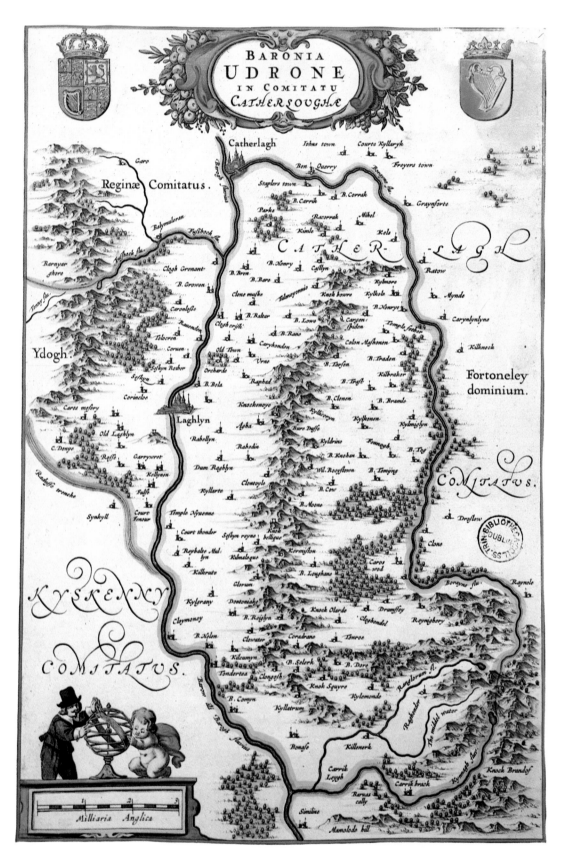

PLATE A Map of the Barony of Idrone, Co. Carlow, c. 1662 (Trinity College Dublin, Atlas of Printed Maps No. 10 C). This map covering central and north-western Carlow (cf. Plate VII) is based on an earlier survey by R. Lythe carried out in the period 1568-1571. It is disappointing for its lack of detail, but it does provide evidence for the survival of tracts of forest in this region up to the end of the sixteenth century.

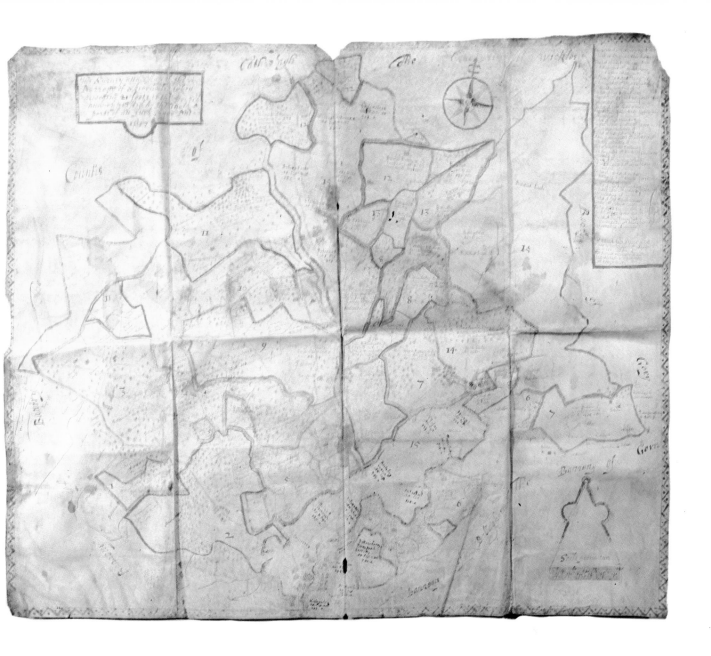

PLATE B Map of the Barony of Scarawalsh, Co. Wexford, *A.D. 1657 (Dublin Public Records Office, Clayton MS No. 27: 28 x 23 ins. parchment). The purpose of the map seems to have been to provide information on Catholic estates in this barony in north Wexford (cf. Plate VII), since the amount of forest, pasture, and arable land is specified for Catholic holdings. The manuscript provides graphic representation for the survival of extensive tracts of woodland on the slopes of the Blackstairs and on the southern extremity of the Wicklow hills. Some information is provided on neighbouring regions such as references to extensive tracts of waste on the Carlow mountains and in the adjoining Wexford*

barony of Bantry. This map shows that the valley of the Slaney was free of forest and formed a natural pass from Bunclody, on the Carlow border in the north, to Enniscorthy in the south. At Bunclody, a break in the forest coincided with the break in the mountain chain which separates the Wicklow hills from the Blackstairs. This was the location of Fid Dorcha *('Dark Forest'), later known as the fastness of* Leverocke, *where a pass led from Carlow into Southern Uí Cheinnselaig (Plate XVI). The* Round O Rath, *north of Bunclody, must have controlled movement along this strategic pass in the Iron Age if not in the Dark Ages.*

CHAPTER VII

Tribes and Dynasties of the North-Western Region

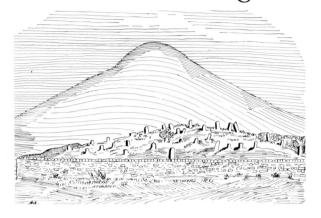

36

Croghan Hill (Cruachán Brí Éle), Co. Offaly, rises above the Bog of Allen as a permanent land-mark of ancient Uí Failge. This hill and its surrounding bog guarded the Leinstermen in the north-west from their enemies, the Uí Néill highkings of Mide. The churchyard, seen here in O'Hanlon's sketch of August 1883 marks the site of the monastery of Mac Caille, an early sixth-century saint associated with Brigit of Kildare.

The rulers of Uí Failge lived in forts and lake-dwellings or crannógs *all over this boggy region, but the chief royal stronghold of Uí Failge in the sixth and seventh centuries was that of Rathangan in Kildare. The following early poem on Rathangan lists its royal occupants from that time:*

> The fort over against the oakwood,
> It was Bruidge's, it was Cathal's,
> It was Áed's, it was Ailill's,
> It was Conaing's, it was Cúilíne's,
> And it was Máeldúin's.
> The fort remains after each king in turn,
> And the hosts sleep in the ground.
>
> *(MS. Rawlinson B 502 fol. 122. b.c. 49; translation by Kuno Meyer)*

The North-Western Region (Plates I and III) was covered largely by peat bogs and forest and was undoubtedly the most remote corner of Leinster. So difficult and inaccessible was the terrain here that the Old Gaelic order held out intact until the middle of the sixteenth century. In spite of being within easy reach of Dublin Castle, even Elizabethan commanders feared risking their men in the great woods of Offaly. The primeval woodland was cleared here in the seventeenth century and the ravages of modern fuel technology have excavated the peat bogs leaving only a raped and impoverished landscape that bears absolutely no relationship to its medieval past. If we want to gain some impression of the medieval environment we must consult the Tudor map (Frontispiece) of this region which presents us with a veritable aerial view of forest, bog and fertile clearings hemmed in between the Barrow and the Slieve Bloom. We shall refer to this map in detail below, but here we may note that the upper reaches of the Barrow, the foot-hills of Slieve Bloom and the western parts of O'Connor's country in Offaly were all still unknown and inaccessible to the Tudor surveyor. We note, too, that while to-day we speak of medieval boundaries in terms of diocesan and baronial limits and as lines on a map, the medieval reality was altogether different. The Slieve Bloom separated Ely O'Carol in Munster from Leix and Offaly; the Slievemargy hills separated Ormond in Ossory from Leix, and a barrier of forest and bog separated Offaly from Westmeath (*Ferical, Kinoliegh* and *Fartoulogh*). The principal tribes occupying this region in medieval times were the Uí Failge and the Loígis. The Uí Failge traced their descent from Cathair Mór, and so along with the Uí Bairrche and Uí Enechglaiss (Chart 2) together with the two major dynasties of Uí Dúnlainge and Uí Cheinnselaig, they constituted the Free Tribes of the Leinstermen. The Loígis, on the other hand, were regarded by the genealogists as aliens to the Province and, therefore, subject to tribute.

The boundaries of Uí Failge on the north and west were also the boundaries of the Province with the Uí Néill kingdom of Mide. The extent of ancient Mide and Brega is well represented by the medieval diocese of Meath (Plate VI), and the Uí Failge border is defined by the boundary between the diocese of Kildare and Meath in the western area. The lands of the Loígis coincided with the north-western extension of Leighlin diocese on Plate VI and the division between the Loígis and Uí Failge survives in the diocesan division between Leighlin and Kildare. Thus, Tinnahinch and Portnahinch, the two northern baronies of Co. Leix (Plate VII), belonged to Uí Failge in ancient times, and this continued to be so into the sixteenth-century as is seen on the Tudor map of Leix discussed below.[1] On the west the Loígis were bordered by the Uí Duach of Ossory (Plate VIII), a kingdom whose extent is well represented by the diocese of Ossory (Plate VI), and which was almost coextensive with the basin of the river Nore (Plate II).

The extent of Uí Failge lands as defined on Plate VIII seems at first to be greater than that of any other kingdom in Leinster. In the centuries before A.D. 700 the territories and political status of Uí Failge was even greater than this map might suggest. The extent, however, as shown on Plate VIII is deceptive, for we see from the soil map on Plate III that the area was one of immense boggy waste and wood (Plate XIV), with restricted pockets of fertile ground. In the east, however, Uí Failge lands came out onto the Kildare Plains beyond the monastery of Kildare itself (Plates XI and XII) and this fertile area, which also included the royal fortress at Rathangan,[2] really formed part of the Northern Region (Plate I). The memory of these Uí Failge lands in Co. Kildare is preserved in the names of the baronies of Offaly East and Offaly West (Plate VII) in western Co. Kildare. The excellence of the open plains about Kildare monastery in Uí Failge drew a comment from Giraldus Cambrensis who saw in their lush pastures an opportunity to enrich his *Topographia Hiberniae* with a quotation from Virgil:

'And all the day-long browsing of thy herds
Shall the cool dews of one brief night repair.'[3]

This eastern section of Uí Failge lands obviously formed the most important part of their kingdom before they were pushed behind the tributaries of the Barrow by the Normans, and the genealogical tracts also point to the importance of Uí Failge lands in Kildare.[4]

It has been assumed since the days of O'Donovan and O'Curry,[5] who inaugurated Irish 69

PLATE C The Festival of St Kevin at the Seven
Churches, Glendalough *by Joseph Peacock, 1813
(Collection Ulster Museum, Belfast). The medieval
Lives of Kevin (Coemgen) of Glendalough tell of the
saint praying waist-deep in the waters of the Upper
Lake and sleeping 'on bare ground, fasting on herbs
and water.' They tell, too, of Kevin bargaining with*

an angel for the salvation of all who lie buried in his cemetery and for the promise that he could lead seven times the full of the valley into Heaven on Judgement Day. Glendalough became one of the four great centres of pilgrimage in medieval Ireland and 'all fighting, quarrelling and rapine' were outlawed there during the days of the óenach which centred on the Festival of Kevin (3 June). Peacock's picture (painted in 1813) testified to the survival of Kevin's Pattern or Fair from the Dark Ages into the modern era in spite of those centuries of 'dungeon, fire and sword' when the majestic ruins of Kevin's monastic city were strewn in so many piles of antiquarian rubble across the valley floor.

topographical studies early in the last century, that the extent of the Anglo-Norman baronies (Plate VII) was based on that of the older Celtic tribal areas or *tuatha*. Entire tribes have been arbitrarily assigned to certain baronial areas for want of more reliable information. Walsh, in his study of the placenames of Westmeath,[6] challenged O'Donovan's methods, but in his study of the Leinster region elsewhere[7] he followed the earlier topographers without great qualification, as did Fr. Ryan.[8] Uí Failge was one of the last Gaelic lordships to fall to the English Crown. Brian Ua Conchobhuir, its last king under Irish law, submitted in 1549.[9] A survey of his forfeited estates, made in the following year, and a map dating to *c.*1563 of the Country of O'Connor and of O'More's lands of Leix (Frontispiece) have both survived. These two valuable sources—the Survey of Cowley, and the slightly later map—allow us to compare the extent of the lesser Irish lordships (or tribes) within Uí Failge at the time of its capitulation with the later baronial divisions established by the English administration. In studying the North-Western Region, then, we have a unique opportunity to examine the ancient *tuatha* that lay within this late medieval Gaelic territory.

Admittedly, the survey is very late, but it comes, firstly, from an area which enjoyed unbroken Gaelic rule under its native kings, who were direct descendants of the Uí Failge aristocracy of the ninth century. Secondly, the survey and cartography were undertaken by the Tudors whose methods were more thorough and more advanced than those of earlier administrations. Thirdly, the internal divisions, by their very names, show themselves to be of the old tribal order of things.

Each of the larger Irish kingdoms such as this, incorporated many smaller *tuatha* which were ruled in turn by their own tribal kings, who owed obligations to the king of the whole confederacy and who might, as in the case of Uí Failge, be related to the kin of their overlord. The names of the internal divisions on the Tudor map incorporate the *Towghe* or *Towte* element direct into English from the Irish *tuath*, the old tribal unit. Finally, the internal divisions and other features of the survey were drawn up on the sworn evidence of tenants before the inquisition, who were, as Curtis pointed out, exclusively Irish.[10] Any detailed discussion, therefore, of the Gaelic territories of this part of Leinster must involve a scrutiny of the unique Tudor map.

We will confine ourselves to studying those aspects of the survey and map which have a bearing on early Leinster. The conclusions may be summarized as follows. No generalizations can be made in regard to the relationship between the older *tuatha* and the later English baronial divisions. Each case must be examined on its merits. The area of the ancient Loígis, marked as *Leis* on the Tudor map, (Frontispiece) (i.e. excluding Yregan and Clanmalier which belonged to Uí Failge), has to-day six baronial divisions, while on the map it can be seen to have at least thirteen Celtic lordships. Whether we take the divisions of the map separately, or attempt groupings, we find little correspondence with the later baronies. In the case of Uí Failge, also, the number of lordships (eight) exceeds that of the subsequent baronies (five), but by and large the English system here seems to have adapted the older Irish divisions in forming baronies. Even in the case of Uí Failge, however, with the exception of Tuath Géisille and Nethertoumuy of the map, at least two and sometimes more lordships have gone to make up a barony. Whether or not this situation was peculiar to the Midlands is difficult to say, but the evidence points, perhaps, to a grouping of three or four adjacent parishes, rather than the barony, as approximating to the old tribal *tuatha* areas. We may note, too, that baronies bearing the same name today may indicate quite distinct earlier regions. Thus, Lower Phillipstown (Plate VII) is based on Tuath Rátha Droma of O'Connor's lands (Frontispiece), while Upper Phillipstown (Plate VII) coincides with Ferann Clainne Diarmata of O'Dempsey's Country (Frontispiece).

70

The lordships for O'Connors Country in the survey and on the Tudor map are as follows:

	TUDOR MAP	COWLEY'S SURVEY	RESTORED IRISH FORMS
1.	Tovogeishel	Towgheyshell	Tuath Géisille
2.	Tovoradrvmmom	Towradroume	Tuath Rátha Droma
3.	Tovanachilie	Tounekyll	Tuath na Cille
4.	Tovocroghan	Towecroghane	Tuath Cruacháin
5.	Vppertovmvy)	Towtemoyeglyncholgen	Tuath muighe
6.	Nethertovmvy)		Cloinne Cholgain
7.	Mviligh	Moylaghe	Magh Léghe
8.	Feranomveghan	Offerynmorchane	Ferann Uí Muircáin
		Towtemoymansterorys	Tuath muighe Mainister Fheorais

Before discussing these earlier divisions further we must examine their natural background of forest and bog for which the Leix-Offaly area was renowned and which are shown on the sixteenth-century map (Frontispiece). This map was drawn up, on its side, so to speak, with the north point on the reader's right and with the top of the map facing west. On the bottom, as the surveyor's base-line, is shown the course of the river Barrow, from Carlow town (Carlogh) in the south (bottom left) to where it turns due west up-stream at Monasterevin (Munestereum) to its source in the Slieve Bloom mountains. A glance at the enormous extent of the woods shown on this map recalls the statement of Giraldus Cambrensis that in comparison with the woodlands the extent of the Irish plains, however fair, was indeed small.[11]

At the time of compilation of this map, the area must have been reduced to a pathetic plight by the recent wars of conquest, as is confirmed by the many references to sites in a ruinous condition in Cowley's survey for Uí Failge. The situation in the main, however, must derive from a period of greater economic stability, and yet it is interesting to see that some of the modern market towns of this region do not appear on the map. The most prominent places— and the centres of communication—are the old monastic sites that date back to the early centuries of Christianity, such as Clonenagh (Cluain Ednech) or Killeigh (Cell Achid). This is of great interest when we consider that the region had developed under an exclusively Gaelic organization. The old monastic sites had obviously become town centres of trade and commerce by the sixteenth-century. This trend was already asserting itself in the case of Armagh and Ferns, for instance, before the Norman Invasion, and the *Vitae Sanctorum* of the eleventh and twelfth centuries speak of Leinster monasteries like St Mullins, Glendalough and Ferns, as prosperous 'cities'.[12] Giraldus speaks of 'townspeople' (*civium*) in Kildare during the earliest days of Strongbow's Invasion, if not before, and the *Three Fragments of Annals* refer to a fuller's workshop in the 'Street of the Stone Step' (*Sraid in céime cloichi*) in the eastern part of that town as early as A.D. 909.[13]

To extract as much information as possible from the Tudor map, I have projected some of its features on to Ordnance Survey sheets of this region (Plate XIV). This presents us with part of the sixteenth-century picture drawn to scale, and I have used as many identifiable placenames as was necessary to achieve accuracy in the projection. The Tudor information relating to roadways and forest has also been transferred to Plate XIV, and superimposed there on the Ordnance Survey mapping of bog and mountain, in conjunction with the monasteries and forts of the pre-Norman period.

We see how the monastery of Kildare (Plate XII) and its surrounding plain was joined to the ancient Mag Rechet in Leix by two trackways, one from Monasterevin (Ros Glas) to Coolban-agher (Cúl Bendchuir) (Plates XII and XIV), the other crossing the Barrow further south and penetrating The Great Wood as shown on the original Tudor map (Frontispiece). On entering The Great Heath of Maryborough (Mag Rechet), easy access was gained to the heartlands of the Loígis and to their centres at Coolbanagher (Cúl Bendchuir), Dysart (Dísert Óengusa) and the Rock of Dunamase (Dún Masc) (Plate XIV). This route continued from Mag Rechet through bog and wood to Clonenagh (Cluain Ednech), the most important monastery of ancient Leix, and from there via Mountrath (Móin Rátha) to Clonfertmulloe (Cluain Ferta Molua), a great centre of scholarship in the seventh century. The road obviously continued a few miles further south through the narrow pass between the Slieve Bloom and Silvermines mountains to Roscrea (Plate XIV). On the half-inch Ordnance sheet the significant placename *Ballaghmore* (*Belach Mór*, 'The great way or pass') occurs in this very area, which was the gateway from North Leinster into Munster, and which led on to the isolated Leinster monas-teries of Inis Celtra, Lorrha (Lothra), and Terryglass (Tír dá Glas) in the Shannon basin. The placename *Ballaghmore* represents the Belach Mór Maige Dála of ancient sources,[14] and leads us to the conclusion that we have been following the line of the Slige Dála Meic Umhoir, a pre-historic trackway and one of the legendary Five Roads of ancient Ireland which were supposed to converge on Tara.

There is no question that the crude *toghers*—causeways or roads— of the Tudor map, which give this very logical itinerary, preserve the line of the Slighe Dála Meic Umhoir of early Irish sources. Ó Lochlainn discovered[15] this great road ran from Dublin to Kildare — Monasterevin (Ros Glas) — Togher — Rathleague — Ballyroan — Abbeyleix — Shanahoe — Aghaboe — Borris–Ballaghmore to Roscrea. We have seen that the map allows us two routes from Kildare to Mag Rechet. On the route via Monasterevin the track is shown on the Tudor map to join Bally-brittas to Shean (Frontispiece and Plate XIV). If we join these two places on the Ordnance Survey half-inch sheet, we find the line passes within a quarter of a mile to the north of Togher Townland, (*tochar*, 'a road or causeway'). This is not only evidence in support of the accuracy of the Tudor surveyor, but it also suggests he was drawing the course of the ancient Slige Dála (Road of the Assemblies).

Ó Lochlainn by no means claimed finality for his survey[16] and we may have to correct his assumption that the Slige Dála ran via Abbeyleix, Aghaboe and Borris. This involved a detour too far south for the traveller coming from Kildare. His route lay, clearly, through Clonenagh and Clonfertmulloe to Roscrea, as indicated by the map and as suggested by ancient topo-graphy. We ought to avoid, however, seeking a too rigid definition of the course of Irish road-ways, since it seems that these achieved importance only when they were confined to passes across otherwise impassable wood or marsh. The open plains must have provided innumerable possibilities to the well-mounted horseman, and this would have held true for considerably later times since it was not until the eighteenth century that the Irish landscape was enclosed with the characteristic banks and hedgerows of to-day. Our map shows us that there was not one, but a choice of routes from place to place. For instance, Ó Lochlainn's itinerary via Aghaboe is quite feasible though not practicable for the northern traveller for, as the map shows, a pass joined Mag Rechet at Timahoe (Tech Mo-Chua, Plate XIV) in Loígis territory, with Mag Lacha in Ossory. West of Timahoe, also, is the Pass of the Plumes (Bernán na gCleti), so called from the plumes on the helmets of English soldiers who were cut down in this pass by the army of Owen O'More, chieftain of Loígis, in 1599.

If a hard-pressed and impoverished Gaelic society of the sixteenth century possessed a com-munication system of the sort illustrated by the Tudor surveyor, surely we can argue as much for the flourishing communities of the ninth century? The location of so many important

37

Clonfertmulloe or Kyle (Cluain Ferta Molua), Co. Leix, was founded by St Lugaid or Molua who came from a tribe in Co. Limerick, and who died in A.D. 609. This monastery became a most important centre of learning in the seventh century and was the home of Laidcend mac Baíth-Bannaig, whose works on biblical commentaries survive in manuscripts preserved all over Europe. Laidcend died on 12 January 661, and was buried here in Clonfertmulloe. The monastery, like other important Leix houses, was built on the line of the Road of the Assemblies (Slige Dála) near where it joined the Midland Corridor at Roscrea. We learn from the Lives of Mo-Chuda *of Rahan and* Colmán *of Lynally that it was a day's journey on foot from Clonfertmulloe to Lynally and from Rahan to Roscrea.*

38

Coolbanagher (Cúl bendchuir) in Co. Leix was immortalized in early Irish tradition by its association with Óengus the Céli Dé. As Óengus travelled along the Road of the Assemblies from Clonenagh on his way to Tallaght in Co. Dublin, he visited Cool-

38

banagher. It was in the churchyard here that he had his vision of angels hovering over a freshly made grave of a man who had venerated the saints. As a result of this vision, Óengus resolved to compile his Félire *or Calendar of Saints, which he duly completed in Tallaght, and which still survives as a major source for ancient Irish ecclesiastical history.*

monasteries on or near the line of the Slige Dála helps to explain the close ecclesiastical alliances that existed, for instance, in the seventh and ninth centuries between Lorrha, Inis Celtra, Clonfertmulloe, Roscrea and Clonenagh. These monasteries were much closer in reality than a superficial glance at their geographical situation would indicate. In the north we see that another pass ran north from Mag Rechet in Loígis, across bog and wood to Geashill (Géisill) in

Uí Failge (Plate XIV), and from Geashill to Daingean and Croghan (Cruachán) in the extreme north of Offaly. The extent of Tuath Géisille (Tovogeishel) of the Tudor map corresponds remarkably well with the later barony of Geashill (Plates XIV and Frontispiece), although the Tudor map shows this lordship to have taken in the fort of Daingean. The Daingean area itself together with Tuath Cruacháin and Tuath Rátha Droma of the map represent very well the extent of the later barony of Lower Phillipstown. The area defined as Tuath Cruacháin on the map is larger than that described in Cowley's survey,[17] but the overall general accuracy of these sources cannot be questioned. For instance, the baronial division between Lower Phillips-town and Warrenstown is based on the division between Tuath Cruacháin and Tuath Muighe Cloinne Cholgain (Nether Tovmvy of the map, Plates VII and Frontispiece). Within the present barony of Lower Phillipstown, and shown as a subdivision of Tuath Rátha Droma on the Tudor map is Tuath na Cille which, as its name implies, was Church land. It is impossible to say how old this allotment of Church land was, but the name Tuath na Cille could indicate some antiquity. The area may refer to Church lands of the nearby site of *Kilcloenfart* on the Tudor map. This was Cluain Ferta Mughaine (Plate XIV) of Irish annals and other early sources, and is Kilclonfert to-day.[18] Curtis regarded these two areas of Church land in O'Connor's Country as not representing ancient tribal divisions.[19] While the case of Tuath na Cille may be in doubt, Curtis was correct in regarding Tuath muighe mainistrech Fheorais as late in so far as Church property was concerned. This land refers to the abbey of Monasteroris, which was a post-Norman Bermingham foundation. It may or may not be significant that, while Tuath na Cille is listed in both the map and the survey, *Towetemoymansterorys* appears in the survey only. We may regard the Church lands of Feranoprior in the Timahoe area of Leix (on the Tudor map) as being of no great antiquity.

We have seen that *Towetemoymansterorys* is omitted on the Tudor map, and a nearby area of *Towtemoyeglyncholgen,* also detailed by the survey, is likewise omitted on the map. The areas are replaced on the map by the lordships of Vppertovmvy and Nethertovmvy. Hogan identified these two later areas with the ancient Tuath dá Maige ('Tuath of the Two Plains').[20] The identification is beyond question. The areas on the Tudor map cover the later baronies of Warrenstown and Coolestown (Plate VII), and these combined baronies do in fact cover two plains which on the Tudor map are joined by a pass-way linking Rathangan, an ancient royal fortress in Uí Failge, with the Drumcooly (Cowley) area on the plain in northern Offaly. If this is Tuath dá Maige, then without doubt the pass-way must be none other than the Tochar etar dá Mag ('Causeway between two Plains') in Uí Failge mentioned in early sources.[21] Drium dá Maige must have been either at Drumcooly or more likely at Ballykilleen Hill on the side of the causeway, in north-eastern Co. Offaly.

The division between the baronies of Warrenstown and Coolestown is based on the older Celtic division between Upper and Nether Tovmvy (Plates VII and Frontispiece). This division does not, however, quite coincide with the natural division between the two plains which are the basis of the duality in the first place. The southern 'plain' has been enlarged to take in some of the northern. The explanation for this may lie in the fact that originally Uí Failge lands were more extensive to the east in Kildare. The territory of the more southerly of the two plains once extended east past Rathangan to include Kildare monastery. The tribe of Uí Failge occupying this area was, according to the Rawlinson MS B. 502, the *Cland Colcan i Liphi*, 'Clann Colgan in the Liffey Plain'.[22] The name of this sept is preserved in Tuath muighe Cloinne Cholgain—the title given in Cowley's survey to this Tuath dá maige (Upper and Nether Tovmvy) of the Tudor map. On being pushed back behind the tributaries of the Barrow by the Anglo-Normans, much of the southern plain of Tuath dá maige in Kildare was lost to Uí Failge, but the ancient idea of the 'Tuath of the two Plains' survived in the modified way in which we

74

see it when Cowley surveyed the area in 1550.

Hogan placed the Tochar etar dá Mag near Geashill on the grounds that it was near Brí Dam, and the fact that Ballintogher is the name of a townland near Geashill.[23] Townland names such as this are of little use in the absence of more certain evidence, and if the Ordnance Survey six-inch sheets of the Irish Midlands are examined countless *togher* elements in place-names will be found. The site of Brí Dam is itself uncertain,[24] and depends on the location of both Tochar etar dá Mag and Druim dá Maige. While Hogan errs in stressing the proximity of this *Tochar* or causeway to the actual site of Geashill, the sources he quotes do demand an explanation when they refer to Tuath Géisille. If we examine the location of Géisill on Plates XIII and XIV in relation to the Tuath Géisille as defined *c.*1560 (Frontispiece) we see that Geashill itself is on the eastern border of its own tribal region. It may be that the area of Tuath Géisille was once larger than its sixteenth-century extent. The plain surrounding Geashill must be the ancient Mag Géisille[25] and this plain extends eastwards of the site, although it lies out-side the present barony of Geashill. If this is correct then the location of the Tochar etar dá Mag south of Monasteroris fulfills all the requirements. In the text of the survey dealing with the *Lordshyp of Towemowe Mansteroryshe*[26] there is mention of *Togherdadowe* (*Toghwadawe*) which may well be a corruption of Tochar etar dá Mag.

The *Lordshyp of Offerynmorchane* of the survey[27] is marked as *Feranomvrghan* on the Trinity College copy of the map and as *Feranomveghan* on the older Cottonian copy of the map. Curtis is correct in deriving this name from Uí Muiricáin who held the district of Fid Gaible.[28] The name *Fid Gaible* is preserved in the Figile river (a tributary of the Barrow) and the territory of *Feranomvrghan* on the map is shown to lie in that part of the barony of Cool-estown in Offaly lying east of the Figile river. There is evidence to show[29] that Fid Gaible originally extended eastwards to take in Rathangan in Co. Kildare, and since the Uí Muiricáin were a sub-sept of the Clann Colgan,[30] this is in keeping with what I have said in connection with Tuath dá Maige and the occupation of part of the Western Liffey Plain by Clann Colgan.

The identification by Curtis of the lordship of *Moylaghe* with the ancient Mag Lége is con-vincing.[31] There is, however, the difficulty that the position of Castle Lea, east of Portarling-ton, must indicate (as Curtis, following Hogan,[32] agreed) the location of Mag Lége. Yet Curtis ignored the fact that the map shows the lordship of *Mviligh* considerably north of this area in the barony of Coolestown. Associated with the Lége area were the Uí Onchon and Uí Cellaig (Plate XIII), other septs of Uí Failge.[33] The remaining portions of the Tudor map were not covered by the survey, although O'Dunne's Country and O'Dempsey's Country at that time, and much earlier in the ninth century, belonged to the Uí Failge complex. O'Dunne's country, or *Yregan* at the top of the map, takes its name firstly from the Uí Riacáin, an Uí Failge sept whose genealogy is given in Rawlinson MS B 502.[34] Riacán, the ninth-century founder of this sept, was the son of Cináed, over-king of the Uí Failge confederacy and the grandson of Mugrón, another Uí Failge king who was slain in battle beside Kildare monastery in 782.[35] The connec-tion with the Curragh is interesting, because according to the genealogists Mugrón's immediate descendants ruled in the Liffey Plain.[36] By the eleventh century, however, the surviving Ua Duinn (O'Dunne) representatives of this sept had been pushed towards the Slieve Bloom in north-west Co. Leix. For the Tudor surveyor O'Dunne's Country of *Yregan* was a *terra incognita* yielding not a single placename (Frontispiece). The only information available to him was the correct location of the source of the river Barrow in the Slieve Bloom mount-ains. From its northern and southern mearing with Tuath Géisille and *Leis* (Loígis) respect-ively, we can deduce that the country of Uí Riacáin coincided with the barony of Tinnahinch Co. Leix (Plate VII).

O'Dempsey's Country and the name of that family derives from Diummasach, an eleventh-century Uí Failge prince of the Clann Máel Ugra.[37] This territory covered the areas of *Feran Clandrmon* (Ferann Clainne Diarmata), *Eni, Eri* and *Clanmali(e)r* of the Tudor map. The Clann Máel Ugra, in turn, took their name from Máelaugrai, an Uí Failge chieftain who flourished in the middle of the ninth century. Máelaugrai's grandfather, Áed, was slain by Óengus son of Mugrón, king of Uí Failge, in the oratory of Kilclonfert in A.D. 789.[38] The centre of Clanmalier (Clann Máel Ugra) territory on the Tudor map was located near Ballybrittas in Co. Leix, and the placename *Glenmalire* on the half-inch Ordnance Survey sheet is located within a quarter of a mile of Ballybrittas. The extension of Ua Diomasaigh (O'Dempsey) power over the barony of Upper Phillipstown may be a late phenomenon.[39]

The map of 1563 covers that part of Leix which lay traditionally within the ancient kingdom of the Leinstermen (Plate VII and Frontispiece) and which in the seventeenth century was dominated by the O'Mores, descendants of the ancient Loígis. The centre of Loígis territory lay on the Great Heath of Maryborough in the area of *Shian* and *Muret* on the Tudor map. *Muret* represents the Irish form of *Mag Réta* or *Mag Rechet* which was the name of the open plain here in Celtic times—a plain that was synonymous with the Loígis. The word *Rechet* has been compared[40] with *Rheged* the name of the Northern British kingdom centred on the Eden valley in Cumbria which was conquered by the Northumbrian Angles in the seventh century. Most modern scholars accept the medieval Irish tradition that the Loígis were *Cruthin* or Picts[41] and remarkably, like the Picts of Scotland, they were believed to consist of seven tribes or segments as enshrined in the phrase *na Secht Laichse Laigen* ('the Seven Loígis of the Leinstermen').[42] The Loígis like the Fothairt were understood in medieval tradition to have been a non-Laginian mercenary tribe settled as fighting men alongside certain Laginian masters. In the case of the Loígis of Mag Réta, they were settled there by the Uí Failge along a stretch of the Slige Dála to defend that trackway against invasion from Ossory and Munster (Plates XIII and XIV).

The genealogical compilations refer to the 'Loígis of the Leinstermen' (*Laíges Laigen*) as synonymous with the 'Loígis of the Uí Enechglaiss' (*Laígis Hua nEnechglais*)[43] and this is a phrase which may hold the key to understanding much of late Leinster prehistory. The Loígis

39

Five bronze figures forming part of a larger group affixed to the shrine of St Manchán, preserved in the Catholic church at Boher near Lemanaghan (Liath Mancháin) in Co. Offaly. The shrine dates to the late twelfth century but the figures have been seen as Irish copies of Continental originals. Yet the treatment of the eyes and beards, and the kilt-like garments strongly suggest that the figures have been given an Irish interpretation by the craftsman. Manchán, who founded Lemanaghan, died in 665.

Manchán's Wish, a poem surviving in its present form from the tenth century, is ascribed to the founder of Lemanaghan. In it a monk asks God for 'a little hut, hidden in the wilderness', with a southern aspect and a stream nearby, together with a wood sheltering 'many-voiced birds'. The produce of his monastery would include 'leeks, hens, speckled salmon and bees'. This poem (ed. G. Murphy, Early Irish Lyrics, pp. 28-31) evokes the spirit of the golden age of Irish monasticism and of the Bogland landscape in which it was composed.

76

of the Uí Enechglaiss would suggest that the Loígis (and their allies the Fothairt) served not only the Uí Failge and Uí Bairrche, but also the Uí Enechglaiss. Such a tradition fits perfectly with other genealogical statements to the effect that a specially close bond existed between these three Free Tribes descended from Cathair Mór, namely, Uí Failge, Uí Bairrche and Uí Enechglaiss.[44] It is these three tribes who, as the original Laigin, occupy a distinct stratum within the genealogies, and who on historical grounds can be shown to have ousted the last of the Dumnonians who ruled in the fifth century under the tribal name of Dál Messin Corb. We may now regard the Loígis and the Fothairt as the mercenary troops who helped to conquer Leinster for the Uí Failge and their Laginian kinsmen; who were rewarded with lands adjacent to those particular masters all over Leinster, and who were remembered in the traditional lore as the 'battlers of the Leinstermen' (cliathaire Lagen).[45] O'Rahilly rightly interpreted the legend of how the Picts or Cruthin conquered the British tribe (tuath de Bretnaib) of Tuath Fhidga in Mag Fea in Carlow (Plates XV and XVI) as preserving a dim memory of the coming of the Fothairt to that central region of Leinster.[46] But the defeated Britons were not the Uí Bairrche as O'Rahilly believed. The Uí Bairrche may well have had a British origin as their Brigantian affinities would suggest, but this legend recalls how the Fothairt as mercenaries of the Uí Bairrche branch of the original Laigin defeated more ancient peoples of British origin who were either part of the Fir Domnann or were at least under their overlordship. This is as far as the records in the present state of our knowledge will allow us to go and it is perhaps prudent to cite Byrne's note of caution at this point, namely, that we are faced with a gap of many centuries between events described in Irish invasion legends and the documentation proper from the historical period.[47]

* * * *

This completes the topographical survey of the natural regions and ancient tribal divisions of the Leinstermen. It may be appropriate to stress here that the reason why we know so much about this ancient topography is because the learned classes and their royal patrons in the Middle Ages were themselves captivated by the landscape which they believed their ancestors had enjoyed from time immemorial. The Life of St. Comgall of Bangor in Ulster relates an incident concerning that Uí Bairrche king of South Leinster, Cormac mac Diarmata, whom we have encountered in another context.[48] Cormac, we are told, left his kingdom to become a monk at Bangor, but he was overcome by home-sickness for his native Leinster. He eventually overcame this temptation to abandon his pious exile, but the temptation itself (in the form of a dream) presents us with a striking picture of the bond which existed between a Dark Age Irish king and the environment in which he exercised his royal authority:[49]

> 'He dreamt that he had been walking round the borders of Leinster visiting his beautiful cities and his fortresses, and that he had traversed the flowering plains and lovely meadows; he dreamt of his kingdom and of his fine war-chariots and he saw himself surrounded by his war-lords, princes and magnates, and with the symbols of his royal power.'

CHAPTER VIII

Geography and Inter-tribal Marriage

The genealogical compilations are of most use to the historical geographer when studied at the level of inter-tribal relationships. The intricacies of each tribal genealogy clearly merit a study in themselves, and there is frequently, as we have already seen, detailed geographical information offered on the whereabouts of each subdivision within a particular tribe. This detailed geographical lore helps to fill out the picture at a very local level, but unfortunately many of the individual settlements mentioned are no longer identifiable, and we may have to wait a long time before we can get down to studying the geography of the component settlements within a tribe. In addition to studying the internal geography of tribal territories, and the geographical relationship between one tribe and another, there is yet another level at which geographical studies can proceed, and this relates to inter-tribal marriage. It is clear from the annals, as well as from the genealogies, that tribal rulers frequently sought their queens from outside their own tribes and even from the ranks of an enemy aristocracy. Such marriages with traditional enemies were probably inspired by political motives, but equally it is clear that royal descent was something kings sought in their wives and this requirement ensured that royal marriage was essentially an inter-tribal phenomenon.[1] Marriage to royal ladies from alien tribes may also have been connected with inheritance laws, since early Irish women were capable of inheriting property and brought their own dowry to a marriage.

The details of Leinster royal marriages are both reliable and comparatively full for the seventh and eighth centuries, and remarkably so in comparison with contemporary Frankish and Anglo-Saxon sources. It was normal for an early Irish king to marry several times, and there is more than a hint that polygamy, or at least a discreet form of it, continued to be practised by the Celtic aristocracy long after the introduction of Christianity.[2] Early Irish laws allowed for a 'chief wife' and concubines in the household at one time, and we see that kings such as Flann-dá-Congal of Uí Failge (+ 740) had at least three queens (Chart 3), although it is almost impossible to determine, from the fragmentary records which survive, whether these ladies lived in a polygamous relationship or whether each reigned in turn as sole queen. That Flann was married to more than one queen is supported by the genealogical and annalistic evidence. We have the names of no less than thirteen of his sons who reached manhood,[3] and five of these succeeded their father as kings of the Uí Failge confederacy. These sons must have differed widely in age, since one, Ailill Corrach, died as king of Uí Failge in 741,[4] while another, Mugrón, who also succeeded to that office, did not die until 782,[5] and it may be that some of Flann's offspring even survived into the ninth century. Even the illustrious Munster king, Brian Boru, seems to have enjoyed the marital privileges of a typical Irish king, although again it may not be possible to prove that he cohabited with more than one of his several wives at any one time.[6]

The genealogical table in Chart 3[*] deals with inter-tribal marriages in early historical Leinster. This is a chart which shows the inter-relationship between tribes based, not on male lines of descent, but on the marriage ties of royal ladies. It is rich in geographical and historical significance. We are fortunate in being able to compile from annals, tribal king-lists and genealogies, a reliable record of the tangled marital relationships which involved tribes from inside and outside the Province; and we may begin by studying the relationship between the two kings, Colmán of Uí Dúnlainge (fl. A.D. 600) and his rival, Brandub of Uí Cheinnselaig. Colmán was married first to Fedelm, an Uí Theig princess, and secondly to Cummine of the Déisi (cf. Plate VIII). While Colmán was Cummine's first husband, on his death she married Brandub, king of Uí Cheinnselaig for her second spouse. If we are to accept a genealogy in the Book of Leinster[7] (Chart 3), Brandub was the half-brother of Áedán mac Gabráin, the Dál Riata king of Scots, who appears in Adomnan's Life of Columba[8]. Such royal marriage tangles seem to have been typical of early Ireland, and recur in the ninth century when Lann, a princess of Ossory, for instance, was married first to the Uí Néill highking, Maelsechnaill I, and later to his successor, Áed Findliath of the Northern Uí Néill.[9] Lann's brother, Cerball, the king of Ossory, was said in the Three Fragments of Irish Annals to have been married to a daughter of Maelsechlainn.[10] This may have meant that the Southern Uí Néill highking, Flann Sinna (879-916), who was the son of Lann and Maelsechlainn, was the half-brother of his Northern Uí Néill rival and successor Niall Glúndub (916-9), the son of Áed Findliath. Niall's son, Muirchertach of the Leather Cloaks (+ 943), married in turn Dub-Daire, a queen from Cerball's House of Ossory.[11] This intense interbreeding between early Irish aristocratic kin-groups must be related to, or at least help to explain, the rotational nature of the highkingship between Northern and Southern Uí Néill factions. I do not follow here exactly the terminology of African historians and anthropologists in the use of the terms 'circulating' and 'rotational kingship'. Circulating kingship is defined as 'a system whereby offices pass between two or more units of organisation',[12] but in the case of pre-eighth-century Leinster, this involved a fairly irregular movement of kingship between different dynasties or kin-groups, such as Uí Máil, Uí Cheinnselaig or Uí Dúnlainge. A strict rotational system as practised in post eighth-century Leinster, or among the Northern and Southern Uí Néill, confined kingship to within two or three dynastic groups, distantly related to each other, while within each group the kingship passed (with interruption) from father to son.

The Northern and Southern Uí Néill were only remotely related to each other through their common descent from Niall of the Nine Hostages, who flourished in the fifth century. The two dynasties were intense rivals, and yet they arrived at an agreement whereby the highkingship 'rotated' with relative ease and regularity between the two related groups (Chart 4) from the eighth to the early eleventh centuries. A similar rotational kingship evolved among the Uí Dúnlainge of Leinster in the early eighth century (Chart 5),[†] which replaced an earlier oscillating (or circulating) kingship. Under the more primitive oscillating system, the kingship of the Province was shared not by a few related dynasties, but by several unrelated hostile groups. Later rotation must have become easier – if it had not been made possible in the first place – by the fact that marriages to the same queens had produced generations of half-brothers succeeding to a continuous line of kingship. For in Leinster, too, we have the example of Fáelan (+ 738), ancestor of Uí Fáeláin, married to the same Munster queen, Tualaith, who had earlier been married to his brother Dúnchad (+ 728),[13] ancestor of Uí Dúnchada (Chart 5). Such marriages were probably much more common than even the surviving records suggest, and produced siblings which bound the diverse segments of the polydynastic systems closer together, and encouraged rotational kingship. There are numerous parallels to early Irish rotational and circulating forms of succession among modern African tribes.[14] The apparently incestuous

79

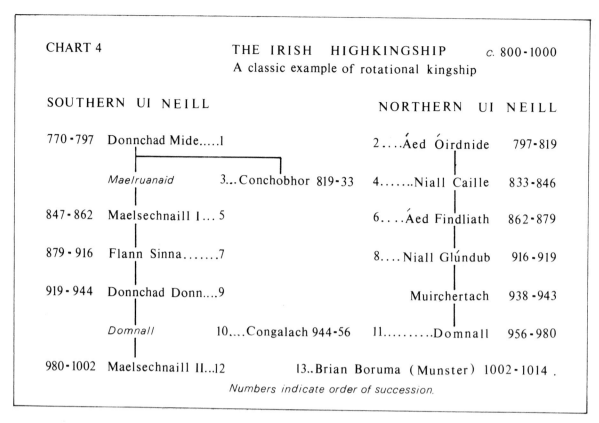

CHART 4   THE IRISH HIGHKINGSHIP   *c.* 800-1000
                          A classic example of rotational kingship

SOUTHERN UI NEILL   NORTHERN UI NEILL

770-797 Donnchad Mide.....1   2....Áed Óirdnide   797-819

         Maelruanaid   3...Conchobhor 819-33 4.......Niall Caille 833-846

847-862 Maelsechnaill I...5   6....Áed Findliath   862-879

879-916 Flann Sinna.......7   8....Niall Glúndub   916-919

919-944 Donnchad Donn....9   Muirchertach   938-943

         Domnall   10....Congalach 944-56 11..........Domnall 956-980

980-1002 Maelsechnaill II...12   13..Brian Boruma (Munster) 1002-1014 .
                          Numbers indicate order of succession.

nature of some of these royal Irish unions and the 'rotation of queens' reminds us, too, of ninth-century Wessex, where Judith, the daughter of the Frankish ruler Charles the Bald, married first King Ethelwulf, and on his death in 858 married her step-son Ethelbald.[15] The Wessex situation in 858 closely parallels that of Leinster in 728. For Fáelán of Leinster and Ethelbald of Wessex both rebelled against close kinsmen and eventually married the queens of their rivals. Royal ladies were indispensable for their royal blood, political alliances, and perhaps their property, and they changed partners within Dark Age aristocratic kin-groups with remarkable ease.

In addition to showing all the known royal Leinster marriages in this period, Chart 3 also sets out the succession to the kingship of Leinster as it oscillated in the seventh century among the Uí Cheinnselaig, Uí Máil and Uí Dúnlainge (cf. Plate VIII). The pattern of marriage alliance is immediately related both to the succession struggle for the kingship of Leinster—in the period pre-A.D. 700, before a proper rotational system was evolved—and to the geography of the Province. We may begin with Dúnlang's marriage to Cuach of the Uí Bairrche of Mag Ailbe (Chart 3, top). The tradition regarding this marriage relates to a period in the late fifth century, before contemporary sources are available. It is an interesting tradition, however, in that it shows the ancestor of the Uí Dúnlainge marrying a princess of the Uí Bairrche of Mag Ailbe in southern Kildare and northern Carlow (Plates XI and XII). The tradition may be an ancient one, since it is enshrined in the genealogies within a short anecdote which claims that Cuach bore three sons to Dúnlang, 'Hence was said Cuach's three leaps in Gabair (*tri lemend Cuache i ngabuir*), each time she bore one of the aforesaid sons'.[16] Cuach was said to have received three forts for bearing each of these sons; none of the forts are identifiable, but one of them, Magen Garbáin, was clearly in Gabair.[17] At any rate, Cuach's homeland in Mag Ailbe and the reference to her 'three leaps in Gabair' takes us back to the same conclusion I have reached earlier,[18] namely, that Uí Dúnlainge origins were centred alongside those of Uí Cheinnselaig on the Carlow-Kildare border (Plate V).

Early Uí Dúnlainge and Uí Cheinnselaig connections are clearly seen in the marriages (Chart 3) of Colmán of Uí Dúnlainge and Brandub king of Uí Cheinnselaig (+ 605). Colmán, as we have seen, was married to Fedelm and also to the Déisi princess, Cummine. Cummine came from a Munster subject-tribe who were neighbours of the southern Leinstermen across the Barrow estuary in modern Co. Waterford (Plate VIII). Yet another princess of this neighbouring Munster people, Failend of the Déisi,[19] married another Leinster king from Uí Cheinnselaig, Crundmáel mac Rónáin, who died in A.D. 656, and who may have ruled from Rathgall hill-fort (? Bolg Luatha) in the barony of Shillelagh in south-west Wicklow.[20] According to the saga of *Fingal Rónáin*, the Uí Máil king, Rónán mac Áeda (Chart 3), was married to Ethne of the Déisi, also in the seventh century.[21] Meanwhile, Colmán's first queen, Fedelm (Chart 3), came from among his northern neighbours, the Uí Théig, who at this time were struggling with Brandub of the Uí Cheinnselaig for control of all Leinster and for west Wicklow and southern Kildare in particular. The Uí Théig were a branch of the Uí Máil (Plate VIII, and Chart 2) and the Uí Máil dominated the Leinster kingship in the seventh century, producing no less than five or six kings of the Province at that time.[22] It is not surprising, therefore, to find early Uí Dúnlainge leaders, such as Cairpre and Colmán, marrying into this dynasty in their bid to win acceptance as contenders for the kingship. For while Colmán married Fedelm of Uí Théig, his father, Cairpre, had married Lassi of Uí Máil (Chart 3).[23]

The marriage of the Uí Máil king, Cellach Cualann, to Mugain of the Uí Bairrche,[24] on the other hand, can be explained on simpler geographical grounds. The Uí Bairrche, although a Free Tribe, had long since ceased to count as a great people in Leinster by A.D. 700, but they had once been powerful and they had been close neighbours of the Uí Máil and Uí Cheinnselaig for centuries (Plate VIII). The Uí Bairrche and Uí Cheinnselaig were traditional enemies, but that did not prevent Failbe,[25] son of Domnall king of Uí Bairrche, from marrying Ethne of the Uí Cheinnselaig (Chart 3). The daughter of that marriage was Mugain, an Uí Bairrche princess who bore several daughters to Cellach Cualann, the last and most famous Uí Máil king of Leinster. Two of these girls married Uí Néill kings in Brega to the north of Leinster. Derbforgaill married Fínsnechta ('Snow Wine'), king at Lagore in Southern Brega,[26] while her sister Muirend, married Írgalach the king of Northern Brega whose palace was near the Boyne at Knowth.[27] Another of Mugain's daughters, Conchenn,[28] married Murchad, that Uí Dúnlainge king who founded an unbroken rotational line of Leinster kings which lasted from 715 to 1042 (Chart 5).

Two major points become clear from this very complex network of inter-tribal marriage. Firstly, none of the Leinster queens came from far afield with the exception of those, as we shall see, from the Scottish Dál Riada, and a few from elsewhere. Several kings married ladies from neighbouring tribes within Leinster, and in one instance we find Conall, son of King Fáelán of Uí Dúnlainge, marrying Conandil from the Uí Maine, a remote sub-group of his own dynasty (Charts 2 and 3). When Leinster kings sought wives outside the Province, or supplied their daughters in turn to non-Leinster kings, they usually did not go further than bordering tribes—the Déisi of Munster, and the Uí Néill of Mide and Brega. To return to the case of King Flann-dá-Congal of Uí Failge who ruled over North-Western Leinster; one of his wives, Érrenchu, was the daughter of Murchad, king of neighbouring Mide; his second queen was 'the daughter of Forannán' (*ingen Forranáin*) from his Leinster neighbours the Uí Dúnlainge; while his third queen was the daughter of Flann Lena.[29] The second element in this Flann's name suggests he was either ruler of Mag Lena near Durrow in Fir Cell in Mide (Plates VIII and XIII), or that he was fostered there. Fir Cell was a tribe in Uí Néill territory in Mide which was separated from Flann-dá-Congal's Uí Failge kingdom by a great belt of bogland in what is now Offaly[30] (Plates VIII and XIII). The Uí Dúnlainge, too, married into royal houses of nearby

Brega, and into Clann Cholmáin, the ruling Uí Néill dynasty of Mide and highkings of Ireland. Fáelán of the Uí Dúnlainge (*fl.* 626) was married to Uasal (+ 643), the daughter of Suibne, son of Colmán Mór of Mide,[31] a king who was probably slain by the Uí Failge at Brí Dam in 600. Fáelán's other queen was Sárnát of the Fothairt of Mag Fea in Carlow[32] –a more modest match, but possibly connected with Fáelán's ambitions to control the nunnery of Kildare where another branch of the Fothairt had a traditional interest. Fáelán's mother was Fedelm of the Uí Théig. This tribe was a branch of the Uí Máil who originally controlled the monastic town of Glendalough, which lay in their territory. The *Lives* of Kevin of Glendalough allege that Fáelán had a close association with both Kevin and his monastery, and that the infant Fáelán was the foster-son of St Kevin.[33] Bran son of Muiredach of the Uí Muiredaig (Chart 5), fifth in descent from Fáelán, was married to Ethne, the daughter of the highking, Domnall Mide (+ 763). Bran and his queen from Mide were burnt to death in 795 in the church of Cell Chúile Dumai in Loígis.[34] But other Uí Dúnlainge marriages were less exotic. Muiredach son of Bran (+ 818) married a princess from nearby Roíriu (Mullaghreelion, southern Kildare)[35] and Muiredach's great aunt, Failend, married Cathal son of Gerthide of Uí Briúin Cualann,[36] a neighbouring and related dynasty in south Dublin (Plate VIII and Chart 2).

In marked contrast to the local flavour of Leinster inter-tribal marriage was the strong northern Irish and Scottish connection with this southern Province. It is true that at least one prominent Munster queen came to Leinster–Tuathlaithe (or Tualaith, + 754) the daughter of Cathal mac Finguine, king of Cashel, who was queen first to Dúnchad the Leinster king who died in 728 and later to his brother Fáelán who died in 738.[37] But the northern and Scottish connection predominated, and may derive from a common origin of the Leinstermen and the *Ulaid* or Ulstermen. I have already referred to the tradition which held that Áedán mac Gabráin, king of Scots Dál Riada and Brandub, king of Uí Cheinnselaig and all Leinster, were half-brothers.[38] Their mother, Feidelm, was the daughter of Fedelmid, a king of the Connachta (in Connaught). Columcille, the missionary saint of the Scots and Picts, had a Leinster mother, Ethne of the Uí Bairrche, who was the queen of king Fedelmid of Cenél Conaill, the grandson of Conall Gulban the founder of that dynasty.[39] Even more firmly rooted in the historical period is the record of the marriage of Bran mac Conaill, the Uí Dúnlainge king of Leinster (+ 693), with Almaith, a princess from Scottish Dál Riada.[40] Rónán, a seventh-century member of the Uí Maine branch of the Leinster Uí Dúnlainge, was married to Lasair, one of the Uí Crimthainn of Airgialla in Ulster,[41] and according to the saga of *Fingal Rónáin*, Rónán the Uí Máil king of seventh-century Leinster, took as his second queen the daughter of the Ulster king, Eochu of Dunseverick (Dún Sobairche).[42] Indeed, Rónán's son, the hero Máel Fothartaig, removed himself to Scotland, according to the saga, to escape the amorous advances of his Ulster stepmother at the Leinster court of the ageing King Rónán.[43] We are reminded, too, of Caintigern (+ 734), yet another of the numerous offspring of the Uí Máil king, Cellach Cualann, who was venerated as a saint (Kentigern) at Loch Lomond.[44] This Scottish connection with Leinster was most likely fostered–as in the case of Iona contacts with Taghmon in Wexford and earlier contacts with the Scottish Dumnonii–by direct communication between south-west Scotland and the Wicklow and Wexford coasts across the Irish Sea.

The extraordinarily detailed record of inter-tribal marriage in seventh and eighth-century Leinster adds to our understanding of a world, which, if we were to rely solely on the annalists, would appear to have witnessed unremitting slaughter in tribal battles, or was otherwise dominated by the leaders of the Church. The picture, however, of queens moving from tribe to tribe and frequently marrying into traditionally hostile tribes, gives us a new insight into a Dark Age world. We realize that clerics, craftsmen, and traders were not the only people who moved across tribal frontiers. Aristocratic women travelled with their retinues to become child-

bearers to the warrior aristocracies of other tribes. These women constituted the most important social class of those who exchanged one tribe for another because as members of the aristocracy they belonged to the dominant social group—and, indeed, the only one that ultimately
mattered, in the Dark Ages. Such royal ladies carried with them books and ideas, and they
must have exercised a profound influence on the spread of fashion and taste in jewellery and
fine arts. The number of these royal women whose names survive is but a tiny fraction compared to those of their warrior menfolk, but they were probably no less numerous in reality
than the warriors whom they quite clearly outlived, and no less influential on certain levels of
society. It is true that aristocratic youths were fostered in early Ireland at the court of some
lord who was an ally of their fathers' house, but fosterage was unlikely to take them outside
their tribes. Royal women, on the other hand, left home and tribe when they reached maturity
and had more experience of the wider world in some respects than their menfolk, who fared
abroad only in pursuit of the heady business of war.

The eventful lives of some of these women left their mark on Irish Dark Age tradition, as in
the case of Gormlaith who began her career as the queen of Cormac, the bishop-king of Cashel,
and after his death became the consort of Cerball, king of Leinster who died in A.D. 909.
Finally, she married the northern Uí Néill highking, Niall Glúndub, who was slain by the
Northmen in 919. Gormlaith was herself the daughter of a king—Flann Sinna, highking of
Ireland from 879 to 916. Her marriage to the ascetic Cormac was merely symbolic, since he
preserved his celibacy, and it ended when that bishop was beheaded in the battle of Ballaugh-
moon in southern Kildare in 908. She was next married—in typical 'reginal rotation'—to
Cormac's enemy, and slayer, Cerball king of Leinster, who himself died in an accident in Kildare town in 909. Finally, she was robbed of her third king, Niall Glúndub, when he was slain
in battle against king Sitric, the grandson of Ivar, at Dublin in 919. Gormlaith is alleged to
have composed a dirge on both Cerball and Niall which survives, and this famous daughter of a
highking, who had been queen to three kings in turn, was remembered enigmatically in sixteenth-century folklore thus: 'After all these royal marriages, she begged from door to door
forsaken of all her friends and allies, and glad to be relieved by her inferiors' *Annals of Clonmacnoise*.[45] A more sober and contemporary observation in the *Annals of Ulster* shows us
that she survived her third husband by thirty years and died an old woman 'in penitence' (i.e.
in a nunnery) in 948.[46]

This tenth-century Gormlaith had an even more famous namesake in the following century—
the Leinster princess, Gormlaith, sister of king Máelmorda of the Uí Fáeláin (who was king of
the Province). Through her first union with Olaf Cuaran, king of Dublin and one-time king of
York, she became the mother of king Sitric Silkenbeard at Dublin. She later became queen or
concubine of Maelsechlainn II, the Irish highking, and finally ended up as the consort of king
Brian Boru. To confuse a complex situation even further, king Brian gave his daughter in
marriage to his stepson, king Sitric of Dublin![47] We are introduced to this veteran queen in
Njáls saga—perhaps the finest of all the Icelandic family sagas—as the divorced consort of king
Brian, who urged her son, Sitric king of Dublin, to slay her ex-husband. In Icelandic tradition[48] she is portrayed as a grim and scheming lady who plays men off against each other in
her ruthless quest for vengeance against Brian Boru, and like early Germanic heroines Gormlaith, too, was alleged to have been the 'fairest of all women', even by her Scandinavian enemies.[49] Gormlaith may, or may not, have had good looks, but she did have the royal blood
of countless generations of Leinster kings in her veins, and it was this which earned her a place
in the beds and counsels of three of the most famous kings of medieval Irish and Scandinavian
tradition—Maelsechlainn II, Olaf Cuaran and Brian Boru.

CHAPTER IX

Midland Ecology in a Golden Age

40

Clonenagh (Cluain Ednech), Co. Leix, was the royal monastery of the Loígis and the monastic home of Óengus the writer and Céli Dé who wrote his Calendar *or* Martyrology of Irish saints *at about A.D. 800.*

Clonenagh continued to enjoy the patronage of the O'Mores, descendants of the Loígis kings, into the sixteenth century. It was founded as a monastery by St Fintán who died in A.D. 603, and its location on the Slige Dála (Road of the Assemblies) ensured it an important place in the life of early medieval Ireland. The Book of Leinster *most likely began life here before being moved to Noghaval.*

Óengus out of the assembly of Heaven   In Clonenagh he was reared,
Here are his tomb and his bed.   In Clonenagh he was buried,
It is from here he went to death   In Clonenagh of the many crosses
On Friday to holy Heaven.   He first read his psalms.

(*Leabhar Breac; translation based on Kuno Meyer)*

There is scarcely a more melancholy experience for a medieval historian than to visit the forgotten monasteries of Ireland in the Bog of Allen. Centres such as Lullymore, Clonenagh, Killeigh or Clonfertmulloe lie neglected and forlorn in a landscape which has been shorn of almost all its natural resources. Even the enduring hills of the Slieve Bloom are now clothed with a sombre blanket of conifers which intrude as an alien species out of keeping with the environment. Only a tiny fraction of the Dark Age monastic centres are in State care, while most are now reduced to a modest heap of overgrown rubble. Official neglect has gone hand in hand with the demise of popular religion, which until the middle of the nineteenth century and even later, ensured that these centres still occupied a place in the lives of

84

local communities. Almost all Early Christian sites were resorted to regularly as places of pilgrimage and their churchyards still provided a last resting place for local communities, who kept faith with their dead generations in a manner reminiscent of ancestor worship in other societies. The recent closing of almost all of these ancient churchyards for burial by Local Authorities, combined with the re-routing of roads and the rehousing of entire communities have all conspired to exclude these historic sites from the everyday experience of local communities. Being no longer a living part of modern society, they inevitably suffer neglect and desecration. For the historical geographer and archaeologist, the problem is to reconstruct the original environment in which these centres flourished; to study them in the ancient landscape in relation to each other; to understand their political setting; and ultimately to achieve the full picture of their significance by associating these pathetic nettle-beds with their manuscript and artistic treasures which now survive in the museums of Europe.

The starting point, yet again, must be the configuration of the peat bogs. A study of Plates III, VIII, XIII and XIV shows that in many cases the bog cover has determined the size of individual tribes or *tuatha*, and in the case of some tribes of Mide in Westmeath it is possible to view the extent of fertile land available to each tribe and to view this in relation to their monastic and secular centres. More detailed cartographical studies in the future will no doubt yield information on individual settlements and on tribal population in this area of Mide and Uí Failge. The tribes of Mide which bordered on northern Leinster were (Plate VIII) the Fir Bile, Fir Tulach and Cenél Fhiachach. Two of these tribal names survive in the Westmeath Baronies of Farbill and Fartullagh (Plate VII), and the extent of Cenél Fhiachach was discovered by Walsh to cover all the barony of Moycashel and to have extended northwards to the Hill of Ushnagh (Plates XIII-XIV).[1] When we compare the distribution of bog with the boundaries of these three baronies (Plates III and VII), we see that the baronial—and even earlier Celtic—divisions were determined by the configuration of the bogs which enclose three large divisions of fertile ground in this region. It is easy to see how such naturally protected areas provided ready-made territorial units for the older tribal *tuatha.* Although this area of Mide forms a continuation with the boglands of Uí Failge, yet the bog here is thinning out and the region was cut off from the ancient Leinstermen by a continuous belt of bog running west from Clonard (Plate XII) to Tyrrellspass (Plate XIV), while in the north it was easily accessible to the Plains of Westmeath (cf. Plate III). In the ninth century this entire Westmeath area belonged to Mide, but a number of its southern tribes claimed a Leinster origin.[2] Looking in more detail at the Plates XIII and XIV we see how the three tribal territories of Fir Bile, Fir Tulach and Cenél Fiachach afforded very restricted access to each other along the Slige Mór or Great Way which ran along the southern border of each territory. The Pass of Kilbride, joining Fir Bile to Fir Tulach, and Tyrell's Pass, joining Fir Tulach to Cenél Fiachach, lost nothing of their strategic importance up to the middle of the seventeenth century. We note that Fir Tulach was enclosed by Lough Ennel and by a circuit of bog some two to eight miles deep. The amount of fertile land available to this tribe was less than sixteen square miles, and perhaps considerably less if we allow for poor drainage and more extensive forest. We may note, too, the location of the fortress of the kings of Fir Tulach at Dún na Cairrge near the safety of Lough Ennel and that its two most important monastic centres at Lann and Clonfad (Cluain Fada Fine Libráin) were well separated from each other in the north and south of the kingdom respectively.

The western boundary of Uí Failge, as in all of this North-Western area, coincided with the limits of the medieval diocese of Kildare (Plate VI), but all of these boundaries in turn were determined by a great diagonal strip of bog running across the modern Co. Offaly (Plates III and XIII). This bog separated the Leinstermen from Fir Cell ('Men of the Churches'), a tribe which belonged to Mide. The linear outline of Fir Cell territory on Plate VIII is strictly theoretical, and on Plates III and XIII we can identify it as a narrow strip of fertile land some twenty miles long, hemmed in by bogs, joining the Uí Neill of the north with Éle Tuaiscert in the Province of Munster to the south. The monasteries of Rahan (Rathan), Durrow (Dairmag) and Lynally (Lann Élo) (Plate XIV), which were situated in Mag Lena in the northern portion of this territory, were connected by a system of passes with Killeigh (Cell Aichid) in Uí Failge (Plate XIV) and ultimately with Mag Rechet in the heart of Leinster territory. While the Leinster monastery of Killeigh opened on to this plain in the north, Clonfertmulloe (Cluain Ferta Molua) in Loígis had easy access to it in the south near Roscrea.

We see from Plate XIV that another narrow plain stretched from Roscrea to Birr, continuing on to Lusma (Lusmag) on the Shannon. Yet other narrow passes wound their way through the bogs from Roscrea south-east into Ossory, and due south into Munster. Lusma, although east of the Shannon, was occupied by the Uí Maine of Connaught, while the region from Birr to Roscrea belonged to the Éle of Munster. This Roscrea area bordered on Fir Cell of Mide in the north, the Leinstermen on the east, and Ossory on the south-east. In this confined area, with its network of narrow passes—many of them formed by the gravelly esker ridges—we have the meeting-place of the Provincial kingdoms of Laigin, Mide, Osraige, Mumu and Connachta. Mac Neill rejected the statement of the seventeenth-century Gaelic historian, Geoffrey Keating, that originally the four Provinces of Ireland met at the Hill of Ushnagh in Westmeath (Plate XIV), on the grounds that it defied geographical realities.[3] Mac Neill was right in rejecting the idea of two Munsters converging on this particular area. But geography, far from ruling out the possibility of all the Provinces meeting in the Irish Midlands, actually leads us to that very conclusion. Indeed, if we were to follow Keating further in his tradition that the original kingdom of Mide was formed from a portion of each of the Provinces where they converged on Ushnagh,[4] we would be left with a political picture not unlike that on Plate XIII. At least the tradition, whether fictional or not, was built upon a reasonable basis.

The findings we have reached by bringing early Irish topography to bear on the Midlands with its bogs and forest reminds us of the perceptive remarks of Dr Andrews in his preliminary study of this region:[5] 'These strips of relatively unattractive country have many times helped to channel the course of Irish History. . . Ideas and attitudes have flowed freely around and between them.' The notion that the Midland bogs constituted an unproductive wilderness in the Middle Ages has arisen from a general ignorance of the needs of a medieval society, and from projecting modern evaluations of land use uncritically backwards in time. Far from being a backwater, the great expanse of bogland was honeycombed with fertile land which offered not only sustenance, but also shelter to monastic communities who were in much need of protection from the violence of a Dark Age society dominated by an irresponsible warrior élite. These narrow, fertile strips of territory also allowed free access from one community to another, from the Shannon in the west to the Liffey Plain in the east, without endangering the overall security of isolated tribal communities. Access was available only to those with detailed knowledge of the labyrinthine pattern of bog, esker and firm ground. Strangers and hostile armies, on the other hand, were forced to use the single clearly-defined route which led through this wilderness from Uí Néill lands in the north into Munster in the south. This route, which I term the 'Midland Corridor', offered some clear advantages to the stranger who was brave enough to leave his tribe and trust himself to the mercies of an uncertain world. Firstly, the way was free from natural obstacles and consisted of a stretch of open fertile countryside, approximately twenty miles long and two to four miles wide. It extended from Clonfad (Cluain fada fine Libráin) and Tyrellspass in Westmeath, past Rahugh (Ráth Áeda) and the Great Esker or gravel ridge, into Fir Cell and ancient Mag Lena. The route continued to run south-westward and the important monasteries which sprung up along this way are in themselves an indication of its prime importance in Celtic Ireland. These included Durrow, Tihilly (Tech Taille), Rathan, Lynally (Lann Élo), Kinitty (Cend Eitig), Seirkieran (Saiger) and finally Birr on the Munster border. It is little wonder that the tribe which occupied this entire Corridor were known as Fir Cell, 'Men of the Churches'.

Evidence for the regular use of this great pass from Munster into Mide is to be found in the *Lives* of Mo-Chuda of Rahan and Colmán of Lann Élo, for instance. Mo-Chuda was a seventh-century Munster saint who first approached Rahan (which lay on the northern end of the Midland Corridor) from the south. As he journeyed north we are told he found Molua of Clonfertmulloe (Cluain Ferta Molua) in Leix harvesting in the fields 'on the borders of Leinster and Munster' (Plate XIV).[6] Clonfertmulloe was on the borders of Leinster, Munster and Ossory. Mochuda's next stop was at Lynally in the centre of the Corridor and not far from his destination at Rahan. We are told that Colmán of Lynally (Lann Élo) and Mo-Chuda frequently visited each other, which is another way of saying that there was frequent communication between the two monasteries in the Early Middle Ages.[7] When Mo-Chuda was expelled from Rahan with his followers, probably in connection with the dispute regarding Easter dating and and other liturgical matters, he headed south along the Corridor and his first stop was at Drumcullen (Druim Cuilinn: Plate XIV) 'on the borders of Munster, Leinster and Mide, but actually in Fir Cell in Mide'.[8] From there he went to Seirkieran and spent his first night on the road in Roscrea, from which we deduce it was a day's journey to traverse the Corridor from Rahan to Roscrea.[9] This estimate is confirmed by the *Life* of Colmán of Lynally which states that when Colmán headed south to visit St Máedóc of Ferns the monks of Clonfertmulloe entreated him to spend the night with them.[10] Lynally is only two miles south-east of Rahan, while Clonfertmulloe is about four miles east of Roscrea (**Plate XIV**). Colmán's *Life* also suggests that the

41a   b   c

The wooden vessel hollowed out of a single piece of yew with an oak bottom (a) was discovered in a bog in Co. Offaly (Dublin Penny Journal, *1833). This, together with the richly decorated leather sandal or cuarán (b)–place of discovery unknown– reminds us of the remarkable richness of perishable organic material which has been preserved for centuries in the peat bogs of Ireland. The medieval* Lives *of Irish saints abound with references to such household items as sandals (*Life *of Ciaran of Saiger); satchels (*Life *of Mochuda of Rahan); and milk pails (*Life *of*

Columba). *The ornamental pail (c) which was found in a river at Kinnegad (Co. Westmeath) was clearly a luxury item very probably looted from Finian's monastic township at nearby Clonard, and helps to complete our picture of the extraordinary richness of material culture in the Bogland Zone in Early Christian times. Numerous simple wooden vessels, made mostly from willow, were discovered in the excavation of Ballinderry crannóg on the borders of Westmeath and Offaly (Plate XIV). (For source of illustrations see List of Figure Plates.)*   87 route from Mag Lena to Uí Cheinnselaig ran south along the Corridor, and from there went past Clonfertmulloe, down the valley of the Nore through the kingdom of Ossory and into south Leinster via Gowran (Belach Gabráin).

Evidence for the existence of the Midland Corridor survives today in the form of a long appendage which forms part of the diocese of Meath (Plate VI) in its south-west corner. This strip of countryside, which almost bisects Co. Offaly, belongs to Meath diocese because the borders of this diocese coincide with the borders of de Lacy's Anglo-Norman lordship of Meath, which in turn was formed out of the twelfth-century kingdom of Mide (Plate IX). Fir Cell, and their strategically important Corridor, was seized by the Uí Néill of Mide in the fifth century[11] (Plate V). This Uí Néill occupation of Fir Cell offered an obvious advantage to travellers from Munster and northern Ireland, who found that by using the Corridor they could avoid passing through the kingdom of the cantankerous Leinstermen. Furthermore, a traveller coming from the northern half of Ireland (Leth Chuinn) had various options open to him as he reached the southern end of the Corridor. He might journey to the end of the Corridor as far as the Brosna river, where he could cross into Munster below Birr, or he might choose to turn off a few miles to the west and enter Connaught territory at Lusma before he had even crossed the Shannon. Equally, he might choose to follow the Corridor to Killyon (Cell Liadaine) and from there cross a tributary of the Brosna and reach the great Ossory monastery of Seirkieran only a few miles to the south. Should the traveller wish to turn off the Corridor to the right or left, he could follow his guides through the labyrinth into Leinster on the one side, or into Delbna on the other. Another advantage, then, which the road through Fir Cell offered the long-distance traveller was—in addition to its safety, and monastic hostelries—its essentially inter-tribal character.

The number of major events—sometimes of national significance—which took place along this twenty-five mile strip of territory also vouches for its strategic importance in the life of

42

The Roscrea Brooch probably dates to the late eighth century and comes from a major monastic settlement which, like Birr and Durrow, lay at the centre of a network of communications in ancient Ireland. Roscrea was also the home of the eighth-century Book of Dimma, Fig. 43c, which was found near that centre. Some of Roscrea's impressive twelfth-century Romanesque architecture still survives today.

About half a mile to the east of the main monastic complex lay Monaincha (Figs. 11 and 12 above), which provided a retreat for anchorites.

ancient Ireland. These were events of an inter-tribal character, which involved either the holding of ecclesiastical synods and the proclamation of ecclesiastical laws, or battles between major political confederacies in the northern and southern halves of Ireland. We might begin by citing the synod of Mag Lena convened in *c*. A.D. 630 to decided the crucial question of the dating of Easter in the Early Irish Church. Mag Lena was the plain constituting the northern end of the Midland Corridor and included the monasteries of Durrow and Rathan. Clearly, the synod was held at a monastery in Mag Lena, and Rathan suggests itself, from the evidence available, as the most likely location for this assembly, whose deliberations were discussed at length in places as far apart as Rome and Iona.[12] In 737 Terryglass (Tír dá Glas) was chosen as the location for a royal parley or *Ríg dál* between the reigning highking, Áed Allán, and Cathal, king of Munster.[13] In the following century (859) the highking, Maelsechnaill I, convened a crisis assembly at Rahugh (Ráth Áeda) on the Great Esker near the northern entrance to the Midland Corridor.[14] The assembly at Rahugh was attended by the abbots of Clonard and distant Armagh, and by the kings of Munster and Ossory, and its purpose was to form a united front against the Vikings. The two southern kings clearly approached the meeting-place via the Midland Corridor. Not all north-south meetings were held on the line of the Midland Corridor, as is evident from the 'great royal assembly' (*Rígdál mór*) attended by the highking, Niall, and the Munster king, Feidlimid, at Cloncurry, (Cluain Conaire Tomáin) in 838.[15] But significantly, Cloncurry, too, was on the borders of Leinster and Brega, at one of the few crossing points between Uí Néill territory and Leinster.

The use of the Midland Corridor for more hostile activities between tribes, and even between corrupt and belligerent monasteries, is amply attested in the annals, particularly during the eighth century. In 742 the men of Ossory devastated the territories of Cénel Fhiachach and Delbna (Plate XIII).[16] The heart of Cenél Fhiachach territory lay in the later barony of Moycashel in Westmeath at the northern entrance to the Midland Corridor, while its ruling dynasty would have been the immediate Uí Néill overlords of Fir Cell, who occupied the Corridor further south. The Delbna were located to the west of the Midland Corridor and the Osraige attacked all of these tribes by entering the Corridor from the region of Seirkieran (Saiger) or Roscrea (Ros Cré) (Plates XIII and XIV). In 760 the monasteries of Clonmacnoise and Birr went to battle against each other at Móin Coisse Blae, and although the particular bog or *móin* has not been identified, it was almost certainly on the Corridor which was probably the only route from one monastery to the other.[17] Four years later Clonmacnoise was again at war, this time busily slaying 200 of the *familia* of Durrow.[18] The cause of this last battle was probably due to the burial of the highking, Domnall, in the cemetery at Durrow. Domnall, who had died in December 763, was the first of the Clann Cholmaín highkings, and he was buried in Durrow 'with honour and veneration'[19], his ancestors most likely being interred in the royal cemetery at Clonmacnoise. The loss of revenue that could ensue from this change in funeral arrangements proved too much for the worldly monks of Clonmacnoise and so they slaughtered their rivals at Durrow in the following year. In 775 the highking, Donnchad, led an invading army almost certainly down the Midland Corridor, when we are told he 'committed great devastation in the borders of the Munstermen'.[20] In the following year this was assuredly the case because in a 'destructive battle' between the Munstermen and the Uí Néill, we are informed that the monastery of Durrow was involved in the conflict, and Durrow was, of course, on the Midland Corridor.[21]

Records such as these underline the importance of a detailed geographical knowledge of early Ireland, since a picture emerges of northern and southern contacts being confined, by the physical barriers of bog and waste, along the lines of a great pass from Mag Lena to Birr. The traveller who crossed Mag Lena in the Dark Ages — just as the traveller who crosses it to-day—

a   b   c   d   e

43

Heads of Evangelists in illuminated Gospel Books for the Bogland Zone. These figures remind us that most of the Gospel Books which it is possible to identify with specific early Irish scriptoria come from the Midland Bogs, or from southern Leinster. The benign figure on the right (a) comes from the eighth-century Book of Moling *(from St Mullins, Co. Carlow). The severe St Matthew (b) from the* Book of Durrow *seems to wear the Early Irish tonsure which involved shaving the head above the forehead from ear to ear–a practice outlawed in England at the Synod of Whitby in A.D. 664. The*
body of the Evangelist in this seventh-century drawing copies contemporary Irish millefiori enamel work. The central portrait (c) is that of St Mark from the Book of Dimma *associated with eighth-century Roscrea (cf. Fig. 42). The portrait of St John (d) from the fragmentary Gospel bound in with the Stowe missal hails from either Lorrha or Terryglass (cf. Fig. 44). St John from the* Book of Mac Regol *(e) is the work of Mac Riagoil, abbot of Birr, who is described as a* scriba *at his death in A.D. 822.*

could not have failed to notice the magnificent line of the Great Esker, a glacial gravel ridge, which is at its most impressive proportions in this particular region. In early Ireland this portion of Eiscir Riada must have made an even deeper impression than it does today, since in ancient times travellers from north to south were virtually compelled to pass that way. It is little wonder, therefore that early Irish tradition believed that Eiscir Riada constituted the line of an ancient division of Ireland into two halves between Conn, the champion of the north, and Mug, the Munster hero, thus giving us the terms *Leth Cuinn* and *Leth Mugha* ('Conn's Half' and 'Mug's Half') for Northern and Southern Ireland respectively.[22] Many prominent Irish monasteries such as Clonard, Clonmacnoise and Rahugh availed of the good drainage of Eiscir Riada and its related eskers for their siting.

The Midland Corridor, then, gave travellers access to the northern and southern halves of Ireland, otherwise separated from each other by miles of marsh and bog. The monasteries which lay within this great area of bogland, however, were in constant touch with each other, not only along the Corridor but also in an east-west direction. We find that the bogland produced its own monastic confederation which flourished within the safety of its intractable wilderness, and which exploited the considerable amount of fertile land which lay sealed off in long meandering strips within the waste. These monasteries stretched from Kildare and Clonard, on the eastern fringes of the bogs, to Clonmacnoise, Lorrha and Terryglass on its western front along the Shannon. To begin with, we find that some of these great houses – although situated many miles apart–were ruled by the same superiors, such as Clonard and Kildare which were governed by Abbot Dodimóc (+ 748),[23] or Killeigh (Cell Achid Drummo Fada) and Birr which were ruled by the same abbot, Senchán (+ 796).[24] It is remarkable that such monastic alliances paid scant attention to political or tribal boundaries. Clonard was a Leinster monastery situated across the border in southern Brega, while Kildare was in Uí Failge and controlled by the dynasty of Uí Fáeláin. Similarly, Killeigh was another great house of Uí Failge and firmly under their control, while Birr was on the border between Uí Néill and Munster territory (Plate XIV).

Sometimes a sudden disaster lifts the curtain of silence on monastic organization in the Bogland Zone and reveals complex monastic alliances, as in the case of the record of a Viking raid in 845 on the Rock of Dunamase (Dún Masc),[25] a fortress in the heart of Loígis territory (Co. Leix, Plate XIV). The vice-abbot or *secnap* 'of Kildare and other monasteries' was slain during that raid, and sheltering along with him in the Loígis stronghold was the abbot of the combined monasteries of Terryglass (Tír dá Glais) near the Shannon in Munster, and of Clonenagh (Cluain Ednech) in Co. Leix. Clonenagh, situated in Loígis territory on the foot-hills of the Slieve Bloom mountains, was relatively near Dunamase, but Kildare and Terryglass were far away at opposite ends of the Bogland Zone. Yet all of these monasteries were represented in that gathering on the Rock of Dunamase in 845. Some of these monastic alliances were probably temporary affairs, but we are still ignorant of the reasons which caused them to form and to dissolve, or re-form along new lines. For instance, while Clonenagh was united, as we have seen, to Terryglass under the rule of Abbot Áed in 845, the *Félire Óengussa* (*Martyrology of Óengus*) commemorates the memory of an earlier alliance in which Clonenagh in Loígis and Saggart (Tech Sacra) in Uí Dúnchada (Co. Dublin, Plate XII) may have both provided a monastic retreat for a holy man, called Mo-Sacru mac Senáin.[26] But one thing is clear: the geography of the Bogland Zone facilitated communication between all these monastic houses.

One reason for the peculiar Leinster qualities of certain monasteries, which lay outside Leinster altogether, and even—as in the case of Clonard—in hostile country, was that these religious houses had been founded by Leinstermen in areas which, in the sixth century, were still under strong Leinster influence. Clonard, founded by Finian, a south Leinster saint, is a case in point;[27] and the association of Brigit of Kildare with houses in Mide and even further afield in Tethba is explained by the same reason, namely Leinster's former extension as far as Ushnagh before the battle of Druim Deirrge in A.D. 516.[28] It is more difficult to explain the close Leinster connections with monasteries in the Shannon basin, such as Terryglass Lorrha and Holy Island on Lough Derg (Inis Celtra). These monasteries were connected with Leinster not only through tales which told of the Leinster origins of their founders, but their essentially Leinster character was preserved through centuries of separation from the territories of the Leinstermen. Mo-Chóeme of Terryglass, Cóemgen (Kevin) of Glendalough and Cóemán of Anatrim (Enach Truimm) in Loígis were all alleged in the *Félire Óengussa* to have been brothers.[29] This information was based on a misreading of their genealogy, but while it is highly unlikely that they were brothers, they were all claimed to belong to the Uí Náir, a branch of the Dál Messin Corb.[30] The Dál Messin Corb, as we have seen, were once the dominant dynasty of Leinster along with the Dál Chormaic, at a time when Leinster's territory was much more extensive than in later times.[31]

Traditions concerning the founding fathers of the monasteries in the Shannon basin are very confused, but even in spite of the confusion a strong Leinster dimension remains. Colum, the founder of Inis Celtra on Lough Derg (+ 549), for instance, was of the Leinster Uí Crimthannáin, and we are told that his successor, Nadcáem, had Colum's body entombed in Terryglass.[32] This is a hagiographical way of stating that Terryglass was the head of a *paruchia* which included Inis Celtra. Yet another tradition ascribed the founding of Inis Celtra to Caimín, a holy man who died in A.D. 644. Rhodán, the patron of Lorrha, is shown in hagiography as a close friend of the Leinsterman, Finian, who founded Clonard,[33] while Fintán (+ 603) of Clonenagh—a key monastery in the Midland confederacy—was alleged to have founded that house in Uí Failge at the instigation of Colum of Inis Celtra and Terryglass.[34] Senán of Scattery Island (Inis Cathaig) in the lower Shannon was claimed in tradition to have succeeded Máedóc of Ferns in Uí Cheinnselaig.[35] We need to be cautious about making too much of the tribal origin of saints, since they were clearly free to move across tribal boundaries in somewhat the same way as entertainers and the learned classes. Nor indeed were all the Midland saints from Leinster. Finán of Kinnity (Cend Eitig) in Fir Cell on the Midland Corridor, for instance, was of the Corcu Duibne, a Kerry tribe who were neighbours of the Ciarraige, while his neighbour, Molua of Clonfertmulloe, hailed from the Corcu Oiche in Co. Limerick.[36]

In the eighth and early ninth centuries the monastic confederacy in the Bogland Zone took on a more clearly defined aspect in the form of the Céli Dé movement. This was a puritanical reform movement born of a reaction to the materialism and decadence of such centres as Clonmacnoise, Birr and Durrow. The founders of the movement, Máelruain of Tallaght (Tamhlachta) and Dublitir of Finglas (Finn Glas), both from monasteries in Co. Dublin (Plate XII), set up centres far away from the Bogland Zone, but these centres and others such as Fahan (Othain) on the Inishowen peninsula in Donegal soon fell victim to Viking attacks. The heart of the movement seems to have grown up across the Bogland Zone and included Terryglass under Máel Ditruib, who died in 840, and who was an anchorite and disciple of Máelruain of Tallaght.[37] Loch Cré, an island near Roscrea (cf. Fig. 11), harboured the Céli Dé ascetic, Elair (+ 807); while Lorrha had close associations with Máelruain of Tallaght.[38] Rathan was connected with the movement through the ecclesiastical dynasty of Uí Suanaigh; while Óengus the famous author of the *Félire* or *Martyrology*, was a monk of Clonenagh in Leix, who had also close associations with Coolbanagher (Cúl Bendchuir) in Mag Rechet on the borders of Loígis and Uí Failge, and with Dysart Enos (Dísert Óengusa) near the Rock of Dunamase in Leix.[39] The obituary of Aedán of Rahan, for instance, and that of Máelruain of Tallaght are entered side by side in the *Annals of Ulster* under A.D. 792, and both are described as *milites Christi* or *Céli Dé*.[40] An ecclesiastical *Law*, presumably designed, like others of its kind, to curb the violence of eighth-century life, was proclaimed by the Uí Saunaigh of Rahan in 743 and yet again in 748.[41] In the latter year Ua Suanaigh's Law was 'proclaimed' over the whole of *Leth Cuinn* or the Northern half of Ireland. Óengus, who wrote his *Félire* in the reign of Áed Oirdnide, the Uí Néill highking (797-819), began his education and novitiate at Clonenagh, and spent his early years as an ascetic among the Loígis and Uí Failge. This phase of his career is enshrined in the names of two monastic retreats or 'deserts' where he sought the solitude of the trackless waste, namely Dísert Bethech on the Nore, a few miles above Ballybrophy, and Dysart Enos near Dunamase.[42] It was while visiting Coolbanagher, to the north of Dunamase, that Óengus was inspired to write his *Félire* or *Calendar of Saints*, and this work was later finished during his stay at Tallaght. In spite of his prominent contribution to the Tallaght scriptorium, Óengus was, from first to last, a saint and scholar of the boggy wilderness of his childhood, as the following verses from the *Leabhar Breac* (*Speckled Book*) illustrate so beautifully:[43]

> Óengus out of the assembly of Heaven
> Here are his tomb and his bed.
> It is hence he went to Death
> On Friday to holy Heaven.
> In Clonenagh he was reared,
> In Clonenagh he was buried,
> In Clonenagh of the many crosses
> He first read his psalms.'

Óengus was not the only Céli Dé who was engaged in literary pursuits; indeed the whole movement was characterized by an interest in liturgical reform and the production of monastic rules which were in keeping with its puritanical ideals. Óengus's superior at Tallaght, Máelruain (+ 792), produced the *Rule of the Céli Dé* and perhaps a hymn and penitential, and he may have had a hand in compiling the *Martyrology of Tallaght*.[44] The so-called *Notes on the*

Customs of Tallaght were probably compiled at Terryglass, and certainly owe much to the hand of Máeldithruib of that monastery, who died in 841.[45] From this period also we have the *Teist Choemáin*, or *Coeman's Testimony on Sinchell's School*, which describes the monastic *Rule* of Killeigh in Uí Failge in the time of Sinchell the Younger in the sixth century. This work was written *c*.A.D. 800.[46]

The ninth century was not the only period in which the monks of the Bogland and their monasteries led the field in the production of books in ancient Ireland. From the earliest times for which documentation survives, ecclesiastics from the Bogland monasteries were either associated with the authorship of important works, or they are mentioned in documents in a context which suggests that seemingly unimportant establishments in later centuries were houses of learning in the Early Christian period.

One of the earliest Irish historical sources, apart from annals and genealogies, is the *Letter of Cummian to Abbot Ségéne of Iona* written in connection with the Easter controversy and the synod of Mag Lena in 632-3. Cummian, the author of this Letter, was a monk either of Durrow or some other monastery in Mag Lena (Plate XIV), while the *Letter* was probably delivered to Iona by Ernéne, a monk of Clonmacnoise.[47] We have another *Letter* written shortly after this period in 640 from John, pope-elect, and the Clergy of Rome to the Clergy of northern Ireland, which is addressed (among others) to Columbanus and Saranus. These are usually identified as Colmán moccu Telduib, bishop and abbot of Clonard (+ 654) from South Leinster, and Sarán Ua Critáin (+ 662) of Tisaran (Tech Saráin) in Delbna Ethra to the west of the Midland Corridor in Offaly (Plate XIV).[48] The so-called *Irish Augustine* was written by a monk of the Bogland Zone as is clear from a reference to his two religious brethern, Bathanus and Manchianus. These have been identified as Báetán moccu Cormaicc (i.e. of the Dál Chormaic of Leinster), abbot of Clonmacnoise who died in 664, and Manchán, abbot of Mundrehid (Men-droichet) on the borders of Loígis and Ossory in Co. Leix (Plate XIV), who died in 652.[49]

Scarcely a mile to the west of Mundrehid is the site of Clonfertmulloe (Cluain Ferta Molua) which was the home of a prominent writer, Laidcenn mac Baíth-Bannaig, who died in 661. Laidcenn is stated in later tradition to have been the author of the so-called *Lorica of Gildas*, and he is also credited with writing an abridgement of the *Moralia* of Gregory the Great, known as *Egloga de Moralibus Job*.[50] In the *Commentary on the Catholic Epistles* written in the second half of the seventh century,[51] Manchian, *doctor noster*, and Lodcen, are cited as authorities consulted, in a list which includes the Church Fathers, and it seems clear that Manchán of Mundrehid and Laidcenn of Clonfertmulloe are referred to here yet again. Indeed, Kenney and Esposito believed that the author of this *Commentary* was the same as the writer of the *Irish Augustine*. The essential Bogland character of the literary circle in which the author moved is borne out by a reference to Bannbán, identified as Bannbán *sapiens* of Kildare, who died in 686.[52] The names of the monks who dominated this literary circle and whose works were carried to Continental monasteries are sufficiently rare to enable us to identify them accurately with Laidcenn, Manchán and Bannbán of the Irish Midlands. While the works in which their names appear may not necessarily have even been written by Irishmen in all cases, nevertheless the references to these men testify to the existence of a high standard of learning in the scriptoria not only of prominent houses such as Clonmacnoise, but also in seemingly lesser places such as Mundrehid and Clonfertmulloe. Monks of these houses achieved a scholarly reputation in the seventh century which went far beyond their Bogland home, and indeed far beyond Ireland itself. The libraries which now house the manuscripts preserving the memory of their learning are as far apart as Rouen, Verona, Vienna, Karlsruhe and Leningrad.

Clearly, the greater houses of the Bogland area were not without their scholars. Bannbán of   93

Kildare has already been mentioned, and his older contemporary, Ailerán the Wise (*sapiens*) from Clonard, who died of plague in 665, is credited with the authorship of at least two ecclesiastical works.[53] These include a work on the mystical interpretation of the genealogy of Christ, and a rhyming Latin discourse on the Eusebian Canons, or those sections of the Gospels which either the evangelists have in common, or which are peculiar to each gospel. Kildare also produced a Latin *Life* of its foundress Brigit, written by Cogitosus in the middle of the seventh century. While this work is of limited historical importance, it testifies to the early growth of Brigit's cult and to the riches and power of Kildare in the early seventh century.[54] The *Old Irish Life of Brigit*, although dating in its present form to the ninth century, is, according to Dr Ó hAodha, a translation of an early eighth-century Latin *Life*, compiled perhaps in nearby Fir Tulach.[55] An apochryphal tradition found in the notes to the *Félire Óengusso* names Conláed, first bishop of Kildare, as one of the 'three chief artisans' of Ireland, and chief craftsman of St. Brigit.[55a] Such a tradition would have been meaningless were it not inspired by the magnificence of Kildare craftsmanship in the Celtic period.

Before leaving the seventh century we may notice two works written outside Ireland at this time which also have some connection with the Bogland Zone. The first of these, Adomnan's *Life of Columba*, written by the Iona abbot some time between 679 and 704, has several references to Leinster ecclesiastics which suggests that Iona felt it important to keep close contact with the monastic houses of that Province. In addition to stories about Munnu, and contacts with the Leinster seaboard, Adomnán mentions Durrow, Clonmacnoise and Terryglass (*Ecclesia Duorum Agri Rivorum*); and he also mentions individuals such as Brendán of Birr and Cainnech of Aghaboe (Achad Bó) in Upper Ossory (Co. Leix) (Plate XIV).[56] There is a reference, too, to *Colmán moccu Loígse* or 'Colman of the tribe of Loígis', a Leinster bishop, and we are told of one Iogenan, a Pictish priest, living among the Leinstermen, who possessed a hymnal written by Columba.[57] Indeed, Adomnán shows such a detailed knowledge of Durrow and its monastic buildings that a convincing case can be made (Appendix) for this royal abbot and scholar to have studied at Durrow in his youth.

The second work referring to Leinster although written outside Ireland, is the *Life of Columbanus* written by Jonas, a monk of Bobbio *c.*A.D. 640, which provides a few vital scraps of information on the Irish background of one of the greatest missionary saints in Continental Europe. Jonas informs us of Columbanus's Leinster origin and states that he studied in Ireland under Comgall of Bangor.[58] The *Life* of Comgall in turn claims that that northern Irish saint began his ecclesiastical and scholarly career under Fintán of Clonenagh, 'situated among the Loígis in Northern Leinster beside the foot-hills of the Slieve Bloom'.[59] It is indeed likely that Columbanus himself grew up close to the great Leinster centres of learning in Uí Failge at the very time when that dynasty controlled the kingship of all Leinster.

Finally, at Clonard, which had especially close contacts with Kildare in the seventh and eighth centuries, later tradition claimed that its founder, the Leinsterman Finian, had tutored all the great monastic founders of Ireland, and that his 'School' at Clonard numbered no less than 3000 students.[60] The number may be exaggerated, but seen in the context of an ecological and historical study of the Bogland Zone, the Clonard tradition can no longer be regarded as an isolated and extravagant claim, but reinforces the picture of the heart of Early Irish learning being located between the Shannon and the Plain of Liffey.

It is now clear that this Bogland region, stretching from Terryglass and Clonmacnoise in the west, to Kildare and Clonard in the east, was unique in the British Isles and in Early Medieval Europe at large, for the extraordinary number of prominent monastic houses which grew up there and which kept the closest contact with each other while paying little heed to tribal or dynastic boundaries. The seventh century in particular saw the flowering of learning in these monastic communities, and for a region which supported such an intense pursuit of scholarship, there is no other parallel in either the rest of the Celtic world or in Anglo-Saxon England. We cannot ignore the existence of very important literary centres elsewhere, such as at Armagh, Bangor or Iona—at which latter house the earliest Irish and Scottish annals came into being.[61] Similarly, St David's in Wales, Lindisfarne, Jarrow, York, Lichfield and Canterbury all housed important scriptoria in the seventh century. But none of these isolated centres of learning can compare with the elaborate monastic network of great houses such as Clonmacnoise, Lorrha, Terryglass, Birr, Seirkieran, Durrow, Kinnity, Killeigh, Clonenagh, Clonard and Kildare, all of which grew to greatness in the safety of the Midland Bogs.

It is in this new historical and geographical context that we must now view the arguments

44

45

Ancient Irish Gospels, like other sacred books of Early Christendom and Islam, were treated as relics in their own right and their pages were embellished with ornament to the point where the words of the actual text became quite obscured (cf. Fig. 48). An Irish illuminated sacred text was enshrined like the bones of a saint, in a reliquary of cumdach, *which in turn was preserved for safe keeping and transport in an ornamental leather satchel.*

The cumdach *or case of the Stowe Missal is made of oak boards plated with silver and inlaid with gems and ornamental metal. The inscription on the left-hand edge of the base (illustrated here) claims it was made by Dunchadh Ó Taccáin of the community of Clonmacnoice* (do muintir Cluana). *Elsewhere on the shrine a prayer for Donnchadh son of Brian Boru, king of Dál gCais, 1014-64, and for Mac Raith, king of Cashel, 1045-52, suggests the case was made c. 1050 by a craftsman from Clonmacnoise. Over three*

centuries later the top cover was replaced or re-decorated under the patronage of Philip O'Kennedy, king of Ormond (c. 1371-1381). Philip, his queen Áine, and the comharba or hereditary abbot, Gilla-Ruadáin Ó Macáin, are commemorated in an inscription on this renovated side. The name of the comharba, 'Servant of Ruadán' shows that he was the hereditary Warden of the church and lands of St Ruadán of Lorrha, Co. Tipperary (Plate XIV).

Even fewer satchels have survived than book-shrines, although references in saints' Lives show that satchels were standard equipment in every monastery and that books might even hang in their satchels in libraries when not in use. The leather satchel or tiag illustrated here was not used for a book, but for the shrine of St Máedóc of Ferns (cf. Fig. 35). Some of its interlace is not unlike that on the satchel for the Book of Armagh, whose metal shrine we know was commissioned by the high-king, Donnchad, in 939. It was Donnchad's father, Flann Sinna, who commissioned the Cross of Flann at Clonmacnoise.

concerning the monastic home of the *Book of Durrow*, which on art-historical grounds is agreed to be a product of the seventh-century Hiberno-Saxon School, but which is variously claimed to be Irish, Northumbrian or Scottish (Dál Riadic) in origin. Arguments based on art-historical grounds are hampered by an undue element of subjective analysis, and in view of the evidence provided by historical geography it seems clear that the most appropriate context for the *Book of Durrow* is provided by the Bogland Zone in the seventh century. Not only was this the time when the study of biblical exegisis was at its height in this region, but Durrow, lying as it was on the Midland Corridor, participated not only in the mainstream of east-west contacts across the monastic confederacy, but also lay on the principal thoroughfare between northern and southern Ireland. Durrow, then, situated on the crossroads in the very heart of this area, was the obvious home for the *Book* that bears its name.

We know that by 764 Durrow had become so degenerate that its monks were engaged in warfare with Clonmacnoise in a struggle to usurp the rights of the latter to house the mausoleum of the Uí Néill highkings.[62] Such an incident bespeaks wealth, which clearly had taken centuries to accumulate. The *Book of Durrow*, however magnificent, reflects a materialism, aesthetic taste, a degree of leisure, and an economic surplus which were against all the principles of the monastic founders. Durrow is likely to have been just such a place where all these elements were likely to flourish in the seventh century. According to O'Flaherty, the author of *Ogygia*, the *Book of Durrow* once had a silver shrine with an inscription to the effect that this case had been commissioned by Flann Sinna who reigned as highking from 879 to 916.[63] We know from other evidence that King Flann was a great patron of monastic craftsmen and artists, and it is significant that his son, the highking Donnchad, had the *Book of Armagh* enshrined in a precious cover in 939.[64] The *Book of Durrow* is mentioned as being at Durrow by O'Clery in the *Martyrology of Donegal* (1628), and Conall Mageoghagan, the compiler and translator of the *Annals of Clonmacnoise*, has left us the horrific anecdote of the use of this manuscript treasure to cure sick livestock when dipped in water.[65] Conall also wrote an entry in the *Book of Durrow* in 1633.[66] We have a clear and impressive historical and geographical context to argue for a Durrow origin for the book in the middle seventh century, and we know the work existed at Durrow from the ninth to the seventeenth century. The new picture which emerges showing Durrow's central position in the monastic ecology of the seventh century does not indeed prove that the gospels were actually penned at Durrow but it does somewhat dramatically shift the burden of proof on to that school of thought which would favour a Northumbrian origin (see Appendix).

The *Book of Durrow* was not the only artistic production of the Bogland monasteries, for what we find true of scholarly production was also true on the artistic front, namely, that the bogs afforded necessary protection for craftsmen and artists to work in comparative peace. The eighth-century *Book of Dimma* is firmly associated by its colophon with the monastery of Roscrea and the work survived in the neighbourhood after the Dissolution of the Monasteries until *c.*1800.[67] Roscrea, lying near the *Belach Mór* or Great Road from Leinster into Fir Cell, Munster and Ossory, was, like Durrow, on a cross-roads of cultural influences. It was but a few miles from Clonfertmulloe and Mundrehid which housed the scholars of the seventh century. The *Stowe Missal* is a liturgical and artistic production sponsored by the Céli Dé movement in the closing years of the eighth century and was housed at Lorrha in the early eleventh century. The work has also Terryglass connections, and the last person commemorated in the *Memento of the Dead* is Máelruain of Tallaght who died in 792.[68] We can be certain, however, that it is a product of the Bogland Zone, even if Tallaght had a hand in its production. Mac Regol, abbot of Birr, who died in 822, was very probably the painter and the scribe of the Gospels which bear his name in the Bodleian Library in Oxford,[69] and the importance of Birr, situated on the frontier between Munster, Ossory and the Uí Néill, makes it virtually certain to have housed talented craftsmen and scholars.

The number of illuminated gospels which survive from the Bogland monasteries represents only a fraction of the original output, just as the names of seventh-century biblical scholars of repute are but a handful that survive, while most of their works are irretrievably lost. In addition to evidence from sources such as the *Cogadh Gaedhel*, for instance, which refers to the 'drowning of shrines, relics and books' seized by Limerick Vikings in the Shannon basin *c*.922,[70] we must also consider the wholesale burning of monastic scriptoria and libraries in the Viking onslaught of the ninth century, and by Irish enemies in every century—not to mention accidental burning. There are also references in Irish sources to individual writers and craftsmen who achieved notoriety for their great output of work and its high quality. We are told of Cairnech Móel (the bald), for instance, alleged to have been a scribe of St Ciarán of Saiger (Seirkieran, Plate XIV) who wrote a 'wondrous book' which was still to be seen at Seirkieran in the eleventh century.[71] Yet another apochcryphal tradition speaks of Daig mac Cairill, 'a smith, a craftsman and excellent scribe' who made 300 bells, 300 croziers and 300 Gospels. He was the chief artist or *primcherd* of Ciarán of Seirkieran[72].No one need seriously accept these legends at their face value, but they are of use to the historian. They reinforce the tradition that Seirkieran, the greatest monastery of Ossory, like Clonmacnoise, the royal chapel of the highkings—both situated in the Bogland Zone—once had impressive scriptoria, and teams of talented craftsmen. This is precisely what we should expect. These legends ought also to suggest to archaeologists one of the reasons why Dark Age metalwork, sculpture and manuscript art of Early Ireland and elsewhere should look so alike. This was not only because artists borrowed ideas from each other, but also because really talented and creative individuals, such as Daig mac Cairill, were capable of working in all three media. The monastic craftsmen and their clerical masters were in turn dependent on patronage from the warrior aristocracy. The lay lords not only endowed the monasteries with land and precious metal, but they might also commission work from monastic craftsmen. We read in the early twelfth-century *Life* of Colmán mac Luacháin,[72a] for instance, that a goldsmith of the Lann community of Tech Conán, in Fir Tulach in Mide, made a bridle of silver and gold which he personally delivered to the king of Uí Failge. This saint's *Life* is unreliable in regard to specific detail, but at least we can say that its compiler considered this incident as a plausible anecdote to present to readers who were themselves still part of a fully blown Gaelic society.

The *Life* of Mochuda presents us with the picture of that saint setting out from Clonfertmulloe, and heading north along the Midland Corridor to found Rahan, with two satchels or *scethas* filled with books on his shoulders.[73] Further south in the wilderness of Dísert Garad in northern Ossory, a note in the *Felire Óengussa* tells us about a holy man, Longarad coisfind, who had a very personal view of learning and who, perhaps with very good reason, hid his books when visited by St Columba! Longarad is described as 'a sage of learning (*súid légind*), of history (*senchais*), of jurisprudence (*brethemnais*) and of poetry (*filidechtai*)'.[74] The number of references to lost books and libraries in the Irish Midlands seems endless, and we might end with the detailed account by Giraldus Cambrensis of a magnificent illuminated Gospel Book (Fig. 46) housed at Kildare.[75] Knowing the richness and political power wielded by that monastery under the rule of royal abbots of the Uí Dúnlainge, we have every reason to expect that the Kildare Gospels could rival the *Book of Kells* or the *Book of Lindisfarne* in magnificence. Already in the time of Cogitosus in the seventh century, Kildare had amassed great wealth and was using it to beautify its church. It was Robin Flower who first recognized nearly half a century ago that it was the Leinstermen who made the most significant contribution to Christian civilization within Ireland.[76] In particular, Flower identified Kildare as the monastic home of Sedulius and his Irish followers who distinguished themselves in the Carolingian Renaissance during the reign of Charles the Bald. The manuscripts with their Christian and Classical texts in Latin and Greek associated with Sedulius and his circle all contain marginal notes with strong Kildare and Leinster affinities, including invocations to St Brigit and sayings of that saint. An entire bardic poem survives from this collection of Continental material which celebrates the glories of a north Leinster ruler, Áed son of Diarmait, who seems to have belonged to the Uí Dúnlainge dynasty.[77] Áed's kingdom is understood in the poem to include the ancient centres of Roériu (Mullagh Reelion) and Maistiu (Mullaghmast), both located in Uí Muiredaig in southern Kildare (Plates XI and XII), as well as Cualu in the north-east, and those rich lands on the Curragh 'where Liffey flows in glory'. Flower believed that a whole contingent of Leinster scholars emigrated to the court of Charles the Bald perhaps as part of an embassy which reached the Frankish ruler from Ireland in 848.

In the field of metalwork and sculpture, too, the surviving evidence in museums and churchyards cannot be taken as truly representative. The annalistic record shows that the late eighth

46

The material which survives of Early Irish manuscript illumination reflects a complex and developed art-form which required centuries of skill and dedication to perfect. That being so, we are certain that what survives is a mere fraction of the original output. For secular literature we have a veritable catalogue of lost books from the Middle Ages. It is more difficult to assess the losses in the range of luxury liturgical productions. The illustration is taken from the British Library manuscript of The Topography of Ireland *by Giraldus Cambrensis which has the caption: 'The scribe writing the marvellous Kildare Gospels.' These Gospels, which are now lost, were described in detail by Giraldus and were once considered to be the same as the* Book of Kells. *This cannot have been the case. The*

Book of Kells *was kept in a Columban monastery in Uí Néill territory in the heart of Brega. Kildare on the other hand, was the ecclesiastical capital of Leinster and patronized by the Uí Dúnlainge kings (cf. Fig. 14). Giraldus knew Kildare well, and it was there he tells us he inspected this lost masterpiece on several occasions. Furthermore, he tells us a miracle story about the* Book of Kildare *which associated it with St Brigit. Clearly, it cannot have dated from her time in the sixth century, but from Gerald's description it must have dated from the Golden Age of Kildare,—from the time of Cogitosus c. 650 up to the opening of the Viking Age at 800. Giraldus tells us the work included illuminations of Christ in Majesty and of the symbols of the Four Evangelists, and he was in no doubt as to its priceless nature:*

> You will find them [these pictures and letters] so delicate and exquisite, so finely drawn, and the work of interlacing so elaborate, while the colours with which they are illuminated are so blended, and still so fresh, that you will be ready to assert that all this is the work of angelic, and not human skill. The more often and closely I scrutinize them, the more I am surprised, and always find them new, discovering fresh causes for increased admiration. [Translation, T. Wright, *Historical Works of Giraldus* (London 1863) p. 99. Text: *Topographia, ed. Dimlock, v, 123-4.*]

This is a rare outpouring of praise from a writer who lost no opportunity to highlight the bizarre and primitive aspects of a civilization he failed to understand. It underlines the loss of what was probably the greatest manuscript treasure of the Leinstermen, representing the finest caligraphic work of a people who had produced an endless stream of scholars, saints, and writers over seven centuries, ranging from Columbanus and Cogitosus in the Dark Ages, to Sedulius, Óengus the Céli Dé, and Archbishop Laurence O'Toole in later times.

47

48

The High Cross of Durrow (47) was probably erect-
ed by Abbot Dubtach, head of the Columban par-
uchia who died in A.D. 938. Although basically of
Northern or Leth Cuinn type, the ring of this cross
has Southern or Leth Mogha characteristics, which
is what we should expect at a monastery on the
crossroads of cultural exchange in the geographical
heart of ancient Ireland. Durrow was founded by
Columcille in the sixth century; it is mentioned by
Adomnán and by Bede in the eighth century; and is

described in medieval Irish sources as a church 'with
its books and learning; a devout city with a hundred
crosses'. This was the home of the seventh-century
Book of Durrow (48), which was preserved for cen-
turies here, and which was enshrined by the high-
king, Flann Sinna (A.D. 879-916). The Book was
still kept near the monastery when the annalist
Conal Mageoghagan saw it in the early seventeenth
century.

and early ninth centuries witnessed an upsurge in the production of shrines and buildings as
the Bogland monasteries grew richer and more decadent. A new gold and silver shrine was
made for the relics of Conláed, the first bishop of Kildare, in 800, while the relics of Finian at
nearby Clonard had been 'translated' in 776.[78] A new oratory (*oratorio novo*) was burnt at
Killeigh in Uí Failge in 805.[79] The late ninth and early tenth centuries saw the monastic
patrons concentrating more and more on stonework in their efforts to produce works of art
which could withstand Viking attack. The new styles in High Cross production which began in
Ossory as a result of new-found wealth from alliances with Scandinavian Dublin, spread north
and west across the Bogland Zone to Lorrha, Monaincha and Clonmacnoise on the Shannon.[80]
Durrow on the borders between Leth Cuinn and Leth Moga has a High Cross which is, in
accordance with its ambivalent geographical position, of transitional type between the Northern
and Southern variety of High Cross.[81] But the surviving fragments of cross-shafts from the
Bogland monasteries is again but a wretched fraction of what must have originally existed. I

99

48a

Daniel Maclise gave a highly romantic interpretation to The Marriage of Strongbow and Eva, *c. 1854 (National Gallery of Ireland). This marriage to Aoife, daughter of Dermot MacMurrough took place after the Anglo-Norman sack of Waterford in 1170. Nevertheless, the artist captured something of the essential ethos of that ceremony, since Irish ladies of royal blood constituted, in their own right, an essential ingredient for lending legitimacy to Celtic kingship. There had been several precedents for conquerors marrying the daughters of former Leinster kings in the Celtic centuries, as witnessed, for instance, by*

the marriage (c. A.D. 710) of Murchad, a leader of the Uí Dúnlainge, to Conchenn, daughter of the last Uí Máil king of Leinster. Murchad usurped that kingship and founded a dynasty which lasted for four centuries in control of the Province. Maclise paid great attention to antiquarian detail in this composition but the walls of Waterford have an authentic Celtic rather than Scandinavian appearance, and many of the weapons and jewellery of the Irish warriors (bottom right) were modelled on genuine artifacts dating to the Early and Late Bronze Ages rather than to the Celtic period.

have already cited the poem on 'Clonenagh of the many crosses' where Óengus the Céli Dé 'first read his psalms'. The allusion to 'many crosses' reminds us of the medieval plan of the monastery of St Mullins in Co. Carlow, which was drawn on a page of the *Book of Moling*, showing several crosses positioned about the old monastic city.[82] The *Life* of Mo-Chuda mentions the Cross of the Angels (*Crux Angelorum*) which stood 'outside the city' of Rahan, and another cross which stood near the door of the church, around which Mochuda promised to return on Resurrection Day and gather all his monks about him before leading them into Heaven.[83] A note in the *Leabhar Breac* on the Ua Suanaigh of Rahan tells how a local magnate, Máel Bresal son of Flann Léna, desecrated the Cross of Ua Suanaig while raiding near Rahan, and the same tract refers to this or another cross as the Cross of the Satirists at the same monastery.[84] Neither Rahan nor Clonenagh show much evidence above ground to-day for the existence of great crosses in stone from the Early Christian period, much less than for the existence of libraries and scholars capable of reading difficult works on biblical commentaries. Yet both of these houses once shared in the intellectual and artistic life which pervaded this entire zone in the Dark Ages. Where the nettle and ivy now luxuriate in the solitude of remote churchyards, was once the setting of a unique monastic civilization which prepared men like Columbanus for the court of the Merovingians.

CHAPTER X

Lords of the Wilderness

The Survival of the Gaelic Environment
from Dermot Mac Morrough to Owen O'Moore
1150 – 1600

49

The Rock of Dunamase, Co. Leix, in Ledwich's Antiquities of Ireland *(1790), showing the ruins of the later medieval stronghold of the O'More's. This impregnable fortress, known to Celtic Ireland as Dún Masc was the centre of Uí Crimthainn Áin power in the Dark Ages and passed under the control of the kings of Loígis by the tenth century. The O'More's, who were descended from the ancient Loígis kings, lost the place to the Anglo-Normans for a brief period, but returned and hung on to defend their rocky crag, rising 200 feet above the Great Heath of Maryborough, until its defences were finally dismantled by Cromwell's army in 1650.*

The end of the eleventh century and the opening of the twelfth ushered in a new era in Irish history. The Scandinavian settlers had become Christian, and while not fully integrated into the Gaelic order of things, nevertheless, they no longer posed a challenge to the survival of Gaelic life. From the Continent new monastic orders were being introduced into Ireland which threatened the existence of indigenous Celtic monasticism and its love of antiquarian learning, which was in turn rooted in the tribal loyalties of traditional scholars. The old tribal order of things was itself on the decline with the rise of new and ambitious dynasties, such as the O'Briens in Munster and MacMurroughs in Leinster, who were bent on establishing strong centralized dynastic monarchies which took little account of tribal autonomy. This was an era which witnessed a literary revival recalling earlier movements of the biblical exegetists and the Céli Dé of the seventh and eighth centuries. Like the new religious orders, the literary movement was continental in origin although local in ethos, and Ireland's

101

twelfth-century renaissance has left us three great manuscript compilations: *Leabor na hUidre* (*The Book of the Dun Cow*), Rawlinson B 502 (now at Oxford) and the *Book of Leinster*. Each of these great works constitutes a whole library of early Irish literature, history and genealogy in its own right, and it is fair to say that if all three codices had been lost in the later Middle Ages, then a sizeable portion of the secular sources for the history of ancient Ireland would have perished. For although these works were compiled in the twelfth century, they incorporate material from as early as the first half of the eighth century.

The cultural rescue operation which launched these three compilations on the Celtic world was based, yet again, in the monasteries of the Bogland Zone, and nowhere is this clearer than in the case of the *Book of Leinster*. The earlier name of this work was *Lebar na Núachong-bála*, or the *Book of Núachongbáil*, a place firmly identified with the townland of Noghaval in the parish of Stradbally, Co. Leix.[1] The earliest recorded name of the place was Tulach meic Comgaill (Plate XIV) and this small monastic foundation lay only two-and-a-half miles away from Dunamase (Dún Masc), headquarters of the Loígis in the twelfth century. The earliest mention of the *Book of Leinster* as *Lebar na Núachongbála* occurs in 1390 in the *Yellow Book of Lecan*[2] and while this title firmly connects the work with the Bogland Zone, it is unlikely that such a great manuscript was actually compiled at that obscure place in the twelfth century. The *Book of Leinster* has internal evidence connecting it with the O'Mores, the hereditary lords of Loígis, and Tulach meic Comgaill was in their territory. But the chief monastery of the Loígis was Clonenagh (Cluain Ednech, Plate XIV) whose founder, Fintán, was the patron saint of the O'Mores, and Clonenagh was a much more likely place for the undertaking of such a work, or part of it—since it was almost certainly not compiled by one scribe, much less than by one researcher. The research and collection of manuscript materials involved in the production of a compilation such as the *Book of Leinster* must have taken not one, but several scholars. Indeed, for the *Book of Leinster*, we know the names of two of these—Áed Ua Crimthainn, *coarb* of Colum of Terryglass, and bishop Finn of Kildare, who died in A.D. 1160.[3] Once again the old pattern reasserts itself, of co-operation between monasteries across the east-west axis of the Bogland Zone, between Terryglass in the extreme west (Plate XIV) and Kildare on the eastern fringe (Plate XII). What better place to co-ordinate the activities of these Bogland scholars than at Clonenagh, which had ancient ties with Terryglass and which must have possessed a treasure-house of ancient manuscripts. The editors of the *Book of Leinster* noted that Rory O'More (Ruaidhri Ó Mordha, slain in A.D. 1567), a chief of the Loígis who flourished as late as the sixteenth century, had a mortgage on Clonenagh then said to have been the residence of Uí Crimthainn, the *coarbs* or ecclesiastical rulers of Terryglass.[4] All this evidence identifies the *Book of Leinster* as a work undertaken among the Loígis, most likely at Clonenagh, with the co-operation of scholars from elsewhere in the monastic Bogland confederacy. Soon after its completion, however, the Book must have been moved for safety to

50

Noghaval or Oughaval (Núachongbáil) about two-and-a-half miles from the Rock of Dunamase in Co. Leix is the earliest recorded home of the Book of Leinster *which was originally called* Lebar na Núachongbáil *or* The Book of Noghaval.

102

Núachongbáil beside the Loígis stronghold at Dunamase.

Lebor na hUidre was also very likely the product of a team of researchers, one of whom was the scribe Máelmuire of Clonmacnoise, who was slain by brigands in that monastery in A.D. 1106.[5] Oskamp has claimed that Máelmuire and his team had access to material from Armagh, Monasterboice—and, significantly, from nearby Durrow.[6] Once again we are dealing with a compilation from the western end of the Bogland Zone, which, among other precious items, has preserved for us the earliest version of the most important epic of ancient Ireland, the *Táin Bó Cuailgne* (*Cattle-Raid of Cooley*). Finally, we come to the Oxford Bodleian compilation known as MS Rawlinson B 502. This impersonal catalogue title refers to two separate works now bound together. The first section, consisting of twelve folios, contains a fragment of the *Annals of Tigernach* and derives from Clonmacnoise. The second and largest part of the book is a Leinster compilation, containing largely material of Leinster interest which was compiled some time after A.D. 1120.[7] Rawlinson B 502 contains the most extensive early genealogical collection covering the whole of Ireland. This great genealogical work which formed the basis of later compilations on a similarly massive scale must be treated as a 'compilation within a compilation' as it were, for it is clear that there are different chronological stages in its composition.[8] A noticeable feature of the Rawlinson genealogies is the minute detail with which the Leinster tribes are dealt with, and the attention that is given to the Uí Failge in particular. The Uí Failge genealogies are shown to be exceptionally rich in collateral lines forming tribal subdivisions such as Uí Failge Iarmotha, Clann Colcan, Uí Colcan ó Tech Cainén, Clann Rotaidi, Clann Colcan i Liphi and Uí Riacáin—all of whom are supplied with pedigrees, together with the mention of numerous other obscure septs of which only the names are given.[9] The Uí Failge section also includes a poem on the royal fortress of Rathangan (Ráth Imgáin, Plate XII), which is a type of metrical king-list on the sixth and seventh-century kings of Uí Failge.[10] Elsewhere in this genealogical compilation there are frequent references to Kildare, which lies only about five miles south-east of Rathangan (Plate XII). There are references to Conláed, first bishop of Kildare, and to Brandub, an Uí Dúnlainge royal bishop of that house in the seventh century.[11] Another Kildare abbot, Áed Dub, is also mentioned, and two abbesses by the name of Muirenn are noted, as well as Brigit the foundress who is mentioned five times.[12] There is a note alongside the name of a certain Gilla Comgaill, son of Donncuan, a prince of the Uí Muiredaig branch of Uí Dúnlainge, who was slain in A.D. 1041 according to the annals.[13] This note states: 'It was he who was taken from Kildare and slain on the Curragh by Murchad mac Dúnlaing.'[14] This Murchad, as is clear from the genealogy, was Gilla Comgaill's uncle. Notes such as this are rare in an Irish genealogical collection, and the presence of this detailed information relating to Kildare, when taken along with numerous other references to that monastery, together with the interest in neighbouring Uí Failge families, is strongly suggestive of a Kildare origin for the Leinster genealogies compiled in Rawlinson B 502. Kildare, although traditionally in Uí Failge and Fothairt territory, was controlled by the Uí Dúnlainge kings of Leinster. It was, therefore, ideally placed to gather information on a wider level dealing with the entire Province and also for collecting local material on Uí Failge and Loígis tribes. The poem on Rathangan is matched by another in the *Book of Leinster* collection of genealogies in which Áed Dub, the Uí Dúnlainge bishop of Kildare, addresses his royal brother, Áed Find.[15] It appears, then, that Rawlinson B 502 has not only a Leinster origin but its genealogies, at least, were very likely compiled at Kildare on the eastern fringes of the Bogland Zone, and Kildare may well have been the monastic home for the entire compilation (apart from the *Tigernach* fragment). This conclusion ties in well with earlier evidence linking the school of Sedulius and his Irish Carolingian circle in the ninth century with the scriptorium of Kildare. It was just such a monastery which could provide historians of the twelfth century with an 103

51a

b

These two antiquities from Clonmacnoise remind us that this monastic city on the banks of the Shannon remained for centuries in the forefront of European craftsmanship and learning. The tombstone commemorates Suibhne mac Máelumai, the hermit and scribe of Clonmacnoise who died in 891. Suibhne's reputation as a writer and a scholar had reached the court of King Alfred of Wessex, where his death as 'the best scholar among the Irish' was noted in the Anglo-Saxon Chronicle. The crozier-top is from the Crozier of the Abbots of Clonmacnoise and dates from the middle of the eleventh century. It displays strong Scandinavian influence in its art-forms. The manuscript output which still survives from Clonmacnoise includes a series of Annals; *various* Lives of the founder, St Ciarán, *and* Lebor na hUidre *or* The Book of the Dun Cow *which dates to c. A.D. 1100. Among the extensive architectural remains that still survive at Clonmacnoise are two High Crosses from the ninth and tenth centuries (cf. Figs. 8 and 44).*

archive suitable for their needs. We may never reach agreement on the precise origin of Rawlinson B 502, but it would seem that a title such as the *Book of Kildare* is much more appropriate for this precious codex than a mere catalogue number in the Bodleian library.

The importance of this Bogland region in the life of Celtic Ireland cannot be overstated. As long as the ecology of this distinctive landscape remained substantially unchanged, Celtic Ireland lingered on alongside Anglo-Normans and English alike, finding the well-springs of its cultural existence deep within this expanse of boggy waste. One of the most ominous events for the future tragic struggle between *Gael* and *Gaill*, or Irish and Foreigners, was the assassination of Hugo de Lacy, first Anglo-Norman lord of Meath, while he was supervising the building of his castle at Durrow.[16] De Lacy may, or may not, have appreciated the immense strategic importance of the Midland Corridor which his Durrow Castle would have dominated. His royal master, Henry II of England, seems to have been largely concerned with securing the Irish sea-ports once held by the Scandinavians, while other Anglo-Norman adventurers conquered Celtic territory piecemeal without any overall strategy guiding their operations. The sea-ports meant little to native Irish kings, whose world centred on landed estates in the interior of the island. Frequently the best land—on the carboniferous limestone of the Central Plain—was separated from the coast by high mountains. So, the cultural life of the Celtic nation had its economic base on the limestone drift surrounding the central mass of Bogland where so many of the ancient kingdoms met in a labyrinth of passes and roads (Plates III and XIII). The failure of the Anglo-Norman invaders and their successors to appreciate the importance of conquering this Bogland Zone meant that Celtic civilization continued to flourish here under traditional Gaelic aristocracies—O'Connor and O'Dempsey in Offaly; O'More in Leix; Mageoghagan, Molloy and Fox in Fir Cell; and Ely O'Carroll in North Munster (Plate X). This was the situation which still prevailed when the Tudor surveyor drew his panoramic map of the Southern Midlands *c.* 1560 (Frontispiece). It meant, in effect, that a Celtic bloc continued to dominate Irish life from its traditional centre of gravity, and formed a bridge between the areas of Celtic survival further east in the Wicklow mountains (O'Byrne and O'Tooles' Country) and the Gaelic families of Connaught and north-west Ulster. The only way in which the Gaelic nation could have been destroyed would have been by extensive and strategic castle-building on a scale such as that adopted later by Edward I in Wales. Indeed the Welsh analogy was very close, since in Wales, too, a central wilderness ensured the survival of the indigenous aristocracy. Extensive castle-building in the Irish Midlands was precisely the strategic advice offered by Giraldus Cambrensis to Henry II in the *Expugnatio Hibernica*.[17] He suggested the building of a network of closely linked castles which would completely subdue the Gaelic lordships as far west as the Shannon, and he implied that the capitulation of Connaught must follow. His advice was ignored. In Ireland, the English administration lacked both the foresight of Giraldus and the resources of Edward I.

The initial onslaught of the Anglo-Normans had achieved the conquest of the whole of the Liffey and Barrow valleys where villages and towns of the new settlers developed under a thoroughly English feudal system. But the invaders had gone further: they had penetrated the eastern fringes of the Bogland Zone establishing tiny marcher lordships or cantreds such as *Tethmoy* (Tuath dá Maige) in de Bermingham's country in north-eastern Uí Failge; and *Oboy* (Uí Buide) and *Slievemargy* (formerly Uí Bairrche) between the Loígis and the new Carlow colony (Plate X). Similarly, *Imaal* was created as a buffer between the Irish who had fled to the Wicklow hills and the settlers in *Omurethy* (Uí Muiredaig) in southern Kildare, while to the east of the mountains, Arklow, Wicklow, and Newcastle provided bases which could be victualled by sea from Dublin and from where the remote coastal wilderness might be cleared of Irish. It seemed inevitable as the colony settled down that the kerns and so-called rebels in the Wicklow wilderness must quickly integrate into the feudal system or be destroyed. This did not prove to be so, however, and the remarkable survival, not of outlaws but of entire tribes and their kings, in the North-Eastern and North-Western regions for four centuries is a phenomenon which has never been adequately studied or explained. This question of Gaelic survival requires a treatment all to itself and is clearly related to the decline of the Anglo-Norman colony in the fourteenth century, a process which was in turn accelerated by England's preoccupation with wars in France and by recurring outbreaks of bubonic plague which wrecked havoc in the Anglo-Norman towns. The decline of the Anglo-Norman colony was one thing, the survival and remarkable recovery of Gaelic society was clearly something different.

The career of Art MacMurrough Kavanagh (Art Mór Mac Murchadha Caomhánach) who dominated Irish politics in the last quarter of the fourteenth century not only epitomizes the phenomenon of Gaelic survival but shows us how closely that survival was linked to the Dark Age Celtic past and to the landscape of Leinster. It was these two factors – Celtic tradition and the landscape which nurtured it – which more than any others account for the resilience of the Gaelic way of life. The decline of the English settlement saw MacMurrough's followers encroaching on the marches of Carlow and *Omurethy* ·as they moved down from the hills of north Wexford and southern Wicklow back into the Slaney and Barrow basins. We read of the burning of Carlow, 'the head and comfort of Leinster', several times from the 1360s onwards and a petition from the commons of Carlow to the King's Council in Ireland in 1392 testifies to the ruinous state of houses in the town; to widespread pillage and arson; to the decay of the town gates; and more ominously to the dwindling number of burghers who were willing to live there for fear of Art MacMurrough.[18] As MacMurrough led his sub-chiefs such as O'Nolan (descended from the Fothairt in Carlow) and O'Byrne (Uí Fáeláin of north Kildare) back into 105

Mag Fea and Uí Máil, the O'Mores of Loígis were pushing slowly eastwards over ancient Uí Buide and Uí Bairrche.[19] Strongbow's failure to conquer the Wicklow highlands and the Midland bogs two centuries before, meant that when Gaelic expansion eventually came it led inevitably to the coalescing of Gaelic territories to the east and west of the central Barrow basin. This is what happened in Carlow under MacMurrough's rule, and with his reconquest of the central Barrow basin, he severed the major access route between Dublin in the north and the southern Anglo-Norman outposts at Kilkenny, Waterford and Wexford.[20] This was the period when the English colony in Ireland came closest to extinction, and to cope with these years of crisis the centre of government was virtually moved from Dublin to the castle at Carlow. We find the Dublin council negotiating with MacMurrough at Moone (Móin Coluimb) in southern Kildare in October 1379 charging him with the supervision of the roads between Carlow and Kilkenny.[21] This was a public admission that the Leinster king controlled the ancient highway from Belach Mugna through Belach Gabráin which provided that lifeline between Dublin, and Kilkenny and Waterford. These were years when Art MacMurrough, however often he might be 'brought to peace' by the Anglo-Norman parliament, was in effect king of Leinster in as full a sense as any of his Laginian royal ancestors. He claimed to be 'captain of the Irish of Leinster' and he frequently extracted tribute in the form of fees or black rents from the English settlers in Dublin, Kildare, Carlow and Wexford. Through the disputed estates in Norragh, of his wife, Elizabeth Veele,[22] he temporarily annexed the old Uí Muiredaig territories centred on Forrach Pátraic, that ancient inauguration site in south central Kildare (Plate XII). He now dominated the Barrow basin from St. Mullins past Dinn Ríg to Mullaghmast (Plate XVI). The powerless Anglo-Norman council may have viewed Mac Murrough as a 'rebel captain', but to his followers he was by descent and position king of the Leinstermen.

Historians have, in the past, over-estimated the Anglo-Norman impact on medieval Ireland and have failed to take into account the limited effect the partial English conquest had on Gaelic areas — even near Dublin — where tribal attitudes and limited tribal political ambitions still survived. From Art MacMurrough's point of view, he could justifiably claim to be as powerful a king as his two most famous Uí Cheinnselaig ancestors, Brandub mac Echach and Diarmait Mac Murchadha. He and his forbears were essentially lords of north Wexford and the Carlow region, and while Art was gradually extending his sway northwards over southern Kildare in the fourteenth century, Brandub had successfully achieved a limited lordship there in the early seventh century and Diarmait Mac Murchada more spectacularly in the twelfth. Both these Uí Cheinnselaig ancestors had made themselves kings of the Province and both had ambitions for highkingship of Ireland. When the French chronicler, Jean Creton, reported that MacMurrough 'called himself lord and king of Ireland' and that he swore he would never submit to Richard II 'for all the treasure of the sea',[23] we recognize the boast of a king who believed he was descended from Cathair Mór, prehistoric ancestor of the Free Tribes of Leinster. Mac Murrough's court poets would have reminded him of such matters daily. We must bear in mind that to Mac Murrough and his followers such claims were not as extravagant as they might appear to Richard. MacMurrough's criteria for what constituted a king of Leinster or even a king of Ireland were clearly different and more modest than those of the Plantagenet ruler, but they were based nonetheless on substantial historical claims. Art MacMurrough's dealings with the Dublin council were probably little different from Diarmait Mac Murchada's dealings with the Dublin Norsemen two centuries before. To Art and Diarmait alike, the political centre of gravity of Leinster lay not at Dublin but in the central Barrow Valley. Dublin was an alien outpost and a political threat whose social and economic function was entirely lost on these tribal war-lords. The scale of medieval Gaelic royal government and political ambitions were of a tribal order which was equally incomprehensible to the English settlers.

106

52

The French chronicler Jean Creton has left us his eyewitness account of Richard II's disastrous expedition against Art Mac Murrough Kavanagh in 1399. This illustration from Creton's manuscript (British Library, Harleian 1319) shows the meeting between Mac Murrough and Richard's envoy, the Earl of Gloucester, in which the two sides vainly sought to come to terms. The picture (the original is in colour) is full of significance for social historian and geographer alike. Creton contrasts the serried ranks of heavily armed Plantagenet knights on the left with the archaic scene of the Leinster king and his two attendants riding barefoot without stirrups, saddle, or body armour, on the right. The meeting took place near the Wicklow coast, probably not far north of Arklow, and Creton's picture also underlines the crucial contrast between the Gaelic and Anglo-Norman environments. Mac Murrough's party is shown charging down from the forested high ground of central Wicklow, while the English knights stand solidly on the level plain.

So much for the Celtic tradition and tribal lore of the *senchus* on which MacMurrough's kingship fed and which sustained an embattled Gaelic society of the later Middle Ages in the belief that little had changed since the coming of the English and that the sacred bond between kings, people and their ancestral lands was destined to withstand anything which the Plantagenet system might throw at them. As it happened the Plantagenet king appeared in Ireland in person to cope with MacMurrough and with the problems facing the dwindling English colony in Ireland generally. Richard came with the unrealistic objective of bringing the Gaelic lordships of Wicklow and the Bog of Allen within the English system.[24] The details of his two Irish campaigns of 1394-5 and 1399 tell us much about the all-important ecological basis of Gaelic society in medieval Ireland. Too often the question of Gaelic survival has been viewed in a Robin Hood context of native Irish surviving in the greenwood by living as brigands off the settlers on the plains. We are not dealing however with mere survival, nor with a band of outlaws living a precarious and inevitably brief existence, but with entire social groups preserving tribal indentities which went back into the remote pre-Norman past. These later medieval Gaelic clans were led by aristocracies who raised armies, collected tribute and patronized their hereditary poets and historians after the manner of their Dark Age forbears. Clearly, then, we are faced with something more complex than a bunch of what Queen Elizabeth scornfully described in later centuries as 'a rabble of rogues'.[25] This forces the realization upon us that medieval Leinster was capable of sustaining two quite separate and self-sufficient societies each with its own distinct economy, for four centuries.

The Gaelic population was almost exclusively confined to the wooded hill country of Wicklow above the 600 foot contour[26] and to the bogs of Offaly. We have already seen that in pre-Norman Ireland there can have been scarcely any permanent settlement in Wicklow above the 500 foot line. Nevertheless, there must have always been the capability for adaptation within the pre-Norman Gaelic economy which allowed for survival in such bleak environments in later centuries. Put another way, it seems clear that had the Anglo-Norman villagers been driven to the hills and bogs instead of the native Irish, their society so dependent on agriculture would have succumbed. Therefore, while recognizing that in pre-Norman times agriculture may well have played a prominent part in the economy of the Uí Dunlainge and Uí Cheinnselaig lords of the Liffey and Barrow valleys, pastoralism must also have played a key rôle even among these lowlands tribes. If that had not been so they could not possibly have adapted so easily to the wilderness of Wicklow in the twelfth century. It has been claimed that the keeping of large herds of cattle by Irish chiefs was peculiar to the sixteenth century when it suited the troubled conditions of the Tudor wars, (whereas agriculture would have left the Gaelic population more vulnerable to attack). This argument does not hold up either for the fourteenth century of for earlier Celtic times. The truth is that early Irish literature abounds with tales of cattle-raiding (*táin*) between tribes, and in any case it could be argued that inter-tribal warfare and feuding was so endemic in Celtic Ireland that then, too, it was more prudent to invest in moveable livestock than in more vulnerable cereals. Creton, who affords us an eyewitness account of the disastrous English treck through MacMurrough's kingdom in 1399, vouches for the strong pastoral element in what must then have been a buoyant Gaelic economy. MacMurrough's horse, we are told, cost him four hundred cows 'for there is little money in the country, wherefore their usual traffic is only with cattle'.[27] Creton also states that MacMurrough's 'abode is in the woods, where he is accustomed to dwell at all seasons',[28] and this cannot be dismissed as a temporary situation to cope with Richard's reckless invasion of his territory, or as a mistake of Creton's, because it ties in with other evidence to the effect that Art's 'principal fortress' back in 1394 was in the wood at Leighlin near the Barrow.[29] So, even at the time of his greatest strength when he dominated the Barrow Valley, Art MacMurrough still preferred the safety of the forest environment. Thus, while Creton vouches for villages and houses in MacMurrough's Wicklow lands, nevertheless, we must assume that the basis of the Gaelic economy which sustained his rule was rooted in a pastoralism centring on those small cattle described in later Tudor documents, whose meat provided food and whose hides could be traded with the English settlers of the lowlands.[30] These cattle grazed the clearings within the forests and bogs, and pork too, must have figured prominently in this economy from the swine who foraged in the deciduous forest.[31] Pork, was regarded as *the* delicacy at Celtic banquets and warriors competed for the champion's portion. One of the most famous sagas of early Ireland dealt with just these matters in the *Tale of Mac Dátho's Swine*, an episode believed to have taken place in the Barrow Valley in central Carlow.[32] Of course the Gaelic and Anglo-Norman economies must have interlocked, the Gaelic clans trading hides and perhaps their coarse wool and cured pork, furs, hawks and hounds, in exchange for such things as horses, weapons, luxury items of clothing and jewellery, wine and grain. Obviously some cereals were grown in

108

Gaelic societies in all centuries, but if we are to believe Fynes Moryson writing at the beginning of the seventeenth century, then oats was the most popular crop, which was burnt rather than threshed at harvest time and which was made into oat cakes. But this observer believed that the growing of oats was quite restricted even in Gaelic Ulster.[33] We know from the details of Lord Deputy Grey's campaigns in Offaly in 1537 that corn grown on the plain of Geashill (Géisill or Mag Gésilli, Plate XIV) was of crucial economic significance for that Gaelic kingdom, but we also note that in the same year O'Connor was expected to pay a fine or tribute to Henry VIII in the form of eight hundred cows.[34] As Lord Mountjoy wallowed in his campaign of genocide in Offaly in 1600 he reported the destruction of ten thousand pounds worth of corn on that same plain of Géisill, which he claimed provided 'almost the only means for them [the native Irish] to live'. Mountjoy also marvelled, incidentally, at the proper fencing and manuring of the Gaelic fields in Offaly and at the good order of the roads (see Frontispiece).[34a] Mag Gésilli, protected as it was by an immense circle of bog, was clearly the granary of the North-Western Region, and given the immutable nature of the landscape with its limited opportunities for agriculture, we can be certain that this was as true for the Dark Ages as it was for Tudor times. Whenever Irish kings were strong enough they supplemented their incomes by extracting tribute in the form of black rents or protection money from their English neighbours. Such payments were not peculiar to the post-Norman era. It was a hallmark of their status as over-kings for early Celtic rulers to demand tribute at similarly irregular intervals from their Celtic neighbours.

Ultimately the survival of Gaelic society for so long under the noses of Angevin, Plantagenet and later administrations was due solely to the protection afforded by that very hostile landscape to which the Gaelic kings proved capable of adapting. It was the combination of difficult terrain — bogs in Offaly and high mountains in Wicklow and Wexford — along with a dense forest cover on the perimeter of these regions which more than anything else saved the Irish from immediate extinction. Richard II, like Giraldus before him and several later writers after him,[35] fully realized that the greatest enemy of the Anglo-Norman colony was the Leinster forest, and it was this forest which was to be his undoing. So pressing was this environmental problem for the safety of the English settlers that when Richard assembled a great host at Leighlin Bridge on 4 April 1395, from all the Leinster counties and Waterford (four men from each ploughland), they were not expected to turn up for battle, but to come equipped with axes and eight days provisions to make an onslaught on the forests in the Barrow Valley which prevented communication with Kilkenny and Waterford.[36] Creton, too, has a graphic description of how four years later, Richard employed two thousand five hundred people in the western part of MacMurrough's kingdom in Wicklow to cut a way through the forest for the royal army on its disastrous treck from the Barrow Valley to the Wicklow coast, most likely via the Glen of Imaal and Glenmalure (Plate XII):[37]

> There were then no roads, neither could any person, however he might be furnished with bold and valiant men, find a passage, the woods are so dangerous. You must know that it is so deep in many places that, unless you are very careful to observe where you go, you plunge in up to the middle, or sink altogether. This is their retreat [i.e. the Irish] and therefore no one can catch them.

This description shows that the Wicklow 'deserts' described in the *Life* of St Kevin (*deserta loca*)[38] had changed nothing over those centuries which separated them from the French chronicler who in 1399 related the tale of Richard's expedition 'into the depths of the desert' or 'into the deserted heights' (*es haulx deserts*) in search of MacMurrough.[39] It was disastrous for Richard to lead his royal army across the Wicklow massif to the east coast: it was tantamount to suicide to lead his famished troops up that coast to Dublin. We have seen how all the

109

rivers in this long coastal region ran transversely across the traveller's path into a multitude of coastal swamps particularly at Newcastle and north of Arklow (Plate XII), and how the entire region was heavily forested. We have few records of early Irish kings ever risking an army in this wilderness and the Dublin council must have long since learnt to avoid it. It is an indication either of Richard's poor judgement or the gross lack of communication between his English retinue and the Anglo-Irish lords that he risked himself and his men on such an insane venture. The result was predictable and inevitable. MacMurrough's troops hung about the flanks and rear of the royal army picking off stragglers at will. Richard's men, including even his magnates ran out of food, and would have surely starved to death had not three ships arrived with food from Dublin, landing probably at Arklow or Wicklow. A diminished, demoralized and famished army eventually reached the safety of Dublin. Little wonder that, as

53

One of the five taboos of the Kings of Leinster – designed to protect these semi-divine rulers from disaster – was that they should never march through the Fortuatha or the Wicklow Hills, widdershins or from south to north 'against the sun'. At a simpler level, this taboo advised against any expedition into this wilderness, and it would not have escaped the notice of Art MacMurrough and his court that Richard II chose to march widdershins through this very region in 1399. The results for Richard and his royal army were disastrous, not because they broke an ancient Irish taboo, but because they ran out of food and were constantly exposed to Irish attack as they trudged through impenetrable forest and marsh, and across countless rivers which ran transversely across their path from the mountains to the sea.

Creton informs us that even the gentlemen and knights in the king's entourage went for five days without food and shared a single loaf between five or six of them. All would have perished had not three ships arrived with provisions from Dublin, and in his illustration Creton shows famished knights wading into the water desperate for food. The chronicler tells us he wished he were penniless at Poitiers or Paris rather than face the horrors of this Leinster campaign.

Creton tells us:[40]

> 'The king could not forget Macmore (Art MacMurrough). He caused three companies of men to be well appointed to go in quest of him, and exhorted them to behave well, saying, that he would readily give that man who should bring him in, a hundred marks in pure gold . . . And if they could not seize his person, should God give him good health, till the season of autumn be gone by, when trees are stripped and bare of their leaves, he would burn all the woods great and small.'

It was a vain threat. Before those autumnal leaves had fallen from the Wicklow trees, Richard was back in England, a ruined man, who by September 1399 was the prisoner of Henry IV. MacMurrough ruled on over his primeval wilderness for another eighteen years. The record of Art's death in early January 1417 as recorded in the *Annals of Ulster* and the *Four Masters*[41] glows with the gratitude of those poets and historians who had benefited from the economic surplus built up by this remarkable Leinster king over his forty-two year reign. Even the Ulstermen were grateful to record that Art 'was the best of hospitality and prowess and charity in his own time'. It was an obituary of which any pre-Norman highking would have been proud. As for the Wicklow forest, precisely two centuries after Richard's invasion of east Wicklow, the woods there although diminished[42] were still sheltering the Leinster clans and still proving a dangerous obstacle to the army of the Earl of Essex in the vicinities of Arklow and Wicklow.[43]

The survival of native kings in the highlands of Wexford and Wicklow called for some adaptation on the part of the MacMurroughs, O'Tooles and O'Byrnes who had formerly ruled in the lowlands of the Liffey and Slaney basins. In the north-west of Leinster a somewhat different situation prevailed, since the O'Connors and O'Mores had always ruled over the Bogland Zone and so the degree of adaptation to the post-Norman situation was clearly less. There were also historical differences between the ruling families of Offaly and Wicklow. MacMurrough, O'Toole and O'Byrne had all claimed the kingship of Leinster in the more recent pre-Norman past, and the MacMurroughs continued to claim the title throughout the medieval period. Nicholls has reminded us that the kingship of Leinster survived longest of all the provincial kingships of Ireland, – the last MacMurrough to have claimed this title died as late as 1631.[44] In the north-west on the other hand, the O'Connors had not ruled as kings of the Province since the sixth century and theirs was a kingdom more distinguished for its cultural achievement than for its political power. Uí Failge and Loígis territory had of course suffered at the hands of Strongbow's followers, and much territory had been lost in the early thirteenth century on the eastern border with the Anglo-Norman county of Kildare. This was at a time, incidentally, when the *Book of Leinster* may not yet have been completed at its monastic home, probably at Clonenagh (Plate XIV). The de Berminghams and the earls of Kildare had seized whatever rich farmland was available in the eastern baronies of modern Co. Offaly, while eastern Leix fell to Meiler Fitz Henry and later to the Marshals. Otway-Ruthven informs us that Dunamase (Dún Masc), the stronghold of the Loígis in the eleventh and twelfth centuries was a flourishing Anglo-Norman manor in 1283, while another important Anglo-Norman settlement was based on Leys.[45]

The Irish throughout the thirteenth century had clearly fallen back towards the border with Fir Cell and the foot-hills of the Slieve Bloom. These were, as Curtis wrote: 'remote places which even the Norman conquerors at their best could neither conquer nor inhabit'[46] and it may be that historians relying too heavily on Anglo-Norman documentation have been misled by the extent and thoroughness of English settlement and administration west of the Barrow. Not only was most of this region reconquered by the Irish in the first quarter of the fourteenth century, but they re-emerged with their tribal organization intact under the leadership of those dynastic groups whose ancestry went back into the far Celtic past – O'Connor, O'Dempsey,

O'Dunne and O'More. The survival of so many dynastic subdivisions of the Uí Failge and Loígis tribes clearly suggests that however much their territory had contracted in the face of the Norman advance, nevertheless, sufficient lands remained to sustain entire social and political groups. The survival of the dominant Gaelic dynasties on either side of the Barrow basin does seem to have been achieved at the expense of weaker Irish tribes. Thus, while O'Byrne, O'Toole and MacMurrough seem to have appropriated the lands of Uí Enechglaiss and Dál Messin Corb in Wicklow, so too in the Bogland Zone the O'Mores seem to have survived at the expense of the Uí Crimthainn Áin and Uí Buide.

As the Gaelic revival gathered pace in the fourteenth century, the O'Mores regained Dunamase and already by 1324, the Anglo-Norman settlement at Leys was virtually in ruins.[47] As the fourteenth century wore on, the O'Mores annexed the old Gaelic territories of Uí Buide and parts of Uí Bairrche, over which they had no traditional claims, while further north the Uí Failge were moving back eastwards into the ancient Tuath dá Maige, which had once been the centre of their homeland, and from there they levied black rents on the settlers of Meath and Kildare. By the middle of the fifteenth century, under their king, Calbach (Calvagh O'Conor), the Uí Failge had recaptured their old royal centre at Rathangan. Just as the MacMurroughs were probably as strong in the fourteenth and fifteenth centuries as they had been in the eleventh and twelfth, so too the Uí Failge under Calbach Ua Conchobuir were more powerful in the fifteenth century than they had ever been in the late Celtic period. Calbach's kingdom extended from the remote borders of Fir Cell in the west to Rathangan in the east. By regaining access to the rich farmland in north-east Kildare and by extorting tribute from his Anglo-Irish neighbours, Calbach revived the ancient power of Uí Failge, and under his rule the region even recovered something of its ancient reputation for the patronage of learning and of the arts.

As late as 1451, we have Dubhaltach Mac Firbisigh's record of a traditional Gaelic feasting of court-poets and historians from all over Ireland by Calbach Ua Conchobuir, king of Uí Failge, and his queen, Margaret, at Killeigh (Plate XIV).[48] Margaret, who was herself the daughter of the nearby king of Ely (i.e. Ely O'Carol, Plate X), stood 'on the garrets of the greate church of Dasinchell [i.e. 'The Two Sinchells,' patrons of Killeigh], clad in cloath of gold with her deerest friends about her, her clergy and judges'. Her husband, Calbach, greeted the learned and artistic throng at the end of the church. The event took place 'in the darke dayes of the yeare to wit on the feast day of Dasinchell [26 March]', and in addition to feast-

54

Killeigh (Cell Achid Drommo Fota) near Tullamore in Co. Offaly was founded by Abbot Sincheall who died in A.D. 549. With the usurpation of Kildare by the Uí Dúnlainge kings of Leinster in the seventh century, Killeigh became the chief church of the Uí

112

Failge and remained so for nine hundred years. A Franciscan friary had been founded at Killeigh under the patronage of O'Conor Faly in 1293 while an earlier Augustinian priory and convent of nuns had existed here from the twelfth century. This royal monastic centre is steeped in historical associations. It was here 'in the dark days of the year', on 26 March 1451, that Queen Margaret of Offaly feasted the poets of Gaelic Ireland. Killeigh found itself in the front line of the Tudor wars as a centre of Gaelic royal power and Roman tradition. The friary was looted in 1537 by Lord Deputy Grey who pilfered the organ and glass from the windows. The Franciscans held on to their buildings until 1598, and friars remained among the people here up to the middle of the seventeenth century. The Holy Wells of Sincheall (above) were sketched by O'Hanlon in August 1888, but by then local pilgrimage to the shrine was on the decline and the feast-day of Sincheall had been forgotten.

ing the intellectual élite of the Gaelic world, Margaret, we are told fed the hungry and clad the orphans, and she was the only woman who was interested in 'preparing highwayes and erecting bridges [and] churches and [making] Mass-books'.[49] Margaret and Calbach's great display of largesse at Killeigh in those 'darke dayes' of 1451 was the twilight of a great tradition already a thousand years old. Killeigh lay on a pass leading into the Midland Corridor (Plate XIV) and was immediately accessible to Gaelic travellers from Westmeath, Connaught, Ossory and Ely. This monastery had become the most important religious and cultural centre in Uí Failge after the church of Kildare had been lost to the Uí Dúnlainge kings in the seventh century. Killeigh retained its position as chief of the holy places of Uí Failge until the collapse of the Gaelic system. As late as 1537 we find the king's Deputy, Lord Leonard Grey, looting this church when, in his frustrated efforts to cow the king of Uí Failge, he turned his fury against this ancient symbol of the Gaelic past.[50] Indeed Grey's expeditions against Brian Ua Conchobhuir show how little things had changed in the four centuries of strife between English and Irish for the domination of Leinster. From their bases in the Wicklow Hills and the Bog of Allen, the Gaelic chieftains terrorized the Liffey and Barrow valleys at will. Even the leaders of the Tudor war machine failed to realize that the Midlands could never be dominated from a castle at Dublin. When Grey led his second expedition in six months against Offaly in October-November 1537 he was prevented from entering the territory for several weeks because continuous rains had made the bogland impassable for horses and men.[51] When the English army eventually got inside they found that Ua Conchobuir had slipped out through the labyrinth into Ely O'Carol in Munster. Thus did climate conspire with landscape to keep the archaic Gaelic order alive. The entire ecological basis for this unique civilization lingered on into the next century, but its death-blow came with the death of Brian Ua Conchobuir, last of the kings of Uí Failge, probably in Dublin Castle in 1559. Brian could trace his ancestry in manuscript sources to the sixth century, and his bards could trace it further back for him to Cathair Mór, lord of the Free Tribes of Leinster. They could remind him, too, of even more shadowy traditions which traced his royal forefathers back into the mists of prehistoric time, to heroes of the Fir Domnann—those mysterious British war-lords who once ruled from Dún Ailinne 'over worlds of men.'

O'Dempseys of Clanmalire and O'Dunnes of Iregan, the ancient tributary septs of Uí Failge survived with the O'More chieftains of Loígis into the seventeenth century. As long as these Gaelic aristocracies could hold out along the western foot-hills of the Slieve Bloom, then the heart of Gaelic Ireland continued to beat. While the demise of O'Connor Faly destroyed the cultural and political unity of the Midland bogs, nevertheless the survival of Gaelic organization among the few remaining clans still provided a rallying point and means of communication radiating from the geographical centre of Ireland out to pockets of Gaelic survival on the periphery in Wicklow, Connaught, Munster, and even as far afield as north-west Ulster. Hugh O'Neill could never have mounted such effective or prolonged opposition from the north-east, if something of the 'Great Irishry' had not survived intact in the Bogland Zone. While the Earl of Essex was losing men as casualties and deserters from his magnificent army on dangerous and fruitless marches through Leinster and Munster, O'Neill was gaining valuable time, and later on he was to come in person to win support from the Gaelic and Gaelicized territories of Leinster and the Midlands.

Essex twice risked his men in the Bogland Zone and eyewitness accounts from the English side show how little the landscape had changed here since the Dark Ages. It was a landscape which fostered the survival of those enemies Essex sought to subdue, and it was landscape which could have proved fatal to an army which was ignorant of the terrain however well equipped it may have been. The Bogland Zone rendered cavalry virtually useless, and men marching in long columns with baggage trains were particularly vulnerable to Gaelic guerilla 113 tactics. Essex led his army into the Leix region across the Barrow at Athy into *Fasaghreban*, 'the wilderness of Rheban' (see Frontispiece). Already at this early stage in the expedition, two hundred rebels were sighted but they retired safely 'to their boggs and from thence to their woods'.[52] The English army then marched to the relief of Maryborough (Port Laoise) and from there Essex decided on a line of march which was to lead him to Viscount Mountgarret's castle at Ballyragget in Co. Kilkenny and from there on to Kilkenny city.

To an English general, unfamiliar with Ireland such a route may have seemed logical and obvious, but to anyone familiar with the physical and political geography of Gaelic Ireland, Essex's decision must have seemed reckless. Indeed, it very nearly proved fatal for many of his men. Essex had chosen to cross the old Leinster provincial border with Ossory at the point (Plates XIII, XIV) where nature had made it strongest, between the Loígis and the Osraige, and where we read of no contact across this region in earlier historical sources. The hills of northern Ossory had no early Christian churches, for instance, and placenames such as *Wolfhill* in northern Ossory to-day testify to the forbidding nature of this desolate terrain in medieval times. And so, instead of leading his troops south-westwards along the Slige Dála and from there moving south to Kilkenny along the Nore valley, Essex decided on a short cut to Ballyragget. His road lay through that pass which to-day, as 'The Pass of the Plumes', recalls the attack on his army here in 1599.

> The nature of the passage is such through a thicke woode a myle long, leadeth a highe waye, in moste places ten going paces broad. . . . To the other two sydes of the woode are adjoyned 2 boggs which served the rebell for a secure retreat from all force of our armye.[53]

Owen O' More had plashed the forest on either side of the pass in the same way as Irish kings four centuries earlier had prepared ambushes against Strongbow's men, and Essex carefully arranged his troops to force the passage. In spite of the small losses which Harrington claimed were sustained,[54] it is painfully obvious from the amount of space which he devotes to this incident, that Essex had led his men into a crisis situation that could have been avoided. The account of Essex 'in all places, flying lyke lightninge from one parte of the army to another, leadinge, directinge and followinge in the vanguarde, batle, and reareguard' reads more like a man at his wit's end than a commander 'at his best' as Falls somewhat naively maintained.[55] Whether or not we accept Irish accounts of a slaughter of English troops, it was clearly a reckless act to risk a vice-regal army by wilfully leading it through an ambush in hill country along a narrow forest pass, a mile long, and surrounded by bogs.

Later in the summer Essex was back in the Bogland Zone once more, this time going across Offaly as far west as Fir Cell, in spite of Elizabeth's disapproval of such ventures. Essex seems to have marched from Philipstown (Daingean) across the bog into *Fartoulogh* (the ancient Fir Tulach, Frontispiece) where he was ambushed marching west along the Slige Mór or 'Great Way' as it ran through that pass leading from Fir Tulach into Cenél Fhiachach (Plates XIII, XIV). The leader of this attack was Captain Tyrrell, whose twelfth-century Anglo-Norman ancestors had replaced the O'Dooley chiefs as rulers of Fir Tulach in de Lacy's Lordship of Meath. Tyrrell, at the close of the sixteenth century, was in rebellion against the English administration and in the pay of O'Neill. The pass where he attacked Essex's army bears his name to-day (Tyrrell's Pass) and was described by Dymmok as being four miles long and flanked by wood and bog.[56]

Having extricated himself from this ambush, Essex moved west and then due south into the Midland Corridor, first to Durrow and then south along the Corridor to Ballycowan near the ancient monasteries of Rathan and Lynally. Here Essex rendezvoused with Sir Conyers Clifford who had forced his way from Connaught with heavy losses, into Fir Cell. Dymmok gives us a description of Fir Cell which shows us that this landscape, which in the heart of the Irish Mid-

114

lands had given much-needed protection to the monasteries of the Golden Age in the seventh century, had changed little over the millennium which separated it from the Tudors:[57]

'A porcion of the county of Ophalye is called Fergall, a place so strong as nature could devise to make yt by wood and bogge, with which yt is environed, which for the naturall strength thereof, the rebells in those partes have ever since the begininge of these warres made a storehowse for all their prayes, peaceably enjoyinge there without molestacion what they had injuriously robbed from other parties.'

That was Fir Cell in 1599 and very soon afterwards, as Fynes Moryson made his way through this countryside on his journey from Armagh to Kinsale, he confessed that the only woods which impressed him on his route were 'the great woods of Ofaly', through which incidentally, he noted that fallow deer were still roaming wild.[58] It was only a matter of a few years until Elizabeth had finally crushed O'Neill who also visited the Midland Corridor in 1600, but for entirely different reasons.

Nothing had changed and no lessons had been learnt in four hundred years of continual strife between Gael and Gaill. In those final hours of Gaelic rule, English and Irish not only failed to understand each other's society, but both sides viewed even the landscape differently. To the English generals Fir Cell was a remote and secure bog, as indeed it was, but to the Irish it was still the ancient gateway from Leth Chuinn, or northern Ireland, into Leth Mugha in the south, and it was also the meeting place of many Provinces. Witness the *Four Masters* account of O'Neill's triumphal progress through Ireland in 1600:[59]

A hosting was made by O'Neill . . . in the month of January in this year, and he proceeded to the south of Ireland, to confirm his friendship with his allies in the war, and to wreak his vengeance upon his enemies. When O'Neill left the Province of Ulster, he passed along the borders of Meath and Breifne and through Delbna Mór [Delvin]. . . . He totally spoiled Machaire Cuircne [western Westmeath, Plate XIV] and all the possessions of Theobald Dillon. O'Neill afterwards marched to the gates of Athlone and along the southern side of Clann Cholmáin [Mide] and through Cenél Fhiachach [Plate XIV] into Fir Cell.

In this country [Fir cell] he remained encamped nine nights and the people of Fir Cell,

55
Detail from the Map of Leix and Offaly c. A.D. 1563 (see Frontispiece). This section covers the area from Mountrath (top) to Port Laoise, marked as Protectour (bottom). Structural details are clearly visible in the Plantation fortress which was built in 1548 and renamed Maryborough in 1557. The road from Mountrath via Clonenagh and Clonkeen was part of a prehistoric trackway known to the ancient Irish as the Slige Dála (Road of the Assemblies) which linked Roscrea with the Liffey Plain. The building of Fort Protector (named after the Lord Protector Somerset) in the heart of O'More's Country in Leix, and of Fort Governor (later Philipstown) at Daingean in O'Connor's kingdom of Offaly a year earlier in 1547 heralded a radical change in English military strategy in Ireland. These forts, built by Bellingham, symbolised a final onslaught on the old Gaelic tribal environment. Their presence in the Midland kingdoms was a recognition that the Castle at Dublin was never capable of controlling this region directly, and more ominously they paved the way for Plantation which was the final solution adopted in the long struggle to sever the bond between the Gaelic population and their ancestral territories.

of Upper Leinster (*Uachtair Laighen*), and Westmeath, made full submission to him, and formed a league of friendship with him.

On leaving this country, O'Neill passed over the upper part of Slieve Bloom westwards.... [to Ely and to Munster]

Just as MacMurrough in the fourteenth century and O'Connor in the fifteenth had been stronger than any of their pre-Norman Gaelic ancestors, so now O'Neill in these last years of Gaelic autonomy was acting out the reality, of what would have seemed fantasy to many of his Northern Uí Néill ancestors. So much of this campaign followed a pattern which was deeply rooted in the Dark Age Celtic past. Here was a Northern Uí Néill highking on a circuit of the territories of his client kings, marching along a route which was older than the oldest historical record in the land. The campaign shows, too, that for the sixteenth-century Irish, Mag Lena in Fir Cell was still the centre of Ireland in so far as it facilitated inter-tribal gatherings – in this case the submission of the Midland chiefs to O'Neill. The incident had other less desirable old tribal overtones, as witnessed by O'Neill's onslaught on the territory of Ely. This attack was in revenge for O'Carol's execution of MacMahon mercenaries,[60] but it can be viewed in the tradition of an Uí Néill over-king making an example of a Munster vassal tribe as he was about to invade southern Ireland. In short, the incident was probably little different in its ethos from the attack of the Uí Néill highking, Donnchad, 'on the borders of the Munstermen' in 775 almost a thousand years before.[61]

The seventeenth century saw the systematic destruction of the Gaelic environment particularly of the forest which provided essential protection for a way of life that was now in full scale retreat. Gaelic culture was dependent for the survival of many of its salient features on a particular type of landscape, and this had always been the case even in the remote Celtic past. There is no doubt whatever, that tribal institutions had been consolidated by the essentially enclosed nature of ancient Ireland, and those tribal lands so naturally enclosed by a circle of forest, mountain, and bog, engendered a strong sense of regionalism and a deep dislike of centralized authority within the people who dwelt there. This enclosed landscape also discouraged communication and population movement, and so Gaelic Ireland remained essentially conservative and rural, and without large urban centres. It is no coincidence that where the landscape was most enclosed by nature's defences Gaelic society survived longest and strongest. This was so, not just because the English failed to penetrate such regions, but for reasons which are shrouded in the subtle relationship between a people and the landscape which they inhabit. Anglo-Norman lords who came to settle in tiny tribal lands such as Fir Tulach or Tuath dá Maige, within easy reach of Dublin, fell in their turn, under the spell of that environment ringed by forest and bog. By the sixteenth century the Tyrrells and Berminghams had become 'degenerate English' in the eyes of the Dublin garrison less than forty miles away. The great Earls of Kildare had inherited the lion's share of Strongbow's conquests in Leinster, and yet they, too, fell under the spell of that unique environment of nearby Móin Almaine (the Bog of Allen), the cradle land of Gaelic civilization.

So strong was the presiding genius of this primeval wilderness in keeping ancient glories and tribal loyalties alive, that eventually the Dublin administration determined on a policy which was to finally sever the bond between the people and the landscape – plantation. Military conquest had been tried by Strongbow and failed, and isolated military victories proved only that an ancient Midland *tuath* might be momentarily taken but never held. Experiments under the auspices of Richard II and Henry VIII had shown that while Irish rulers were always flattered to be offered titles or privileges by English kings, it was impossible to turn them into 'good Englishmen' as long as they were left to rule their people in their ancestral kingdoms. This was the paradox of the medieval Irish 'problem': Irish kingship required nothing more than a tiny territory no bigger than an English parish, with a tiny ancestral population to be ruled over. Such requirements seemed modest, and for centuries they blinded English monarchs to the amazing strength and resilience of the Irish political system. But a powerful tribal dimension to Gaelic kingship lurked behind the very modesty in the scale of its operation. It was the local flavour of Irish kingship which wedded the king to his people and to their ancient tribal territory. It was the function of the hereditary caste of genealogists, poets and historians, to consolidate tribal bonds by harping on the intimate relationship between the ruling dynasty and the evocative historical places in the landscape. They stressed too the real or imagined descent of the king and his people from countless generations of war-lords and holy men whose blood had either flowed in defence of their territory or whose bones had sanctified monastic cemeteries across the land. These social bonds and the institutions which sustained them were impervious to either military oppression or centuries of feudal legislation. Only the complete removal of a tribe and the destruction of the natural wilderness which promoted such intense local loyalties could achieve the elusive conquest of Ireland. And so, plantation and transplantation were seen by Tudor and Stuart governments as the final solution for eliminating the problem of the Irishry. It is significant that this divisive experiment which was to cast such a long shadow over later centuries of Irish history, was first implemented in Offaly and Leix.[62] It was in effect, a blow struck at the geographical heart of Gaelic civilization which had continued to beat for so long on the very borders of the English Pale.

*   *   *   *

EPILOGUE

These are the five taboos of the king of the Leinstermen:
> To travel withershins around the Wicklow Hills on Wednesday
> To sleep between the Dodder and Dublin with his head to one side
> To encamp for nine days on the plains of Cualu
> To travel along the Dublin road on Monday
> To ride on a dirty black-hooved horse across the plain of Mullaghmast

These are his five lucky things:
> The fruit of the Hill of Allen
> The deer of Glenn Serraig
> To drink by the light of wax candles at Dinn Ríg on the banks of Barrow
> To drink the ale of Cualu
> To preside over the Games of Carman
>> *Geasa agus Urgartha ríg Érenn*
>> The Taboos and Lucky Things of the Kings of Ireland
>> (*Book of Lecan*, facsimile 194.a.1)

*   *   *   *

Appendix

ADOMNÁN, KING ALDFRITH,
AND THE HOME OF THE BOOK OF DURROW

It now appears likely that it was the library and school at Durrow which helped shape the mind of one of the greatest literary figures of Dark Age Ireland, namely, Adomnán, the writer, diplomat and ninth abbot of Iona. It is possible to deduce from Adomnán's *Life of Columba* that Adomnán may not have reached Iona before 669 at the earliest. Adomnán tells us that he was on Iona during a great spring drought, some seventeen years before he wrote *Columba's Life,* which would date the drought to 671 or later (*Adomnán's Life of Columba*, ed. Anderson and Anderson, pp. 450-1). In spite of the wealth of detail which he provides on Iona life and topography, he does not profess a personal knowledge of any abbot before the time of his immediate predecessor, Failbe (ibid., p. 93). Failbe came to the abbacy in 669 which strongly suggests that this leader of the Columban church invited Adomnán from Ireland to Iona perhaps as his deputy there as soon as Failbe himself came to power *c.* 670. But Adomnán was already forty-two by that year—an old man by Dark Age standards—and even if he were ten years younger, men of that age have already absorbed most of the learning they are ever likely to possess. Adomnán had therefore been trained to cope with the *Dialogues* of Pope Gregory and the writings of Sulpicius, Evagrius and Constantius—to name but some of his sources—in some Irish monastery of his youth and early manhood. He can scarcely have studied at Derry since he never mentions that monastery although he does refer three times in passing to the actual place (ibid., p. 71). His later career took him into close contact with the Southern Uí Néill kingdoms of Brega and Mide which is puzzling for a churchman whose tribal origins were in the extreme north-west of Ireland unless we accept that earlier in his life he had travelled south to the Irish Midlands. This in turn is supported by late and sometimes inconsistent anecdotes such as that in the *Three Fragments of Annals* (ed. O'Donovan, pp. 74-5) which shows Adomnán as a schoolboy fagging for other boys at a school somewhere in the territory of the Southern Uí Néill king, Fínsnechta (675-95). Adomnán's contacts with the Irish Midlands show that his career followed that of Columba quite closely, because that saint, too, studied in Leinster and perhaps also under Finian of Clonard—whose monastery was in the Bogland Zone (Anderson, op. cit., pp. 68-70). Columba eventually founded Durrow in the heart of that zone and, clearly, Durrow must have provided the major training ground for Irish Columban monks after its foundation. In the light of this background evidence, it is significant that Adomnán refers to Durrow several times, offering us detailed information on that monastery of a kind possessed only by a writer with first-hand knowledge of the place. He first mentions Durrow in a long and detailed story involving Columba's visit to nearby Clonmacnoise which took place while that saint was founding Durrow. The details are many, and Adomnán cites his predecessor, the abbot Failbe, as his immediate source for this tale (ibid., pp. 214-9). He next relates a miracle story of how Columba was able to see from Iona 'the construction of a large

118

building' (*majoris domus*) at Durrow under the direction of the monk Laisrán on a cold winter's day (ibid., pp. 264-7). Adomnán returns later on to this theme of building activity at Durrow when he tells us how Columba dispatched an angel from Iona to save a monk falling from the top of a round building (*monasterii rotundi*) under construction at Durrow (ibid., pp. 494-5). These tales were clearly inspired or embroidered by the presence of real buildings at Durrow in Adomnán's own day, and his personal knowledge of that monastery shines through in yet another anecdote which tells how Columba once visited Durrow in the autumn and blessed a particular fruit-tree 'near the monastery of Durrow on its southern side' (ibid. pp. 326-9). Adomnán also relates how a monk of Columba's on the Hebridean Island of Tiree eventually travelled to Durrow by way of the Brega coast and when he died at Durrow he was buried among the 'elect' monks—presumably in a special plot in the monastic cemetery (ibid., pp. 432-5). It could, of course, be argued that Adomnán found some of these Durrow anecdotes in an earlier source such as the *Life* of Columba written by Adomnán's predecessor, Cumméne. Even if that were true it would do nothing to undermine the case for arguing that Durrow had the closest connections with Iona of all other Irish Columban houses. While Adomnán claims he heard one Durrow anecdote (which originated with Abbot Ségene) from his predecessor, Failbe, he also very significantly tells us, in another rare instance where he cites the source of his information, that he had personally heard a particular miracle story from a certain Finán 'who had lived for many years as an anchorite beside the monastery of Durrow' (ibid., pp. 318-9). It is the detail in these anecdotes rather than mere quantity which suggests that Adomnán may have been as familiar with Durrow as he was with Iona, and the topographical element in that detail suggests that Adomnán wrote with the interest of one who was personally familiar with Durrow rather than as a compiler who would have been expected to drop such irrelevant matter from his text. There are other detailed passages in Adomnán's work which may well have a hidden Durrow connection, if not indeed a Durrow origin. The traditions concerning the voyages of Cormac Ua Liatháin through the Scottish Isles and into the North Atlantic are a case in point. Cormac visited Columba in his Scottish home, and Adomnán's account of his travels constitutes very early evidence for monastic voyages of this kind. It is significant that a note in the *Félire Óengusso* associates Cormac with Durrow, where presumably he was buried (*Félire Óengusso*, ed. Stokes, p. 156). If there is a single monastery in Ireland which can claim to have provided Adomnán with a monastic home, it is surely Durrow, and Adomnán may have begun his studies there as early as the 640s. As a kinsman of Columba, a great scholar, and a man of spiritual leadership, it must have been already apparent from the 650s that he was a serious candidate for the abbacy of Iona. That being so, he would have held an important position at Durrow if he stayed on there after his novitiate, and the post of master of the scriptorium or of the monastic school would have suited a man of his learning and intellectual curiosity.

It is at this point that we may tie in the career of Adomnán with that of his friend, King Aldfrith of Northumbria who ruled the northern English from 685 until 705. Adomnán knew the English king well enough to describe him as his friend (Anderson, op. cit., p. 460) before he visited the Northumbrian court in 686. Clearly, the two men had met before, and according to the *Anonymous Life of Cuthbert* Aldfrith was staying on Iona in the year before he was summoned back to Northumbria to succeed his hostile brother Ecgfrith (*Two Lives of Saint Cuthbert*. ed. B. Colgrave, New York reprint, 1969, p. 104). A letter from the English scholar Aldhelm is thought to congratulate King Aldfrith on returning from a six-year exile among the Irish (ibid., p. 329). Remarkably, if Aldfrith had spent a six-year exile on Iona immediately before becoming king of Northumbria, he would have gone to Iona in 679, the very year in which Adomnán became abbot there. But there is evidence to suggest that Aldfrith and Adomnán's friendship went back even further. According to William of Malmesbury (*De Gestis Regum Anglorum* in *Willelmi Malmesbiriensis monachi*, ed. W. Stubbs, Rolls Ser., 1887, i, 57) Aldfrith acquired his great learning in Ireland. Later Irish sources call Aldfrith the *dalta* or 'pupil' of Adomnán which would imply that the Northumbrian king had studied under Adomnán as a youth in Ireland, and that, too, is supported by other Irish traditions claiming Aldfrith's mastery of the Irish language and his ability as a poet in that tongue (*Baedae Opera Historica*, ed. C. Plummer, Oxford, reprint 1969, ii, 263). For Aldfrith was the son of King Oswiu and an Irish princess, Fína, daughter of the Northern Uí Néill highking, Colmán Rímid, who died in A.D. 604 (cf. F.J. Byrne, *Irish Kings and High-Kings,* London, 1973, p. 111). That tradition has been preserved in Rawlinson B 502, one of the more reliable genealogical compilations (*C.G.H.i.,* 135). As a result of his Irish connections, which he clearly kept in touch with throughout his life, Aldfrith was unique among English kings for enjoying a distinct Irish personal name, that of Flann Fína. None of this evidence can be used to *prove* that Aldfrith studied as a youth at Durrow under Adomnán's supervision nor is it my purpose to argue for such a precise equation. Those who seek proof of such matters in Dark Age history fail to understand the discipline. But all this evidence, however unsatisfactory it may be, does help to explain the general context in which Durrow was likely to have found itself in the middle of the seventh century. It is quite clear from Adomnán's own writings and from contemporary annals, that Durrow and not Derry was the most important Columban house on the Irish mainland, from its foundation up to the ninth century. Furthermore, an abundance of historical and geographical evidence shows that Durrow occupied a key geographical position (Plate XIV) at the centre of a complex monastic ecology in the Irish Midlands. Adomnán had a detailed and personal knowledge of the place and he almost certainly studied there and may well have risen to a position of authority within its scriptorium in the period 640-670. King Aldfrith of Northumbria was a good friend of Adomnán ever since the latter became abbot of Iona in 679. But Irish tradition believed that friendship between the two men went back to Aldfrith's schooldays. King Oswiu most likely fathered his son, Aldfrith (regarded by medieval English historians as illegitimate), before Oswiu himself became king of Bernicia in 642. For Oswiu, too, had been an exile and fugitive among the Irish prior to the defeat and death of Cadwallon, from 616 until 632-3 and it was during that time he formed a union with his Irish princess, and Aldfrith was his eldest son.

If Irish tradition is correct about Aldfrith's early relationship with Adomnán, then the most likely monastery to have housed both master and pupil was Durrow and the most likely time was the period 650-60, for by 665, Aldfrith had returned to England and was then a pupil of the Anglo-Saxon scholar, Aldhelm of Malmesbury. Aldhelm in a letter written to King Aldfrith early in his reign claims that some twenty years before then he had taken the king as his adopted son (Plummer, op. cit., ii, 312). We thus arrive at a possible and indeed very probable context in which the Book of Durrow came into being, for that illuminated Gospel Book has been dated on palaeographical and art historical grounds to about the middle of the seventh century. This was a time when the Irish Bogland monastic confederacy was reaching its greatest scholarly output; and Durrow, enjoying the closest possible ties with Iona, was situated in the heart of the Irish cultural zone. Durrow was not only an important Irish monastery in the centre of the Bogland confederacy, but as the most important Columban house in Ireland, Northumbrian travellers coming via Iona would have been certain to make their way there.

If Aldfrith had studied among the Southern Uí Néill at Durrow and had established friendly connections with the Irish Midlands, then we may at last have an explanation for the otherwise extraordinary expedition which Ecgfrith of Northumbria dispatched against the churches of Brega in June 684 (*Ann. Ulst.,* ed. Hennessy i, 134). Admittedly, the evidence points to

Aldfrith being at Iona when that raid took place, and of course his student days were by then long over. But the raid may suggest he had close connections with the Southern Uí Néill whose Brega coastline was vulnerable to an Anglian sea-borne attack. Ecgfrith then would have launched a punitive raid against the Southern Uí Néill in the belief that they had harboured his rival and older brother for many years. In this the career of Aldfrith would have resembled that of his distant relative Adomnán, for while both men had the royal blood of the Northern Uí Néill highkings in their veins, they would also have shared an exile of scholarship among the Southern Uí Néill. A friendship forged in those early days was later to flourish when one man became head of the Columban church and the other, king of the Northumbrians. Therefore, if William of Malmesbury was right in thinking Aldfrith studied in Ireland, Durrow fits his description well of that 'place where, safe from the hatred of his brother, he became deeply versed in literature, and had enriched his mind with every kind of learning' (*De Gestis Regum*, ed., Stubbs, i, 57). Aldfrith ruled as one of the greatest scholar kings in English history. It was of him that Stenton wrote:

> He is the most interesting member of the most remarkable dynasty to which he belonged, and he stands beside Alfred of Wessex among the few Old English kings who combined skill in warfare with desire for knowledge.   (F.M. Stenton, *Anglo-Saxon England*, p. 89)

It was those very things—politics and the pursuit of knowledge—which led Aldfrith to the gates of an Irish monastery and to a long-standing friendship with the learned Adomnán.

Even if Aldfrith never reached Durrow, Northumbrian influence was bound to have been strong there since constant communication with Iona was bound to have opened up contacts with Lindisfarne. It is significant that Bede must have had either personal contact with Irish monks who provided him with information on Durrow, or more likely he had access to a manuscript source relating to that house. This is the only explanation which accounts for Bede's knowledge that the Irish name, *Dearmach*, of that distant monastery, signified *campus roborum* ('Plain of Oak-trees') in Latin (*Historia Ecclesiastica*, iii, 4, ed., B. Colgrave and R.A.B. Mynors, Oxford, 1970, p. 222). The phrase reminds us of Adomnán's use of *monasterium roboris campi* and *roboreti monasterium campi* to describe Durrow in his *Life of Columba*. But Bede did not get his information from Adomnán and the two writers appear to differ on the precise time in Columba's career at which he founded Durrow. If the atheling, Aldfrith, had studied at Durrow then we may be sure he was attended there by warriors from his household and by Northumbrian clergy. Such men as these, and less exotic travellers from Northumbria, would have taken books and ornaments from their English homeland which were eagerly studied and copied in the monastic workshops then entering their Golden Age in the Irish Midlands, and this in turn would help to explain the Germanic influence on some of the art in the Durrow Gospels. Indeed the question as to whether the Book of Durrow was written in the Durrow scriptorium or at Lindisfarne becomes somewhat irrelevant when the true cultural context of Durrow itself is properly understood.

Sadly, under nationalistic influences, scholars—often for other very good reasons—have passionately argued that this or that manuscript or fragment of metal originated or was inspired by craftsmen in this or that corner of the British Isles. Disputes inspired by such sentiments can never be resolved, simply because the so-called Hiberno-Saxon cultural zone pervaded most of the British Isles in the seventh and eighth centuries. Thus, it is possible to argue, on perfectly sound academic grounds, that the earliest Irish annals were in fact Scottish; that much early British and Anglo-Saxon enamel work was Irish, and that the Book of Durrow is as English as the Tyne. But just as the dominant cultural strain in medieval Scandinavian historiography was clearly Icelandic rather than Norwegian or Danish; and just as the major cultural impulses in   121 the British Isles in the Elizabethan era were English; it is equally apparent that the Irish element was the dominant and parental strain in the monastic culture of Northern Britain in the Dark Ages. That being so, regardless of where the Durrow Gospels were actually penned, there is no gainsaying their fundamental Irish ethos or the fact that their medieval monastic home lay at the centre of a monastic ecology which dominated the cultural life of the British Isles in the seventh century. For even if the codex had begun life in Northumbria, the fact that such a magnificent work had been allowed to gravitate towards Durrow at an early stage in its life would in itself be suggestive of the pre-eminent position of the Irish Midlands in the cultural life of the British Isles in the Dark Ages.

Chart 5

Rotational Kingship in Leinster A.D. 700 - 1050

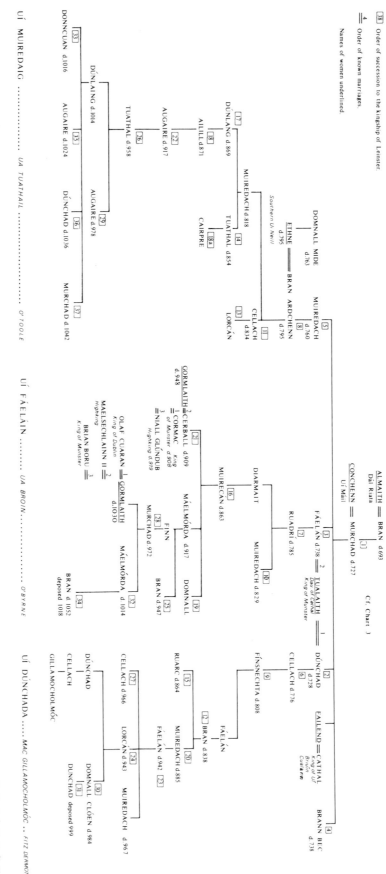

38 Order of succession to the kingship of Leinster.

= Order of known marriages.

Names of women underlined.

The Leinstermen developed a more orderly and restricted system of royal succession to the overlordship of their Province from A.D. 700 onwards. In place of the random circulation of overlordship between rival tribes in the Dark Ages (see Chart 3) this new system confined the kingship within three dynastic groups all of whom descended from Murchad son of Bran, who died in 727.

123

(i)

Knockaulin Hillfort (i) in central Kildare consists of an oval earthworth enclosing 34 acres (cf. Fig. 22). The bank runs on the outside of the ditch, as at Tara and Emain Macha, suggesting these centres had a social or ritual function and were not true forts. Archaeological excavations directed by Professor Bernard Wailes have revealed a series of three superimposed henge-like circular wooden monuments near the top of the hill. They show no evidence for domestic or industrial use and may have had a ritual function. The more recent of these monuments shows up in the detailed photograph (ii) as a series of massive post holes laid out in a circular plan and surrounded by two pallisade trenches. This structure, some 38 metres in diameter enclosed a small central chamber of uncertain function built with massive posts. A maze of earlier pallisade trenches from Phase 2 can also be seen, and Phase 2 included a ceremonial avenue leading from this hilltop building down in the direction of the main entrance through the outer enclosure (i). Archaeological and historical evidence combine to suggest that Knockaulin was a ritual site used for periodic assemblies and perhaps also for inauguration ceremonies of the kings of the Leinstermen and the Fïr Domnann during the La Tène Iron Age from the first to the fifth or sixth centuries A.D.

(ii)

Killeigh, Co. Offaly (Cell Achid Drummo Fota) – (iii) – has for long remained unnoticed by historians and archaeologists alike. This important religious and cultural centre enjoyed continuous patronage from the kings of Uí Failge from the sixth until the sixteenth century (Fig. 54), and so had a far longer Gaelic life than, say, Clonmacnoise or Armagh. The aerial photograph shows the Dark Age monastic enclosure running along the line of the curved hedgerow in the right foreground, and continuing into the centre foreground as a ploughed-out bank and ditch. The church and cemetery (hidden by trees in the centre of the enclosure) mark the nucleus of this lost monastery, but the impressive size of the enclosing earthwork testifies to the former extent of the monastic settlement. Aerial photography has revealed similar enclosures around numerous other monasteries such as Lorrha in north Tipperary (iv). Almost the entire enclosure can still be seen here along the line of curved hedgerows and ploughed out ditches (left foreground). Cf. Fig. 10.

(iii)

(iv)

Photographs copyright D.L. Swan, Archaeological Air Survey

Notes

CHAPTER I

1 *Armes Prydein: The Prophecy of Britain*, ed. I. Williams, transl., R. Bromwich (Medieval and Modern Ser., vi, Dublin, 1972), pp. 14-5.

2 O'Rahilly, *EIHM*, pp. 101-17. O'Rahilly believed that while the saga dealing with the destruction of Dinn Ríg (*Orgain Denda Ríg*) told the origin tale of the Leinstermen from their own (invading) point of view, yet another saga, *Togail Bruidne Da Derga (The destruction of Da Derga's Hostel)*, told the same story from the point of view of the invaded. Ibid., pp. 117-30.

3 See p. 18.

4 *Onomasticon*, ed. Hogan, p.33. Cf. O'Rahilly, op. cit., pp. 20-1, who questioned the Laginian descent of the Dál Cairpre Arad, in spite of the strong genealogical tradition to that effect, as found for instance in Rawl. B. 502, (119.a.6 - 119.ab.30), *C.G.H.* i, 26-7.

5 See pp. 19, 91-2.

6 A.P. Smyth, 'The Húi Néill and the Leinstermen in the Annals of Ulster, 431-516 A.D.', *Études Celtiques*, XIV, i (1974), 137-42.

7 The significance of the 'reign' of Cormac mac Airt in Irish proto-history is still quite obscure and several able scholars have advanced different views on the subject. O'Rahilly (op. cit., pp. 137-40) saw Cormac as a ruler of the Érainn but did recognize his geographical association, at least, with North Leinster. Professor Byrne, on the other hand, accepted Cormac as a genuine ancestor of the Connachta and Uí Néill in the kingship of Tara: F.J. Byrne, *Irish Kings and High-Kings* (London, 1973), pp. 65-6.

8 See p. 18 below.

9 O'Rahilly, op. cit., pp. 93-4.

10 J. Ryan, 'The Early History of Leinster', *The Past*, no. 4 (Wexford, 1948), 19. O'Rahilly saw the Welsh placename *Lleyn* deriving from the Irish *Lagin*—the Welsh name deriving, in his opinion, from Irish settlers in north-west Wales: O'Rahilly, op. cit., p. 113, n. 5.

11 O'Rahilly, op. cit., pp. 321, 527.

12 *V.S.H.*, ed., Plummer, ii, 144-7.

13 Ibid., p. 219.

14 Ibid., i, cxxv.

15 *Onomasticon*, ed. Hogan p. 191; *Loca Patriciana*, pp. 259-60.

16 In the *Additions to Tírechán's Collections*, it is quite clear that Iserninus alias Bishop Fith set up his own independent mission in southern Leinster based on a tribe called the Catrige in Clíu in Uí Dróna in northern Carlow (Plates XII, XVI). His mission stations there are named as Toicuile, Ráth Fálascich and Lathrach Dá Arad (Laragh, Barony of Shillelagh, south-west Wicklow, Plates XII, XVI): *Tripartite Life*, ed. Stokes, ii, 342-3.

17 Patrick is said to have landed at Inber Dee, or Arklow, in Muirchu's *Notes*, (ibid., ii, 275) and in the *Lebar Brecc* (ibid., ii, 448). In the *Vita Tripartita* proper, Palladius is first taken to Inber Dee, and shortly afterwards Patrick is made to land at the same place: (*Bethu Phátraic: The Tripartite Life of Patrick*, ed. K. Mulchrone, (R.I.A., Dublin, 1939), i, 19, 23).I have shown elsewhere, that the association of Inber Dee with the earliest Christian mission in Leinster may be quite late (Smyth, op. cit., pp. 131-3). The basis of the tradition, however, that it was Palladius and not Patrick who introduced Christianity to the Uí Garrchon or Dál Messin Corb is likely to be genuine.

18 Rawl. B. 502 (121, bb. 33) in *C.G.H.*, i, 49.

19 O'Rahilly, op. cit., pp. 34, 37-8. O'Rahilly identified the Uí Bairrche as a branch of the Brigantes, but he was quite wrong in regarding this tribe as non-'Laginian' in its origins.

20 The anchorite, Áed of Sleaty (Sleibte), who died in A.D. 700, supplied the church of Armagh with early Leinster traditions dealing with the first Christian mission to the Clíu area in Carlow, and involving the Dál Chormaic, Dál Messin Corb, Uí Bairrche and Uí Cheinnselaig: (*Muirchu's Notes, Tripartite Life*, ed. Stokes, ii, 269, 271. From the *Additions to Tírechán* (ibid., p. 346), it is clear that this same Áed committed his church at Sleaty to a political alliance with Armagh during the abbacy of Ségene (+688). The implication of Áed's bequest to Armagh of 'his kin and his church to Patrick forever' seems to be that, up to that time, the important *paruchia* of Sleaty had nothing whatever to do with either Patrick or Armagh.

21 *Ann. Ulst.* A.D. 770 (sub anno 769), i, 238.

22 Ibid., A.D. 838 (sub anno 837), i, 340.

23 *V.S.H.*, ed. Plummer, ii, 191.

24 *Ann. Ulst.*, A.D. 858 (sub anno 857), i, 368; A.D. 870 (sub anno 869), i, 382.

25 Ibid., A.D. 906 (sub anno 905), i, 420.

26 Ibid., A.D. 908 (sub anno 907), i, 420-2. The extensive account of this battle in the *Three Fragments* suggests that the Munster invaders may have avoided Gowran as being too obvious a route, and crossed by a shorter and more dangerous pass over the Slievemargy

hills (Plate XVI) to the north of Gowran, descending into Leinster at Old Leighlin in Carlow (Plates XII and XVI): *Annals of Ireland: Three Fragments*, ed. J. O'Donovan (Dublin, 1860), p. 204.

27 *Ann. Ulst.*, A.D. 941 (sub anno 940), i, 460: *The Circuit of Ireland by Muirchertach Mac Neill, Prince of Aileach*, ed. J. O'Donovan, (Dublin, 1841), p. 38.

28 G.H. Orpen, *Ireland under the Normans*, (Oxford, reprint 1968), i, 157-8.

CHAPTER II

1 The oldest Uí Failge genealogy is found in Rawl. B 502 (122.b. 32-123, f.35), *C.G.H.*, i, 56-66. The major sub-divisions consist of Uí Máeletopair, Uí Maine, Uí Báeth, Uí Failge Iarmotha, Uí Máelceithirnaich, Clann Colgan, Clann Colgan i Liphi, Clann Colgan ó Thig Cainén, Clann Rotaidi, Uí Riacáin, Uí Timmíne, Clann Mugróin—all of whom are supplied with a genealogy.

2 Rawl. B 502 (119.a.25), ibid., pp. 25-6: O'Rahilly, *EIHM*, pp. 23, 34-5.

3 Rawl. B 502 (118.a.25-119.a.l) *C.G.H.*, i, 19-25.

4 Rawl. B 502 (117.a.1-30); (117.c.l-117.e.39); (124.a.22-124.b.55); *C.G.H.* i, 10, 12-5, 70-5. The *Book of Leinster* has a most extensive genealogical collection relating to the Uí Cheinnselaig: ibid., pp. 334-55.

5 The 'genealogy of the kings of Uí Dróna' is given in the *Book of Leinster* (LL.337.b. 19: ibid., p. 430) as that of the line of Rián and his descendants (Ua Riáin) who occupied this Carlow territory until the Anglo-Norman Invasion (Plates VIII, IX, XV). Rián was part of the Uí Cheinnselaig direct line, but in earlier times the Síl Alténi were regarded as the rulers of Uí Dróna and were alleged to descend from Drón, the brother of Énna Cennselach (progenitor of the Uí Cheinnselaig, LL. 317.b.1: ibid., p. 350). This brotherly relationship to Enna, as opposed to belonging to the direct line of descent, was, in early Irish genealogical terms, equivalent to saying that the Uí Dróna were quite distinct from Uí Cheinnselaig proper. Similarly, the Uí Dega were alleged to descend from Daig, yet another brother of Énna Cennselach (LL. 316.b. 55-60: ibid., p. 343), or, alternatively, they were supposed to descend from Énna's son (LL. 337.a.41: ibid., p. 429). This quite remote branch of the Uí Cheinnselaig line were the earliest known rulers of Uí Dega and were possibly related to the Uí Dega of Ossory. There is a gloss, however, on the name of Dondgal, king of Uí Cheinnselaig, at his place in the genealogy of the main line of the kings of South Leinster (Síl Chormaic) to the effect that he was 'ruler of Uí Dega' [*Taísech Ua nDega*, (LL.317.a.16): ibid., p. 347]. This king of South Leinster died in A.D. 761, so that by then at least the Uí Cheinnselaig had already taken over Uí Dega tribal lands. This Dondgal was a great-great-uncle of Rián, whose people had taken over Uí Dróna territory, and the activities of this family in

the late eighth century can be seen to represent a determined drive on the part of the Uí Cheinnselaig to over-run most of Carlow and Wexford (see Plate V and also pp. 60-5).

6 Ibid., pp. 71-2. Bressal Bélach's death is dated by the *Annals of Ulster* to A.D. 435, but this date is entirely arbitrary (*Ann. Ulst.*, A.D. 435, i, 6).

7 Rawl. B 502 (124.a.49), *C.G.H.*, i, 71.

8 The position of Cathair Mór and his alleged *Timna (Testament)* in Leinster tradition is discussed in some detail in A.P. Smyth, 'Húi Failgi relations with the Húi Néill in the century after the Loss of the Plain of Mide', *Études Celtiques*, XIV, ii (1975), 515-22.

9 Ibid., pp. 503-22; cf. Smyth, 'Húi Néill and the Leinstermen', *Études Celtiques*, XIV, i (1974), 137-42.

10 Smyth, 'Húi Failge relations with Húi Néill', *Études Celtiques*, XIV, ii (1975), 517-9.

11 Kildare monastery had been taken over by the Uí Dúnlainge from as early as the second quarter of the seventh century, and it is difficult not to accept that the Uí Dúnlainge had taken over the Curragh, from at least as early as the eighth century. In A.D. 782, for instance, two rival branches of Uí Dúnlainge fought for the kingship of Leinster on the Curragh. In this conflict, Ruaidhri son of Fáeláin (of Uí Fáeláin) took captive his rival, Bran of Uí Muiredaig. Significantly, the Uí Failge were involved in the battle, but only in a subsidiary rôle. The king of Uí Failge, Mugrón son of Flann, was slain in single combat. Mugrón's territory still included the Curragh in 782, but he almost certainly held it in a tributary position to his Uí Dúnlainge overlords: *Ann. Ulst* A.D. 782 (sub anno 781), i, 256. Yet Mugrón's immediate descendants, at any rate, held lands in the Liffey Plain (see p. 75 and *n.* 36 Chapter VII).

12 A.P. Smyth, *The Laigin or Early Leinstermen* (Unpublished M.A. History thesis, University College Dublin, 1969), pp. 275-326. Cf. P. Walsh, 'Leinster States and Kings in Christian Times', *Irish Ecclesiastical Record*, liii (1939), 57.

13 For a detailed discussion on ancient sites within Uí Máil see L. Price, *The Place-names of Co. Wicklow*, iii (1949), 118-26, 162-5, 183; vii (1967), vii-x.

14 Rawl. B 502 (118.b.32-119.a.l), *C.G.H.* i, 24-5.

15 The earliest traditions relating to Cú Corb and his sons are found, not in the prose tracts of the genealogies, but in a collection of archaic genealogical poems found in Rawlinson B 502, and ascribed in part to Laidcenn mac Bairceda: K. Meyer, *Über die älteste irische Dichtung* (aus den Abhandlungen der Königlich-preussischen Akademie der Wissenschaften, Berlin, 1913). The poems are edited without translation in *C.G.H.* i, 1-9.

16 Smyth, 'Húi Néill and the Leinstermen', *Études Celtiques*, XIV, i (1974), 129-36.

17 O'Rahilly, *EIHM*, pp. 139-40.

18 Rawl. B 502 (118.b.43; 119.bb.22), *C.G.H.*, i, 24-5; 32. Cf. Smyth, op. cit., p. 136.

19 Ryan, 'Early History of Leinster', *The Past*, no. 4 (1948), pp. 15-9; O'Rahilly, *EIHM*, pp. 93-4. Kuno Meyer was aware of a Dumnonii origin for the Fir Domnann as early as 1914: Meyer, op. cit., p. 5.

20 Rawl. B 502 (118.a.29), *C.G.H.*, i, 20. Cf. K. Meyer, *Hail Brigit: an Old Irish Poem on the Hill of Allen* (Halle and Dublin, 1912), p. 6 and *n.* 2.

21 *C.G.H.*, loc. cit; Ryan, op. cit., pp. 18-9.

22 Rawl. B 502 (118.a.47), *C.G.H.*, i, 21.

23 Ibid. Find File and his brothers are discussed in Rawl. B 502 (118.b.2-118.b.17), *C.G.H.* i, 22-3.

24 Ibid., i, 23 Rawl. B 502 (118.b.15-17).

25 O'Rahilly, *EIHM*, pp. 92-9.

26 Ibid., p. 96.

27 Ryan, op. cit., p. 17.

28 O'Rahilly, op. cit., pp. 22-3, 95.

29 LL. 311.a.29; *C.G.H.*, i, 334.

30 See *n.* 10, Chapter I.

31 Smyth, 'Húi Failgi relations with Húi Néill', *Études Celtiques*, XIV, ii (1975), 518, *n.* 1.

32 Ibid., pp. 517-9.

33 Ibid., pp. 503-22.

34 D. Ó Corráin, 'Topographical Notes II: Mag Femin, Femen and Some Early Annals', *Ériu*, xxii (1971), 98.

35 Smyth, 'Húi Néill and the Leinstermen', *Études Celtiques*, XIV, i (1974), 132-3.

36 Rawl. B 502 (120.a.4); (120.a.6). *C.G.H.* i, 35.

37 Rawl B 502 (121.bc.49); (128.b.7); *C.G.H.*, i, 50, 99. Cf. Smyth, 'Húi Failgi relations with Húi Néill', *Études Celtiques*, XIV, ii (1975), 518.

38 M. Richards, 'Places and Persons of the Early Welsh Church', *Welsh Hist. Rev.,* v (1970), 334.

39 Smyth, op. cit., pp. 520-1; ibid., *Études Celtiques*, XIV, i (1974), 131-2.

40 Ibid.

41 Smyth, *Études Celtiques*, XIV, ii (1975), 518.

42 Ibid.

CHAPTER III

1 A. J. Otway-Ruthven, 'The Medieval County of Kildare', *Irish Hist. Stud.*, xi (1959), 185-8; W. Fitzgerald, 'The ancient territories out of which the present County of Kildare was formed and their septs', *Kildare Archaeol. Soc. Jrnl.*, i (1891-5), 159.

2 E. Curtis, 'The Survey of Offaly in 1550', *Hermathena*, xliv (1926), 313.

3 L. Price, *The Place-names of Co. Wicklow*, vii (Dublin, 1967), p. lxxxiv.

4 C. Ó Lochlainn, 'Roadways in Ancient Ireland' in *Essays to Eoin Mac Neill*, ed. Ryan, p. 465.

5 E. McCracken, 'The Woodlands of Ireland circa 1600', *Irish Hist. Stud.*, xi (1959), 289-91.

6 Ibid.

7 J.H. Andrews, 'The Irish Surveys of Robert Lythe', *Imago Mundi*, xix (1965), 22-31.

8 Three copies of this map survive: (a) BM Cottonian Augustus I. Vol. II, art. 40. Date: c. A.D. 1563; (b) TCD Hardiman Atlas no. 9 (Catalogue p. 232), Carew copy. Date: somewhat later than (a); (c) National Maritime Museum, Greenwich. Dartmouth Collection. Unfinished copy of (a) lacking all placenames.

9 P.R.O. Dublin, MS Clayton, No. 27, parchment. This manuscript is in a very faded condition and I am grateful to the authorities in the Dublin P.R.O. for having it recently cleaned to enable the best possible photographic plate to be prepared from it. This map of the barony of Scarawalsh, Co. Wexford (cf. Plate VII), dates to A.D. 1657.

10 *Baronia Udrone in Comitatu Catherloughlae*, T.C.D. (MS Room) Atlas of printed maps, no. 10. C. Folio, *c.* A.D. 1662. This map is based on the original survey of Lythe, the survey itself surviving only in two derivitive maps: one c. 1580 in the London P.R.O (M.P.F. 70) and another published in Mercator's atlas of 1595. Andrews, *op. cit.*, p. 31. Plate A illustrates Blaeu's version of the map (1662) which was almost certainly derived from Mercator's edition.

11 *V.H.S.*, ed. Plummer, i, 194; ii, 105, 232.

12 Ibid., ii, 194.

13 Ibid., i, 225.

14 *Onomasticon*, ed. Hogan, p. 587.

15 *Ann. Ulst.*, A.D. 1514, iii, 512.

16 Ros Corr and Fid Elo are mentioned in the *Tract on the Sons of Ua Suanaig* (*Bethada Náem*, ed, Plummer, i, 312). Coill an Cláir is mentioned in the *Life* of Colmán of Lynally (Lann Éló), (ibid., i, 172).

17 *V.S.H.*, ed. Plummer, i, 241-2, 253-4.

18 T.P. Le Fanu, 'The Royal Forest of Glencree', *Roy. Soc. Antiq. Irel. Jrnl.*, xxiii (1893), 268-80.

18a Giraldus, *Topographia*, ed. Dimlock, v, 28.

19 G. Mitchell, 'Post-boreal Pollen Diagrams from Irish Raised-bogs', *Roy. Irish Acad. Proc.*, lvii, B, no. 14 (1959), 244-5.

20 J.R. Kilroe, *A description of the Soil Geology of Ireland based upon Geological Survey maps and Records with notes on Climate,* (H.M.S.O., Dublin, 1907), pp. 168-9.

21 See p. 49 below.

22 G.R.J. Jones, 'Historical Geography and our Landed Heritage', *University of Leeds Review*, xix (1976), 59-62.

23 W. Rees, *An Historical Atlas of Wales, from Early to Modern Times,* (London, reprint 1966), Plates 25-27.

24 Jones, *op. cit.*, pp. 58, 66-8.

25 L. Price, 'Glendalough: Saint Kevin's Road' in *Essays to Eoin Mac Neill*, ed. Ryan, pp. 244-71.

26 M. Richards, 'Places and Persons of the Early Welsh Church', *Welsh Hist. Rev.,* xx (1970), 337-8.

27 Ibid.

28 Farne Island served as an ascetic retreat for Lindisfarne; St Kevin's Bed and Temple na Scellig for Glendalough; and Monaincha for Roscrea.

29 S. Caulfield, *The Rotary Quern in Ireland* (unpublished M.A. thesis in Archaeology, University College Dublin, 1966).

30 *Onomasticon*, ed. Hogan, p. 262. The modern placename is given as Clonown or Cloonowen.

31 *Milliud Mide, mórad Lagen, léim dar Lulchach. The Book of Leinster*, ed. R.I. Best, O. Bergin and M.A. O'Brien (Dublin, 1954), i, 218.

32 E. O'Curry, *Lectures on the Manuscript Materials of Ancient Irish History* (Dublin, 1861), p. 491, *n.* 61.

33 Smyth, 'Húi Néill and the Leinstermen', *Études Celtiques*, XIV, i (1974), 122-5.

34 P. Walsh, *The Placenames of Westmeath* (Dublin, 1957), p. 230.

35 *Onomasticon*, ed. Hogan, p. 463 (under *Inis Cré*).

36 Jones, op. cit., pp. 58-9.

37 *Bethu Brigte*, ed. D. Ó hAodha (Dublin, 1978), pp. 6, 24.

38 Walsh, op. cit., p. 182.

39 Ibid., pp. 181-2.

40 Richards, op. cit., pp. 341-3.

41 *Tripartite Life*, ed Stokes, ii, 342-3.

42 *Bethada Náemh*, ed. Plummer, i, 157. The *brughaidh* or yeoman is said to have driven his herds from Mide or modern Westmeath, but there is clearly confusion in this late Irish *Life* between Brega (modern Co. Meath) and Mide proper (Westmeath).

43 The Wicklow evidence will be found in Price, *Placenames of Wicklow*, ii, 93; iii, 114; iv, 219, 237; vii, 386. For Ballynaboley, Co. Carlow, and Boley Co. Wexford, cf. E. St. John Brooks, *Knight's Fees in Counties Wexford, Carlow and Kilkenny* (Irish Manuscripts Commission, Dublin, 1950), pp. 75, 89. The word *baile* ('place') may have replaced many Leinster *buaile* placenames.

44 *Ancient Laws of Ireland*, ed., R. Atkinson (Dublin Rolls Ser., 1901), v. 482-3.

45 M. Herity, 'Prehistoric Fields in Ireland', *Irish University Review* i (1970), 258-65. Cf. F.H.A. Aalen, *Man and the Landscape in Ireland* (London and New York, 1978), p. 36. I am grateful to Professor M. Herity and to Dr. S. Caulfield for discussing the results of their important excavations with me.

46 *V.S.H.* ed. Plummer, i, xcvi, note 6.

47 Giraldus, *Topographia,* ed. Dimlock, v, 32-3; 34-9.

48 Ibid., pp. 46-7.

49 *Four Masters*, ed. O'Donovan, i, 680 (sub anno 960).

50 Plummer, *op. cit.*, i, cxlvi.

51 Ibid., pp. 244, 238-9.

52 *Félire Óengusso Céli Dé: the Martyrology of Óengus the Culdee*, ed. W. Stokes (Henry Bradshaw Soc., London, 1905), pp. 128, 156.

53 A.P. Smyth, *The Laigin or Early Leinstermen* (unpublished M.A. History thesis, University College Dublin, 1969).

CHAPTER IV

1 E. MacNeill, *Phases of Irish History* (Dublin, 1919), pp. 107-9.

2 *Onomasticon*, ed. Hogan, p. 670.

3 Ibid., p. 668. ´

4 *Ann. Ulst.*, A.D. 999 (sub anno 998), i, 504.

5 Ibid., A.D. 1042, i, 580. *The Annals of Ulster* name the Ossory king as Gillapátraic mac Donnchada.

6 *Onomasticon*, loc. cit.; Price, *Place-Names of Wicklow*, vii, xxxiv-vi.

7 *Lebor na Cert: The Book of Rights*, ed. M. Dillon, (Irish Texts Soc., Dublin, 1962), p. 10.

8 Ibid., p. 118. (lines 1738 and 1763).

9 *Four Masters*, ed. O'Donovan, A.D. 1146, ii, 1080.

10 *Ann. Ulst.*, A.D. 1171, ii, 166-8.

11 Price, op. cit., iv, 263; v, 287.

12 Ibid., v, 297, 319, 325.

13 *Onomasticon*, ed. Hogan, (under *Glais inasc*). p. 438.

14 Orpen, *Ireland under the Normans*, i, 367-71.

15 See p. 63 below.

16 McCracken, 'Woodlands of Ireland', *Irish Hist. Stud.*, xi (1959), 285.

17 *Onomasticon*, ed. Hogan, p. 581. In the saga, *Cath Ruis na Ríg*, the Ulstermen pursued the defeated Leinstermen south to the Ryewater, boasting: 'We are satisfied to have followed them thus far.' *Cath Ruis na Ríg: The Battle of Ross na Ríg*, ed. E. Hogan (Dublin, Roy. Irish Acad., Todd Lecture Ser., iv, 1892), pp. 54-5; 104-5.

18 *Ann. Ulst.*, A.D. 781 (sub anno 780), i, 254.

19 *Four Masters*, ed. O'Donovan, (sub anno 776), i, 382.

20 Ibid., A.D. 1072, ii, 904.

21 Smyth, 'Húi Néill and the Leinstermen', *Études Celtiques*, XIV, i, (1974), 131; see p. 10 above.

22 *Ann. Ulst.*, A.D. 804 (sub anno 803), i, 286-8.

23 Smyth, op. cit., pp. 128-9.

24 Ibid., pp. 122-5.

25 The Isle of Allen is so marked on the map of Co. Kildare in *Lewis's Atlas comprising the Counties of Ireland* (London 1837).

26 K. Meyer, *Fianaighecht . . . Poems and Tales relating to Finn and his Fiana* (R.I.A. Todd Lecture Ser., Dublin, 1910, reprint 1937), p. xv.

27 Ibid., p. xviii.

28 O'Rahilly, *EIHM*, pp. 275-7, and cf., ibid., p. 74, *n.* 1.

29 Meyer, op. cit., p. ix.

30 Ibid., p. 52.

31 *Leabhar Branach: The Book of the O'Byrnes*, ed. S. Mac Airt (Dublin, 1944), line 3365, p. 127; line 3760, p. 142; line 6765, p. 259 (references to Maistiu or Mullaghmast). Line 5447, p. 207 (reference to Nás or Naas); Line 6173, p. 235 and cf. lines 898, 1231, 2104, 2824, 4938, 6252, 6445 (references to Almhu or the Hill of Allen).

CHAPTER V

1 *Book of Leinster*, ed. Best, Bergin and O'Brien, i, 181-9.
2 *Onomasticon*, ed. Hogan, pp. 457-8.
3 Ibid. Price (*Place-names of Wicklow*, vii, 478-9) is unusually non-committal on this important placename and on that of Ráth Inbhir, which must also refer to the Arklow area.
4 J. Otway-Ruthven, 'The Medieval County of Kildare', *Irish Hist. Stud.*, xi (1959), 193, and map facing p. 196; ibid., 'Knight's Fees in Kildare, Leix and Offaly', *Roy. Soc. Antiq. Irel. Jrnl.*, xci (1961), 179, and map facing p. 166. The cantreds of Arklow and Wicklow were originally reserved by Henry II as part of his royal demense, but after 1173 they seem to have been granted to Strongbow, whose headquarters was most likely at Kildare. Price, *Place-names of Wicklow*, vii, xxvi-xxxii.
5 Smyth, 'Húi Néill and the Leinstermen', *Études Celtiques*, XIV, i, (1974), 127-36.
6 Ibid., pp. 132-3; *Onomasticon*, ed. Hogan (Under Cell Fine), p. 192; Price, op. cit., vii, 494.
7 *V.S.H.*, ed. Plummer, i, 241; Price, op. cit., vii, p. xv.
8 O'Rahilly, *EIHM*, p. 26, *n.* 3; Price, 'Glendalough: Saint Kevin's Road' in *Essays to Eoin Mac Neill*, ed. Ryan, pp. 244-71; ibid., *Place-names of Wicklow*, vii, pp. xi-xii.
9 Ibid., i, 24-5.
10 Ibid., v, 336-7.
11 Ibid., iii, 162-5.
12 *Fingal Rónáin and other Stories*, ed. D. Greene, (Med. and Mod. Irish Ser., xvi, Dublin, 1955), p. 1.
13 Ó Lochlainn, 'Roadways in Ancient Ireland' in *Essays to Eoin Mac Neill*, ed. Ryan, p. 473.
14 O'Rahilly, op. cit., pp. 25-6.
15 *Onomasticon*, ed. Hogan, p.442; Kevin's *Vita* strongly suggests that in its early days Glendalough was under the control of Uí Máil, and some later abbots may also have belonged to that dynasty. Price, op. cit., vii, 507.
16 The *Lives* of Kevin bring Fáelán, an early seventh-century Uí Dúnlainge king, into close association with Glendalough. Fáelán's mother, Fedelm, was of the Uí Máil in whose territory Glendalough lay. *V.S.H.*, ed. Plummer, i, 250-2; *Bethada Náem* ed. Plummer, i, 128-9, 150-1, 164.
17 O'Rahilly cites a note from the *Félire Óengusso* to the effect that the river Dael, a few miles north of Arklow (Plate XVI), marked the boundary between Uí Enechglaiss and Dál Messin Corb: O'Rahilly, op. cit., p. 30, *n.* 2. The boundary either followed the river to the coast, or, more likely, may have run along the high ground parallel to the Dael and to the south of it (Plates XI, XV). Domnach Rignaige (Templerainy) a few miles north of Arklow (Price, op. cit., vii, 472-3) lay in Uí Enechglaiss.
18 Rawl. B 502 (120.bb.6), *C.G.H.*, i, 39.

19 T.C.D. Hardiman Atlas No. 2, p. 231.
20 Le Fanu, 'Royal Forest of Glencree', *Roy. Soc. Antiq. Irel. Jrnl.*, xxiii (1893), 270.
21 *V.S.H.*, ed. Plummer, i, 241.
22 J. Ryan, 'The Ancestry of St. Laurence O'Toole', *Reportorium Novum*, i, 70.
23 *Ann. Ulst.*, A.D. 1021, i, 546.
24 *Four Masters,* ed. O'Donovan, A.D. 1170, ii, 1178.
25 *C.G.H.*, i, 39. (Alternative readings from LL and BB in note *a* to Rawl. B 502 (120. ba. 1)).
26 *Four Masters* A.D. 1072, ii, 902; A.D. 1095, ii, 950.
27 Ibid., A.D. 1043, ii, 842.
28 Ibid., A.D. 1039, ii, 836; A.D. 1127, ii, 1026. The Ua Tauthail abbot of Glendalough who was slain by the Fortuatha in 1127 was Giolla Comhghaill Ua Tuathail of the main royal line of Uí Muiredaig and grandfather of St Laurence O'Toole, archbishop of Dublin at the time of the Norman Invasion: Ryan, op. cit., p. 72.
29 *Four Masters*, A.D. 1154, ii, 1110. Muirchertach Ua Tuathail, who slew the Uí Enechglaiss king in this year, was the father of St Laurence O'Toole.
30 *Ann. Ulst.*, A.D. 827 (sub anno 826), i, 324.
31 *Four Masters*, A.D. 917 (sub anno 915), i, 590.
32 Domnaill's chief slayer is named as the king of Uí Cheinnselaig (*Ann. Ulst.*, (sub anno 983), i, 494), but *Four Masters* (sub anno 983, i, 716) name the king of the Fortuatha as an accomplice. The correct date is 984.
33 *Ann. Ulst.*, A.D. 1014, i, 532.
34 Price, op. cit., v, 300; vii, xi-xii.

CHAPTER VI

1 The Uí Cheinnselaig king, Cairpre mac Laidhgnéin, is called *Rí Laigen Desgabair* at his death in 793 (*Ann. Ulst.* A.D. 793 (sub anno 792), i, 272), as is Echtigern mac Guaire at his death in 853 (Ibid., A.D. 853 (sub anno 852), i, 362). Uí Cheinnselaig is used either in a territorial sense or ambiguously in the *Lives* of Kevin (*VSH.*, ed. Plummer, i, 254); Máedóc of Ferns (ibid., ii, 148-9); and Moling (ibid., ii, 193). For a similar use of the term in the *Lives* of Munnu and Abban, see notes 23 and 24 below.
2 O'Rahilly, *EIHM*, pp. 23-4.
3 M.E. Dobbs, 'Women of the Uí Dúnlainge of Leinster', *Irish Genealogist*, i, no. 7, 196-206.
4 Ibid., p. 197.
5 *Onomasticon*, ed. Hogan, p. 661.
6 *Book of Rights*, ed. Dillon, p. 148.
7 O'Rahilly, op. cit., p. 24.
8 LL. (337.b.19), in *C.G.H.*, i, 430.
9 See *n.* 5, Chapter II
10 *Onomasticon*, ed. Hogan, p. 667 (under Uí Dega and Uí Dega Móir Laigen).
11 *Ann. Ulst.*, A.D. 761 (sub anno 760), i, 226. See also *n.* 5, Chapter II

12 LL. (317.a.15) in *C.G.H.*, i, 347.

13 In the *Additions to Tírechán*, we are told that Crimthann son of Énna Cennselach was converted to Christianity at Rathvilly (*Tripartite Life*, ed. Stokes, ii, 342). The later *Vita Tripartita* proper does not mention Rathvilly by name, but clearly the traditions concerning the early evangelization of Uí Cheinnselaig as found in this source also assume a southern Kildare and northern Carlow location for these events, ibid., i, 188-94.

14 Ryan, 'Early History of Leinster', *The Past*, no. 4 (1948), 36.

15 Kilroe, *Soil Geology of Ireland*, p. 230.

16 *V.S.H.*, ed. Plummer, ii, 191.

17 Orpen, *Ireland under the Normans*, i, 66 and *n.* 1; 141-2.

18 Ibid., i, 141, *n.* 2.

19 See n. 9, Chapter III

20 Le Fanu, 'Royal Forest of Glencree', *Roy. Soc. Antiq. Irel. Jrnl.*, xxiii (1893), 271, 274.

21 *Adomnan's Life of Columba*, ed. A.O. Anderson and M.O. Anderson (London, 1961), pp. 212, 490.

22 *Onomasticon*, ed. Hogan, pp. 602, 177-8; Price, (*Place-names of Wicklow*, vii, 475) identified Cell Bicsige with Kilbixy near Arklow.

23 *V.S.H.*, ed. Plummer, ii, 102-3. The *vita* of Fintán of Taghmon claims that Cormac, the Uí Bairrche king, was king of South Leinster or Uí Cheinnselaig, while his enemy, Colmán of the Uí Cheinnselaig proper, was king of North Leinster. The *vita* confirms, therefore, that the Uí Cheinnselaig originally invaded Wexford from the north and that they displaced the Uí Bairrche as rulers of South Leinster. Colmán kept Cormac prisoner at his palace at Ráth Mór, very likely the same place as Ráth Mór Maige Fea or Rathmore, east of the Slaney, and about a mile south of Rathvilly (another Uí Cheinnselaig stronghold) in Co. Carlow (Plate XVI).

24 Ibid., i, 23-4. Cormac of Uí Bairrche is described as king of Uí Cheinnselaig in this *vita* also.

25 *Ann. Ulst.*, A.D. 769 (sub anno 768), i, 234.

26 Ibid., A.D. 722 (sub anno 721), i, 172.

27 Smyth, 'Húi Failgi relations with Húi Néill', *Études Celtiques*, XIV, ii, (1975), 515-22.

28 Smyth, *Early Leinstermen* (unpublished M.A. History thesis. University College Dublin, 1969), pp. 310-26.

29 Ibid., pp. 304-5.

30 LL. (316.a.24), *C.G.H.*, i, 339; Rawl. B 502 (124.b. 27), *C.G.H.*, i, 73.

31 LL. (316.a.20), *C.G.H.*, i, 339.

32 Rawl. B 502 (124.b.39), *C.G.H.*, i, 74.

33 *Book of Ballymote*, cited in *C.G.H.*, i, 340, in conjunction with LL. (316.a.47), ibid.

34 Ibid.

CHAPTER VII

1 See pp. 70, 75-6 below.

2 For the importance of Rathangan and its occup-

ation by the early kings of Uí Failge, see Smyth, 'Húi Failgi relations with Húi Néill', *Études Celtiques*, XIV, ii, (1975), 509-12.

3 *The First Version of the Topography of Ireland by Giraldus Cambrensis*, transl., J.J. O'Meara (Dundalk, 1951), pp. 65-6. The quotation is from Virgil *Georg.* II, 201-2 (ibid., *n.*38, p. 116).

4 See pp. 16-17, 74-5, and n. 11, Chapter II

5 E. O'Curry, *On the Manners and Customs of the Ancient Irish* (Dublin, Celtic Soc., 1855), i, xcviii and notes.

6 Walsh, *Placenames of Westmeath*, p. xxviii.

7 P. Walsh, 'Leinster States and Kings in Christian Times, I.', *Irish Eccl. Rec.*, xxiv, 5th Ser. (1924), 1-12; ibid., 'Leinster States and Kings in Christian Times, II'. *Irish Eccl. Rec.* liii, 5th Ser. (1939), 47-61.

8 Ryan, 'Early History of Leinster', *The Past*, no. 4. (1948), 13-37; ibid., 'Ancestry of St. Laurence O'Toole', *Reportorium Novum*, i, 64-75.

9 Curtis, 'Survey of Offaly, 1550', *Hermathena*, xliv (1926), 312.

10 Ibid.

11 Giraldus, *Topographia*, ed. Dimlock, v, 26.

12 St Mullins is referred to as a *civitas* in *V.S.H.*, ed. Plummer, ii, 191; Glendalough, as a *civitas magna* full of wealth and royal treasure, ibid, i, 246; Ferns as a *civitas*, ibid., ii, 151, 162, 193.

13 Giraldus, *Topographia*, v, 122; *Three Fragments*, ed. O'Donovan, p. 222

14 *Onomasticon*, ed. Hogan, p. 102.

15 Ó Lochlainn, 'Roadways in Ancient Ireland' in *Essays to Eoin Mac Neill*, ed. Ryan, p. 471.

16 Ibid., p. 465.

17 Curtis, op. cit., pp. 322-3, 327.

18 *Onomasticon*, ed. Hogan, p. 263.

19 Curtis, op. cit., pp. 315-6.

20 *Onomasticon*, pp. 650-1.

21 Ibid., p. 641.

22 Rawl. B 502 (123. e.30), *C.G.H.* i, 64.

23 *Onomasticon*, loc. cit.

24 Ibid., p. 127.

25 Ibid., p. 521.

26 Curtis, op. cit., p. 324.

27 Ibid., pp. 344-5.

28 Ibid., p. 315, *n.* 6.

29 *Onomasticon*, p. 417.

30 Rawl. B 502 (123.c.50), *C.G.H.* i, 62.

31 Curtis, op. cit.

32 *Onomasticon*, p. 482.

33 Rawl B 502 (122.bb.48), *C.G.H.*, i, 57.

34 Rawl B 502 (123.f.3), *C.G.H.*, i, 65.

35 *Ann. Ulst.*, A.D. 782 (sub anno 781), i, 256.

36 The *Book of Leinster* and the *Book of Ballymote* both describe the Clann Mugróin as being *i mMaig Liphi* (in the Liffey Plain), note to Rawl. B. 502 (123.e.30), *C.G.H.*, i, 64. See also *n.*11, Chapter II above.

37 LL. (314.d.7), *C.G.H.*, i, 337.
38 *Ann. Ulst.*, A.D. 789 (sub anno 788), i, 266.
39 *Onomasticon*, p. 244.
40 I am grateful to Professor F.J. Byrne for drawing my attention to this point at the time of going to press.
41 O'Rahilly, *EIHM*, pp. 30, n.5; 34. F.J. Byrne (*Irish Kings and High-Kings* (London, 1973), p. 39) was more cautious about the Pictish origins of the Loígis.
42 *The Problem of the Picts*, ed. F.T. Wainwright (Edinburgh and London, 1955), pp. 46-7.
43 *C.G.H.*i, 256, note *h* to Rawl. B 502 (155.a.10).
44 A poem, *Clanna Falge Ruis na ríg*, in the *Book of Leinster*, claims that Rus Failge, Bressal Enechglass and Dáire Barrach (the supposed ancestors of Uí Failge, Uí Enechglaiss and Uí Bairrche) shared the same mother's womb together. This was another way of saying that the three tribes had very close political and perhaps ethnic affiliations. *The Book of Leinster: formerly Leabar na Nuachongbála*, ed. R.I. Best, O. Bergin and M.A. O'Brien (Dublin, 1954), i, 241-2.
45 Rawl. B 502 (119.a.5), *C.G.H.*i, 26. Cf. O'Rahilly, *EIHM*, p. 34.
46 Ibid., p. 35.
47 Byrne, *op. cit.*, p. 45.
48 See p. 65 above.
49 *V.S.H.*, ed. Plummer, ii, 16; cf. R. Flower, *The Irish Tradition* (Oxford, 1966, reprint of 1947 edn.), pp. 22-3.

CHAPTER VIII

1 G. Mac Niocaill, *Ireland before the Vikings* (Dublin, 1972), pp. 57-8.
2. N. Power, 'Classes of Women described in the *Senchas Már*', in *Studies in Early Irish Law,* ed. R. Thurneysen *et. al.* (Dublin and London, 1936), pp. 81-108. Some five or ten types of marriages were defined for women in Early Irish Law depending on whether the criterion was one of status or of property. The precise number of wives recognized in law is more difficult to establish, but in addition to a 'chief wife' (*cétmuinter*) and her substitute in the case of illness, there might also be a 'secondary wife' (*adaltrach*) as well as at least two kinds of concubines (*airech* and *carrthach*), not to mention abducted women who were also a feature of aristocratic households. There were other concubines who were not recognized by the chief wife; had servile status (*cumal*); or had a secret relationship with the head of the house.
3 Twelve of Flann's sons are named in Rawl. B 502 (123.a.8-123.a.25), *C.G.H.*, i, 58-9, and the death of a thirteenth son, Ailill Corrach, is recorded in the *Annals of Ulster* in the year 741: *Ann Ulst.*, A.D. 741 (Sub anno 740), i, 200.
4 See last note.
5 See *n.* 11, Chapter II, above.

6 According to the *Cogadh Gaedhel*, Gormlaith was Brian's queen [the word *ben* is used in Early Irish literature not merely to signify 'woman' (its usual meaning) but also to signify 'queen' or 'consort'] in the crucial months before the battle of Clontarf in A.D. 1014, and the same source adds that she was the mother of Brian's son, Donnchadh. Donnchadh was old enough to lead a contingent at Clontarf (ibid., p. 154), a point which is confirmed by the contemporary evidence from the *Annals of Ulster* to the effect that Donnchadh won a battle in his own right in 1015 (*Ann. Ulst.* A.D. 1015, i, 536). This suggests that Donnchadh was born before the year 1000 at the very latest. Yet king Brian had another queen, Dubhcobhlaigh daughter of king Cathal of Connaught, who did not die until 1009: *Four Masters*, ed. O'Donovan, A.D. 1009 (sub anno 1008), i, 760. This evidence when viewed in the light of other Irish royal marriages suggests that Brian either divorced one of his queens or practised polygamy.
7 LL. (317.cc.18), *C.G.H.*, i, 55.
8 *Adomnan's Life of Columba*, ed. Anderson and Anderson: see under *Aidan son of Gabran* in Index, p. 554, ibid.
9 A.P. Smyth, *Scandinavian Kings in the British Isles 850-880* (Oxford, 1977), Chart VII, p. 134.
10 *Three Fragments*, ed. O'Donovan, p. 128.
11 *Circuit of Ireland by Muircheartach mac Neill*, ed. O'Donovan, pp. 51-2, and n. 173, ibid.
12 *Succession to High Office*, ed. J. Goody (Cambridge, 1966), p. 157. The comparative African material in this book sheds a great deal of light on early Irish kingship. Cf. ibid., pp. 157-64. Goody's doubts about the reliability of early Irish sources and about the precise meaning of the term *mac* or son are unfounded. This Dark Age evidence from Ireland is on the contrary more accurate and more extensive than that which we can recover for nineteenth-century Africa.
13 *Three Fragments*, ed. O'Donovan p.56. The dynastic marriage of Queen Tualaith sheds much light on the political, and perhaps ritual, nature of these alliances. Tualaith was the daughter of Cathal mac Finguine, a powerful king of Munster who died in A.D. 742. Her first marriage to Dúnchad, king of Leinster, ended with his death from wounds shortly after his defeat in the battle of Knockaulin (Dún Ailinne), Co. Kildare, in 728 (*Ann. Ulst.*, A.D. 728 (sub anno 727), i, 180). In that battle Dúnchad was assisted by his father-in-law, King Cathal of Munster, who shared in his defeat. The victor was none other than Fáelán, a younger brother of Dúnchad who then seized the kingship of Leinster and married Tualaith his brother's queen. Since Fáelán was opposed by king Cathal of Munster in his bid to oust Dúnchad from the Leinster kingship, we may safely assume that on his victory he seized his dead brother's queen and forcibly married her in spite of her father's opposition. This and other evidence from Irish sources

suggests that widowed queens, themselves of royal blood, had high ritual status, and marriage to such a queen by a contender for kingship was almost a prerequisite for consolidating one's position in a royal office.

14 Goody, loc. cit.

15 F.M. Stenton, *Anglo-Saxon England* (Oxford, 2nd edn., 1947), p. 243; cf. A.P. Smyth, *Scandinavian York and Dublin: the History and Archaeology of Two Related Viking Kingdoms* (New Jersey and Dublin, 1980), ii, Chart. II, 'West Saxon Kings', end of volume.

16 Dobbs, 'Women of the Uí Dúnlainge', *Irish Genealogist*, i, 197.

17 See p. 59 and ns. 3 and 4, Chapter VI above.

18 See pp. 65-7 above.

19 Dobbs, op. cit., p. 198.

20 *Ann. Ulst.* A.D. 656 (sub anno 655), i, 112. Cf. Price, *Place-names of Wicklow* vi, 363-4.

21 *Fingal Rónáin*, ed. Greene, p. 3.

22 Smyth, *Early Leinstermen* (unpublished M.A. History thesis, University College Dublin, 1969), pp. 310-26.

23 Dobbs, op. cit., p. 199.

24 Ibid., p. 198.

25 Ibid.

26 Fínsnechta was slain in battle in 695: *Ann. Ulst.* A.D. 695 (sub anno 694), i, 142.

27 Muirend died in 748: *Ann. Ulst.* A.D. 748 (sub anno 747), i, 210; and her husband, king Írgalach, was slain by British raiders on Ireland's Eye (Plate XII) forty-six years earlier in 702: ibid., A.D. 702 (sub anno 701), i, 150. Muirend was the mother of Cináed son of Írgalach, the Irish highking who predeceased his mother in 728: ibid., A.D. 728 (sub anno 727), i, 180.

28 Dobbs, op. cit., pp. 198, 203-4.

29 *C.G.H.*, i, 59.

30 For a detailed discussion of Fir Cell territory, see pp. 85-90, 114-6 below.

31 *Chronicum Scotorum: A Chronicle of Irish Affairs from the Earliest Times to A.D. 1135* ed. W.M. Hennessy (London, Rolls Ser., 1866), A.D. 643 (sub anno 641), p. 88.

32 Dobbs, op. cit., pp. 199, 205.

33 *V.S.H.*, ed. Plummer, i, 250-2. Fáelán is called the *dalta* or foster-child of Kevin of Glendalough in the Leinster genealogies of Rawl. B 502 (124.b.35), *C.G.H.*, i, 74.

34 *Ann. Ulst.* A.D. 795 (sub anno 794), i, 274.

35 Dobbs, op. cit., p. 203; Muiredach is described as 'half-king of the Leinstermen' at his death in 818: *Ann. Ulst.* A.D. 818 (sub anno 817), i, 308.

36 LL. (316.b.34), *C.G.H.*, i, 342.

37 See p. 79 above.

38 Ibid.

39 Rawl. B 502 (128.b.7), *C.G.H.*, i, 99.

40 Dobbs, op. cit., pp. 199, 205.

41 Ibid.

42 *Fingal Rónáin*, ed. Greene, pp. 3-4.

43 Ibid., p. 4.

44 Dobbs, op. cit., p. 204; *Ann. Ulst.*, A.D. 734 (sub anno 733), i, 188 and *n*. 9, p. 189, ibid.

45 *The Annals of Clonmacnoise, being Annals of Ireland, from the Earliest Period to A.D. 1408.*, ed. D. Murphy (Dublin, 1896), (sub anno 905), p. 145.

46 *Ann. Ulst.*, A.D. 948 (sub anno 947), i, 466. For Gormlaith's supposed dirge on King Cerball of Leinster, see *Three Fragments*, ed. O'Donovan, p. 223.

47 A. Stopford Green, *History of the Irish State to 1014* (London, 1925), pp. 355-6. Cf. *Cogadh Gaedhel*, ed. Todd, p. clxi, *n*. 1. A poem concerning the three 'leaps' or marriages of Gormlaith–first to Olaf of Dublin, secondly to Maelsechlainn, and lastly to Brian, is found in LL. (334.c.), *C.G.H.*, i, 13. Sitric's marriage to Brian's daughter is mentioned in the *Gogadh Gaedhel* (ed. Todd, p. 192).

48 *Njáls saga*, ed. M. Finnbogason (Reykjavík, 1944), pp. 241-5.

49 Ibid., p. 241.

CHAPTER IX

1. Walsh, *Placenames of Westmeath*, p. 89.

2 Ua Dubhlaoich, the eleventh-century kings of Fir Tulach, claimed descent from Énna Cennselach, progenitor of the royal house of Southern Leinster, ibid., pp. 95 *n*. 1, 162; cf. Smyth, 'Húi Failgi relations with Húi Néill', *Études Celtiques*, XIV, 2 (1975), 505.

3 MacNeill, *Phases of Irish History*, p. 103. Cf. Stopford Green, *Irish State to 1014*, p. 18, where that writer also rejects the idea of Ushnagh being the common boundary of the ancient Provinces.

4 *E.I.H.M.*, pp. 167-8.

5 J.H. Andrews, 'A Geographer's view of Irish History' in *The Course of Irish History*, ed. T.W. Moody and F.X. Martin (Dublin, 1967), p. 18.

6 *V.S.H.*, ed. Plummer, i, 176.

7 Ibid., p. 177.

8 Ibid., p. 194.

9 Ibid.

10 Ibid., p. 270, n. 1. The passage relating to Colmán's visit to Máedóc of Ferns is found only in the *Codex Salmanticensis* version of the *Vita*. The full text of this version is edited in *V.S.H. ex Codice Olim Salmanticensi*, ed. Heist, p. 221.

11 Smyth, 'Húi Néill and the Leinstermen', *Études Celtiques*, XIV, 1 (1975), 137-42.

12 Kenny, *Sources*, i, 220-1.

13 *Ann. Ulst.*, A.D. 737 (sub anno 736), i, 194.

14 Smyth, *Scandinavian Kings*, pp. 135-6.

15 See pp. 10 and 45-6 above.

16 *Ann. Ulst.*, A.D. 742 (sub anno 741), i, 200.

17 Ibid., A.D. 760 (sub anno 759), i, 224.

18 Ibid., A.D. 764 (sub anno 763), i, 228.

19 *Four Masters*, ed. O'Donovan, A.D. 763 (sub anno

758), i, 360.

20 *Ann. Ulst.*, A.D. 775 (sub anno 774), i, 242.

21 Ibid., A.D. 776 (sub anno 775), i, 244-6.

22 *Onomasticon*, ed. Hogan, pp. 484-5.

23 *Ann. Ulst*, A.D. 748 (sub anno 747), i, 210.

24 Ibid., A.D. 796 (sub anno 795), i, 276.

25 Ibid., A.D. 845 (sub anno 844), i, 348.

26 *Félire Óengusso Céli Dé: The Martyrology of Oengus the Culdee*, ed. W. Stokes (Henry Bradshaw Soc., London, 1905), xxix, p. 86 [ambiguous note on Mo-Machru (*sic*) mac Senain who appears under 3 March (p. 80, ibid)]

27 Finian had founded Aghowle in south-west Wicklow before he moved north to Clonard, where he died of the Great Plague in A.D. 549. His monastery continued to have close ties with Leinster and with nearby Kildare, until it was taken over by the Uí Néill highking, Donnchad, in 775 when he quarrelled with the *familia* there.

28 Smyth, 'Húi Néill and the Leinstermen', *Études Celtiques*, XIV, 1 (1975), 137-42. Brigit's excursion into Mide and Tethba is narrated in the *Old Irish Life* of that saint, for which, and also for a commentary on the text, see *Bethu Brigte*, ed. Ó hAodha, pp. x-xii, 6-13, 47-55.

29 *Martyrology of Óengus*, ed. Stokes, p. 240; cf. *Life of Fintán of Clonenagh* (*V.S.H.* i, 97) where Fintán, Mo-Chóeme and Cóemán are all said to have been disciples of Colum of Terryglass.

30 Rawl. B 502 (120.b.25-32), *C.G.H.*, i, 41.

31 See pp. 17-8, 20 above

32 Rawl. B 502 (122.bb.12); *V.S.H., ex Codici Salmanticensi*, ed. Heist, pp. 232-3.

33 *V.S.H.*, ed. Plummer, ii, 244-5.

34 Ibid., 97-8.

35 Kenney, *Sources*, i, 365.

36 *V.S.H.*, ed. Plummer, ii, 87, 206.

37 Kenney, *Sources*, i, 469, 471-2.

38 Ibid., pp. 468-9, 699 *n.*194.

39 Ibid., pp. 468, 471, 480.

40 *Ann. Ulst.*, A.D. 792 (sub anno 791), i, 270.

41 Ibid., A.D. 743 (sub anno 742), i, 202-4; A.D. 748 (sub anno 747), i, 210.

42 A good account of the places associated with Óengus the Céli Dé is given in J. Healy, *Insula Sanctorum et Doctorum, or Ireland's Ancient Schools and Scholars* (Dublin, 1893), pp. 404-13. An account of his *Martyrology* or *Félire* is given in K. Hughes, *Early Christian Ireland: Introduction to the Sources* (Sources of History, London, 1972), pp. 205-10.

43 *Martyrology of Óengus,* ed. Stokes, p. xxiv.

44 Kenney, *Sources*, i, 469, 472, 482.

45 Ibid., pp.471-2. Máeldithruib's death is noted by *Four Masters*, ed. O'Donovan, A.D. 841 (sub anno 840), i, 460.

46 Kenney, op. cit., pp. 475-6.

47 Smyth, 'The Earliest Irish Annals', *Roy. Irish Acad. Proc.*, lxxii, C (1972), 40.

48 Kenney, op. cit., *n.*192. p. 222.

49 Ibid., p. 276.

50 Ibid., pp. 271-2, 278-9.

51 Ibid., p. 278.

52 *Ann. Ulst.*, A.D. 686 (sub anno 685), i, 136.

53 Ibid., A.D. 665 (sub anno 664), i, 120. Kenney, op. cit., pp. 279-281.

54 Ibid., pp. 359-60.

55 *Bethu Brigte*, ed. Ó hAodha, pp. xxiv-xxvii.

55a *Martyrology of Óengus,* ed. Stokes pp. 128, 186.

56 *Adomnan's Life of Columba*, ed. Anderson and Anderson, pp. 215, 265, 319, 327, 435, 495 (references to Durrow); pp. 215, 219 (refs. to Clonmacnoise); pp. 409-11 (Terryglass); pp. 469, 487-9 (Brendán of Birr); pp. 221, 353-5, 501 (Cainnech of Aghaboe).

57 Ibid., pp. 343-5, 489.

58 *Sancti Columbani Opera*, ed. G.S.M. Walker, (*Scriptores Latini Hiberniae*, 2, Dublin, 1957), pp. xii-xiii. At the time of going to press I have had to make do with the imperfect text in *Patrologiae*, ed. J-P. Migne, lxxxvii (Paris, 1851), chap. ix, col. 1016.

59 *V.S.H.* ed. Plummer, ii, 4-6.

60 Healy, *Ireland's Ancient Schools and Scholars*, p. 201. The *vita* of Finian, dating to the ninth or tenth century, names the following saints who studied the Scriptures or monastic discipline under Finian at Clonard: Ciarán of Clonmacnoise, Ciarán of Seirkieran, Columcille of Iona, Colum of Terryglass, Brendán of Clonfert, Brendán of Birr, Mobhi of Glasnevin, Rhodán of Lorrha, Mo-Laise (Lasrianus) of Old Leighlin, Sinell of Cleenish, Cainnech of Aghaboe, Nainnid, Mugenoch of Cell Cumli, and Senach (Senán) of Inishcathy (*Vita S. Finniani*, in *V.S.H., ex Codice Salmanticensi*, ed. Heist, p. 101).

61 Smyth, op. cit., pp. 33-41.

62 See p. 89 above.

63 Kenney, op. cit., p. 631.

64 *Chronicum Scotorum*, ed. Hennessy, A.D. 939 (sub anno 938), p. 202.

65 Mageoghagan's account of the *Book of Durrow* is as follows: 'I have seen partly myselfe of that book of them [New Testaments alleged to have been written by Columba] which is at Dorow in the Ks County [i.e. Co. Offaly], for I saw the Ignorant man that had the same in his Custody, when sickness came upon cattle, for their Remedy putt water on the booke & suffered it to rest there a while & saw alsoe cattle returne thereby to their former or pristin state & the booke to receave no loss' (*Annals of Clonmacnoise*, ed. Murphy, p. 96).

66 Kenney, op. cit., p. 631, *n.* 18.

67 F. Henry, *Irish Art in the Early Christian Period, to 800 A.D.* (London, 1965), p. 201. Kenney, op. cit., p. 633.

68 Ibid., pp. 692-9 and *n.* 169, p. 696.

69 Ibid., p. 642. Henry, op. cit., p. 198.

70 *Cogadh Gaedhel*, ed. Todd, p. 38.

71 *Martyrology of Óengus,* ed. Stokes, p. 90, 5th Mar. Cairnech's Book, since lost, was called the *Imirche*

Ciaráin or 'Ciarán's Penitential Journey'.

72 Ibid., p. 186. 18th Aug. In the *vita* of Daig, we are told that this bishop, who eventually settled at Inis Cáin Dego (Inishkeen, Co. Louth), was remarkable for making the following items of ecclesiastical metalwork: 'bronze bells (*campanas*), cymbals, croziers, crucifixes, shrines, repositories or satchels (*capsas*), small boxes for the Sacred Hosts (*pixides*), chalices, patens, portable altars (*altariola*), chrism jars (for holy oils), and book covers which were either plain or covered with gold or silver and encrusted with precious stones' (*V.H.S., ex Codice Salmanticensi*, ed. Heist, pp. 389-90). Daig was also credited in his *Vita* with being an excellent calligrapher or scribe (ibid., p. 390).

72a *Betha Colmáin maic Lúacháin, Life of Colmán son of Luachán,* ed. K. Meyer, Roy. Irish Acad., Todd Lecture Ser., xvii (1911), pp. 38-9. For royal patronage of Irish monasteries see, Smyth, *Scandinavian York and Dublin,* ii (1980), 136-151.

73 *V.S.H.* ed. Plummer, i, 177.

74 *Martyrology of Óengus,* ed. Stokes, 3rd Sept. When Longarad died, all the book-satchels or *tiaga lebar* of Ireland were alleged to have fallen down (ibid., p. 198).

75 Giraldus, *Topographia,* ed. Dimlock, v, 123-4.

76 R. Flower, *The Irish Tradition* (Oxford, 1966, reprint of 1947 edn.), pp. 24-40.

77 Ibid., pp. 27-8.

78 *Ann. Ulst.,* A.D. 776 (sub anno 775), i, 244; A.D. 800 (sub anno 799), i, 282.

79 Ibid., A.D. 805 (sub anno 804), i, 290.

80 Henry, op. cit., pp. 138-9.

81 I discuss the archaeological and historical significance of the Northern and Southern types of Irish High Crosses in: Smyth, *Scandinavian York and Dublin,* ii, (1980), 284-91.

82 Henry, op. cit., pp. 134-5.

83 *V.S.H.* ed. Plummer, i, 192-3.

84. *Martyrology of Óengus,* ed. Stokes, p. 466. Cf, the tract, *Of the Sons of the Ua Suanaig (Bethada Náem,* ed. Plummer, i, 312-3), where Máel Bresal is described as the grandson of Flann Lena and not his son.

CHAPTER X

1 Tulach meic Comgaill was believed to have been founded as an obscure monastery in the early centuries of Irish Christianity by two brothers, Senach and Colmán, the sons of a certain Lugna of the nearby tribe of Loígis. These brothers are stated to have resided at Tulaigh meic Comgaill i nDruimnibh Togha. i. isin Nuacongbháil: P. Walsh, *Genealogiae Regum et Sanctorum Hiberniae* (1928), p. 102. Cf. *Book of Leinster,* ed. Best, Bergin, and O'Brien, i, xii-xiv.

2 Ibid., p. xiii.

3 Ibid., pp. xv-xvii. Áed of Terryglass ceased his compilation or died, sometime between A.D. 1201 and 1224, so the Book was continued into the post-Norman era. Best believed the *Book of Leinster* was the work of a single scribe, Áed, (ibid., p. xv), but O'Sullivan has argued that the compilation involved the team-work of several scribes: W. O'Sullivan, 'Notes on the Scripts and Make-up of the Book of Leinster', *Celtica,* vii (1966), 1-31; especially, pp. 6-13, 20-5. Hughes, *Early Christian Ireland: Sources,* pp. 274-5.

4 *Book of Leinster,* ed. Best, Bergin and O'Brien, i, xiv-xv.

5 Hughes, op. cit., p. 273.

6 H.P.A. Oskamp, 'Notes on the History of Lebor na hUidre', *Roy. Irish Acad. Proc.,* lxv (1967), C., 117-37. Oskamp suggested (ibid., pp. 119, 130) that one of the principal scribes of *Lebor na hUidre* (Scribe A) had close contacts with Glenn Uissen, by which presumably he meant the monastery of Cell Eision or Killeshin, Co. Leix (Plate XVI).

7 Hughes, op. cit., p. 274.

8 I examined the Leinster genealogies in Rawl. B 502 for the period 500-800: Smyth, *Early Leinstermen* (unpublished M.A. History thesis, University College Dublin, 1969).

9 Rawl. B 502 (122.b.32)-(123.f.18), *C.G.H.,* i, 56-65.

10 Smyth, 'Húi Failgi Relations with Húi Néill', *Études Celtique,* XIV, ii (1975), 509-12.

11 Rawl. B 502 (120.b.33, 120.b.45), *C.G.H.,* i, 41, 42; (124.b.27), *C.G.H.,* i, 73.

12 Rawl. B 502 (124.b.37), *C.G.H.,* i, 74; (126.b.12), *C.G.H.,* i, 86; (126.a.54), *C.G.H.,* i, 85; references to Brigit occur at 125.b.53; 126.a.28; 127.b.37; 137.b.47; 139.b.33, *C.G.H.* i, 82, 84, 94, 130, 133.

13 *Ann. Ulst.,* A.D. 1041, i, 578.

14 Rawl. B 502 (117.c.6), *C.G.H.* i, 12.

15 L.L. (316.a.26), *C.G.H.,* i, 339.

16 Orpen, *Ireland Under the Normans,* ii, 67-8.

17 Giraldus Cambresis Opera, *Expugnatio Hibernica* ed. J.F. Dimlock (Rolls Series, 1867) V, 397.

18. *A Roll of the Proceedings of the King's Council in Ireland for a portion of the sixteenth year of the reign of Richard the Second A.D. 1392-93,* ed. J. Graves (Rolls Ser., London, 1887), pp. 8-9. A.J. Otway-Ruthven, *A History of Medieval Ireland* (London, 1968), pp. 287, 302, 309-11, 324.

19. K. Nicholls, *Gaelic and Gaelicised Ireland* (Dublin, 1972), p. 174.

20. Ibid., p. 171.

21. Otway-Ruthven, op. cit., p. 313. The roads from Carlow, presumably to Dublin, were described as 'perilous' in a petition to the council in 1392. *King's Council in Ireland, 16th Richard II,* ed., Graves, pp. 12-3.

22. Otway-Ruthven, op. cit., p. 330 and *n.* 41.

23. J. Webb, 'Translation of a French Metrical History of the Deposition of King Richard the Second', *Archaeologia,* xx (1824), 35, 302.

24. Cf. J.F. Lydon, *The Lordship of Ireland in the*

Middle Ages (Dublin, 1972), pp. 236-8.

25. R. Bagwell, *Ireland under the Tudors* (London, 1963 reprint of 1885-90 edn.), iii, 333.

26. J. Otway-Ruthven, 'The Medieval County of Kildare', *Irish Historical Studies*, xi (1958-9), 184 and *n.* 13.

27. Webb, op. cit., pp. 40, 305. See E. Curtis, *A History of Medieval Ireland from 1110 to 1513* (Dublin and Cork, 1923), pp. 317-8, for the general background to Richard's second Irish expedition.

28. Webb, op. cit., pp. 27-8, 298.

29. Otway-Ruthven, *Medieval Ireland*, p. 327.

30. A detailed account of Irish cattle at *c.* 1600 is found in *Fynes Moryson's Description of Ireland*, ed., H. Morley, in *Ireland under Elizabeth and James the First* (London, 1890) p. 421.

31. *A Treatise of Ireland by John Dymmok*, ed. R. Butler, in *Tracts relating to Ireland*, II (Dublin, Irish Archaeological Society, 1843), pp. 5, 54.

32. *Scéla Mucce Meic Dathó*, ed. R. Thurneysen (Medieval and Modern Irish Ser., vi, Dublin, 1969), pp. 1-20.

33. *Fynes Moryson's Description*, pp. 425, 427.

34. Bagwell, op. cit., i, 206, 213.

34a G.A. Hayes-McCoy, 'The Completion of the Tudor Conquest, and the Advance of the Counter-Reformation, 1571-1603', in *A New History of Ireland: iii, Early Modern Period, 1534-1691*, eds. T.W. Moody, F.X. Martin, and F.J. Byrne (Oxford, 1976), p. 131.

35. Webb, op. cit., pp. 27-8, *n. n.*

36. Otway-Ruthven, op. cit., p. 332.

37. Webb, op. cit., pp. 32, 300. It is highly unlikely that Richard could have led a large army through any of the more southerly passes over the Wicklow hills on his way from Kilkenny.

38 See p. 25 above.

39. Webb, op. cit., pp. 27, 298.

40. Ibid., pp. 45, 308-9. A thousand marks in 1399 was the equivalent of approximately half a million pounds sterling in the currency of 1981, if the calculation is based on the cost of labour.

41. *Ann. Ulst.,* A.D. 1417, iii, 72-3; *Four Masters*, ii, 830-1 (sub anno 1417).

42. Dymmok informs us that the Leinster forest had been greatly diminished by the close of the sixteenth century because they were 'ready harboures for the Irish rebell.' (*Dymmok's Treatise*, ed. Butler, p. 6). We have seen how inroads had been made into the woods in the lower Barrow Valley in the late fourteenth century and how the Great Wood in Leix was partially felled by the Fitzgeralds in 1514 (see pp. 25 and 109 above). In 1537, there was a proposal to repair the castle at Trim with several hundred great oaks to be felled in the forest of Offaly. (*Dymmok's Treatise*, editorial note, p. 78). This Offaly forest was still regarded as the best preserved of Irish woodlands by Moryson when he visited Ireland in the early seventeenth century. *Fynes Moryson's Description*, p. 423.

43. *Dymmok's Treatise*, pp. 38-42.

44. The last MacMurrough to be recognized by the English administration was executed in 1557. Nicholls, op. cit., p. 172.

45. Otway-Ruthven, 'Medieval County of Kildare', *Irish Hist. Stud.*, xi (1958-9), 182, 184.

46. Curtis, *Medieval Ireland* (1st. edn.), p. 315.

47. Otway-Ruthven, op. cit., p. 184.

48. Kenney, Sources, i, 22.

49. Ibid., p. 23.

50. Bagwell, op. cit., i, 304.

51. Ibid., p. 213.

52. *Dymmok's Treatise*, ed. Butler, p. 31.

53. Ibid., p. 32.

54. Ibid., p. 33. Dymmok's account of the Leinster march is based on Harrington's journal. Bagwell, op. cit., iii, 323, *n.* 1.

55. Dymmok, loc. cit. C. Falls, *Elizabeth's Irish Wars* (New York and London, reprint, 1970), p. 234.

56. *Dymmok's Treatise*, ed. Butler, p. 43.

57. Ibid.

58. *Fynes Moryson's Description*, pp. 421, 423.

59. *Four Masters*, ed. O'Donovan, (1st edn.), iii, 2146-7, (sub anno 1600).

60. Ibid.

61 See p. 89 above.

62. M. MacCurtain, *Tudor and Stuart Ireland* (Dublin, 1972), pp. 51-61.

Historical Atlas

Historical Atlas

Contents

Plate   Page

I   The natural regions of ancient Leinster   141
II   Mountains and river basins   142
III   Soils and settlement   143
IV   Geology   144
V   Migration of peoples A.D. 300-550   145
VI   Medieval Dioceses   146
VII   Baronies   147
VIII   Tribes A.D. 800   148
IX   Irish dynasties A.D. 1150   149
X   Anglo-Norman conquest in Leinster and Meath c. A.D. 1200   150
       Key to Plates XI - XVI   151
XI   Northern and North-Eastern Regions: Political   152
XII   Northern and North-Eastern Regions: Topographical   153
XIII   North-Western Region: Political   154
XIV   North-Western Region: Topographical   155
XV   Southern Region: Political   156
XVI   Southern Region: Topographical   157

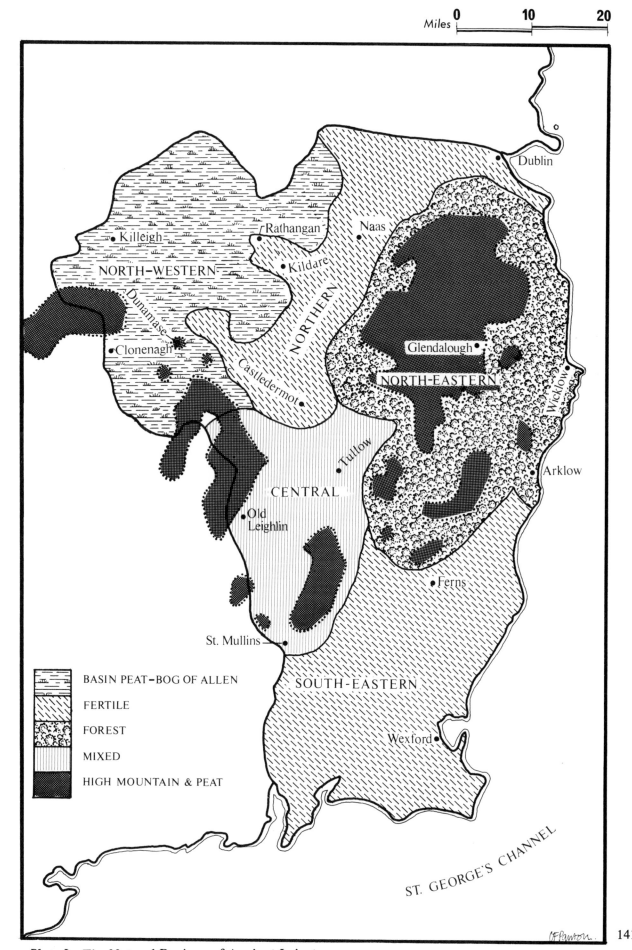

Miles 0 10 20

Killeigh

Rathangan

Naas

Dublin

NORTH-WESTERN

Kildare

Dunamase

NORTHERN

Clonenagh

Castledermot

Glendalough

NORTH-EASTERN

Wicklow

Tullow

CENTRAL

Arklow

Old Leighlin

St. Mullins

Ferns

SOUTH-EASTERN

BASIN PEAT—BOG OF ALLEN

FERTILE

FOREST

MIXED

HIGH MOUNTAIN & PEAT

Wexford

ST. GEORGE'S CHANNEL

141

Plate I   The Natural Regions of Ancient Leinster

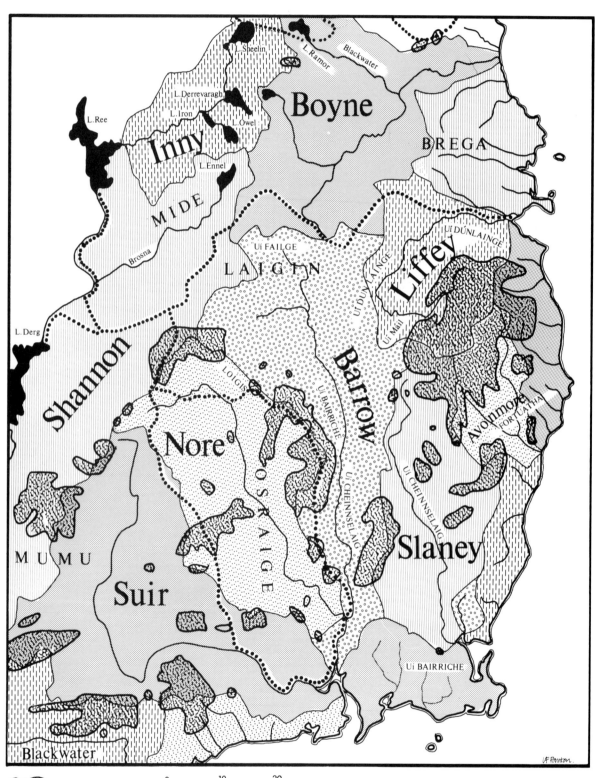

LAND ABOVE 600ft   0   10   20   Miles   BOUNDARIES OF MAJOR KINGDOMS ●●●●●●●●

Plate II   Mountains and River Basins

Boyne

Inny

BREGA

L.Ree

L.Sheelin

L.Ramor

Blackwater

L.Derrevaragh

L.Iron

Owel

L.Ennel

MIDE

Brosna

Uí DÚNLAINGE

Liffey

Uí FAILGE

LAIGIN

Uí DÚNLAINGE

Uí Máil

L.Derg

Shannon

Nore

Barrow

Uí BAIRRICHE

Uí CHEINNSELAIG

Avonmore

FORTUATHA

MUMU

Suir

Uí CHEINNSELAIG

Slaney

Blackwater

Uí BAIRRICHE

LOIGIS

OSRAIGE

I.F. Ponton.

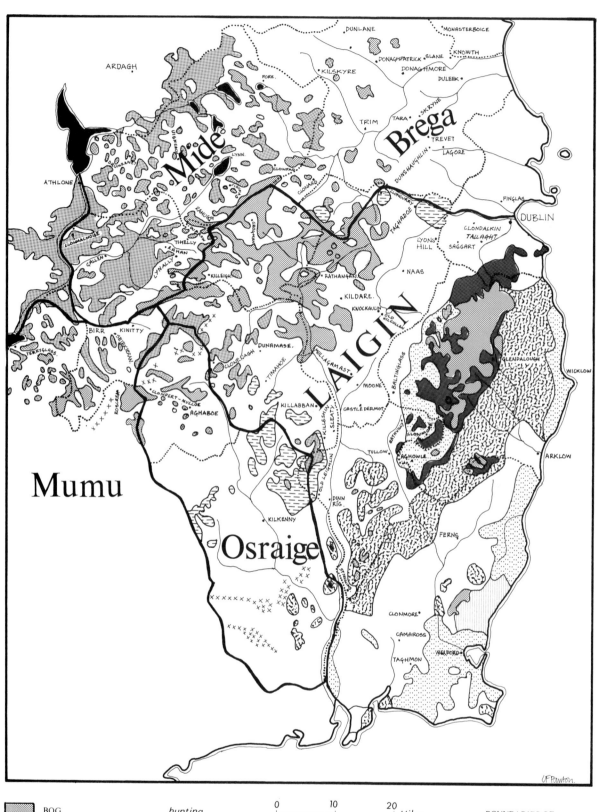

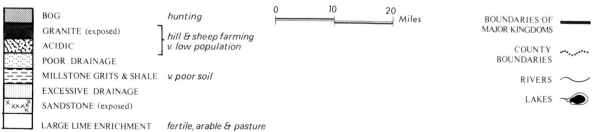

BOG	*hunting*	
GRANITE (exposed)	⎫ *hill & sheep farming*	
ACIDIC	⎬ *v. low population*	
POOR DRAINAGE		
MILLSTONE GRITS & SHALE	*v. poor soil*	
EXCESSIVE DRAINAGE		
SANDSTONE (exposed)		
LARGE LIME ENRICHMENT	*fertile, arable & pasture*	

BOUNDARIES OF MAJOR KINGDOMS ▬▬▬

COUNTY BOUNDARIES ⋯⋯⋯

RIVERS 〜

LAKES 🌢

0   10   20
Miles

Plate III Soils and Settlement

143

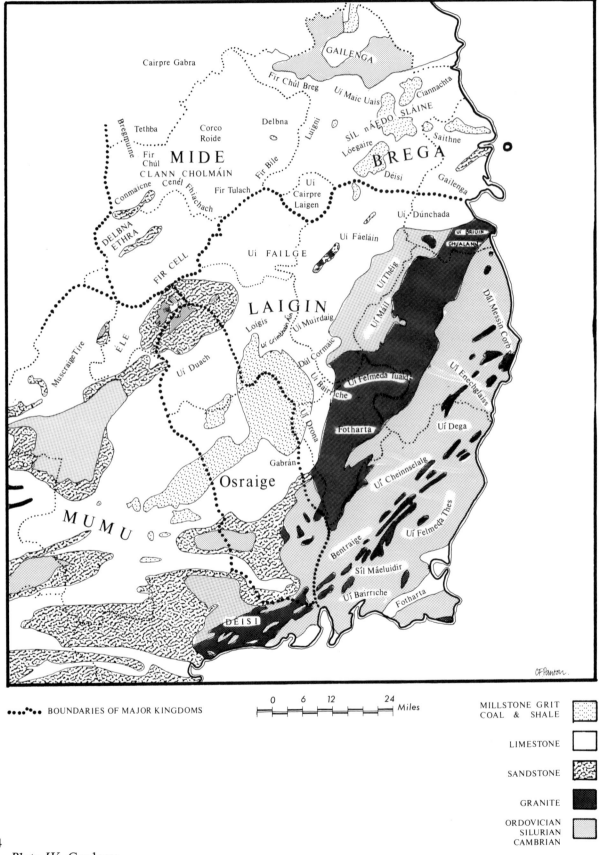

Plate IV Geology

Map labels:

Cairpre Gabra

GAILENGA

Fir Chúl Breg

Uí Maic Uais

Ciannachta

SÍL nÁEDO SLÁINE

Saithne

Tethba

Corco Roíde

Delbna

Luigni

Lóegaire

BREGA

Breemuine

Fir Chúl

MIDE

CLANN CHOLMÁIN

Fir Bile

Déisi

Gaílenga

Conmaicne

Cenél Fhíachach

Fir Tulach

Uí Cairpre Laigen

Uí Dúnchada

DELBNA ETHRA

Uí Fáeláin

Uí Bruin

FIR CELL

Uí FAILGE

Chualann

Muscraige Tíre

ÉLE

LAIGIN

Loígis

Uí Muirdaig

Uí Thúig

Uí Máil

Dál Messin Corb

Uí Duach

Uí Crimthain Áin

Dál Cormaic

Uí Enechglaiss

Uí Bairrche

Uí Felméda Tuaid

Uí Dega

Uí Drona

Fotharta

Gabrán

Osraige

Uí Cheinnselaig

MUMU

Bentraige

Uí Felméda Thes

Síl Máeluidir

Uí Bairrche

Fotharta

DÉISI

●●●●●● BOUNDARIES OF MAJOR KINGDOMS

0 6 12   24 ⌐ Miles

MILLSTONE GRIT COAL & SHALE

LIMESTONE

SANDSTONE

GRANITE

ORDOVICIAN SILURIAN CAMBRIAN

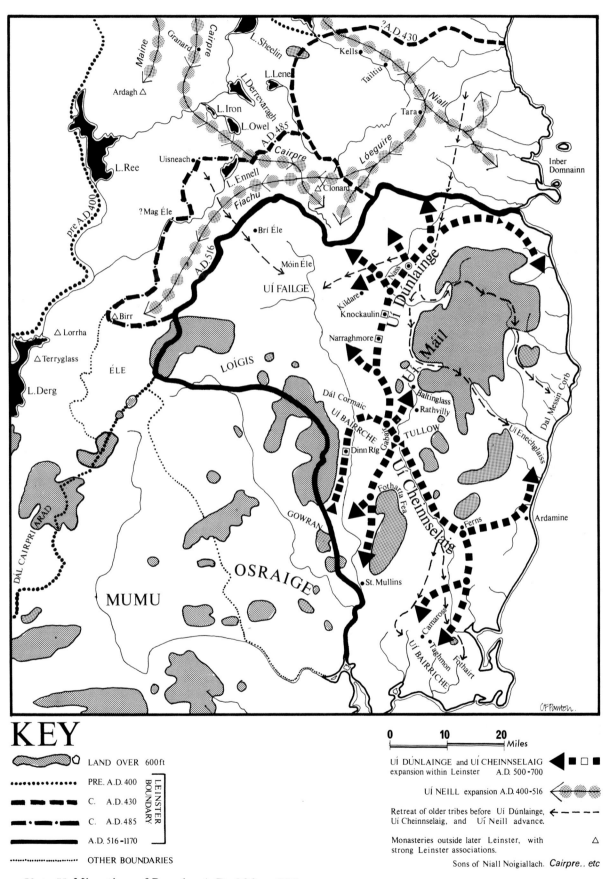

KEY

	LAND OVER 600ft	
●●●●●●●●●●	PRE. A.D. 400	
▬ ▬ ▬ ▬	C. A.D. 430	LEINSTER BOUNDARY
▬·▬·▬·	C. A.D. 485	
▬▬▬▬▬	A.D. 516 -1170	
●●●●●●●●	OTHER BOUNDARIES	

0   10   20   Miles

UÍ DÚNLAINGE and UÍ CHEINNSELAIG
expansion within Leinster   A.D. 500 -700   ◄ ■ □ ■

UÍ NEILL expansion A.D. 400 -516   ⇐≪≪≪

Retreat of older tribes before Uí Dúnlainge,
Uí Cheinnselaig, and Uí Neill advance.   ← ─ ─ ─

Monasteries outside later Leinster, with   △
strong Leinster associations.

Sons of Niall Noígiallach.   *Cairpre.. etc*

Plate V Migration of Peoples A.D. 300 − 550

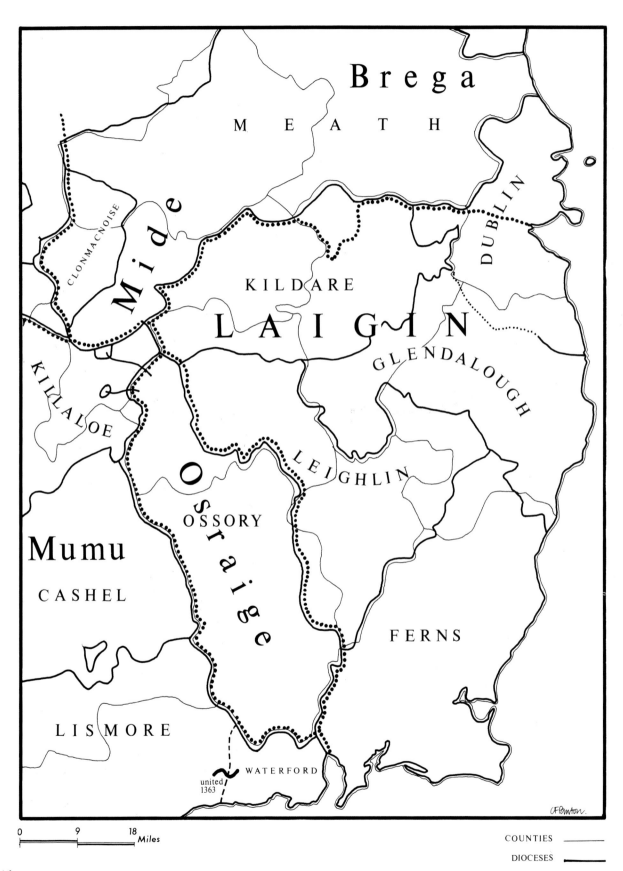

B r e g a

M E A T H

CLONMACNOISE

Mide

DUBLIN

KILDARE

L A I G I N

GLENDALOUGH

KILLALOE

LEIGHLIN

OSSORY

Osraige

Mumu

CASHEL

FERNS

LISMORE

WATERFORD

united 1363

0   9   18 Miles

COUNTIES _____

DIOCESES ▬▬▬

MAJOR KINGDOMS ••••••••

Plate VI Medieval Dioceses

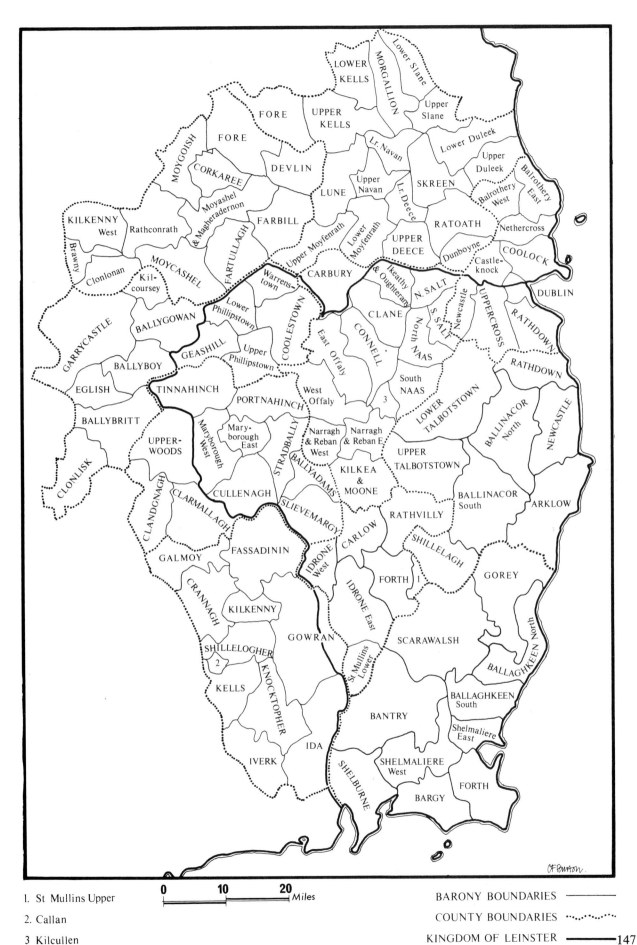

Plate VII Baronies

1. St Mullins Upper

2. Callan

3 Kilcullen

BARONY BOUNDARIES ————

COUNTY BOUNDARIES ·····•·····

KINGDOM OF LEINSTER ————147

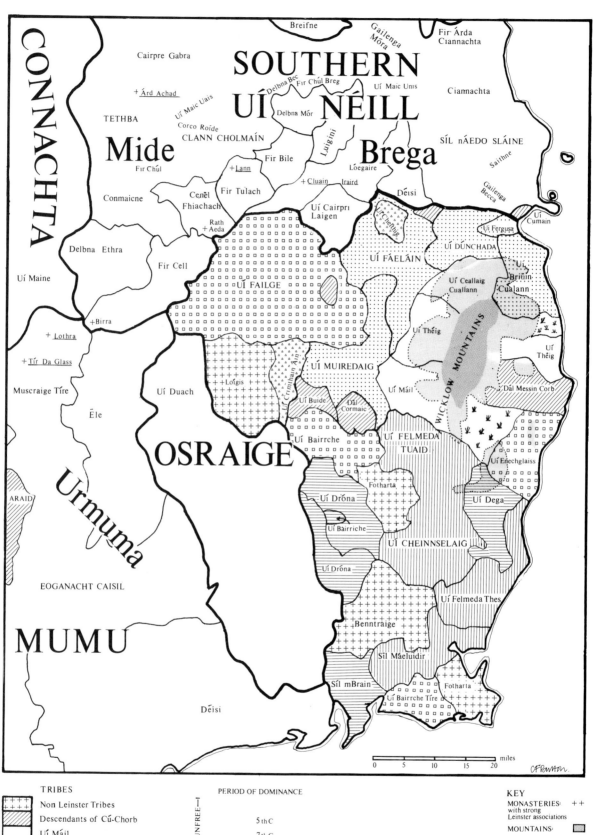

Plate VIII Tribes A.D. 800

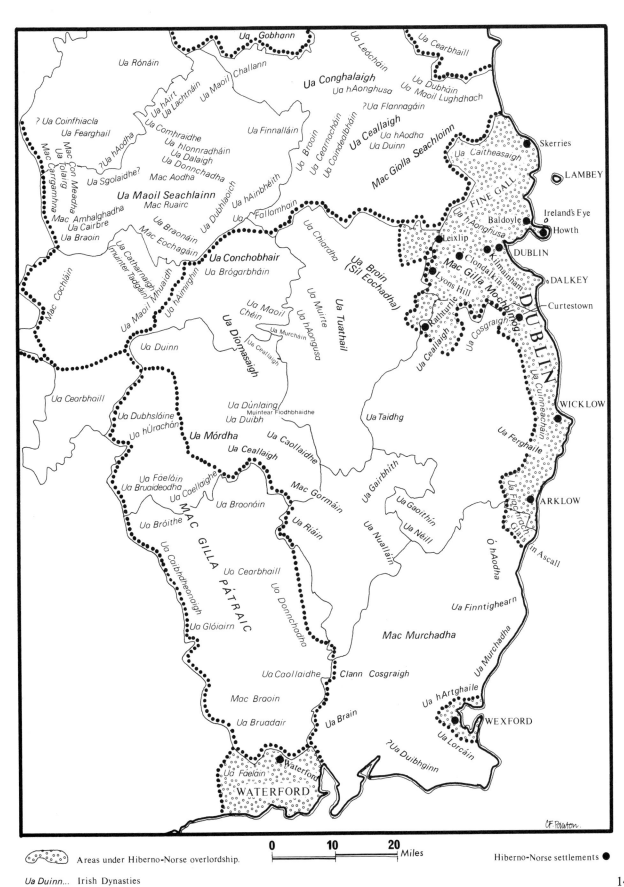

Ua Gobhann

Ua Rónáin

Ua Cearbhaill

Ua Leócháin

Ua Conghalaigh
Ua hAonghusa

Ua Dubháin
Ua Maoil Lughdhach

Ua hAirt
Ua Lachtnáin
Ua Maoil Challann

?Ua Flannagáin

? Ua Coinfhiacla
Ua Fearghail
Ua Comhraidhe
Ua hIonnradháin
Ua Braoin
Ua Cearnacháin
Ua Ceallaigh
Ua hAodha
Ua Duinn

Ua Finnalláin
Ua Coindealbháin

Mac Con Meadha
Ua Tolairg
Mac Cargamhna
?Ua hAodha
Ua Dalaigh
Ua Donnchadha
Mac Aodha

Ua Sgolaidhe?

FINE GALL
Ua Caitheasaigh

Skerries

LAMBEY

Mac Amhalghadha
Ua Cairbre
Ua Braoin
Ua Maoil Seachlainn
Mac Ruairc
Ua Dubhlaoich
Ua hAinbhéith

Ireland's Eye

Ua hAonghusa
Baldoyle
Howth

Mac Giolla Seachloinn

Leixlip
DUBLIN

Mac Braonáin
Ua Fallamhain

Mac Cochláin
Mac Eochagáin
Ua Conchobhair
Ua hAimirghin

Ua Chiardha

Ua Broin
(Síl Eochadha)

Clondalkin
Kilmainham
Mac Gilla Mocholmog
Lyons Hill
DALKEY

Ua Catharnaigh
(muinter Tadgáin)
Ua Maoil Mhuaidh
Ua Brógarbháin

Rathfarnham
Curtestown

Ua Maoil
Chéin
Ua Muirte
Ua hAonghusa
Ua Tuathail
Rathturtle
Ua Ceallaigh
Ua Cosgraigh

Ua Murcháin
Ua Ceallaigh

Ua Duinn
Ua Díomasaigh

WICKLOW

Ua Cearbhaill

Ua Dúnlaing
Muintear Fiodhbhaidhe
Ua Duibh

Ua Taidhg

Ua Ferghaile

Ua Dubhsláine
Ua hÚracháin
Ua Mórdha
Ua Ceallaigh

Ua Caollaidhe

ARKLOW

Ua Faeláin
Ua Bruaideodha
Ua Caellaighe
Ua Broonáin

Ua Gairbhíth

Ua Gaoithín

Glais in Ascall
Ua Fiaghrach

Mac Gormáin

Ua Néill
Ó hAodha

Ua Bróithe

Ua Riáin

Ua Nualláin

MAC GILLA PÁTRAIC

Ua Cearbhaill

Ua Donnchadha

Ua Finntighearn

Ua Caibhdheanaigh

Mac Murchadha

Ua Glóiairn

Ua Murchadha

Ua Caollaidhe
Clann Cosgraigh

Mac Braoin

Ua hArtghaile

Ua Bruadair
Ua Brain

WEXFORD

?Ua Duibhginn

Ua Lorcáin

Waterford
Ua Faeláin
WATERFORD

C.F. POWTON.

0   10   20
                    Miles

Areas under Hiberno-Norse overlordship.

Hiberno-Norse settlements ●

Ua Duinn... Irish Dynasties

149

Plate IX Irish Dynasties A.D. 1150

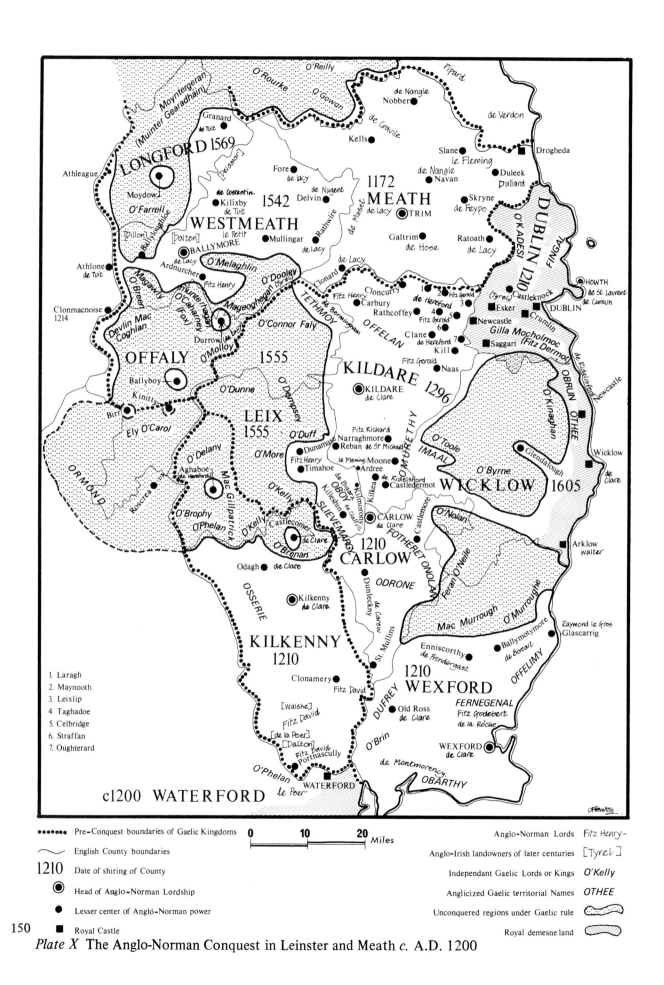

O'Reilly
Moyntergeran (Muinter Gearadhain)
O'Rourke
O'Gowan
de Nangle
Nobber
Pipard
de Verdon
Granard
de Tuit
LONGFORD 1569
Kells
de Craville
Slane
le Fleming
Drogheda
Athleague
Moydow
O'Farrell
Fore
de Lacy
1542
Delvin
de Nugent
1172
MEATH
de Lacy
Navan
de Nangle
Duleek
Dullard
Skryne
de Feypo
DUBLIN 1210
FINGAL
Kilixby
de Tuit
WESTMEATH
le Petit
Mullingar
Rathwire
de Lacy
Galtrim
de Hose
Trim
Ratoath
de Lacy
O'KADESI
Dillon
[Dalton]
BALLYMORE
de Lacy
O'Melaghlin
de Lacy
HOWTH
de St. Laurent
de Cursun
Athlone
de Tuit
Ardnurcher
Fitz Henry
O'Dooley
Clonard
Fitz Henry
Cloncurry
de Hereford
(Tyrel) Castleknock
DUBLIN
Magawly
O'Breen
Muinter Thagan (O'Cataney) (Fox)
Mageoghegan (Tyrel)
TETHMOY
de Bermingham
Carbury
1 2
3
Fitz Gerald
Esker
Crumlin
Clonmacnoise 1214
Devlin Mac Coghlan
Durrow (de Lacy)
O'Molloy
O'Connor Faly
OFFELAN
Rathcoffey
4
5
Fitz Gerald 6
Newcastle
Saggart
Gilla Mocholmoc (Fitz Dermot)
de Ridelesford Newcastle
OBRUN
OTHEE
O'Kinaghan
Clane
de Hereford
7
Kill
KILDARE 1296
Fitz Gerald
Naas
Ballyboy
1555
O'Dunne
O'Dempsey
KILDARE
de Clare
OMBRETHY
IMAAL
O'Toole
Glendalough
O'Kinaghan
Wicklow
de Clare
Birr
Kinitty
LEIX
1555
O'Duff
Fitz Richard
Narraghmore
Reban de St Michael
WICKLOW 1605
Ely O'Carol
O'Delany
O'More
Dunamase
Fitz Henry
Timahoe
le Fleming Moone
Ardree
O'Byrne
ORMOND
Roscrea
Aghaboe (de Hereford)
Mac Gillapatrick
O'Kelly
Kilkea
Kilmoroony
Killeshin de Carew
OBOY
de Bigot
de Ridelsford
Castledermot
IMAAL
Castlemore
FOTHERET ONOLAN
O'Nolan
Arklow
walter
O'Brophy
O'Phelan
O'Kelly
SLIEVEMARGY
CARLOW
de Clare
1210
CARLOW
Feran O'Neile
O'Nolan
Odagh
de Clare
Castlecomer
de Clare
O'Brenan
Dunleckny
de Carew
ODRONE
Mac Murrough
O'Murroughe
Raymond le Gros
Glascarrig
Kilkenny
de Clare
St. Mullins
Enniscorthy
de Prendergast
Ballymotymore
de Bocart
OFFELIMY
KILKENNY 1210
Clonamery
Fitz David
1210
WEXFORD
FERNEGENAL
Fitz Godebert
de la Roche
[Walshe]
Fitz David
DUFREY
Old Ross
de Clare
[de la Poer]
[Dalton]
Fitz David
Portnascully
O'Brin
WEXFORD
de Clare
O'Phelan
le Poer
de Montmorency
OBARTHY

c1200 WATERFORD

1. Laragh
2. Maynooth
3. Leixlip
4. Taghadoe
5. Celbridge
6. Straffan
7. Oughterard

●●●●●● Pre-Conquest boundaries of Gaelic Kingdoms

〜 English County boundaries

1210 Date of shiring of County

◉ Head of Anglo-Norman Lordship

● Lesser center of Anglo-Norman power

150 ■ Royal Castle

0   10   20 Miles

Anglo-Norman Lords *Fitz Henry*-

Anglo-Irish landowners of later centuries *[Tyrel]*

Independant Gaelic Lords or Kings *O'Kelly*

Anglicized Gaelic territorial Names *OTHEE*

Unconquered regions under Gaelic rule

Royal demesne land

Plate X The Anglo-Norman Conquest in Leinster and Meath *c.* A.D. 1200

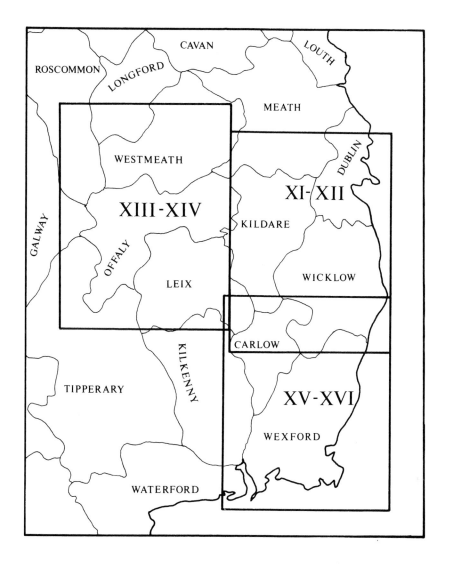

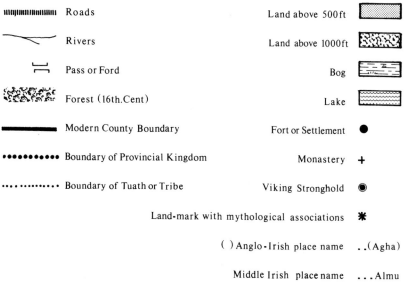

ⅲⅲⅲⅲⅲⅲⅲ	Roads	Land above 500ft	▨
⌒⌒	Rivers	Land above 1000ft	▨
⌐⌐	Pass or Ford	Bog	▨
▨	Forest (16th.Cent)	Lake	▨
▬▬	Modern County Boundary	Fort or Settlement	●
•••••••••	Boundary of Provincial Kingdom	Monastery	+
••••••••••	Boundary of Tuath or Tribe	Viking Stronghold	◉
		Land-mark with mythological associations	✳
		( ) Anglo-Irish place name	. .(Agha)
		Middle Irish place name	. . .Almu

Key to Plates XI — XVI

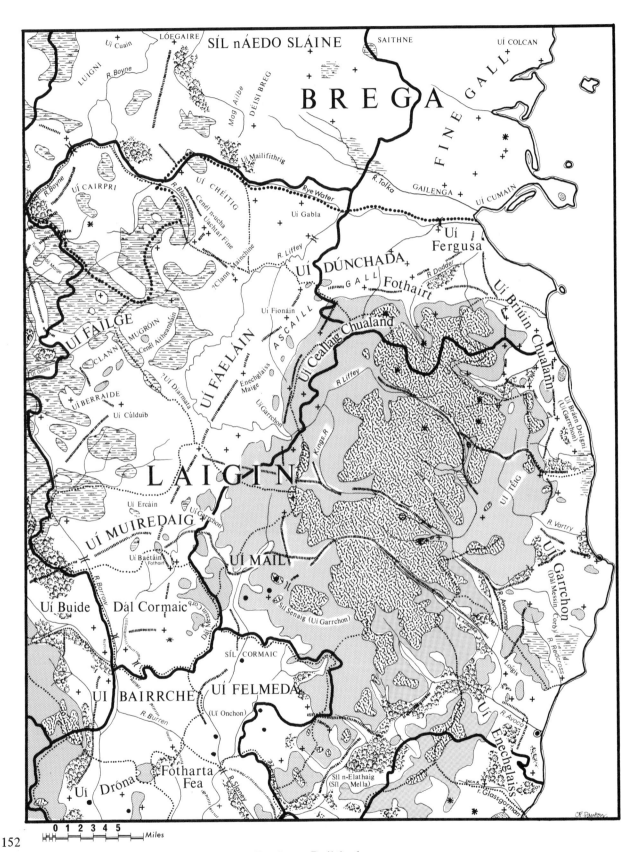

Map labels (as visible):

Uí Cuáin • LÓEGAIRE • SÍL nÁEDO SLÁINE • SAITHNE • Uí COLCAN
LUIGNI • R. Boyne • Mag Ailbe • DÉISI BREG • BREGA • FINE GALL
Uí Mailifithrig • Uí CAIRPRI • R. Boyne • R. Blackwater • SÍL CHÉITIG • Rye Water • R. Tolka • GAILENGA • Uí CUMAIN
Tuath Dá Maige • Cenél n-ucha • Uachtar Fine • Uí Gabla • Uí Fergusa
Clann Mainchíne • R. Liffey • Uí DÚNCHADA • GALL • Fothairt • R. Dodder • Uí Briúin Chualann
Uí FAILGE • MUGRÓIN • Cenél Aithemáin • Uí Fionáin • ASCAILL • Uí Cellaig Chualand • Uí Briúin Chualann • (Uí Garrchon) • Uí Briéen Deilgni
Uí Gabla • CLANN • Uí Diarmata • Uí FÁELÁIN • Enechglaiss Maige • R. Liffey
Uí BERRAIDE • Uí Cúlduib • Uí Garrchon • LAIGIN • R. Liffey • Kings R. • Uí TÉIG • R. Vartry
Uí Ercáin • Uí Garrchon • Uí MUIREDAIG • Uí Garrchon • Uí Baetáin Fothairt • Uí Garrchon (Dál Messin Corb)
Uí MÁIL • R. Avonmore • R. Vartry
Uí Buide • Dál Cormaic • Dál Messin Corb • Síl Senaig (Uí Garrchon) • R. Avonbeg • R. Redcross
SÍL CORMAIC • R. Barrow • Loigis
Uí BAIRRCHE • Uí FELMEDA • R. Avoca
R. Burren • (Uí Onchon) • Uí Enechglaiss
Síl n-Elathaig (Síl Mella) • INCH R. • R. Glassgorman
Uí Dróna • Fotharta Fea • R. Slaney • R. Glassgorman

0 1 2 3 4 5 Miles

152

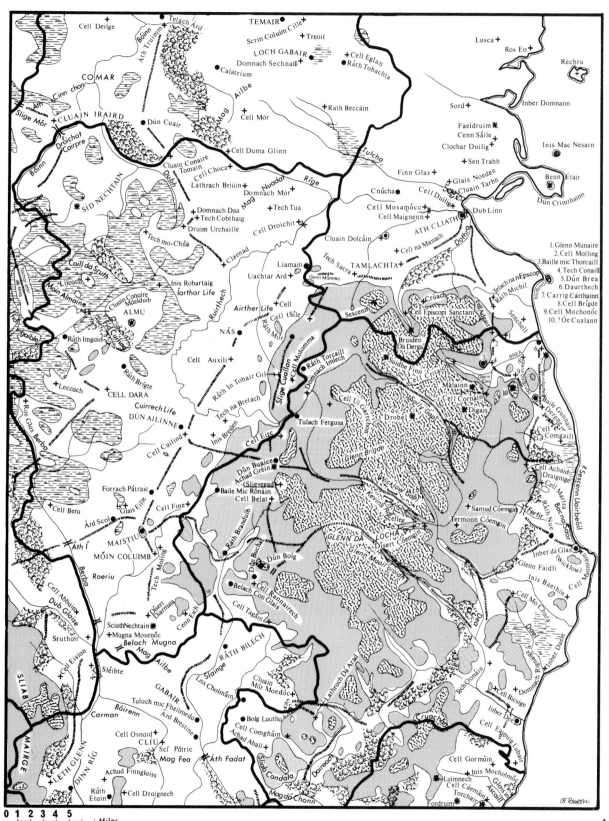

Plate XII Northern and North Eastern Regions: Topographical

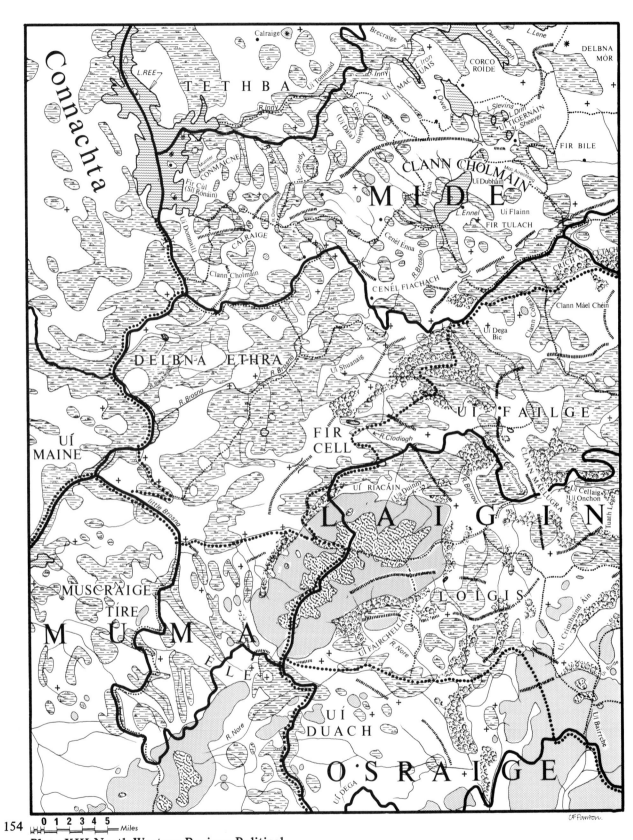

Connachta

Calraige ⊛

TETHBA

L.REE

Brecraige

L. Derravaragh
L. Lene

DELBNA
MÓR

R. Inny
Uí MAC UAIS
CORCO
ROÍDE

L. Iron

R. Inny

Uí Tommaid

Corcu Adaim
(Uí Dala)

L. Owel

L. Slevins
L. Drin
Uí TIGERNÁIN
L. Sheever

Fir Cúl
(Síl Rónáin)

Muinter
Melsinne
CONMAICNE

R. Tang

Sevily

R. Dungoina

FIR BILE

CLANN CHOLMÁIN
Móc Airechtaig
Uí Dubháin

MIDE

Uí Muca

L. Ennel Uí Flainn

FIR TULACH

Uí Donnaili

CALRAIGE

Cenél Enna

R. Brosna

CENÉL FIACHACH

CRÍCH NA CETACH

Clann Cholmáin

Clann Colgan

Clann Máel Chein

Uí Dega
Bic

DELBNA · ETHRA

R. Brosna

Uí Shuanaig

R. Brosna

Blackwater

Uí · FAILGE

FÍR
CELL

R. Clodiogh

CLANN MÁELUGRA

Uí Cellaig
Uí Onchon

Uí
MAINE

little Brosna

Uí RIACÁIN

Ua Duinn

R. Barrow

Clann Colgan

Tuath Legce

L · A · I · G · I · N

MUSCRAIGE
TIRE

M · U · M · A

ÉLE

Uí FAIRCHELLÁIN

R. Nore

LOÍGIS

Uí Crimthann Áin

Uí Bairrche

R. Nore

R. Bróge

UÍ
DUACH

O · S · R · A · I · G · E

Uí DEGA

CFPawton.

0 1 2 3 4 5 Miles

Plate XIII North-Western Region: Political

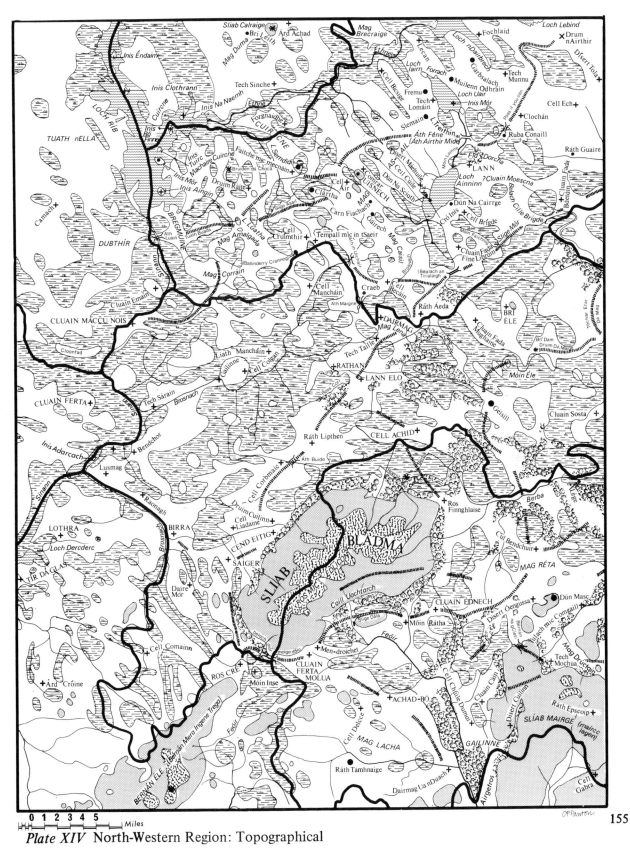

Sliab Calraige
Árd Achad
Brí Léith
Mag Duma
Mag Brecraige
Loch Lebind
Fochlaid
Drum nAirthir
Dísert Tola
Inis Éndaim
Tech Sinche
Loch nDairbrech
Ecen
Garbsalach
Tech Munnu
Loch Íairn
Forrach
Ethne
Inis Clothrann
Inis Na Naemh
Cell Bicsige
Fremu
Muilenn Odhráin
Cell Ech
Ethne
Tech Lománn
Loch Uair
Inis Mór
Clochán
CUIRCNE
Slemain
L Treithin
Ruba Conaill
LOCH RIB
Cuircne
Forgnaidhe
Áth Féne
(Áth Airthir Mide)
TUATH nELLA
Inis Bó Finne
L Semdidi
Dísert Maeltuile
Ráth Guaire
Inis Túirc
Faitche mic mecnáin
Cell Cúile
Fíd Dorcha
Machaire Cuircne
Bruiden da Chocá
KComrar
LANN
Inis Mór
Drum Ráite
Cell
Áir
CUISNECH
Dún Na Sciath
Loch Ainninn
?Cluain Moescna
Cluain Fada Boctáin
Inis Aingin
Clártha
MAG
Cárech
Cró Inis
Cell Brígde
Camach
Cárn Fíachach
Dún Na Cairrge
Belach Cille Brígde
DUBTHÍR
L Uartha
Crumthir
Móin Faichnig
Slige Mór
Áth Luain
Tuath Buada
Mag Amalgada
Tempall mic in tSaeir
Cluain Fada
Fine Libráin
Mag Corráin
(Ballinderry Crannóg)
Cell
Mancháin
Craeb
Cell
Becáin
BRÍ
Cluain Emain
Áth Maigne
Ráth Áeda
ÉLE
CLUAIN MACCU NOIS
DAIRMAG
Cluain Fada
Mugtháine
Cloonfad
Liath Mancháin
Gáilinne
Cell Colgan
Mag Lenai
Tech Táille
Brí Dam
Druim Dá M
Móin Éle
CLUAIN FERTA
Tech Sárain
Brosnach
RATHAN
LANN ELO
Cluain Sosta
Inis Adarcach
Ráth Lipthen
CELL ACHID
Géisill
Lusmag
Bendchor
Áth Buide
Ros
Finnghlaise
Berba
Raonagh
Cell Corbmaic
Cúl Bendchuir
Drum Cuilinn
BLADMA
LOTHRA
BIRRA
Liadaine
MAG RÉTA
Loch Dercderc
Cell Cuilinn
CEND EITIG
Coill Uachtarach
Cluain Ednech
Dún Masc
SAIGER
SLÍAB
Dísert Óengussa
TÍR DÁ GLAS
Daire Mór
ROS MIC ELIGIN
Slige Dála
Móin Rátha
Tulach mic Comgaill
Cell Comainn
Men-droichet
Fedír
Tech Mochua
Árd Cróine
ROS CRE
CLUAIN
FERTA
MOLUA
Cell Cháile Dumai
Cluain Cáin
Dísert Cuilinn
SLÍAB MAIRGE
Ráth Epscoip
Móin Inse
ACHAD-BÓ
(mairce laigen)
BERNÁN ÉLE
Fedír
Cell Deirce
MAG LACHA
GAILINNE
(Bernán Mera Ingene Trego)
Ráth Tamhnaige
Cell Gabra
Dairmag Ua nDuach
Airgenros

0 1 2 3 4 5 Miles

Plate XIV North-Western Region: Topographical

155

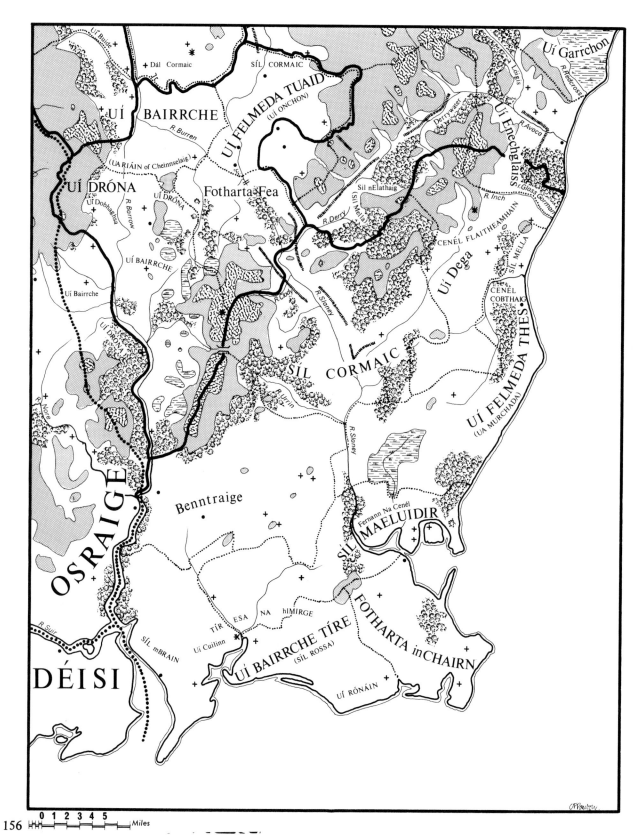

Uí Garrchon

Uí Buide

+ Dál Cormaic   SÍL CORMAIC

UÍ FELMEDA TUAID
(UÍ ONCHON)

UÍ BAIRRCHE

R. Burren   Uí Enechglaiss

(UA RIÁIN of Cheinnselaig)

UÍ DRÓNA   Fotharta Fea   Sil nElathaig

Uí Dobhaghsa   R. Barrow   UÍ DRÓNA   (SÍL MELLA)   R. Inch

R. Derry

CENÉL FLAITHEAMHAIN

UÍ BAIRRCHE   Uí Dega   SÍL MELLA

CENÉL
COBTHAIG

Uí Bairrche

R. Slaney

R. Boro

SÍL   CORMAIC   UÍ FELMEDA THES
(UA MURCHADA)

UÍ DRÓNA

R. Urrin

R. Nore

R. Slaney

O S R A I G E

Benntraige

Fernann Na Cenél

SÍL   MAELUIDIR

TÍR   ESA   NA   hIMIRGE   FOTHARTA in CHAIRN

R. Suir   SÍL mBRAIN   Uí Cuilinn

UÍ BAIRRCHE TÍRE
(SÍL ROSSA)

DÉISI   Uí RÓNÁIN

0 1 2 3 4 5 ⌐Miles

Plate XV Southern Region: Political

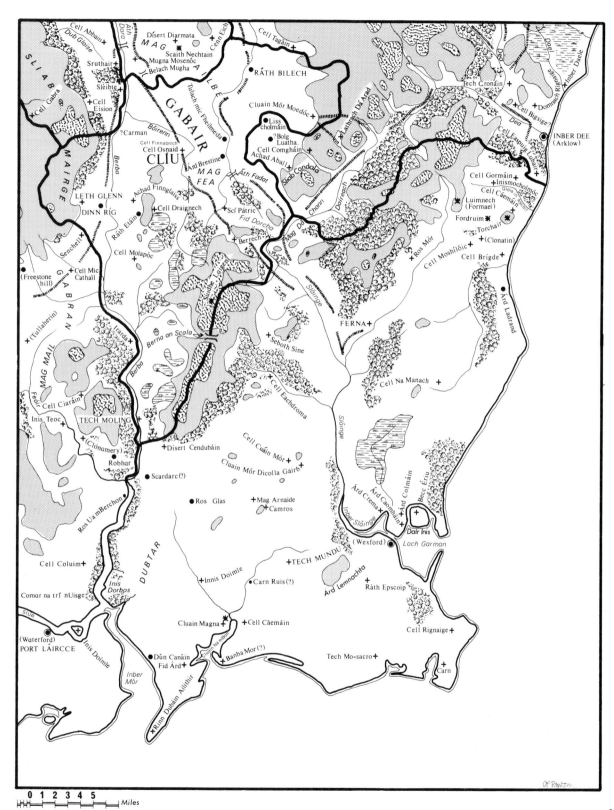

Cell Abbáin
Dub Gloise
Cell Cara
SLIAB MAIRGE
Cell Eision
Ath Dara
Sruthair
Sléibte
?Carman
Bóirenn
Cell Finnabrach
Cell Osnaid
CLÍU
LETH GLENN
DINN RÍG
Ráth Etáin
Cell Draignech
Cell Molapóc
Senchell
GABRAN
(Freestone hill)
Cell Mic Cathall
(Tullaherin)
MAG MAIL
Feóir
Cell Ciaráin
Inis Teoc
Trarda
TECH MOLING
(Clónamery)
Robhar
Scardarc (?)
Ros Ua mBerchon
Cell Coluim
Inis Dorbas
DUBTAR
Comar na trí nUisge
SIÚR
(Waterford)
PORT LÁIRCCE
Inis Doimle
Inber Mór
R.im Dubáin Ailithir
Dún Canáin
Fid Árd
Cluain Na mBoc
Banba Mor (?)
Cluain Magna
Cell Cáemáin

MAG AILBE
Dísert Diarmata
Cenn Eich
Cell Tagáin
Scaith Nechtain
Mugna Mosenóc
Belach Mugha
RÁTH BILECH
GABAIR
Cluain Mór Moedóc
Liss cholmáin
?Bolg Luatha
Cell Comgháin
Achad Aball
Tulach mic Fheilmeda
Ard Brestine
MAG FEA
Áth Fodat
Sciab Condala
Doireach
Scí Pátric
Fid Dorcha
Achad Finnglaiss
Berrech
Mag Da Chonn
Slaine
Uinne Toirenn
Berba
Berna an Scala
Seboth Sine
Cell Eachdroma
FERNA
Cell Na Manach
Slóinge
Ard Crema
Ard Caomháin
Ard Colmáin
Becc Ériu
Inber Slóinge
Dair Inis
Loch Garman
(Wexford)
TECH MUNDU
Ard Lemnachta
Ráth Epscoip
Cell Cáemáin
Dísert Cendubáin
Cell Cuáin Mór
Cluain Mór Dicolla Gairb
Ros Glas
Mag Arnaide
Camros
Carn Ruis (?)
Innis Doimle
Cell Rignaige
Tech Mo-sacro
Carn

Dee
Tech Cronáin
Cell Bigsige?
Domnach Ríagaile
Inber Daele
Cell Easpuig Libairi
INBER DEE
(Arklow)
Cell Gormáin
Inismocholmóc
Glais in Scáil
Cell Cáemáin
Luimnech (Formael)
Fordruim
Torchair
(Clonatin)
Cell Moshílóic
Cell Brígde
Ard Ladrand
Ros Mór

0 1 2 3 4 5 Miles

Plate XVI Southern Region: Topographical

157

Indexes

English-Irish Index to the Historical Atlas

See also *Irish-English Index to the Historical Atlas* and *General Index*

ABBREVIATIONS

Cl.	Clare	Kd.	Kildare	Ltm.	Leitrim	Ty.	Tipperary
Cv.	Cavan	Kk.	Kilkenny	Lx.	Leix	Wk.	Wicklow
Cw.	Carlow	Lf.	Longford	Mth.	Meath	Wm.	Westmeath
Du.	Dublin	Lk.	Limerick	Oy.	Offaly	Wt.	Waterford
G.	Galway	Lth.	Louth	Rc.	Roscommon	Wx.	Wexford

NOTE ON THE ORIGIN OF IRISH FAMILY NAMES

The distribution of the major Gaelic and Anglo-Norman families of South-East Ireland is shown on Plates IX and X.

In the earliest Irish records (prior to the eighth century), a man was known by his personal name and by his tribal designation. Thus, *Colmán moccu Loígse*, a Leinster bishop mentioned in Adomnán's *Life of Columba* (c.A.D. 700), was 'Colman of the tribe of Loígis' in modern Co. Leix (Plate VIII). The oldest tribal names have first elements such as *dál*, (Dál Messin Corb of Wicklow), or *Corcu*, (Corcu Roíde of Westmeath); or end in – *rige*, (Benntraige of Wexford). Later tribes of more developed dynastic composition, from the eighth century onwards, were distinguished by a first element *Uí*, as in *Uí Muiredaig*. Men and women were identified within their communities by the use of a patronymic. This was not a surname, since the form changed in every generation. Thus, *Cormac mac Diarmata* ('Cormac son of Dermot') had a father known to his contemporaries as, say, *Diarmait mac Dúnlainge* ('Dermot son of Dúnlang'). Proper surnames developed in Ireland in the tenth and especially in the eleventh and twelfth centuries – much earlier than in many other parts of Europe. These surnames were formed from the name of illustrious members of tenth and eleventh century dynasties. Kings and princes of Dark Age Irish dynasties often bore personal names which were chosen at random from a family repertoire and were therefore not necessarily related to older tribal or dynastic names. It follows, then, that most Irish surnames (Plate IX) bore little relationship to the names of parent tribes and dynasties (Plate VIII) to which the founders of those surnames belonged. So, for instance, the O'Ryans of Carlow (Ua Riáin, Plates IX, X) took their surname from Rián, a tenth-century ruler of the Uí Cheinnselaig sept which occupied the territory of Uí Dróna (Barony of Idrone, Carlow, Plates VII and VIII), while the O'Tooles of Wicklow (Ua Tuathail, Plate IX) derive from Tuathal mac Aughaire, a king of Leinster of the Uí Muiredaig branch of the Uí Dúnlainge (Plate VIII), who died in A.D. 958.

The vast majority of Irish surnames contain the patronymic *mac* ('son') or *ua* ('grandson') but as surname elements these prefixes signify 'descendant of'. Thus, Art Mac Murchadha Caománach, the fourteenth-century Leinster king, was 'Art, descendant of Murchad'. Art's ancestor, Murchad, who lived c.1060, was the grandfather of Dermot MacMurrough. The nickname, *Caománach*, distinguished Art's branch of the Mac Murroughs as descendants of Domnall Cáemánach, a son of Dermot Mac Murrough, so called because he had been fostered at Kilcavan (Cell Cáemáin) near Gorey in Wexford. The *Caománach* element in this name provides us with a rare instance where an Irish nickname relating to a place, gave rise to a family name in its own right (*Caománach* gave rise to *Kavanagh*). Such a process was common in the development of surnames in medieval England.

The names of over two hundred medieval Irish families from the kingdoms of Leinster, Meath and Ossory are given in the Index and their geographical distribution is shown on Plates VIII-X. Surnames (both Anglo-Irish and Gaelic) are accompanied by cross-references to the territories ruled by these families, which for Leinster, Westmeath and Meath can be examined in more detail on Plates XI-XVI. Other cross-references will lead the reader backwards in time to indicate the parent dynasties or tribes from which families of the eleventh and twelfth centuries evolved (Plate VIII). The development of Irish surnames from earlier dynastic and tribal forms is best studied for Leinster in conjunction with the inter-tribal genealogy set out on Chart 2. The arrival of the Anglo-Normans created a new landowning aristocracy in the fertile lowlands of South-East Ireland and the distribution of these Anglo-Irish families, together with the movement of the older Gaelic dynasties and their retainers, is outlined on Plate X for the period A.D. 1200-1600. Readers investigating the geographical and dynastic origins of modern Irish surnames should look under *Mac* or *O'* in the Index to the Historical Atlas regardless of whether the modern surnames still preserve these patronyms.

161

A Abbeyleix (formerly Clon Kyne), Lx. Cluain Cáin, XIV
Adamstown, Wx. Mag Arnaide, XVI
Agha, Cw. Achad Finnglaiss, XII, XVI
Aghaboe, Lx. Achad Bó, III, X, XIV
Aghade, Cw. Áth Fádat, XII, XVI
Aghowle, Wk. Achad Aball, III, XII, XVI
Allen, Bog of, Kd-Oy. Móin Éle or Móin Almaine, V, XII, XIV
Allen, Hill of, Kd. Almu, XII
Ardagh, Lf. Árd Achad, III, V, VIII, XIV
Ardamine, Wx. Árd Ladrand, V, XVI
Ardcavan, Wx. Árd Caomháin, XVI
Ardcolm, Wx. Árd Colmáin, XVI
Ardcrony, Ty. Árd Cróine, XIV
Ardnurcher *alias* Horseleap, Wm. Áth in Urchair, X, XIV
Ardree, Kd. Árd Ri, X
Ardristan, Cw. Árd Brestine, XII, XVI
Ardscull, Moat of, Kd. Árd Scol *alias* Árd na Macraide, XII
Arklow, Wk. Inber Dee, I, III, X, XII, XVI; Arklow Barony, VII; (see also *Dea* and *Glenn Dea*)
Artramon, Wx. Árd Crema, XVI
Ask Hill, Wx. Fordruim, XII, XVI
Athgreany Stone Circle, Wk. Achad Gréine, XII
Athleague (Lanesborough), Lf. Áth Líag, X
Athlone, Wm--Rc. Áth Luain, III, X, XIV
Athy, Kd. Áth Í, XII
Avoca (Avonmore), R., Wk. Dea, XI-XII, XV-XVI; (see also *Inber Dee*)
Avonmore (Avoca) R., Wk. Dea, XI-XII, XV-XVI; Avonmore Drainage Basin, II; (see also *Inber Dee*)

B Ballaghkeen Barony, North and South, Wx. VII
Ballaghmoon, Kd. Belach Mugna, XII, XVI
Ballaghmore, Lx. Belach Mór Maige Dála, XIV
Ballinacor Barony, North and South, Wk., VII. See *Baile na Corra*
Ballinderry Crannog, Wm-Oy., XIV
Ballyadams Barony, Lx., VII
Ballyboy, Oy. Áth Buide, X, XIV
Ballyboy, Barony, Oy., VII
Ballybritt Barony, Oy., VII
Ballycowan Barony, Oy., VII
Ballyglass (near Mullingar), Wm. Áth Féne *alias* Áth Airthir Mide *alias* Áth Glas, XIV
Ballyloughloe, Wm. Loch Lúatha, X,XIV
Ballymore (Loughsewdy), Wm. Baile Mór, X; (see also *Faitche meic Mecnáin, Loch Semdidi*)
Ballymotymore, Wx., X
Balrothery Barony, East and West, Du., VII
Baltinglass, Wk. Belach Con Glais, III, V, XII
Banagher, Oy. Bennchor, XIV
Bannow, Wx. Banba Mór, XVI
Bannow Bay, Wx. Cluain na mBan, XVI
Bantry Barony, Wx., VII; (see also *Benntraige, Clann Cosgraigh*)
Bargy Barony, Wx. VII; (see also *Ferann Deisceartach, Obarthy, Ua Duibhginn, Uí Bairrche Tíre*)
Barragh, Cw. Berrech, XVI
Barrow R., Lx-Kd-Cw-Wx. Berba, XI-XVI; Barrow Drainage Basin, II

Beggerin Is. Wexford Harbour, Wx. Becc Ériu, XVI
Bellevue, Wk. Baile Gunnair, XII
Bergen (Berrigan, *O'Havergan, O'Hemergin*) of Geashill, Oy. (*q.v.*). Ua hAimhirghin, (Ó Beirgin, Ó Meirgin), of Tuath Géisille in Uí Failge, IX
Berrigan, see *Bergen*
Birr, Oy. Birra, III, V, VIII, X, XIV
Black, see *O'Duff*
Blackwater R., Mth. Séle, II
Blackwater R., Mth-Oy. Dubh (Abha), XI, XII
Blackwater R., (Munster), Abha Mór, II
Blackwater R., Oy, Dub, XIII-XIV
Bohernabreena, Du. see *Bruiden Dá Derga*
Boughna Bog, Parish of Kilbride, Wm. Móin Faíchnig, XIV
Boyne R., Mth-Oy. Bóinn, XI, XII; Boyne Drainage Basin, II
Brannixtown, Kd. Tech na Bretnach, XII
Brawny Barony, Wm. VII; (see also *Bregmuine*)
Bray, Wk. Dún Brea, XII
Bray, (Old Court), Wk. Daurthech, XII
Bray Head, Wk. (part of) Carrig Cárthainn, XII
Bray R., Wk. Brea
Breen, see *Mac Breen, O'Breen, O'Brin*
Breenmore, Wm. Bruiden Dá Choca, XIV
Breffny, (Breifney), Cv-Ltm. Breifne, VIII
Brinan, see *O'Brennan*
Briody, see *O'Brody*
Broder, see *O'Bruadar*
Broderick, see *O'Bruadar*
Brooder, see *O'Bruadar*
Brosna R., Oy-Wm. Brosnach, II, XIII-XIV; (see also *Lámh Airgid*)
Brother, see *O'Bruadar*
Brusselstown Ring, Spinnans Hill, Wk. Dún Bolg, XII
Burgage, Wk. Domnach Imlech, XII
Burgage Moat, Cw. Dinn Ríg, III, V, XII, XVI
Burns, see *O'Byrne*
Burren R., Cw. Bóirenn, XI-XII, XV-XVI

C Callan Barony, (or Liberty), Kk., VII
Callan, Kk., Calland. See *O'Gloherny*
Camaross, Wx., Camros, III, V, XVI
Camma, Rc. Camach (Brígde), XIV
Carbury Barony, Kd., VII; (see also *Uí Cairpri Laigen*)
Carbury Hill, Kd. Síd Nechtain, X, XII
Carey, see *Keary*
Carlow, Cw. Cetharlach, X
Carlow Barony, Cw., VII; Carlow County, X
Carn, Parish of Conry, Wm. Carn Fiachach, XV; (see also *Cenél Fhiachach*)
Carney, see *O'Caharney*
Carnsore Point, Wx. Carn, XVI
Carrick, near Lough Ennell, Wm. Dún na Cairrge, XIV
Carvill, see *O'Carroll, Lth.*
Cashel Diocese, Caisel, VI
Castlecomer, Kk., X
Castledermot, Kd. Dísert Diarmata, I, III, X, XII, XVI
Castlekevin, Wk. Samud Coemgin, XII
Castleknock, Du. Cnúcha, X, XII; Castleknock Barony, VII

162

C

Castlemore, Cw., X

Castletown Kindalen, Wm. Cenél nÉnna, XIII; (see also *Ua Braonáin* of *Craeb*)

Caulfield, see *MacCaron*

Celbridge, Kd. Cell Droichit, X, XII

Church Is., Lough Owel, Wm. Inis Mór, XIV

Church Mountain, Wk. *Slievegad*, XII

Clandonagh Barony, Lx. VII

Clane, Kd. Claenad, X, XII; Clane Barony, VII

Clanmaliere, Oy-Lx. Clann Máelugra, XIII; (see also *Ua Díomasaigh, Uí Failge*)

Clare, Killare Parish, Wm. Clártha, XIV

Clarmallagh Barony, Lx., VII,(see also *Mag Lacha*)

Clody, R., Wx., XV

Cloghan *alias* Cloghanumera, Wm. Clochán (an Imrim), XIV

Cloghanumera, Wm., see *Cloghan*

Clonamery, Kk., X,

Clonard, Mth. Cluain Iraird, V, VIII, X, XII

Clonatin, Wx., XVI

Cloncurry, barony of East Offaly, Kd. Cluain Conaire Máelduib, XII

Cloncurry, barony of Ikeathy and Oughterany, Kd., Cluain Conaire Tomáin, III, X, XII

Clondalkin, Du. Cluain Dolcáin, III, XII

Clonenagh, Lx. Cluain Édnech, I, III, XIV

Clonfad, barony of Farbill, Wm. Cluain Fada Báetáin Abha, III, XIV

Clonfad, barony of Fartullagh, Wm. Cluain Fada Fine Libráin, III, XIV

Clonfert, G. Cluain Ferta (Brénainn), XIV; Clonfert Diocese, VI

Clonfertmulloe, Lx. Cluain Ferta Molua, III, XIV

Clon Kyne, Lx., see *Abbeyleix*

Clonlisk Barony, Oy., VII

Clonlonan Barony, Wm., VII

Clonmacnoise, Oy. Cluain maccu Nois, III, X, XIV; Clonmacnoise Diocese, VI

Clonmines, Wx. Cluain Magna, XVI

Clonmore, Cw. Cluain Mór Máedóc, III, XII, XVI

Clonmore, Wx. Cluain Mór Dicolla Gairb, III, XVI

Clonown, see *Cloonowen*

Clonsast, Oy. Cluain Sosta, XIV

Clontarf, Du. Cluain Tarbh, XII

Cloonfad, Rc. Cluain Fada, XIII

Cloonowen, (Clonown), Rc. Cluain Emain, XIV

Cloran, see *O'Gloherny*

Conellan, see *O'Kenellan*

Conlon, see *O'Kenellan*

Connaught, Connachta, VI, VIII, XIII

Connell Barony, Kd. VII

Conry, Wm. Comrar (Mide), XIV

Coolbanagher, Lx. Cúl Bendchuir, XIV

Coole, nr Abbeyleix, Lx. Cell Chúile Dumai, XIV

Coolestown Barony, Oy., VIII

Coolock Barony, Du., VI

Corkaree Barony, Wm., VII; (see also *Corco Roíde*)

Cormorant Is., Lough Ennell, Wm. Cró Inis, XIV

Corry, see *O'Cowry*

Cosgrave, see *O'Coskry*

Coughlan, see *MacCoughlan*

Courtown, Wx., see *Kilbride*

Coveney (Keveny, ? Keverney) in Crannagh Barony (*q.v.*), Kk. Ua Caibhdheanaigh (Coibhdheanaigh) of Mag Airb in Osraige (*q.v.*), IX

Crannagh Barony, Kk., VII; (see also *Mag Airb*)

Creeve (Crew), Wm., Craeb (?Teine), XIV; (see also *Ua Braonáin*)

Croghan Hill, Oy. Brí Éle *alias* Cruachán, III, V, XIV

Croghan Mountain, Wk-Wx. Cruachán, XII, XVI

Cruagh, Du. Crúach, XII

Crumlin, Du., X

Cullenagh Barony Lx., VII

Curragh of Kildare, Cuirrech Life, XII

Curtlestown, Wk. Baile mac Thorcaill, IX, XII

D

Dalkey Is., Du. Deilginis Cualann, XII

Dalton, Kk., Wm., X

de Bermingham, Oy., X

de Bigarz, Lx., X

de Boreart, Wx., X

de Carew, Cw., X

de Clahull, Lx., X

de Clare, Cw., Kd., Kk., Wk., Wx., X

de Costentin, Wm., X

de Cravile, Mth., X

de Cursun, Du., X

de Feypo, Mth., X

de Hereford, Kd-Lx., X

de Hose, Mth., X

de Lacy, Cv-Mth-Oy-Wm., X

de la Poer, Kk-Wt., X

de la Roche (Fitz Godebert), Wx., X

de Montmorency, Wx., X

de Muset, Mth., X

de Nangle, Mth., X

de Nugent, Wm., X

de Prendergast, Wx., X

de Ridelsford, Du., Kd., Wk., X

de St. Laurent, Du., X

de St. Michael, Kd., X

de Tuit, Lf., X

de Verdon, Lth., X

Decies, Wt. Déisi, IV, VIII, XV

Deece Barony, Upper and Lower, Mth. VII; (see also *Déisi Breg*)

Deegan, see *Diggin*

Delamar, Lf., X

Delgany, Wk. Deilgne Mogoróc (Dergne), XII

Delvin, Wm. X; (see also *Delbna Mór, Delvin Barony*)

Delvin Barony, Wm. VII; (see also *Delbna Mór*)

Delvin Mac Coghlan, Oy. X; (see also *Delbna Ethra, Mac Cochláin, MacCoughlan*)

Derry R., Wk-Wx-Cw. Daireach, XI-XII, XV-XVI

Devil's Bit Mountain, Ty. Bernán Éle *alias* Bernán Méra Ingena Trega, XIV

Devine, see *O'Doane*

Diggin (Deegan, Duigan, Duggan, O'Duygin) of ?Bargy, Wx. Ua Duibhginn of Ferann Deisceartach (*q.v.*), IX

Dillon, Wm., X

Disert Gallin, Lx. Dísert Cuilinn, XIV

Djouce Mountain, Wk. Digais, XII

D

Dodder R., Du. Dothra, XI, XII
Donadea, Kd. Domnach Daa, XII
Donagh, see *Dunphy*
Donaghmore, Kd. Domnach Mór, XII
Donaghmore, Mth. Domnach Mór, III
Donaghpatrick, Mth. Domnach Pátraicc, III
Donaghy, see *Dunphy* and *O'Donoghue*
Donohoe, see *Dunphy*
Doolan, see *O'Dowling*
Doolin, see *O'Dowling*
Donn, Wm. Dún na Sciath, XIV
Douglas R., Lx. Dub Glaise, XI-XII, XV-XVI
Dowling, see *O'Dowling*
Downes, see *O'Doane*
Drogheda, Lth-Mth. Drochat Átha, X
Drumcaw, *alias* Mount Lucas, Oy. Druim dá Maige, XIV.
    Site of Brí Dam *q.v.*, (see also *Tochar etar dá Mag* and
    Tuath dá Maige)
Drumcree, Wm. Druim nAirthir *alias* Druim Criaich, XIV
Drumcullen, Oy. Druim Cuilinn, XIV
Drumraney, Wm. Druim Ráite, III, XIV
Dublin, Dub Linn and Áth Cliath, I, III, XII. Dublin
    County, X; Dublin Diocese, VI
Duff, see *O'Duff*
Duffry, Wx. Dubtar, X, XVI
Duggan, see *Diggin*
Duigan, see *Diggin*
Dulane, Mth. Tuilean III
Duleek, Mth. Damliac (Cianáin), III, X
Duleek Barony, Upper and Lower, Mth. VII
Dullard, Mth., X
Dumphy, see *O'Donoghue*
Dunamase (Rock of), Lx. Dún Masc, I, III, XIV
Dunboyke, Wk. Dún Buaice, XII
Dunboyne Barony, Mth., VII
Duncannon, Wx. Dún Canáin, XVI
Dungarvan, Wt. Dún Garbháin, X
Dungolman R., Wm. Inniuin, XIII-XIV
Dunleckny, Cw., X
Dunmanoge, Kd. Mugna Mosenóc, XII, XVI
Dunmurraghill, Kd. Druim Urchaille, XII
Dunphy (*O'Donochowe, O'Dunaghy, O'Donoghue,
    Donohoe, Donagh*) of Ossory, Kk. Ua Donnchadha of
    Mag Mail (*q.v.*), IX
Dunshaughlin, Mth. Domnach Sechnaill, III, XII
Durrow, Lx. Dairmag Ua nDuach, XIV
Durrow, Oy. Dairmag (Coluim Cille), III, X, XIV
Dysart, Lx. Dísert Óengussa, XIV
Dysart, Wm. Dísert Máeltuile, XIV
Dysart (Taula), Wm. Dísert Tola, XIV
Dysart-Gallen (Gallen), Lx. Gailinne, XIV

E

Eglish Barony, Oy., VII
Ely O'Carol, see *O'Carroll*
Ennereilly, Wk. Inber Daele, XII, XVI
Ennis, see *O'Hennessy*
Ennisboyne, Wk. Inis Báethín, XII
Enniscorthy, Wx. Inis Corthadh, X
Esker, Du. X
Esker, see *Escir Riada*

F

Faloon, see *O'Fallon*
Fanaghan, see *O'Finoghane*
Farann O'Neill, see *Feran O'Neile*
Farbill Barony, Wm. VII; (see also *Fír Bile*)
Farrow, Leny Parish, Wm. Forrach, XIV
Fartullagh Barony, Wm., VII; (see also *Fír Tulach*)
Fassadinin Barony, Kk., VII
Faughalstown, Wm. Fochlaid, XIV
Feary, see *O'Fieghraie*
Feerey, see *O'Fieghraie*
Feighcullen, Kd. Fid cuilind, XII
Feighery, see *O'Fieghraie*
Feltrim, Du. Faeldruim, XII
Fenihan, see *O'Finoghane*
Fenlon, see *O'Fynnolane*
Feran O'Neile, Cw-Wk-Wx. Ferann Uí Néill, X; (see also
    Ua Néill of Mag dá Chonn)
Fernegenal, Wx. Ferann na Cenél, X, XV; (see also
    Shelmaliere Barony)
Ferns, Wx. Ferna (Mór), I, III, V, XVI
Ferns Diocese, VI
Fethard, Wx. ? Fid Árd, XVI
Figile R., Kd-Oy. Fid nGaible, XI, XII
Fingal, Du. Fine Gall, IX, XI
Finglas, Du. Finn Glas, III, XII
Finneran, (*O'Finaran*), Wx. Ua Finntighearn of Síl Mella
    (*q.v.*), of Uí Cheinnselaig, IX
Fitz David, Kk., X
Fitz Dermot, see *Gilla Mocholmóc*
Fitz Gerald, Kd., X
Fitz Godebert, (de la Roche), Wx., X
Fitz Henry, Kd., Lx., Wm., X
Fitzpatrick, see *Mac Gillapatrick*
Fitz Richard, Kd., X
Fitz Walter, see *Walter*
Fleming, see *le Fleming*
Fore, Wm. Fobar, III, X
Fore Barony, Mth., VII
Fore Barony, Wm. VII
Forgney, Lf. Forgnaidhe, XIV
Forth Barony, Cw., VII; (see also *Fotharta Fea, Fotheret
    Onolan, Ua Nualláin*)
Fort Barony, Wx., VII; (see also *Fotharta in Chairn, Ua
    Lorcáin*)
Forth Mountain, Wx. ? Árd Lemnachta, XVI
Fotheret Onolan, Cw., X; (see also *Fotharta Fea, Ua
    Nualláin*)
Fox, see *O'Caharney* Foxes' Country, see *Muinter Tadgáin*
Freestone Hill, hillfort, Kk., XVI
Frewin Hill, Fremu, Wm., XIV

G

Gaffney, see *Mac Caron*
Gahan (*O'Gighine, O'Gehin*, Guiheen, Gihon, Wynne),
    of Shillelagh, Wk. and later of Wexford, Ua Gaoithín
    of Síl Ealaigh (Síl nElathaig) (*q.v.*), IX
Gallen, Lx. see *Dysart-Gallen*
Gallen, Oy. Gailinne na mBretan, III, XIV
Galmoy Barony, Kk., VII
Galtrim, Mth. Calatruim, X, XII
Garhy, Parish of Castletown Kindalen, Wm. Gáirech,
    XIV

G Garrycastle Barony, Oy., VII
Garrysallagh, Wm. Garbhsalach, XIV
Garvey, see *O'Garvey*
Geashill, Oy. Géisill, and Mag Gésilli, XIV
Geashill Barony, Oy. Tuath Géisille, VII
Gee, see *MacGee*
Geraghty, see *Mac Geraghty*
Gihon, see *Gahan*
Gilla Mocholmóc (Fitz Dermot), Du-Wk. Mac Gilla Mo-
    Cholmóg, IX, X; (see also *Uí Dúnchada*)
Gilltown, Kd. Inis Breslén, XII
Glascarrig, Wx., X
Glasnevin, Du. Glais Noeden, XII
Glasseli, Kd. Glais Eille, XII
Glassgorman R., (and Inch R.), Wx. Glaiss in Ascail, XII,
    XVI
Glenbride, Wk. Glenn Brígde, XII
Glencap, Wk. Glenn Capaich *alias* Glenn dá Gruad, XII
Glencree, Wk. See *Cell Critaich*
Glendalough, Wk. Glenn dá Locha (formerly Glenn Dea),
    I, III, X, XII; Reefert Church (Dísert Coemgin) and
    cemetery (Ríg Ferta); Templenaskellig (Scelleg), XII;
    Glendalough Diocese, VI
Glenealy, Wk. Glen Faidli, XII
Glenmalure, Wk. Glenn Maoil 'oraidh, XII
Glen of Imail, see *Imaal, Uí Máil*
Glorney, see *O'Gloherny*
Glory, see *O'Gloherny*
Gorey Barony, Wx., VII
Gowran, Kk. Gabrán (Belach Gabráin), IV-V, XVI
Gowran Barony, Kk., VII
Granard, Lf. Graneret, V, X
Grangegorman, Du. Cell Duilig, XII
Gravale Mountain, Wk. Drobél, XII
Great Island. Wx. Inis Dorbas *alias* Inis Eirne, XVI
Grourke (*M'Royrke, M'Groirke*) of Kinalea (*q.v.*), Wm.
    Mac Ruairc (Mag Ruairc, Mag Ruadhraic) of Cenél
    nÉnna, IX
Guiheen, see *Gahan*

H Hanafy, see *O'Hanvey*
Hanrahan, see *O'Heneran*
Hanway, see *O'Hanvey*
Hare Is., Lough Ree, Wm. Inis Aingin, XIV
Hartley of Shelmaliere East (*q.v.*), Wx. Ua hArtghaile of
    Ferann na Cenél (*q.v.*), IX
Hayes, see *O'Hay*
Henrion, see *O'Heneran*
Hinchy, see *O'Hennessy*
Holland, see *O'Mulchallan*
Holy Is., Lough Derg on Shannon, Cl. Inis Celtra, V, VIII
Hook Head, Wx. Rinn Dubáin Ailithir, XVI
Horan, see *O'Heneran*
Horetown, Wx. Carn Ruis
Horgan, see *O'Heneran*
Horseleap, Wm. See *Ardnurcher*
Howth, Du. Benn Étair. See also Dún Crimthainn, X, XII
Hughes, see *O'Hay*
Hunt, see *O'Fieghraie*

I Ibercon (Uí Bercháin of Osraige), former barony now
    occupying northern Ida, Kk. See also *Ua Caollaidhe*,
    VII, XV
Ida Barony, Kk., VII. Northern Ida was formerly Barony
    of Ibercon (Uí Bercháin: *q.v.*). See also *Ua Caollaidhe*
Idrone (*Odrone*), see *Uí Dróna*
Idrone Barony, East and West, Cw., VII; (see also Uí
    Dróna)
Ikeathy Barony, Kd., VII; (see also *Uí Chéithig*)
Imaal, (Glen of Imail) Kd-Wk., X; (see also *Uí Máil*)
Inch, barony of Gorey, Wx. Inis Mocholmóc, XII, XVI
Inch, barony of Shelmalier, Wx. Inis Doimle, XVI
Inch R., (and Glassgorman R.), Wx. Glais in Ascail, XII,
    XVI
Inchbofin Is., Lough Ree, Wm. Inis Bó Finne, XIV
Inchcleraun Is., Lough Ree, Lf. Inis Clothrann, XIV
Inchenagh Is., Lough Ree, Lf. Inis Endaim, XIV
Incherky, on the Shannon R., Oy. Inis Adarcach, XIV
Inchmore Is., Lough Ree, Wm. Inis Mór, XIV
Inchturk Is., Lough Ree, Wm. Inis Tuirc, XIV
Inistioge (Innistiogue), Kk. Inis Teoc, XVI
Innistiogue, see *Inistioge*
Inny R., Lf-Wm. Ethne, XIII-XIV. Inny Drainage Basin,
    II
Iregan (Yregan), Lx. Uí Riacáin, XIII; (see also *Ua
    Duinn, Uí Failge*)
Ireland's Eye Is., Du. Inis mac Nesáin, XII
Island Bridge, Du. A ford near Cell Mosamócc, XII
Iverk Barony, Kk. Uí nEirc in Osraige, VII; (see also *Ua
    Bruadair*)

K Kavanagh, Caomhánach, see *MacMurrough Kavanagh*
Keary (Carey, *O'Kirry, O'Kerry*) of Carbury, Kd. (*q.v.*);
    Ua Chiardha of Uí Cairpri Laigen (*q.v.*) of Southern
    Uí Néill
Kellistown, Cw. Cell Osnaid, XII, XVI
Kells, Mth. Cenandas, III, V, X
Kells Barony, Kk., VII
Kells Barony,, Upper and Lower, Mth., VII
Kernon, see *MacKiernan, O'Kernaghan*
Keveny, see *Coveney*
Keverney, see *Coveney*
Kiernan, see MacKiernan, (otherwise Mac Tighernáin),
    O'Kernaghan
Kilbaylet, Wk. Cell Bélat, XII
Kilbeggan, Wm. Cell Becáin, XIV
Kilberry, Kd. Cell Bera, XII
Kilbixy, Wk., see *Whitsun Hill*
Kilbixy, Wm. Cell Bicsige, X, XIV
Kilbride, Wk. Cell Brígde, XII
Kilbride (Courtown), Wx. Cell Brígde, XVI
Kilbride, Wm. Cell Brígde, XIV. St Brigit's nunnery in
    Fir Tulach
Kilcavan, barony of Bargy, Wx. Cell Cáemáin, XVI
Kilcavan, barony of Gorey, Wx. Cell Cáemáin, XII, XVI
Kilclare, Kilbride Parish, Oy. Coill an Chláir, XIV
Kilclonfert, Oy. Cluain Ferta Mughaine, XIV
Kilcoanmore, Wx. Cell Cuáin Mór, XVI
Kilcock, Kd. Cell Choca, XII
Kilcolgan, Oy. Cell Colgan, XIV
Kilcolman, Oy. Daire Mór, XIV
Kilcolumb, Kk. Cell Coluim, XVI

K

Kilcommon, Oy. Cell Comainn, XIV
Kilcoole, Wk. Cell Comgaill, XII
Kilcooly, Wm. Cell Chúile, XIV
Kilcormac, Oy. Cell Corbmaic, XIV
Kilcoursey Barony, Oy., VII
Kilcullen Barony, Kd., VII; (see also *Old Kilcullen*)
Kilcumreragh, Wm. Cell Cruimthir, XIV
Kildalkey, Mth. Cell Deilge, XII
Kildare, Kd. Cell Dara, I, III, V, X, XII
Kildare County, X
Kildare Diocese, VI
Kildellig, Lx. Cell Delcce, XIV
Kildreenagh, Cw. Cell Draignech, XII, XVI
Kileencormac, Kd. Cell Fine (Cormaic), XII
Kilglinn, Mth. Cell Duma Glinn, XII
Kilgorman, Wx. Cell Gormáin, XII, XVI
Kilgory, Lx. Cell Gabra, XVI
Kilkea. Kd., X
Kilkea and Moone Barony, Kd., VII; (see also *Moone*)
Kilkenny, Kk. Cell Cainnig, III, X
Kilkenny Barony (County of the City of Kilkenny), Kk., VII
Kilkenny County, X
Kilkenny West, Barony, Wm., VII
Kilkieran, Kk. Cell Ciaráin, XVI
Kill, Kd. Cell, X, XII. Royal cemetery of Uí Dúnlainge kings of Naas (Cell Náis)
Killabban, Lx. Cell Abbain, III, XII, XVI
Killadreenan, Wk. Cell Achaid Draignige, XII
Killagh, Wm. Cell Ech, XIV
Killaghy, see *Killeigh*
Killaloe Diocese, Cell dá Lua, VI
Killare, Wm. Cell Áir, XIV
Killashee, Kd. Cell Auxili, XII
Killaughey, see *Killeigh*
Killegar, Wk. Cell Adgair, XII
Killeglan, Mth. Cell Eglan, XII
Killeigh (Killaughey, Killaghy), of Druim Fota, Oy. Cell Achid (Cell Achid Drommo Foto), I, III, XIV
Killenora, Cw. Cell Finnabrach, XII, XVI
Killerk, Wk. Cell Eirc, XII
Killeshin, Lx. Cell Eision, III, X, XII, XVI
Killoughrum, Wx. Cell Eachdroma, XVI
Killyon, Oy. Cell Liadaine, XIV
Kilmacahill, Kk. Cell mic Cathail, XVI
Kilmacanoge, Wk. Cell Mochonóc, XII
Kilmacurragh, Wk. Cell Mo Chura, XII
Kilmainham, Du. Cell Maignenn, XII
Kilmalin, Wk. Cell Moling, XII
Kilmalum, Kd. Cell Molomma, XII
Kilmanaghan, Oy. Cell Manchráin, XIV
Kilmartin, Wk. Cell Martra, XII
Kilmeelchon, Oy. Cell Ua Mílchon, XIV
Kilmichaelogue, Wx. Cell Moshílóic, XVI
Kilmolappogue, Lorum, Cw. Cell Molapóc, XVI
Kilmore, Cv. Cell Mór, X
Kilmore, Mth. Cell Mór, XII
Kilmorony, Lx., X
Kilnamanagh, Du. Cell na Manach, XII
Kilnamanagh, Wx. Cell na Manach, XVI
166 Kilquiggin, Wk. Cell Comhgáin, XII, XVI

Kilrane, Wx. Cell Rignaige, XVI
Kilranelagh, Wk. Cell Rannairech, XII; (see also Dún Buchat)
Kilskeer, see *Kilskyre*
Kilskyre, (Kilskeer), Mth. Cell Scíre, III
Kilteel, Kd. Cell tSíle, XII
Kiltegan, Wk. Cell Tagáin, XII, XVI
Kinalea, Wm. Cenél nÉnna, XIII; (see also *Castletown Kindalen* Wm. *Mac Ruairc*)
King's R., Wk. Ríge, XI, XII
Kinlan, see *O'Kenelkan*
Kinnegad, Wm. Áth Cinn Chon, XII
Kinneigh, Kd. Cenn Eich (? *alias* Imlech Eich), XII, XVI
Kinnity, Oy. Cenn Eitig, III, X, XIV
Kinsaley, Du. Cenn Sáile, XII
Knockaulin Hillfort, Kd. Dún Ailinne, III, V, XII; cf *Allen, Hill of*
Knocktopher Barony, Kk., VII
Knowth, Mth. Cnodba, III; (see also *O'Connolly, O'Doane)*

L

Lackagh, Kd. Leccach, XII
Lackan, Wm. Lecan (Mide), XIV
Lagore (lake and crannog), Mth. Loch Gabair, III, XII
Lambay Is., Du. Rechru, XII
Lanesborough, see *Athleague*
Laragh (barony of Shillelagh), Wk. Lathrach dá Arad, XII, XVI
Laragh (bryan), Kd. Lathrach Briúin, X, XII
Larkin (Lorkan, O'Lurkaine), of Forth, Wx. (*q.v.*); Ua Lorcáin of Fotharta in Chairn, IX
Lawton, see *O'Loughnane*
Lea, (Ley, Leys) Lx., Lége, XIV
le Fleming, Mth., X
le Gros, Raymond, Cw. Wx., X
le Petit, Wm., X
Leighlin Diocese, VI; (see also *Old Leighlin*)
Leinster Bridge, Mth-Oy. Drochat Cairpre, XII
Leix County, X; (see also *Loígis, O'More, Ua Mórdha*)
Leixlip, Kd. (Old Norse *Lax-hlaup*, 'Salmon-leap'), IX, X
Lemanaghan, Oy. Liath Manchráin, *alias* Tuaim nEirc, XIV
Leys, see *Lea*
Liffey R., Du-Kd. Ruirthech and (later) Life (*q.v.*), XI, XII; Liffey Drainage Basin, II
Limerick Hill, Wx. Luimnech *alias* Formael, XII, XVI
Liscolman, Wk. Liss Cholmáin, XII, XVI
Lismore Diocese, Liss Mór, VI
Lismore, Wt. Liss Mór, X
Lismoyny, Wm. Áth Maigne and Liss Maigne, XIV
Little Brosna R., Oy-Ty. Brosnach, XII-XIV
Little Island, Waterford Harbour, Wt. Inis Doimle, XVI
Loftus, see *O'Loughnane*
Loghan, see *O'Loughan*
Longford County, X
Lorkan, see *Larkin*
Lorrha, Ty. Lothra, V, VIII, XIV
Lorum, Cw., see *Kilmolappogue*
Lough Derg (on the Shannon), Ty-G-Cl. Loch Dercderc, II, V, XII-XIV

L Lough Derravaragh, Wm. Loch nDairbrech, II, V, XIII-XIV

Lough Ennell, Wm. Loch Ainninn, II, V, XIII-XIV; (see also *Cró Inis, Dún na Cairrge, Dún na Scíath*)

Lough Iron, Wm. Loch Íairn, II, V, XIII-XIV

Lough Lene, Wm. Loch Lebind, II, V, XIII-XIV

Lough Owel, Wm. Loch Uair, II, V, XIII-XIV; (see also *Loch Treithin*)

Lough Ramor, Cv. Loch Muinremair, II, V

Loughrane, see *O'Loughnane*

Lough Ree, Lf-Wm-Rc. Loch Ríb, II, V, XIII-XIV; (see also under *Loch Ríb* for the islands in the Lake)

Lough Sewdy, see *Lough Sunderlin*

Lough Sheelin, Lf-Mth-Cv. Loch Sighlenn, II, V

Lough Sunderlin (Sewdy), Wm. Loch Semdidi, XIV; (see also *Ballymore Loughsewdy*)

Lullymore, Kd. Lilcach, XII

Lune Barony, Mth. VII; (see also *Luigni*)

Lusk, Du. Lusca, XII

Lusma, Oy. Lusmag, XIV

Lynally, Oy. Lann Elo, III, XIV

Lynn Bog, at Lynn, Wm. Móin Lainne, XIV

Lynn, Wm. Lann, III, XIV

Lyon's Hill, Kd. Liamain, III, XII

M Mac   Irish patronymic

MacAuley, see *Magawly*

Mac Breen (*M'Brewne, M'Brune, M'Breane*), of Knocktopher Barony (*q.v.*), Kk. Mac Braoin of Na Clanna in Osraige, IX

MacCaron (MacCaroon, O'Growney, *M'Crony*, Gaffney, Caulfield), Wm. Mac Carrgamhna of Muinter Mailsinna (*q.v.*), IX

MacCaroon, see *MacCaron*

Mac Clachlin, see *Mac Glaughlin*

MacClafflin, see *MacGlaughlin*

Mac Convey, see *MacConway*

MacConway (MacConvey, MacNama), Lf-Wm. Mac Con Meadha of Muinter Laoghacháin, IX

MacCoughlan (Coughlan) of Delvin Mac Coghlan, Oy. Mac Cochláin, IX, X; (see also *Delbna Ethra*)

MacElfatrick, see *Mac Gillapatrick*

MacEvoy (*M'Eboy, M'Ewy*, MacVoy), of Leix, Mac Fíodhbhaidhe (Fíodhbhadhaigh) of Tuath Fíodhbhaidhe, Lx. (*q.v.*), IX

MacGee (Magee, *M'Gay*, Gee), Wm. Mac Aodha (Mag Aodha) of Muinter Tlámáin, IX

MacGeraghty (Geraghty) of Lynn (*q.v.*), Wm. Mac Airechtaigh of Lann, hereditary wardens or erenaghs of Lynn, XIII

Mac Gillapatrick of Ossory (MacElfatrick, Fitzpatrick, Kirkpatrick), Lx-Kk. Mac Gilla Pátraic of Osraige, IX, X

Mac Glaughlin (MacClachlin, MacClafflin, MacTaghlin, *M'Gillaghlin, M'Kintaghlin*) of Southern Brega (*q.v.*). Mac Giolla (t)Seachlainn of Síl nÁedo Sláine, IX; (later confused with *Mac/Mag Lochlainn*)

Mac Gorman (O'Gorman), Lx-Cw. Mac Gormáin of Uí Bairrche (*q.v.*), IX

Mac Kiernan (Kernon, Kiernan) of western Breifne (*q.v.*), Cv. Mac Tighearnáin related to O'Rourke (*q.v.*); (see also *O'Kernaghan*)

Mac Loughlin, see *O'Melaghlin*

MacMurrough Kavanagh, Wk-Wx. Mac Murchadha Caomhánach. Branch of MacMurrough (*q.v.*), descended from Domhnall Caomhánach son of Dermot MacMurrough.

MacMurrough (*MacMoroghe, M'Murphewe*, Morrow), Wx. Mac Murchadha of Uí Cheinnselaig (*q.v.*), IX, X

MacNama, see *MacConway*

MacTaghlin, see *MacGlaughlin*

MacVoy, see *MacEvoy*

M'Breane, see *Mac Breen*

M'Brewne, see *MacBreen*

M'Brune, see *MacBreen*

M'Crony, see *MacCaron*

M'Eboy, see *MacEvoy*

M'Ewy, see *MacEvoy*

M'Gay, see *MacGee*

M'Gillaghlin, see *Mac Glaughlin*

M'Groirke, see *Grourke*

M'Kintaghlin, see *MacGlaughlin*

M'Royrke, see *Grourke*

Magawly (MacAuley), Wm. Mac (Mag) Amhalghadha, IX, X

Magee, see *Mac Gee*

Mageney, Kd. Áth Dara, XII, XVI

Mageoghegan, Wm. Mac Eochagáin, IX, X; (see also *Cenél Fhiachach*)

Magheradernon Barony, Wm., VII; (see also *Uí Tigernáin*)

Malahide Bay, Du. Inber Domnann, XII

Maryborough Barony, East and West, Lx., VII

Maryborough, Great Heath of, Lx. Mag Réta (Mag Rechet, Morett), XIV

Maulin Mountain, Wk. Málainn (Málu), XII

Maynooth, Kd. Mag Nuadat, X, XII

Meath County, X

Meath Diocese, VI; (see also *Brega* and *Mide*)

Monaincha, Ty. Móin Inse (Cré) *alias* Inis Cré, III, XIV

Monasterboice, Lth. Mainister Buite, III

Monasterevin, Kd. Ros Glas (Glaisi), XII

Mondrehid, Lx. Mendroichet, XIV

Moone, Kd. Móin Coluim (Cille), III, X, XII; (see also *Kilkea and Moone Barony*)

Moran, see *Morrin*

Morett, (and Great Heath of Maryborough), Lx. Mag Réta, Mag Rechet, XIV

Morgalion Barony, Mth. VII; (see also *Gailenga, Ua Leócháin*)

Morkan, see *Morrin*

Morrin (Moran, Morkan, Murchan, *O'Moraghan, O'Morghane*) of Figile River area, Oy. Ua Murcháin of Fid nGaible in Uí Failge, IX

Mount Leinster, Cw-Wx. Suidhe Laigen, XVI

Mountrath, Lx. Móin Rátha (Bresail), XIV

Mount Seskin, Du. Sescenn ? Uarbeoil, XII

Moyacomb parish, Wk-Cw. Mag dá Chonn, XII, XVI

Moyashel Barony, Wm., VII; (see also *Mag Asail*)

Moycashel Barony, Wm., VII, XIV; (see also *Mag Caisil*)

Moydow, Lf. Mag Duma, X, XIV

Moyelly, Oy. ? Mag Éle, V

Moyfenrath Barony, Upper and Lower, Mth., VII

Moygoish Barony, Wm., VII; (see also *Uí Maic Uais Mide*)

Moyntergeran, Lf. Muinter Gearadháin, X

M Mulholland, see *O'Mulchallan*
Mullaghmast Hill, Kd. Maistiu, III, XII. Fortress of kings
    of Leinster in Uí Muiredaig
Mullagh Reelion, Kd. Róeriu, XII
Mullingar, Wm. Muilenn Cerr, X
Mullinoran, Wm. Muilenn Odhráin, XIV
Mulqueen, see *O'Mulkeen*
Mulquin, see *O'Mulkeen*
Munster, Mumu, II-VI, VIII, XIII; (see also *Ormond*)
Munterhagan, Oy. Muinter Tadgáin, IX, X
Murchan, see *Morrin*
Murphy, see *O'Murroughe*

N Naas, Kd. Nás, I, III, V, X, XII; Naas Barony, North and
    South, VII
Narragh and Reban Barony, East and West, (Norragh),
    Kd., VII; (see also *Narraghmore*)
Narraghmore, (Norragh), Kd. Forrach Pátraic (formerly
    Bile macc Crúaich), V, X, XII; (see also *Narragh and
    Reban Barony*)
Navan Barony, Upper and Lower, Mth., VII
Navan, Mth. Núachongbáil, X
Nethercross Barony, Du., VII
Newcastle Barony, Du., VII
Newcastle Barony, Wk., VII
Newcastle (Lyons), Du. X; (see also *Lyon's Hill, Kd.;
    Newcastle Barony, Du.*)
Newcastle, Wk. X; (see also *Newcastle Barony, Wk.*)
Nobber, Mth. Obair, (an Obair), X
Nore R., Kk-Lx-Ty., Feóir, XIII-XIV, XV-XVI; Nore
    Drainage Basin, II
Norragh, see *Narragh and Reban,* and *Narraghmore*
Nowal, Lx. See *Oughaval*

O O'   Irish patronymic
O'Birne, see *O'Byrne*
O'Breen (O'Brien), of Brawny, Wm. Ua Braoin of Breg-
    muine (*q.v.*), IX, X
O'Breen (O'Brien), of Lune, Mth. Ua Braoin of Luigni
    (*q.v.*), IX
O'Breen, see also *O'Brin*
O'Brennan (Brinan), of Creeve, Wm. Ua Braonáin of
    Craeb (?Teine) (*q.v.*), IX
O'Brennan (Brinan), of Ossory, Kk. Ua Braonáin of Uí
    Duach in Osraige, IX, X
O'Brien, see *O'Breen*
O'Brin (O'Breen), of the Duffry (*q.v.*), Wx. Ua Brain or
    Síl mBrain, IX, X, VIII, XV; (see also *Shelburne
    Barony*)
O'Brody (Briody, O'Broudin), of Rathdowney, Lx. Ua
    Bruaideadha of Ráth Tamnaige (*q.v.*), in Osraige, IX
O'Broha, see *O'Brophy*
O'Brophy (*O'Broha*), of Ballybrophy, Lx. (post-Norman
    era). Ua Bróithe (Bróigthe) of Mag Sédna, Kk., IX, X
O'Broudin, see *O'Brody*
O'Bruadar (Broder, Brooder, Brother, Broderick) of
    Iverk Barony (*q.v.*), in Ossory, Kk. Ua Bruadair of Uí
    nEirc in Osraige, IX
O'Byrne (*O'Birne,* Burns), of Offelan (*q.v.*), Kd. Ua
    Broin of Uí Fáeláin and earlier of Uí Dúnlainge, IX, X
O'Caharney (Carney, Fox), Wm-Oy. Ua Catharnaigh, IX,
    X, *alias* Sinnach of Muinter Tadgáin

O'Cahessy, see *O'Kadesi*
O'Carbery, of Twyford (*q.v.*), Wm. Ua Cairbre of Tuath
    Buada, IX
O'Carroll (Carvill), Lth. Ua Cearbhaill, IX, X
O'Carroll (Ely O'Carol), Oy-Ty. Ua Cearbhaill Éile, IX,
    X; (see also *Éle*)
O'Carroll (*O'Carrowill*), of Ossory, Kk. Ua Cearbhaill of
    Osraige, IX
O'Carrowill, see *O'Carroll*
O'Casey, see *O'Kadesi*
O'Coely, see *O'Kealy*
O'Connolly of Northern Brega, Mth. Ua Conghalaigh of
    Síl nÁedo Sláine (*q.v.*). Retreated to Monaghan in
    post-Norman era, IX
O'Conor Faly, Oy. Ua Conchobhair Failghe, IX, X; (see
    also *Uí Failge*)
O'Coskry (Cosgry, Coskerry, Cosgrave), of Bantry Bar-
    ony, Wx. Clann Cosgraigh of Benntraige (*q.v.*), IX
O'Coskry (Cosgry, Coskerry, Cosgrave), Wk. Ua Cosgraigh
    of *Uí Briúin Chualann*, IX
O'Cowry (O'Curry, Corry), of Moygoish (*q.v.*), Wm. Ua
    Comhraidhe of Uí Maic Uais Mide, IX
O'Curry, see *O'Cowry*
O'Daly, Wm. Ua Dálaigh of Corco Adaim (*q.v.*), of Uí
    Maine of Southern Uí Néill, IX
O'Delany (*O'Dowlaney*), Lx. Ua Dubhsláine of Coill
    Uachtarach (q.v.), IX, X
O'Dempsey of Clanmaliere, Oy-Lx. Ua Díomasaigh of
    Clann Máelugra (q.v.) in Uí Failge, IX, X, XIII
O'Doane (*O'Dovayne*, Devine, Downes), of Knowth
    (q.v.), Mth. Ua Dubháin of Cnodba (*q.v.*), IX
O'Donochowe, see *Dunphy*
O'Donoghue (Donaghy, Dumphy), Wm. Ua Donnchadha
    of Tellach Modharáin (*q.v.*), IX
O'Donoghue, see also *Dunphy*
O'Dooley of Fartullagh (q.v.), Wm. Ua Dubhlaoich of
    Fir Tulach, IX, X
O'Dovayne, see *O'Doane*
O'Dowling (Dowling, Doolin, Doolan), of Leix, Ua Dún-
    laing of Lagán (*q.v.*), IX
O'Duff (Duff, Black), Lx. Ua Duibh of Cenél Crimthainn
    (*q.v.*), IX, X
O'Dunaghy, see Dunphy
O'Dunne, Mth. Ua Duinn of Brega (*q.v.*), IX
O'Dunne, of Iregan (*q.v.*), Lx. Ua Duinn of Uí Riacáin in
    Uí Failge, IX, X, XIII
O'Duygin, see *Diggin*
O'Fallon (Faloon), Mth-Oy. Ua Fallamhain of Crích na
    Cétach (*q.v.*), IX
O'Farrell, Lf. Ua Fearghail, IX, X
O'Farrelly (O'Farrell), of east Wicklow, Ua Ferghaile of
    Uí Garrchon of Dál Messin Corb (*q.v.*), IX
O'Fieghraie (Feighery, Feerey, Feary, Hunt), Wk-Wx. Ua
    Fiachrach of Uí Enechglais (*q.v.*), IX
O'Finaran see *Finneran*
O'Flanagan, (?) Mth. or of Tethba, Lf-Wm. Ua Flannagáin
    of An Comar, IX
O'Fynnolane (Fenlon), of Delvin, Wm. Ua Fi(o)nnalláin
    of Delbna Mór, (*q.v.*), IX
O'Garvey (Garvey) of Rathvilly Barony, Cw. Ua Gairbíth
    (Gairbheith) of Uí Felmeda Tuaid (*q.v.*), of Uí Cheinn-
    selaig, IX

O

O'Gehin, see *Gahan*

O'Gighine, see *Gahan*

O'Gloherny (Glory, *O'Gloran, Cloran,* ? Glorney), of Callan, Kk. Ua Glóiairn of Calland in Osraige, IX

O'Gloran, see *O'Gloherny*

O'Gorman, see *MacGorman*

O'Gowan (McGowan, Smith, Smyth), of Breifney O'Reilly, Cv., IX, X

O'Growney, see *MacCaron*

O'Guindelane, see *O'Kenellan*

O'Hanvey (Hanafy, Hanway), of Farbill (*q.v.*), Wm. Ua hAinbhéith of Fir Bile, IX

O'Havergan, see *Bergen*

O'Hay (Hayes, Hughes), Lf-Wm. Ua hAodha of Eastern Tetbha (*q.v.*), IX

O'Hay (Hayes, Hughes), Mth. Ua hAodha of Odba in Brega, IX

O'Hay (Hayes, Hughes) of Gorey Barony, Wx. Ua hAodha of Uí Dega (q.v.), IX

O'Hemergin, see *Bergen*

O'Heneran (Henrion, Hanrahan, Horgan, Horan, O'Hourigan), Wm. Ua hIonnradháin (Ua hIonráin, Ua hAnradháin) of Corco Roíde, (*q.v.*), IX

O'Hennessy (Hinchy, Ennis), Du. Ua hAonghusa of Gailenga Becca (*q.v.*), IX

O'Hennessy (Hinchy, Ennis) from Lower Philipstown (about Croghan Hill), Oy. and (?) from East Offaly, Kd. Ua hAonghusa of Clann Colgan (*q.v.*) in Uí Failge

O'Hennessy (Hinchy, Ennis), Mth. Ua hAonghusa of Uí Maic Uais Breg (*q.v.*), IX

O'Hourigan, see *O'Heneran*

O'Kadesi (O'Cahessy, O'Casey), Du-Mth. Ua Caitheasaigh of Saithne (*q.v.*), IX, X

O'Kealy (*O'Coely,* Quealy), Lx. Ua Caollaidhe of Uí Buide (*q.v.*), IX

O'Kealy (*O'Coely,* Quealy) of Ida Barony (*q.v.*), Kk. Ua Caollaidhe of Uí Bercháin in Osraige (*q.v.*), IX

O'Kelly, Kd-Wk. Ua Ceallaigh of Uí Théig (*q.v.*), IX

O'Kelly, Lx. Ua Ceallaigh of Mag Drúchtain, IX

O'Kelly of Gallen, Lx. Ua Ceallaigh of Gailinne (*q.v.*), IX, X

O'Kelly of Lea, (*q.v.*) Lx. Ua Ceallaigh Léighe, IX

O'Kelly of Southern Brega, Du-Mth. Ua Ceallaigh of Síl nÁedo Sláine (*q.v.*), IX

O'Kenellan (*O'Quinelane, O'Guindelane,* Conlon, Connellan, Kinlan), Mth. Ua Coindealbháin (Caoindealbháin) of Lóegaire Breg (*q.v.*), and of Southern Uí Néill, IX

O'Kernaghan (Kernon, ?Kiernan) of Lune (*q.v.*), Mth. Ua Cearnacháin of Luigni, IX

O'Kerry, see *Keary*

O'Kinaghan, (*O'Cnigon, O'Finoghane,* Fanaghan, Fenihan), Wk. Ua Finnacáin of Uí Brúin Cualann (*q.v.*); (see next entry)

O'Kinaghan (O'Kynaghan), Wk. Ua Cuinneacháin of Uí Briúin Cualann (q.v.), X; (see previous entry)

O'Kirry, see *Keary*

O'Loughan (Loghan), Mth. Ua Leócháin of Gailenga Móra (*q.v.*), IX

O'Loughnane (Loughrane, Lawton, Loftus), Wm. Ua Lachtnáin, IX

O'Lurkaine, see *Larkin*

O'Melaghlin (Mac Loughlin), Wm. Ua Maoil Seachlainn, IX, X; (see also *Clann Cholmáin*)

O'Molloy, Oy. Ua Maoil Mhuaidh, IX, X; (see also *Fir Cell*)

O'Moraghan, see *Morrin*

O'More of Leix, Ua Mórdha of Loígis of Mag Réta, IX, X

O'Morghane, see *Morrin*

O'Mulchallan (Mulholland, Holland), Mth-Wm. Ua Maoil Challann of Delbna Bec (*q.v.*), IX

O'Mulkeen (Mulqueen, Mulquin), Oy. Ua Maoil Chéin of Tuath da Maige (*q.v.*) in Uí Failge

O'Murroughe (Murphy, *O'Moroghoe* , Wx. Ua Murchada of Uí Felmeda Thes (*q.v.*), IX, X, XV

O'Neill of Moyacomb (*q.v.*), Cw-Wk-Wx. Ua Néill of Mag dá Chonn (*q.v.*), IX, X; (see also *Feran O'Neile*)

O'Nolan of Forth, Cw. Ua Nualláin of Fotharta Fea, IX-X; (see also *Forth Barony,* Cw. and *Fotheret Onolan*)

O'Phelan (Whelan), of Clarmallagh (*q.v.*), Lx. Ua Fáeláin IX, X

O'Phelan (Whelan), of Decies, Ty-Wt. Ua Fáeláin of Déisi (*q.v.*), IX, X

O'Quinelane, see *O'Kenellan*

O'Reilly, Cv. Ua Raghallaigh of Breifne, X

O'Ronan (Ronayne), Lf. Ua Rónáin of Cairpre Gabra (*q.v.*), IX

O'Rourke, Cv. Ua Ruairc of Breifne (*q.v.*), X

O'Ryan, of Idrone (*q.v.*), Cw. Ua Riáin of Uí Dróna, IX

O'Scully, Wm. Ua Scolaidhe of Delbna Iarthair (*q.v.*), IX

O'Teige (Tighe, Teague, Tye), of Imaal, Kd-Wk. Ua Taidhg of Uí Máil (*q.v.*), IX

O'Toole (*O'Toughill,* Touhill, Toale), of Omurethy (*q.v.*), Kd-Wk. Ua Tuathail of Uí Muiredaig (*q.v.*), and earlier of Uí Dúnlainge, IX, X

O'Toughill, see *O'Toole*

Obarthy Wx., X; (see also *Bargy* and *Uí Bairrche Tíre*)

Oboy, Lx., X; (see also *Uí Buide*)

Obrun, Wk., X; (see also *Uí Briúin Chualann*)

Odagh, Kk., X; (cf. *Uí Duach*)

Odrone, (Idrone), Cw., X; (see also *Uí Dróna*)

Offaly Barony, East and West, Kd., VII; (see also *Uí Failge*)

Offaly County, X

Offelimy, Wx. Uí Felmeda Thes, IV, VIII, X, XV; (see also *Ua Murchada*)

Offerlane, Lx. Uí Fairchelláin in Osraige, XIII; (see also *Ua hUrachán*)

Old Kilcullen, Kd. Cell Cuilind, III, XII; (see also *Kilcullen Barony*)

Old Leighlin, Cw. Leth Glen, I, III, XII, XVI; (see also *Leighlin Diocese*)

Old Ross, Wx. Ros Glas, X, XVI

Omurethy, Kd-Wk., X; (see also *Uí Muiredaig*)

Ormond ('East Munster'), Urmuma, (Air-Muma), VIII, X; (see also *Munster*)

Osserie, see *Ossory*

Ossory (*Osserie*), Osraige, Kk-Lx., II-VI, VIII-IX, XIII, XV; Ossory Diocese, VI

Othee, Wk., X; (see also *Uí Théig*)

O

Oughaval (Nowal), Lx. Tulach mic Comgaill *alias* Núachongbáil, XIV
Oughterany Barony, Kd., VII;(see also *Uachtar Fine*)
Oughterard Hill, Kd. Uachtar Árd X, XII

P

Pass if you can, Wm., XIV
Pass of Kilbride, Wm. Belach Čille Brígde, XIV
Pass of the Plumes, Lx. Bernán na gCleti (post-medieval name), XIV
Petit, see *le Petit*
Philipstown Barony, Upper and Lower, Oy., VII
Pipard, Lth., X
Poer, see *de la Poer*
Portloman, Wm. Tech Lomáin, XIV
Portnahinch Barony, Lx., VII
Portnascully, Kk., X
Powerscourt, Wk. See *Cell Cornáin, Glenn Esa,* and *Tech Conaill*

Q

Quealy, see *O'Kealy*

R

Rahan, Oy. Rathan, III, XIV
Rahugh, Wm. Ráth Áeda III, VIII, XIV
Rathangan, Kd. Ráth Imgain, I, III, XII
Rathaspik, Lx. Ráth Epscoip, XIV
Rathaspick, Wx. Ráth Epscoip, XVI
Rathbeggan, Mth. Ráth Beccáin, XII
Rathbran, Goldenfort, Wk. Ráth Branduib, XII
Rathbride, Kd. Ráth Brígte, XII
Rathcoffey, Kd. Tech Cobthaig (meic Cholmáin), X, XII
Rathconnell, Wm. Ruba Conaill, XIV
Rathconrath Barony, Wm. VII
Rathcore, Mth. Dún Cuair, XII
Rathdown Barony, Du., VII
Rathdown Barony, Wk., VII
Rathdowney, Lx. Ráth Tamhnaige, XIV; (see also *Ua Bruaideadha*)
Rathedan, Cw. Ráth Etáin, XII, XVI
Rathgall Hillfort, Wk. ?Bolg Luatha, XII, XVI
Rathline, Oy. Ráth Lipthen, XIV
Rathmichael, Du. Ráth Michil, XII
Rathmore, Kd. Ráth Mór, XII
Rathnew, Wk. Ráth Nue, XII
Rathturtle, Wk. Ráth Torcaill, IX, XII
Rathvilly, Cw. Ráth Bilech, III, V, XII, XVI; Rathvilly Barony, Cw. VII
Rathwire, Wm. Ráth Guaire, X, XIV
Ratoath Barony, Mth., VII
Ratoath, Mth. Ráth Tobachta, X, XII
Reban, (Rheban), Kd., X (see also *Narragh and Reban*)
Redcross R., Wk. Dael, XI-XII, XV-XVI
Reefert Church, Glendalough, Wk. Dísert Cóemgin (Ríg ferta), XII
Rerymore *alias* Reary, Lx. Róeriu, XIV
Reynagh, Oy. Raonagh, XIV Rheban, see *Reban*
Robertstown, Kd. Inis Robartaig, XII
Roche, see *de la Roche*
Ronayne, see *O'Ronan*
Rosbercon, Kk-Wx. Ros Ua mBerchon, XVI
170 Roscore Wood, Oy. Ros Corr, XIV

Roscrea, Ty. Ros Cré, III, X, XIV
Rosenallis, Lx. Ros Finnghlaise, XIV
Rosminogue, Wx. Ros Mór (Moenóc), XVI
Rower, The, Kk. Robhar, XVI
Rush, Du. Ros Eo, XII
Ryewater R., Mth-Kd. Ríge (Laigen), XI, XII

S

Saggart, Du. Tech Sacra, III, X, XII
St Anne's, Du. Cell Episcopi Sanctani, XII
St Boodin's Well, Wk. Cell Uí Garrchon, XII
St Doolagh's, Du. Clochar Duilig, XII
St Kevin's Bed, see *Scelleg*
St Kevin's Road, Wk. XII
St Mullin's, Cw. Tech Moling I, III, V, X, XVI; St Mullin's Barony, Upper and Lower, Cw., VII
Saints Is., Lough Ree, Lf . Inis na Naemh, XIV
Sally Gap, Wk., XI, XII
Salt Barony, North and South, Kd., VII
Santry, Du. Sen Trabh, XII
Scarawalsh Barony, Wx., VII
Scark, Wx. ?Scadarc, XVI
Sculloge Gap, Cw-Wx. Berna an Scala, XVI
Seefin Mountain, Wk. Suidhe Finn, XII
Seirkieran, Oy. Saiger (Chiaráin), III, XIV
Shankill, Du. Senchell, XII
Shankill, Kk. Senchell, XVI
Shannon R., Sinann, XIV; Shannon Drainage Basin, II
Shelburne Barony, Wx., VII; (see also *Síl mBrain*)
Shelmaliere Barony, East and West, Wx., VII; (see also *Ferann na Cenél, Fernegenal, Síl Máeluidir, Ua hArtghaile, Uí Cheinnselaig*)
Shilelagh Barony, Wk., VII; (see also *Síl nElathaig*)
Shillelogher Barony, Kk., VII
Shrule, Lx. Sruthair, XII, XVI
Skea-nagun, Kd. Sciath Nechtain, XII, XVI
Skreen, see *Skryne*
Skryne, hill of, Mth. Scrin Coluim Cille, formerly Achall, III, X, XII; Skryne (Skreen) Barony, VII
Slane, Mth. Sláine, III, X; Slane Barony, Upper and Lower, VII
Slanemore, Wm. Slemain, (Slemu), XIV
Slaney R.. Wk-Cw-Wx. Sláinge, XI-XII, XV-XVI; (see also *Inber Sláinge*); Slaney Drainage Basin, II
Sleaty, Lx. Sleibte, III, XII, XVI
Slieve Bloom Mountains, Lx-Oy. Sliab Bladma *alias* Ros mic Edlicon, XIV
Slieve Golry, Lf. Sliab Calraige *alias* Brí Léith, XIV
Slievemargy, Anglo-Norman lordship, Lx-Cw., X
Slievemargy Barony, Lx., VII
Slievemargy Hills, Lx-Cw-Kk., XI-XVI
Smith, see *O'Gowan*
Smyth, see *O'Gowan*
Southern Uí Néill, VIII; (see also *Cenél nÉnna, Cenél Fiachach, Clann Cholmáin, Lóegaire Breg, Muinter Mailsinna, Síl nÁedo Sláine, Uí Cairpri Laigen, Uí Maine*)
Spinnans Hill, see *Brusselstown Ring*
Stagonil, Wk., Tech Conaill, XII
Stradbally Barony, Lx., VII
Straffan, Kd., X
Sugarloaf Mountain, Wk. ? Óe Cualann, XII

S Suir R., Kk-Wt. Siúr, XVI. Suir Drainage Basin, II
Swords, Du. Sord Coluim Cille, XII

T Taghadoe, Kd. Tech Tua, III, X, XII
Taghmon, Wm. Tech Munnu, XIV
Taghmon, Wx. Tech Mundu, III, V, XVI
Taghshinny, Lf. Tech Sinche, XIV
Talbotstown Barony, Upper and Lower, Wk., VII
Tallaght, Du. Tamlachta, III, XII
Tara, hill of, Mth. Temair, (Temair na Ríg) III, V, XII
Tara Hill, Wx. Torchair, XII, XVI
Teague, see *O'Teige*
Telltown, Mth. Tailtiu, V
Templeludican, Wx. Dísert Cendubáin, XVI
Templemacateer, Wm. Tempall meic in tSaeir, XIV
Templeshanbo, Wx. Senboth Sine, XVI
Terryglass, Ty. Tír dá Glas, V, VIII, XIV
Tethmoy, Oy. Tuath dá Maige, X, XI
Tighe, see *O'Teige*
Tigroney, Wk. ?Tech Cronáin, XII, XVI
Tihelly, Oy. Tech Taille, III, XIV
Timahoe, Kd. Tech Mo-Chúa, XII
Timahoe, Lx. Tech Mo-Chúa, III, X, XIV
Timolin, Kd. Tech Moling, XII
Tinnahinch Barony, Lx. VII
Tipperkevin, Kd. Ráth in Tobair Gil, XII
Tisaran, Oy. Tech Sáráin, XIV
Toale, see *O'Toole*
Tolka R., Du-Mth. Tulcha, XI, XII
Tomhaggard, Wx. Tech Mo-Sacro, XVI
Tornant Moat, Wk. Baile mic Rónáin, XII
Touhill, see *O'Toole*
Trevet, Mth. Treoit, III, XII
Trim, Mth. Áth Truimm, III, XII
Trooperstown, Wk. Termonn Cóemgin, XII
Tuaith, Wm., see *Twyford*
Tulfarris, Wk. Tulach Fergusa, XII
Tullaherin, Kk., XVI
Tullow, Cw. Tulach Mic Fheilmeda, I, III, V, XII, XVI
Tully, Du. Telach na nEpscop, XII
Tullyard, Mth. Telach Árd, XII

Twyford (Twy, Tuaith), Wm. Tuath Buada, XIV
Tye, see *O'Teige*
Tyrel (Tyrrell), Du., Wm., X
Tyrrell, see *Tyrel*
Tyrellspass, Wm. Bealach an Tirialaigh, XIV

U Ullard, Kk. Irarda, XVI
Uppercross Barony, Du ., VII
Upperwoods Barony, Lx., VII; (see also *Coill Uachtarach*)
Urrin R., Wx., XV
Ushnagh, hill of, (Uisnech), Wm., III, V, XIV

V Vartry R., Wk.   ?Fertir, XI, XII; (see also *Bac na Saor* and *Inber dá Glas*)

W Walshe, Kk., X
Walter, (Fitz Walter), Wk., X
Warrenstown Barony, Oy., VII
Waterford County, X
Waterford Diocese, VI
Waterford Harbour, Wt-Kk-Wx. Inber Mór, IX, X, XVI; (see also *Inis Doimle*)
Waterford, Wt. Port Láircce, IX, X, XVI
Westmeath County, X. See *Mide*
Wexford County, X
Wexford Harbour, see *Becc Ériu, Dairinis, Inber Sláinge, Loch Garman*, XVI
Wexford, Wx. Loch Garman, I, III, IX, X, XVI
Whelan, see *O'Phelan*
Whitsun Hill, Shelton Abbey (?Kilbixy), Wk. Cell Bigsige, XII
Wicklow County, X
Wicklow Gap, Wk., XII
Wicklow Town, Wk. (*Víkingr Ló*), I, III, IX, X, XII; Harbour, (Inber dá Glas and Bac na Saor), Church, (Cell Manntáin), XII
Windgates, Wk., XII
Wynne, see *Gahan*

Y Yregan, see *Iregan*

Irish-English Index to the Historical Atlas

See also *English-Irish Index to the Historical Atlas* and *General Index.*

See *Note on the Origin of Irish Family Names* at the beginning of the *English-Irish Index to the Historical Atlas.*

NOTE: The modern placename given after the early Irish name frequently represents the Anglo-Irish form of the ancient Celtic name today (e.g. Cluain Dolcáin, Clondalkin). Sometimes the modern name represents a variant form of the older name (Dún Cuair, Rathcore), but frequently a modern form is given which bears no relationship to the medieval Irish name. This is because the true Anglo-Irish name is either lost or unknown to the writer, or because the modern form is obscure and of little help for purposes of identification. When this is so, I have substituted a modern placename relating to a nearby townland, parish or village.

ABBREVATIONS

Cl.	Clare	Kd.	Kildare	Ltm.	Leitrim	Ty.	Tipperary
Cv.	Cavan	Kk.	Kilkenny	Lx.	Leix	Wk.	Wicklow
Cw.	Carlow	Lf.	Longford	Mth.	Meath	Wm.	Westmeath
Du.	Dublin	Lk.	Limerick	Oy.	Offaly	Wt.	Waterford
G.	Galway	Lth.	Louth	Rc.	Roscommon	Wx.	Wexford

A

Abha Mór, Blackwater R., Munster, II
Achad Aball, Aghowle, Wk., III, XII, XVI
Achad Bó, Aghaboe, Lx., III, X, XIV
Achad Finnglaiss, Agha, Cw., XII, XVI
Achad Gréine, Athgreany Stone Circle, Wk., XII
Achall, see *Scrín Coluim Cille*
Airgetros, Lx-Kk., XIV
Airther Life, Easter Plain of R. Liffey, Kd., XII; (see also *Íarthar Life* and *Ruirthech*)
Almu, Hill of Allen, Kd., XII
an Obair, see *Obair*
Araid (Ara Clíach), Lk., VIII
Árd Achad, Ardagh, Lf., III, V, VIII, XIV
Árd Brestine, Ardristan, Cw., XII, XVI
Árd Caomháin, Ardcavan, Wx., XVI
Árd Colmáin, Ardcolm, Wx., XVI
Árd Crema, Artramon, Wx., XVI
Árd Cróine, Ardcrony, Ty., XIV
Árd Ladrand, Ardamine, Wx., V, XVI
Árd Lemnachta, ?Forth Mountain, Wx., XVI
Árd na Macraide, see *Árd Scol*
Árd Ri, Ardree, Kd., X
Árd Scol *alias* Árd na Macraide, Moat of Ardscull, Kd., XII
Asal, see *Mag Asail* and *Slige Asail*
Ascaill Gall, Du-Kd-Wk-Wx., X, XI
Áth Airthir Mide, (Áth nIrmidi), see *Áth Féne*
Áth Buide, Ballyboy, Oy., X, XIV; (see also *Ballyboy Barony*)
Áth Cinn Chon, Kinnegad, Wm., XII
Áth Cliath, Dublin, (see Dub Linn), I, III, XII
Áth Dara, Mageney, Kd., XII, XVI
Áth Fádat, Aghade, Cw., XII, XVI

Áth Féne *alias* Áth Airthir Mide *alias* Áth Glas, Ballyglass (near Mullingar), Wm., XIV
Áth Glas, see *Áth Féne*
Áth Í, Athy, Kd., XII
Áth in Urchair, Ardnurcher *alias* Horseleap, Wm., X, XIV
Áth Líag, Athleague, (Lanesborough), Lf., X
Áth Luain, Athlone, Wm-Rc., III, X, XIV
Áth Maigne, Wm-Oy., Lismoyny, Wm., XIV
Áth nIrmidi, see *Áth Airthir Mide*
Áth Truimm, Trim, Mth., III, XII

B

Bac na Saor, Mouth of Vartry R. at Wicklow, Wk., XII
Baile Gunnair, Bellevue, Wk., XII
Baile mac Thorcaill, Curtlestown, Wk., IX, XII
Baile mic Rónáin, Tornant Moat near Dunlavin, Wk., XII
Baile Mór, Ballymore (Loughsewdy), Wm., X
Baile na Corra, (Baile na Cuirre), Ballinacor, stronghold of O'Byrne chiefs of Gabhal Raghnaill, Wk., near Ballinacar House in Glenmalure, XII. See also *Ballinacor Barony.*
Banba Mór, ?Bannow, Wx., XVI
Bealach an Tirialaigh (post-medieval name), Tyrellspass, Wm., XIV
Becc Ériu, Beggerin Is. Wexford Harbour, Wx., XVI
Belach Cille Brígde, Pass of Kilbride, Wm., XIV
Belach Con Glais, Baltinglass, Wk., III, V, XII
Belach Gabráin, see *Gabrán*
Belach Mór Maige Dála, Ballaghmore, Lx., (see also *Slige Dála*), XIV
Belach Mugna, Ballaghmoon, Kd., XII, XVI
Bennchor, Banagher, Oy., XIV
Benn Étair, Howth, Du., X, XII

B Benntraige, Wx., IV, VIII, XV; (see also *Bantry Barony, Wx.,Clann Cosgraigh*)

Berba, Barrow R., Lx-Kd-Cw-Wx., XI-XVI; Barrow Drainage Basin, II

Berna an Scala, Sculloge Gap., Cw-Wx., XVI

Bernán Éle, *alias* Bernán Méra Ingene Trega, Devil's Bit Mountain, Ty., XIV

Bernán na gCleti (post-medieval name), Pass of the Plumes, Lx., XIV

Berrech, Barragh, Cw., XVI

Bile macc Crúaich, see *Forrach Pátraic*

Birra, Birr, Oy., III, V, VIII, X, XIV

Bóinn, Boyne R., Mth-Oy., II, XI, XII

Bóirenn, Burren R., Cw., XI-XII, XV-XVI

Bolg Luatha, ? Rathgall Hillfort adjoining Knockloe, (*Cnoc Luatha*), Wk., XII, XVI

Brea, Bray R., Wk., (later for Bray town), XII; see *Dún Brea*

Brecraige, Lf-Wm., XIII

Brega, Mth., II, III, IV, VI, VIII, XI; (see *Meath*)

Bregmuine, Wm., IV, XIV; (see also *Brawny Barony*)

Breifne, (Breifney), Cv-Ltd., VIII

Brí Dam, at Druim dá Maige, Drumcaw, Parish of Bally-nakill, Oy., XIV

Brí Éle *alias* Cruachán, Croghan Hill, Oy., III, V, XIV

Brí Léith *alias* Sliab Calraige, Slieve Golry, Lf., XIV

Brosnach, Brosna R.., Oy-Wm., II, XIII-XIV; (see also *Lámh Airgid*)

Brosnach, Little Brosna R., Oy-Ty., XIII-XIV

Bruiden dá Choca, Breenmore, Wm., XIV

Bruiden dá Derga, nr. Bohernabreena, Du., XII

C Cairpre Gabra, Lf., IV, VIII

Cairpre son of Niall (lands and expenditions of), V; (see also *Cairpre Gabra, Uí Cairpri Laigen*)

Caisel, Cashel Diocese, VI

Calatruim, Galtrim, Mth., X, XII

Calraige of Bregmuine (*q.v.*), Wm., XIII

Calraige of Brí Léith (*q.v.*) in Tethba, Lf., XIII; (see also *Slíab Calraige*)

Camach (Brígde), Camma, Rc., XIV

Camros, Camaross, Wx., III, V, XVI

Caomhánach, see *Mac Murchadha Caomhánach*

Carman, ?Cw., XII, XVI

Carn, Carnsore Point, Wx., XVI

Carn Fiachach, Carn, Parish of Conry, Wm., XIV; (see also *Cenél Fhiachach*)

Carn Ruis, Horetown, Wx., XVI

Carrig Cárthainn, part of Bray Head, Wk., XII

Cell, (Cell Náis), Kill, Kd., X, XII

Cell Abbain, Killabban, Lx., III, XII, XVI

Cell Achaid Draignige, Killadreenan, Wk., XII

Cell Adgair, Killegar, Wk., XII

Cell Achid of Druim Fota, Killeigh (Killaughey, Killaghy) Oy., I, III, XIV

Cell Áir, Killare, Wm., XIV

Cell Auxili (Ausaili), Killashee, Killossy, Kd., XII; *alias* Cell Uasaille

Cell Becáin, Kilbeggan, Wm., XIV

Cell Bélat, Kilbaylet, Wk., XII

Cell Bera, Kilberry, Kd., XII

Cell Bicsige, Kilbixy, Wm., X, XIV

Cell Bigsige, Kilbixy, ?Whitsun Hill, Shelton Abbey, Wk., XII, XVI

Cell Brígde, Kilbride, Courtown, Wx., XVI

Cell Brígde, Kilbride, Wk., XII

Cell Brígde, Kilbride, Wm., XIV

Cell Cáemáin, Kilcavan (Barony of Bargy), Wx., XVI

Cell Cáemáin, Kilcavan (Barony of Gorey), Wx., XII, XVI

Cell Cainnig, Kilkenny, Kk., III, X

Cell Choca, Kilcock, Kd., XII

Cell Chúile, Kilcooly, Wm., XIV

Cell Chúile Dumai, Coole, Abbeyleix, Lx., XIV

Cell Ciaráin, Kilkieran, Kk., XVI

Cell Colgan, Kilcolgan, Oy., XIV

Cell Coluim, Kilcolumb, Kk., XVI

Cell Comainn, Kilcommon, Oy., XIV

Cell Comgaill, Kilcoole, Wk., XII

Cell Comhgáin, Kilquiggin, Wk., XII, XVI

Cell Corbmaic, Kilcormac, Oy., XIV

Cell Cornáin, at Powerscourt Waterfall, Wk., XII

Cell Critaich, in Glencree, Wk., XII

Cell Cruimthir, Kilcumreragh, Wm., XIV

Cell Cuáin Mór, Kilcoanmore, Wx., XVI

Cell Cuilind, Old Kilcullen, Kd., III, XII

Cell dá Lua., Killaloe Diocese, VI

Cell Dara, Kildare, Kd., I, III, V, X, XII; Kildare County, X; Kildare Diocese, VI

Cell Deilge, Kildalkey, Mth., XII

Cell Delcce, Kildellig, Lx., XIV

Cell Draignech, Kildreenagh, Cw., XII, XVI

Cell Droichit, Celbridge, Kd., X, XII

Cell Duilig, Grangegorman, Du., XII

Cell Duma Glinn, Kilglinn, Mth., XII

Cell Eachdroma, Killoughrum, Wx., XVI

Cell Easpuig Iubair, Killapeckure, Wk., XII, XVI

Cell Ech, Killagh, Wm., XIV

Cell Eglan, Killeglan, Mth., XII

Cell Eirc, Killerk, Wk., XII

Cell Eision, Killeshin, Lx., III, X, XII, XVI

Cell Episcopi Sanctani, St Anne's, Du., XII

Cell Fine (Cormaic), Kileencormac, Kd., XII

Cell Finnabrach, Killenora, Cw., XII, XVI

Cell Gabra, Kilgory, Lx., XIV, XVI

Cell Gormáin, Kilgorman, Wx., XII, XVI

Cell Liadaine, Killyon, Oy., XIV

Cell Maignenn, Kilmainham, Du., XII

Cell Mancháin, Kilmanaghan, Oy., XIV

Cell Manntáin, Wicklow, Wk., XII

Cell Martra, Kilmartin, Wk., XII

Cell mic Cathail, Kilmacahill, Kk., XVI

Cell Mochonóc, Kilmacanoge, Wk., XII

Cell Mo Chura, Kilmacurragh, Wk., XII

Cell Molapóc, Kilmolappogue, Lorum, Cw., XVI

Cell Moling, Kilmalin, Wk., XII

Cell Molomma, Kilmalum, Kd., XII

Cell Mór, Kilmore, Cv., X

Cell Mór, Kilmore, Mth., XII

Cell Mosamócc, near Island Bridge, Du., XII

Cell Moshílóic, Kilmichaelogue, Wx., XVI

173

Cell na Manach, Kilnamanagh, Du., XII
Cell na Manach, Kilnamanagh, Wx., XVI
Cell Osnaid, Kellistown, Cw., XII, XVI
Cell Rannairech, Kilranelagh, Wk., (see also Dún Buchat), XII
Cell Rignaige, Kilrane, Wx., XVI
Cell Scíre, Kilskyre, (Kilskeer), Mth., III
Cell Tagáin, Kiltegan, Wk., XII, XVI
Cell tSíle, Kilteel, Kd., XII
Cell Ua Mílchon, Kilmeelchon, Oy., XIV
Cell Uasaille (Cell Usaili), see *Cell Auxili*
Cell Uí Garrchon, St Boodin's Well, Wk., XII
Cenandas, Kells, Mth., III, V, X; (see also *Kells Barony, Mth.*)
Cenél Aitheamhain, at Fid Cuilind (*q.v.*), Kd., XI (see also *Ua Muirte*)
Cenél Cobthaig, of Árd Ladrand (*q.v.*), of Uí Cheinnselaig, XV
Cenél Crimthain, see *Uí Crimthainn Áin*
Cenél Fhiachach, Wm., IV, VIII, XIII; (see also *Carn Fiachach* and *Mac Eochagáin*)
Cenél Flaitheamhain, Wx., XV
Cenél nÉnna, of Castletown Kindalen, Wm., (? and of Kinalea near Uisnech, Wm.), XIII; (see also *Mac Ruairc, Ua Braonáin*)
Cenél nUcha, Kd., XI
Cenn Eich (*alias* Imlech Eich), Kinneigh, Kd ., XII, XVI
Cenn Eitig, Kinnity, Oy., III, X, XIV
Cenn Sáile, Kinsaley, Du., XII
Cetharlach, Carlow, Cw., X
Ciannachta (Breg), Mth., IV, VIII; (see also *Fir Árda Ciannachta*)
Claenad, Clane, Kd., X, XII; (see also *Clane Barony*)
Clann Cholmáin, of Southern Uí Néill of Mide, Wm., IV, VIII, XIII; (see also *Ua Maoil Seachlainn*)
Clann Colgan, of Uí Failge (*q.v.*), Lower Philipstown, about Croghan Hill, and earlier in East Offaly, Kd., XIII
Clann Cosgraigh, Wx., of Benntraige (*q.v.*), O'Coskry (Cosgry, Coskerry, Cosgrave), of Bantry Barony, Wx., IX
Clann Máel Chéin, of Uí Failge in Tuath dá Maige (*q.v.*), Oy-Kd., XIII
Clann Máelugra, of Uí Failge, Oy-Lx., Clanmaliere, XIII; (see also *Ua Díomasaigh*)
Clann Mainchine, Kd., XI
Clann Mugróin, of Uí Failge (*q.v.*), Kd., XI
Clár Maige Lache, see *Mag Lacha*
Clártha, Clare, Wm., XIV
Clíu, in Uí Dróna, Cw., XII, XVI
Clochán (an Imrim), Cloghan *alias* Cloghanumera, Wm., XIV
Clochar Duilig, St Doolagh's, Du., XII
Cluain Cáin, Clon Kyne *alias* Abbeyleix, Lx., XIV
Cluain Conaire Máelduib, Cloncurry, Barony of East Offaly, Kd., XII
Cluain Conaire Tomáin, Cloncurry, Barony of Ikeathy and Oughterany, Kd., III, X, XII
Cluain Dolcáin, Clondalkin, Du., III, XII
Cluain Édnech, Clonenagh, Lx., I, III, XIV
Cluain Emain, Cloonowen, (Clonown), Rc., XIV

Cluain Fada, Cloonfad, Rc., XIV
Cluain Fada Báetáin Abha, Clonfad, Barony of Farbill, Wm., III, XIV
Cluain Fada Fine Libráin, Clonfad, Barony of Fartullagh, Wm., III, XIV
Cluain Ferta (Brénainn), Clonfert, G., XIV; Clonfert Diocese, VI
Cluain Ferta Molua, Clonfertmulloe, Lx., III, XIV
Cluain Ferta Mughaine, Kilclonfert, Oy., XIV
Cluain Iraird, Clonard, Mth., V, VIII, X, XII
Cluain maccu Nois, Clonmacnoise, Oy., III, X, XIV; Clonmacnoise Diocese, VI
Cluain Magna, Clonmines, Wx., XVI
Cluain Moescna, in Fir Tulach, Wm., XIV
Cluain Mór Dicolla Gairb, Clonmore, Wx., III, XVI
Cluain Mór Máedóc, Clonmore, Cw., III, XII, XVI
Cluain na mBan, ?Bannow Bay, Wx., XVI
Cluain Sosta, Clonsast, Oy., XIV
Cluain Tarbh, Clontarf, Du., XII
Cnodba, Knowth, Mth., III; (see also *Ua Conghalaigh, Ua Dubháin*)
Cnúcha, Castleknock, Du., X, XII; (see also *Castleknock Barony*)
Coill an Chláir, Kilclare, Kilbride Parish, Oy., XIV
Coill dá Sruth, near Lullymore (*q.v.*), Kd., XII
Coill Uachtarach, Forest at foot of Slieve Bloom (*q.v.*), which gives name to the Barony of Upperwoods (*q.v.*), Lx., XIV
Comar, Mth., XII
Comar na Trí nUisge, Meeting of Barrow, Nore, and Suir R.s. Kk-Wt-Wx., XVI
Comrar (Mide), (Comraire) Conry, Wm., XIV
Conmaicne (Bec), in Cuircne (*q.v.*), Wm., IV, VIII, XIII
Connachta, Connaught, VI, VIII, XIII
Corco Adaim (Adain), Corkaree-Magheradernon (*q.v.*), Wm., Precise location unknown
Corco Roíde, Wm., IV, VIII, XIII; (see *Corkaree Barony, Ua hIonnradháin*)
Craeb (?Teine), Creeve, (Crew), Wm., XIV; (see also *Ua Braonáin*)
Crích na Cenél, see *Ferann na Cenél*
Crích na Cétach, Mth-Oy., VIII, XIII; (see also *Ua Fallamháin*)
Críoch Bhranach, territory of senior branch of O'Byrne in east Wicklow in later Middle Ages extending from Delgany and the Vartry river in the north, to Arklow in the south, (XII). See also *Ua Broin* of Uí Fáeláin, and *Gabhal Raghnaill*
Cró Inis, Cormorant Is., Lough Ennell, Wm., XIV
Crúach, Cruagh, Du., XII
Cruachán, *alias* Brí Éle, Croghan Hill, Oy., III, V, XIV
Cruachán, Croghan Mountain, Wk-Wx., XII, XVI
Cualu, The Wicklow Hills from Arklow in the south-east to the Dublin Mountains in the north; especially the northern fringe of this mountain chain, Du-Kd-Wk., XI-XII. See also *Óe Cualann, Slige Cualann, Uí Briúin Chualann, Uí Ceallaig Cualann*
Cuircne, Lf-Wm., XIV; (see also *Machaire Cuircne*)
Cuirrech Life, Curragh of Kildare, Kd., XII
Cúl Bendchuir, Coolbanagher, Lx., XIV

D Dael, Redcross R., Wk., XI-XII, XV-XVI
Daireach, Derry R., Wk-Wx-Cw., XI-XII, XV-XVI
Daire Mór, Kilcolman, Oy., XIV
Dairinis Is., in Wexford Harbour, Wx., XVI
Dairmag (Coluim Cille), Durrow, Oy., III, X, XIV
Dairmag Ua nDuach, Durrow, Lx., XIV
Dál Cairpre Arad, Lk., V
Dál Chormaic, Kd-Lx., IV, V, VIII, XI, XV; (see also *Uí Buide, Uí Gabla*)
Dál Messin Corb, (Uí Garrchon), Wk., Wk-Kd., IV, V, VIII, XI, XV; Dál Messin Corb of Cenn Eich (*q.v.*), Kd.; see also *Síl Senaig, Uí Bráen Deilgni, Uí Garrchon* at Cell Uí Garrchon (*q.v.*), and Cell Fine (*q.v.*), and *Ua Ferghaile*)
Damliacc (Cianáin), Duleek, Mth., III, X
Daurthech, Old Court, Bray, Wk., XII
Dea, Avonmore, (Avoca), R., Wk., XI-XII, XV-XVI; (see also *Inber Dee* and *Glenn Dea*)
Deilginis (Cualann), Dalkey Is., Du., XII
Deilgne Mogoróc (Dergne), Delgany, Wk., XII
Déisi, The Decies, Wt., IV, VIII, XV
Déisi (Breg), Mth., IV, VIII, XI; (see also *Deece Barony, Upper and Lower*)
Delbna Bec, Mth-Wm., VIII; (see also *Ua Maoil Challann*)
Delbna Ethra, Oy., IV, VIII, XIII; (see also *Mac Cochláin*)
Delbna Iarthair, ('West Delvin'); (see also *Ua Scolaidhe* Wm-Lf.,)
Delbna (Mór), Wm., IV, VIII, XIII; (see also Delvin Barony, *Ua Fionnalláin*)
Dergne, see *Deilgne Mogoróc*, Wk., XII
Digais, Djouce Mountain, Wk., XII
Dinn Ríg, *alias* Duma Sláinge, *alias* Túaim Tenba, Burgage Moat, Cw., III, V, XII, XVI
Dísert Cendubáin, Templeludican, Wx., XVI
Dísert Cóemgin, Reefert Church, Glendalough, Wk., XII
Dísert Cuilinn, Disert Gallin, Lx., XIV
Dísert Diarmata, Castledermot, Kd., I, III, X, XII, XVI
Dísert Máeltuile, Dysart, Wm., XIV
Dísert Óengussa, Dysart, Lx., XIV
Dísert Tola, Dysart (Taula), Wm., XIV
Domnach Daa, Donadea, Kd., XII
Domnach Imlech, Burgage, Wk., XII
Domnach Mór, Donaghmore, Kd., XII
Domnach Mór, Donaghmore, Mth., III
Domnach Pátraicc, Donaghpatrick, Mth., III
Domnach Rignaige, Templerainy, Wk., XII, XVI
Domnach Sechnaill, Dunshaughlin, Mth., III, XII
Dothra, Dodder R., Du., XI, XII
Drobél, Gravale Mountain, Wk., XII
Drochat Átha, Drogheda, Lth-Mth., X
Drochat Cairpre, Leinster Bridge, Mth-Oy., XII
Druim Criaich, see *Druim nAirthir*
Druim Cuilinn, Drumcullen, Oy., XIV
Druim dá Maige, Drumcaw, *alias* Mount Lucas, Oy., XIV Site also of Brí Dam (*q.v.*); (see also *Tochar etar dá Mag* and *Tuath dá Maige*)
Druim nAirthir, *alias* Druim Criaich, Drumcree, Wm., XIV
Druim Ráite, Drumraney, Wm., III, XIV
Druim Urchaille, Dunmurraghill, Kd., XII
Dub Glaise, Douglas R., Lx., XI-XII, XV-XVI

Dubh (Abha), Blackwater R., Mth-Oy., XI, XII
Dubh, Blackwater R., Oy., XIII-XIV
Dub Linn, *alias* Áth Cliath, Dublin, XII
Dubtar, *Duffry,* Wx., X, XVI; (see also *Síl mBrain*)
Dubthír, Rc., XIV
Duma Sláinge, see *Dinn Ríg*
Dún Ailinne, Knockaulin Hillfort, Kd., III, V, XII; cf. Allen, Hill of
Dún Bolg, Brusselstown Ring, Spinnans Hill, Wk., XII
Dún Brea, Bray, Wk., XII
Dún Buaice, Dunboyke, Wk., XII
Dún Buchat, Kilranelagh, Wk., XII
Dún Canáin, Duncannon, Wx., XVI
Dún Crimthainn, tumulus on Howth Head, Du., XII
Dún Cuair, Rathcore, Mth., XII
Dún Garbháin, Dungarvan, Wt., X
Dún Masc, (Rock of) Dunamase, Lx., I, III, XIV
Dún na Cairrge, Carrick, near Lough Ennell, Wm., XIV
Dún na Sciath, Doon, by Lough Ennell, Wm., XIV

E Éle, Ely (O'Carroll), Oy-Ty., IV, V, VIII, XIII; (see also *Bernán Éle, Brí Éle, Mag Éle, Móin Éle, Ua Cearbhaill*)
Éoganacht Caisil, Ty., VIII
Escir Riada, Great Esker running across the Irish Midlands and coinciding in part with the *Slige Mór* (q.v.),
Ethne, Inny R., Lf-Wm., XIII-XIV; (see also *Inny Drainage Basin*)

F Faeldruim, Feltrim, Du., XII
Faitche meic Mecnáin, at Lough Sunderlin, Wm., XIV
Feóir, Nore R., Kk-Lx-Ty., XIII-XIV, XV-XVI
Ferann Deisceartach, probably Uí Bairrche Tíre, Bargy Barony, Wx.; (see also *Ua Duibhginn*)
Ferann na Cenél, *Fernegenal*, Wx., *alias* Crích na Cenél, XV; (see also *Shelmaliere Barony East, Síl Máeluidir, Ua hArtghaile, Uí Cheinnselaig*)
Ferann Uí Néill, *Feran O'Neile*, Cw-Wk-Wx., X; (see also *Ua Néill* of Mag dá Chonn)
Ferna (Mór), Ferns, Wx., I, III, V, XVI; (see also *Ferns Diocese*)
Fertir, ?Vartry R., Wk., XI, XII
Fiachu, son of Niall, (lands and expeditions of), V; (see also *Cenél Fhiachach*)
Fid Árd, ?Fethard, Wx., XVI
Fid Cuilind, Feighcullen, Kd., XII
Fid Dorcha, near Lann (*q.v.*), Wm., XIV
Fid nGaible, Figile R., and surroundings, Kd-Oy., XI, XII
Fine Gall, *Fingal,* Du., IX-XI
Finn Glas, Finglas, Du., III, XII
Fir Árda Ciannachta, Lth-Mth., VIII
Fir Asail, see *Mag Asail*
Fir Bile, Wm., IV, VIII, XIII; (see also *Farbill Barony, Ua hAinbhéith*)
Fir Cell, Oy., IV, VIII, XIII; (see also *Ua Maoil Mhuaidh*)
Fir Chúl Breg, Mth., IV, VIII
Fir Chúl of Tethba, Wm., IV, VIII, XIII; see also *Síl Rónáin*
Fir Tulach, Wm., IV, VIII, XIII; (see also *Fartullagh* 175

F *Barony*, Ua Dubhlaoich)

Fobar, Fore, Wm., III, X; (see also *Fore Barony*)

Fochlaid, Faughalstown, Wm., XIV

Fordruim, Ask Hill, Wx., XII, XVI

Forgnaidhe, Forgney, Lf., XIV

Formael, see *Luimnech*, (*Limerick Hill*), Wx.

Forrach, Farrow, Leny Parish, Wm., XIV

Forrach Pátraic, (formerly Bile macc Crúaich), Narragh-more, Kd., V, X, XII; (see also *Narragh and Reban Barony*)

Fortuatha, Wk., II; (see also *Uí Enechglaiss* and *Dál Messin Corb*)

Fothairt (Laigen), Du., XI

Fothairt, see *Fotharta, Uí Báetăin, Uí Cúlduib Cille Dara, Uí Diarmata, Uí Ercáin*

Fotharta Fea, (Fothairt), Cw., IV-V, VIII, XI, XV; (see also *Forth Barony*, Cw., *Fotheret Onolan, Ua Nualláin*)

Fotharta in Chairn, (Fothairt), Wx., IV-V, VIII, XV; (see also *Forth Barony*, Wx., *Ua Lorcáin*)

Fremu, Frewin Hill, Wm., XIV

G Gabair (Laigen), Cw., V, XII, XVI

Gabhal Raghnaill, junior branch of O'Byrne, ruling from Rathdown to Shillelagh in later Middle Ages and centred on Ballinacor in Glenmalure, Wk., XII. See also *Ua Broin* of *Uí Fáeláin* and *Críoch Bhranach*

Gabrán (Belach Gabrán), Gowran, Kk., IV-V, XVI; (see also *Gowran Barony*)

Gailenga Becca, Du., IV, VIII, XI; (see also *Ua hAonghusa*)

Gailenga Móra, Mth-Cv., IV, VIII; (see also *Morgalion Barony, Ua Leócháin*)

Gailinne, Gallen (Dysart-Gallen), Lx. Originally name of region, XIV; Ua Cellaigh of (*q.v.*)

Gailinne na mBretan, Gallen, Oy., III, XIV

Gáirech, Garhy, Parish of Kindalen, Wm., XIV

Garbsalach, Garrysallagh, Wm., XIV

Géisill, (Mag Gé(i)silli) Geashill, Oy., XIV

Glais Eille, Glasseli, Kd., XII

Glais in Ascail, Glassgorman R., (and Inch R.), Wx., XII, XVI

Glais Noeden, Glasnevin, Du., XII

Glenn Brígde, Glenbridge, Wk., XII

Glenn Capaich (Caipche), *alias* Glen dá Gruad, Glencap, Wk., XII

Glenn dá Gruad *alias* Glen Capaich, Glencap, Wk., XII

Glenn dá Locha (formerly Glenn Dea), Glendalough, Wk., I, III, X, XII; (see also *Glendalough Diocese, Dísert Cóemgin, Ríg Ferta, Scelleg*)

Glenn Dea, see *Glenn dá Locha*

Glenn Esa, Powerscourt Deerpark, Wk., XII

Glenn Faidli, Glenealy, Wk., XII

Glenn Mámma, (between Saggart and Lyons Hill), Du., XII

Glenn Maoil 'oraidh, Glenmalure, Wk., XII

Glenn Munaire, Ballyman, north of Bray, Du., XII

Glenn Ua Máil, Glen of Imail, Wk. See *Uí Máil*

Graneret, Granard, Lf., V, X

I Íarthar Life, Western Plain of Liffey, Kd., XII; (see also *Life, Airther Life* and *Ruirthech*)

176 Imlech Eich, in Uí Bairrche, see *Cenn Eich*

Inber Daele, Ennereilly, Wk., XII, XVI

Inber dá Glas, Wicklow Harbour, Wk., I, III, XII

Inber Dee, Estuary of Avonmore (Dea) R., at Arklow, Wk., I, III, X, XII, XVI; (see also *Dea* and *Glenn Dea*)

Inber Domnann, Malahide Bay, Du., XII

Inber Mór, Waterford Harbour, Wt-Wx., XVI

Inber Sláinge, Slaney Estuary, Wexford Harbour, Wx., XVI

Inis Adarcach, Incherky, on the Shannon R., Oy., XIV

Inis Aingin, Hare Is., Lough Ree, Wm., XIV

Inis Báethín, Ennisboyne, Wk., XII

Inis Bó Finne, Inchbofin Is., Lough Ree, Wm., XIV

Inis Breslén, Gilltown, Kd., XII

Inis Celtra, Holy Is., Lough Derg, on Shannon, Cl. V, VIII

Inis Clothrann, Inchcleraun Is., Lough Ree, Lf., XIV

Inis Corthadh, Enniscorthy, Wx., X

Inis Cré, see *Móin Inse* (*Cré*)

Inis Doimle, Inch, barony of Shelmaliere, Wx., XVI

Inis Doimle, Little Is., Waterford Harbour, Wt., XVI

Inis Dorbas, *alias* Inis Eirne, Great Island, Wx., XVI

Inis Eirne, see *Inis Dorbas*

Inis Éndaim, Inchenagh Is., Lough Ree, Lf., XIV

Inis mac Nesáin, Ireland's Eye, Is., Du., XII

Inis Mocholmóc, Inch, Wx., XII, XVI

Inis Mór, Church Is., Lough Owel, Wm., XIV

Inis Mór, Inchmore Is., Lough Ree, Wm., XIV

Inis na Naemh, Saints Is., Lough Ree, Lf., XIV

Inis Robartaig, Robertstown, Kd., XII

Inis Teoc, Inistioge, (Innistiogue), Kk., XVI

Inis Tuirc, Inchturk Is.., Lough Ree, Wm., XIV

Inniuin, Dungolman R., Wm., XIII-XIV

Irarda, Ullard, Kk., XVI

Irmide, (Airthir Mide), 'East Mide', XIII-XIV

L Lagán, East of the Barrow in Barony of Stradbally, Leix. Precise location not known. See *Ua Dúnlaing* of Lagán.

Laigin, Kingdom of the Leinstermen, I-X. Detailed areas XI-XVI

Lámh Airgid, Brosna R., south of Lough Owel, Wm., XIV; (see also *Brosnach*)

Lann, Lynn, Wm., III, VIII, XIV

Lann Elo, Lynally, Oy., III, XIV

Lathrach Briúin, Laragh (bryan), Kd., X, XII

Lathrach dá Arad, Laragh, Barony of Shillelagh, Wk., XII, XVI

Lecan (Mide), Lackan, Wm., XIV

Leccach, Lackagh, Kd., XII

Lége, *alias* Tuath Léghe, Lea, (Ley, Leys), Lx., XIII, XIV

Leth Glenn, Old Leighlin, Cw., I, III, XII, XVI; (see also *Leighlin*)

Liamain, Lyon's Hill, Kd., III, XII

Liath Mancháin, *alias* Túaim nEirc, Lemanaghan, Oy., XIV

Life, Plain of R. Liffey, Kd., XII; (see also *Íarthar Life, Airther Life, Mag Life,* and *Ruirthech*)

Lilcach, Lullymore, Kd., XII

Liss Cholmáin, Liscolman, Wk., XII, XVI

Liss Maigne, Lismoyny, Wm., at Áth Maigne (*q.v.*)

L Liss Mór, Lismore, Wt., X; (see also *Lismore Diocese*)

Loch Ainninn, Lough Ennell, Wm., II, V, XIV; (see also *Cró Inis, Dún na Cairrge, Dún na Scíath*)

Loch Dercderc, Lough Derg (on the Shannon), Ty-G-Cl., II, V, XIII-XIV

Loch Gabair, Lagore (lake and crannog), Mth., III, XII

Loch Garman, Wexford, Wx., I, III, XVI

Loch Íairn, Lough Iron, Wm., II, V, XIII-XIV

Loch Lebind, Lough Lene, Wm., II, V, XIII-XIV

Loch Lúatha, Ballyloughloe, Wm., X, XIV

Loch Muinremair, Lough Ramor, Cv., II, V

Loch nDairbrech, Lough Derravaragh, Wm., II, V, XIII-XIV

Loch Ríb, Lough Ree, Lf-Wm-Rc., II, V, XIII-XIV; (see also *Inis Aingin, Inis Bó Finne, Inis Clothrann, Inis Éndaim, Inis Mór, Inis na Naemh* and *Inis Torc*)

Loch Semdidi, Lough Sunderlin (Sewdy), Wm. (See also *Ballymore Loughsewdy, Faitche meic mecnáin*)

Loch Sighlenn, Lough Sheelin, Lf-Mth-Cv., II, V

Loch Treithin, dried-up lake south of Lough Owel (*q.v.*), Wm., XIV; (formerly wrongly identified with Lough Drin)

Loch Uair, Lough Owel, Wm., II, V, XIII-XIV; (see also *Inis Mór*)

Lóegaire (Breg), Mth., IV, VIII, XI; (see also *Ua Coin-dealbháin*)

Lóeguire, son of Niall (lands and expeditions of), V; (see also *Lóegaire Breg*)

Loígis, of Mag Reta (*q.v.*), Lx., II, IV, V, VIII, XIII; (see also *Leix, O'More, Ua Mórdha*)

Loígis Ua nEnechglaiss, Wk., north-west of Arklow, XI, XV

Lothra, Lorrha, Ty., V, VIII, XIV

Luigni, Mth., IV, VIII, XI; (see also *Lune Barony, Ua Braoin, Ua Cearnacháin*)

Luimnech, *alias* Formael, Limerick Hill, Wx., XII, XVI

Lusca, Lusk, Du., XII

Lusmag, Lusma, Oy., XIV

M Mac Airechtaigh of Lann (*q.v.*), MacGeraghty of Lynn, Wm., XIII

Mac (Mag) Amhalghadha, Magawly, MacAuley, Wm., IX, X. Cf. *Mag Amalgada*

Mac Aodha (Mag Aodha) of Muinter Tlámáin, MacGee (Magee, *M'Gay*, Gee), Wm., IX

Mac Braoin of Na Clanna, in Osraige, MacBreen (*M'Brewne, M'Brune, M'Breane*) of Knocktopher Barony (*q.v.*), Kk., IX

Mac (Mag) Carrgamhna of Muinter Mailsinna (*q.v.*), MacCaron (MacCaroon, O'Growney, *M'Crony*, Gaffney, Caulfield), Wm., IX

Mac Cochláin, (Delvin) MacCoghlan, Coughlan, Oy., IX, X; (see also *Delbna Ethra*)

Mac Conn Meadha of Muinter Laoghacháin, MacConway, (MacConvey, MacNama), Lf-Wm., IX

Mac Eochagáin, Mageoghegan, Wm., IX, X; (see also *Cenél Fhiachach*)

Mac Fíodhbhaidhe (Fíodhbhadhaigh) of Tuath Fíodhb-haidhe (*q.v.*), MacEvoy (*M'Eboy, M'Ewy,* MacVoy) of Leix, IX

Mac Gilla Mo-Cholmóg, Gilla Mocholmóc, (Fitz Dermot), Du-Wk., IX, X; (see also *Uí Dúnchada*)

Mac Gilla Pátraic of Osraige, Mac Gillapatrick, MacElfatrick, Fitzpatrick, Kirkpatrick, Lx-Kk., IX, X

Mac Giolla (t)Seachlainn of Síl nÁedo Sláine (q.v.), Mac Glaughlin (MacClachlin, MacClafflin, MacTaghlin, *M'Gillaghlin, M'Kintaghlin*) of Southern Brega, IX. (Later confused with *Mac/Mag Lochlainn*)

Mac Gormáin of Uí Bairrche (*q.v.*), Mac Gorman (O'Gorman), Lx-Cw., IX

Mac Murchadha Caomhánach, Mac Murrough Kavanagh, Wk-Wx. Branch of Mac Murchadha (*q.v.*), descended from Domhnall Caomhánach son of Dermot MacMurrough, X

Mac Murchadha of Uí Cheinnselaig (*q.v.*), MacMurrough (*Mac Moroghe, M'Murphewe*, Morrow), Wx., IX, X

Mac Ruairc (Mag Ruairc, Mag Ruadhraic) of Cenél nÉnna (q.v.), of Southern Uí Néill. Grourke, (*M'Royrke, M'Groirke*), of Kinalea, Wm., IX

Mac Tighearnáin of western Breifne (q.v.), MacKiernan (Kiernan, Kernon), Cv., related to Ua Ruairc (*q.v.*). See also *Ua Cearnacháin*

Machaire Cuircne, Wm., XIV; (see also *Cuircne*)

Machaire Ua dTigernáin, see *Uí Tigernáin*

Mag Ailbe, Kd-Cw., XII, XVI

Mag Ailbe, Mth., XII

Mag Airb in Osraige, in Crannagh Barony, Kk., (*q.v.*); (see also *Ua Caibhdheanaigh*)

Mag Amalgada, Wm., XIV. Cf. the dynastic name *Mac Amhalghadha* from the same locality.

Mag Aodha, see *Mac Aodha*

Mag Arnaide, Adamstown, Wx., XVI

Mag Asail, Wm., XIV; (see also *Moyashel Barony*)

Mag Brecraige, Lf-Wm., XIV

Mag Caisil, Wm., XIV; (see also *Moycashel Barony*)

Mag Corráin, Wm., XIV

Mag dá Chonn, (Moyacomb parish), Wk-Wx-Cw., XII, XVI

Mag Drúchtain, Lx., XIV. Ua Cellaigh of (*q.v.*)

Mag Duma, Moydow, Lf., X, XIV

Mag Éle, ?Moyelly, Oy., V

Mag Fea, in Fotharta, Cw., XII, XVI

Mag Géisilli, see *Géisill* and *Tuath Géisille*

Mag Lacha *alias* Clár Maige Lache, Clarmallagh Barony, Lx., (together with parts of Clandonagh), VII, XIV

Mag Laigen, The Plain of Leinster, which included Clane, Lyon's Hill, Old Kilcullen, and Oughterard (*q.v.*), Kd., XII; *alias* Mag Life (q.v.)

Mag Lena, Oy., XIV

Mag Life (Mag Liphi), The Plain of Liffey, which included Uí Fáeláin and Uí Ercáin, and places from Moone and Narraghmore in south Kildare, to Killashee and Lyon's Hill in the north of that county (q.v.), Kd., XI-XII. See also *Ruirthech, Life,* and *Mag Laigen*

Mag Máil in Osraige, Kk., XVI; (see also *Ua Donnchadha*)

Mag Nuadat, Maynooth, Kd., X, XII

Mag Rechet, see *Mag Réta*

Mag Réta, Morett (Mag Rechet), and Great Heath of Maryborough, Lx., XIV

Mag Ruadhraic, see *MacRuairc*

Mag Ruairc, see *Mac Ruairc*

Maine son of Niall, (lands and expeditions of), V

177

M
Mainister Buite, Monasterboice, Lth., III
Maircc Lagen, see *Sliab Mairge*
Maistiu (Mullach Maisten), Mullaghmast Hill, Kd., III, XII
Málainn, (Málu), Maulin Mountain, Wk., XII
Mendroichet, Mondrehid, Lx., XIV
Mide, II, III, IV, VI, VIII, XIII; (see also *Westmeath*)
Móin Almaine *alias* Móin Éle, Bog of Allen, Kd-Oy., V, XII, XIV
Móin Coluimb (Cille), Moone, Kd., III, X, XII; (see also *Kilkea and Moone Barony*)
Móin Éle *alias* Móin Almaine, Bog of Allen, Kd-Oy., V, XII, XIV; cf. *Éle* and *Brí Éle*
Móin Faíchnig, Boughna Bog, Parish of Kilbride, Wm., XIV
Móin Inse (Cré) *alias* Inis Cré, Monaincha, Ty., III, XIV
Móin Lainne, Lynn Bog, at Lynn, Wm., XIV
Móin Rátha (Bresail), Mountrath, Lx., XIV
Mugna Mosenóc, Dunmanoge, Kd., XII, XVI
Muilenn Cerr, Mullingar, Wm., X
Muilenn Odhráin, Mullinoran, Wm., XIV
Muinter Cearbhaill, see *Ua Cearbhaill (Éile)*
Muinter Fíodhbhaidhe, (Fíodhbhadhaigh), see *Mac Fíodhbhaidhe*
Muinter Gearadháin, *Moyntergeran*, Lf., X
Muinter Laoghacháin, Lf-Wm., on southern Longford-Westmeath border; (see *Mac Con Meadha*)
Muinter Mailsinna, in Cuircne (of Uí Maine of Southern Uí Néill), XIII; (see also *Mac Carrgamhna*)
Muinter Tadgáin, *Munterhagan*, Oy., IX, X
Muinter Tlámáin, Wm. Precise location unknown; in or near Magheradernon (*q.v.*)
Mullach Maisten, see *Maistiu*
Mumu, Munster, II-VI, VIII, XIII
Muscraige Tíre, Ty., IV, VIII, XIII

N
Nás, Naas, Kd., I, III, V, X, XII
Niall Noígiallach ('of the Nine Hostages'), lands and expeditions of, V; (see also *Southern Uí Néill*)
Núachongbáil, Lx., see *Tulach mic Comgaill*
Núachongbáil, Navan, Mth., X

O
Ó Beirgin, see *Ua hAimhirghin*
Ó Meirgin, see *Ua hAimhirghin*
Obair, (an Obair), Nobber, Mth., X
Óe Cualann, ?Sugarloaf Mountain, Wk., XII
Óenach Carman, see *Carman*
Óenach Tailten, see *Tailtiu*
Osraige, Ossory, Kk-Lx., II-VI, VIII-IX, XIII, XV

P
Port Láircce, Waterford, Wt., XVI; (see also *Inber Mór* and *Waterford Diocese*)

R
Raonagh, Reynagh, Oy., XIV
Ráth Áeda, Rahugh, Wm., III, VIII, XIV
Rathan, Rahan, Oy., III, XIV
Ráth Beccáin, Rathbeggan, Mth, XII
Ráth Bilech, Rathvilly, Cw., III, V, XII, XVI
Ráth Branduib, Rathbran, Goldenfort, Wk., XII
Ráth Brígte, Rathbride, Kd., XII
Ráth Epscoip, Rathaspik, Lx., XIV

Ráth Epscoip, Rathaspick, Wx., XVI
Ráth Etáin, Rathedan, Cw., XII, XVI
Rath Guaire, Rathwire, Wm., X, XIV
Ráth Imgain, Rathangan, Kd., I, III, XII
Ráth in Tobair Gil, Tipperkevin, Kd., XII
Ráth Lipthen, Rathline, Oy., XIV
Ráth Michil, Rathmichael, Du., XII
Ráth Mór, Rathmore, Kd., XII
Ráth Nue, Rathnew, Wk., XII
Ráth Tamhnaige, Rathdowney, Lx., XIV; (see also *Ua Bruaideadha*)
Ráth Tobachta, Ratoath, Mth., X, XII; (see also *Ratoath Barony*)
Ráth Torcaill, Rathturtle, Wk., IX, XII
Rechru, Lambay Is., Du., XII
Ríg Ferta, Reefert, cemetery at Dísert Cóemgin, Glendalough, Wk., XII
Ríge, King's R., Wk., XI, XII
Ríge (Laigen), Ryewater R., Mth-Kd., XI, XII
Rinn Dubáin Ailithir, Hook Head, Wx., XVI
Robhar, The Rower, Kk., XVI
Róeriu, Mullagh Reelion, Kd., XII
Róeriu, Rerymore *alias* Reary, Lx., XIV
Ros Corr, Roscore Wood, Oy., XIV
Ros Cré, Roscrea, Ty., III, X, XIV
Ros Eo, Rush, Du., XII
Ros Finnghlaise, Rosenallis, Lx., XIV
Ros Glas (Glaisi), Monasterevin, Kd., XII
Ros Glas, Old Ross, Wx., X, XVI
Ros mic Edlicon, see *Sliab Bladma*
Ros Mór (Moenóc), Rosminogue, Wx., XVI
Ros Ua mBerchon, Rosbercon, Kk-Wx., XVI
Ruba Conaill, Rathconnell, Wm., XIV
Ruirthech, R. Liffey, (later *Life*), Kd-Du., XI, XII

S
Saiger (Chiaráin), Seirkieran, Oy., III, XIV
Saithne, Du-Mth., IV, VIII, XI; (see also *Ua Caitheasaigh*)
Samud Cóemgin, Castlekevin, Wk., XII
Scadarc, ?Scark, Wx., XVI
Scelleg, Templenaskellig, under St. Kevin's Bed, Glendalough, Wk., XII
Sciath Nechtain, Skea-nagun, Kd., XII, XVI
Sci Patric, (location uncertain), Cw., XII, XVI
Scrín Coluim Cille, *alias* Achall, Skryne, (Skreen), Mth., III, X, XII
Séle, Blackwater R., Mth., II
Senboth Sine, Templeshanbo, Wx., XVI
Senchell, Shankill, Du., XII
Senchell, Shankill, Kk., XVI
Sen Trabh, Santry, Du., XII
Sescenn (?Uairbeoil), Wk., XII
Sescenn (? Uarbeoil), Mount Seskin, Du., XII
Síd Nechtain, Carbury Hill, Kd., X, XII
Síl nÁedo Sláine, of Southern Uí Néill, Mth., IV, VIII, XI; (see also *Ua Ceallaigh, Ua Conghalaigh, (?) Ua Dubháin, Mac Giolla (t)Seachlainn*)
Síl mBrain *alias* Ua Brain, of Dubtar, O'Brin of the Duffry, Wx., VIII, IX, X, XV; (see also *Shelburne Barony*)
Síl Cormaic of Ráth Bilech (*q.v.*), of Uí Cheinnselaig, Cw., XI, XV

S Síl Cormaic of Uí Cheinnselaig, at Ferna Mór (*q.v.*), XV
Síl Ealaigh, see *Síl nElathaig*
Síl nElathaig, (Sil Ealaigh), of Síl Fáelchon, of Síl Mella of Uí Cheinnselaig, Shillelagh Barony, Wk.; (see also *Ua Gaoithín*), XI, XV
Síl Máeluidir, Wx., IV, VIII, XV; (see also *Ferann na Cenél, Shelmaliere Barony, East and West; Ua hArtghaile, Uí Cheinnselaig*)
Síl Mella of Uí Cheinnselaig (q.v.), Wk., (Síl nElathaig) (*q.v.*), XI; Wx., XV
Síl Rónáin of Fir Chúl, Tethba, Wm., XIII
Síl Rossa of Uí Bairrche Tíre, Wx., XV
Síl Senaig, of Uí Garrchon at Cell Rannairech (*q.v.*), Wk., XI
Sinann, Shannon R., XIV; see also *Shannon Drainage Basin*
Siúr, Suir R., Kk-Wt., XVI
Sláine, Slane, Mth., III, X; (see also *Slane Barony*)
Sláinge, Slaney R., Wk-Cw-Wx., XI-XII, XV-XVI
Sleibte, Sleaty, Lx., III, XII, XVI
Slemain (Slemu), Slanemore, Wm., XIV
Sliab Bladma *alias* Ros mic Edlicon, Slieve Bloom Mountains, Lx-Oy., XIV
Sliab Calraige, see *Brí Léith*
Sliab Condala, Wk., XII, XVI
Sliab Mairge *alias* Mairce Laigen, Slievemargy Hills, Lx-Cw-Kk., XIV, XVI
Slievegad, Church Mountain, Wk., XII
Slige Asail, Wm., XIV
Slige Cualann, Du-Kd., XII
Slige Dála, Lx., XIV; (see also *Belach Mór Maige Dála*)
Slige Mór *alias* Escir Riada, Wm., XII, XIV
Sord (Coluim Cille), Swords, Du., XII
Sruthair, Shrule, Lx., XII, XVI
Suidhe Finn, Seefin Mountain, Wk., XII
Suidhe Laigen, Mount Leinster, Cw-Wx., XVI

T Tailtiu (Óenach Tailten), Telltown, Mth., V
Tamlachta, Tallaght, Du., III, XII
Tech Cobthaig (meic Cholmáin), Rathcoffey, Kd., X, XII
Tech Conaill, Stagonil, Wk., XII
Tech Cronáin, ?Tigroney, Wk., XII, XVI
Tech Lomáin, Portloman, Wm., XIV
Tech Mo-Chúa, Timahoe, Kd., XII
Tech Mo-Chúa, Timahoe, Lx., III, X, XIV
Tech Moling, St Mullins, Cw., III, V, XVI
Tech Moling, Timolin, Kd., XII
Tech Mo-Sacro, Tomhaggard, Wx., XVI
Tech Mundu, Taghmon, Wx., III, V, XVI
Tech Munnu, Taghmon, Wm., XIV
Tech na Bretnach, Brannixtown, Kd., XII
Tech Sacra, Saggart, Du., III, X, XII
Tech Sáráin, Tisaran, Oy., XIV
Tech Sinche, Taghshinny, Lf., XIV
Tech Taille, Tihelly, Oy., III, XIV
Tech Tua, Taghadoe, Kd., III, X, XII
Telach Árd, Tullyard, Mth., XII. Fortress of Ua Coindealbháin kings of Lóegaire Breg
Telach na nEpscop, Tully, Du., XII

Tellach Modharáin, nr. Corkaree, Wm. Precise location unknown; (see also *Ua Donnchadha*)
Temair, (Temair na Ríg), Tara, Mth., III, V, XII
Tempall meic in tSaeir, Templemacateer, Wm., XIV
Termonn Cóemgin, Trooperstown, Wk., XII
Tethba, Lf-Wm., IV, VIII, XIII
Tír dá Glas, Terryglass, Ty., V, VIII, XIV
Tír Esa na hImirge, Wx., in Shelburne and Bargy Baronies, XV
Tóchar etar dá Mag, Oy., XII, XIV; (see also *Druim dá Maige* and *Tuath dá Maige*)
Torchair, Tara Hill, Wx., XII, XVI
Treoit, Trevet, Mth., III, XII
Túaim nEirc, see *Liath Mancháin*
Túaim Tenba, see *Dinn Ríg*
Tuath Buada, Twyford (Twy, Tuaith), Wm., XIV
Tuath dá Maige, *Tethmoy,* Oy., X, XI
Tuath nElla, Rc., XIV
Tuath Fíodhbhaidhe, (Fidbuide), in Loígis (*q.v.*). Probably in Stradbally Barony (*q.v.*). Precise location unknown; (see also *Mac Fíodhbhaidhe*)
Tuath Géisille, Geashill Barony, Oy., VII; (see also *Géisill*)
Tuath Léghe, see *Lége*
Tuilean, Dulane, Mth., III
Tulach Fergusa, Tulfarris, Wk., XII
Tulach mic Comgaill *alias* Núachongbáil, Oughaval, (Nowal), Lx., XIV
Tulach Mic Fheilmeda, Tullow, Cw., I, III, V, XII, XVI
Tulcha, Tolka R., Du-Mth., XI, XII

U Ua Brain, see *Síl mBrain*
Ua Braoin of Bregmuine (*q.v.*), O'Breen (O'Brien) of Brawny, Wm., IX, X
Ua Braoin of Luigni (*q.v.*), O'Breen (O'Brien) of Lune, Mth., IX
Ua Braonáin of Craeb (?Teine) (*q.v.*), of *Cenél nÉnna* (*q.v.*), O'Brennan (Brinan) of Creeve, Wm., IX
Ua Braonáin of Uí Duach in Osraige, O'Brennan (Brinan) of Ossory Kk., IX, X
Ua Brógarbháin of Uí Failge, Oy., IX
Ua Broin of Uí Fáeláin (*q.v.*), and earlier of Uí Dúnlainge, O'Byrne (*O'Birne*, Burns) of *Offelan* (*q.v.*), Kd., IX, X. Major line of Leinster Kings. Dispossessed by de Clare, FitzGerald, etc. Retreated to mountains of Fortuatha in Anglo-Norman era and resettled in Críoch Bhranach (q.v.) (Newcastle and Arklow Baronies), Wk. The junior branch of O'Byrne, Gabhal Raghnaill (q.v.), was centred in Ballinacor in Glenmalure (XII), in the sixteenth century.
Ua Bróithe (Bróigthe) of Mag Sédna, Kk., O'Brophy (*O'Broha*) later of Ballybrophy, Lx., IX, X
Ua Bruadair of Uí nEirc (*q.v.*), in Osraige, *O'Bruadar* Broder,, (Brooder, Brother, Broderick) of Iverk Barony (*q.v.*), Kk., IX
Ua Bruaideadha of Ráth Tamhnaige (*q.v.*), O'Brody (Briody, O'Broudin) of Rathdowney, Lx., IX
Ua Caibhdheanaigh (Coibhdheanaigh) of Mag Airb in Osraige, Coveney (Keveny, ? Keverney), in Crannagh Barony (*q.v.*), Kk., IX
Ua Cainebáin, see *Ua Coindealbháin*

U Ua Cairbre of Tuath Buada (*q.v.*), O'Carbery of Twyford, Wm., IX

Ua Caitheasaigh, (Ua Cathasaigh), of Saithne (*q.v.*), *O'Kadesi*, O'Cahessy; O'Casey Du-Mth., IX, X

Ua Caoindealbháin, see *Ua Coindealbháin*

Ua Caollaidhe of Uí Bercháin (*q.v.*), in Osraige, O'Kealy (*O'Coely*, Quealy), of Ida Barony, Kk., IX

Ua Caollaidhe of Uí Buide (*q.v.*), O'Kealy (*O'Coely, Quealy*) Lx., IX

Ua Catharnaigh, O'Caharney, Carney, Fox, Wm-Oy., IX, X; *alias* Sinnach of Muinter Tadgáin (Kilcoursey)

Ua Ceallaigh of Gailinne (*q.v.*), O'Kelly of Gallen, Lx., IX, X

Ua Ceallaigh of Mag Drúchtain (q.v.), O'Kelly , Lx., IX

Ua Ceallaigh of Síl nÁedo Sláine (q.v.), O'Kelly of Southern Brega, Du-Mth., IX

Ua Ceallaigh of Tuath Léghe (q.v.), O'Kelly, Lx., IX

Ua Ceallaigh of Uí Théig (q.v.), O'Kelly, Kd-Wk., IX

Ua Cearbhaill, O'Carroll, Carvill, Lth., IX, X

Ua Cearbhaill (Éile), *alias* Muinter Cearbhaill, O'Carroll, (Ely O'Carol), Oy-Ty., IX, X

Ua Cearbhaill of Osraige, O'Carroll, (*O'Carrowill*), of Ossory, Kk., IX

Ua Cearnacháin of Luigni (q.v.), O'Kernaghan, (Kernon, ?Kiernan), of Lune, Mth., IX

Ua Chiardha of Uí Cairpri Laigen (q.v.), of Southern Uí Néill, Keary (*Carey, O'Kirry, O'Kerry*), of Carbury, Kd., (later in Mth., Wm., etc), IX

Ua Coibhdheanaigh, see *Ua Caibhdheanaigh*

Ua Coindealbháin (Caoindealbháin, Cainebáin), of Lóegaire Breg (q.v.), and Southern Uí Néill, O'Kenellan (*O'Quinelane, O'Guindelane*, Conlon, Connellan, Kinlan) Mth., IX

Ua Coinfhiacla of Tethba, IX. Precise location unknown

Ua Comhraidhe of Uí Macc Uais Mide (q.v.), O'Cowry (O'Curry, Corry) of Moygoish, Wm., IX

Ua Conchobhair Failghe, O'Conor Faly, Oy., IX, X. Major line of Uí Failge kings surviving into the sixteenth century; (see also *Uí Failge*)

Ua Conghalaigh of Síl nÁedo Sláine (q.v.), O'Connolly Mth., of Northern Brega. Retreated to Monaghan in post-Norman era, IX

Ua Cosgraigh, (Ua Coscraigh), of Uí Briúin Chualann, *O'Coskry*, (Cosgry, Coskerry, Cosgrave)., IX

Ua Cuinneacháin of Uí Briúin Cualann (q.v.), O'Kinaghan (O'Kynaghan), Wk., IX-X. But see *Ua Finnacáin*

Ua Dálaigh of Corco Adaim (q.v.), (of Uí Maine and Southern Uí Néill), O'Daly, Wm., IX

Ua Díomasaigh of Clann Máelugra, in Uí Failge, O'Dempsey of Clanmaliere, Oy-Lx., IX, X, XIII

Ua Donnchadha of Mag Máil (q.v.), in Osraige, Dunphy (*O'Donochowe, O'Dunaghy,* O'Donoghue, Donohoe, Donagh) of Ossory, Kk., IX

Ua Donnchadha of Tellach Modharáin (q.v.), O'Donoghue (Donaghy, Dumphy), Wm., IX

Ua Dubháin of Cnodba (q.v.), O'Doane (*O'Dovayne*, Devine, Downes) of Knowth (q.v.), Mth., IX

Ua Dubhlaoich of Fir Tulach (q.v.), O'Dooley of Fartullagh, Wm., IX, X

Ua Dubhsláine (Dubhsláinge), O'Delany (*O'Dowlaney*) of Coill Uachtarach (q.v.), Lx., IX, X

Ua Duibh, O'Duff (Duff, Black), Lx., of Cenél Crimthainn (*q.v.*), IX, X

Ua Duibhginn of Ferann Deisceartach (q.v.), Diggin, (Deegan, Duigan, Duggan, *O'Duygin*) of ? Bargy, Wx., IX

Ua Duinn of Brega (q.v.), O'Dunne, Mth., IX

Ua Duinn of Uí Riacáin in Uí Failge (q.v.), O'Dunne of Iregan, Lx., IX, X, XIII

Ua Dúnlaing of Lagán (q.v.), *O'Dowling* (Dowling, Doolin, Doolan) of Leix, IX

Ua Fáeláin of Déisi (q.v.), Ty-Wt., O'Phelan, (Whelan), of Deicies, IX, X

Ua Fáeláin of Mag Lacha (q.v.), O'Phelan, (Whelan), Lx., IX, X

Ua Fallamhain of Crích na Cetach (q.v.), O'Fallon, (Faloon), Mth-Oy., IX

Ua Fearghail, O'Farrell, Lf., IX, X

Ua Ferghaile of Uí Garrchon and Dál Messin Corb (q.v.), O'Farrelly (O'Farrell) of east Wicklow, IX

Ua Fiachrach of Uí Enechglaiss (q.v.), O'Fieghraie (Feighery, Feerery, Feary, Hunt), Wk-Wx., IX

Ua Finnacáin of Uí Briúin Cualann, Wk., O'Kinaghan, *O'Cnigon, ?O'Finoghane* (Fanaghan, Fenihan), XI; (but see also *Ua Cuinneacháin*)

Ua Finntighearn of Síl Mella (q.v.), of Uí Cheinnselaig, Finneran (*O'Finaran*), Wx., IX

Ua Fionnalláin of Delbna Mór (q.v.), *O'Fynnolane,* (Fenlon), of Delvin, Wm., IX

Ua Flannagáin of An Comar, O'Flanagan, (?) Mth., or Tethba, Lf-Wm., IX

Ua Gairbíth (Gairbheith) of Uí Felmeda Tuaid (q.v.), of Uí Cheinnselaig, *O'Garvey,* (Garvey), of Rathvilly Barony, Cw., IX

Ua Gaoithín of Síl Ealaigh, (Síl nElathaig), (q.v.), Gahan (*O'Gighine, O'Gehin,* Guiheen, Gihon, Wynne) of Shillelagh, Wk., and later of Wexford, IX

Ua Glóiairn of Calland in Osraige, *O'Gloherny* (Glory, O'Gloran, Cloran, ? Glorney) of Callan, Kk., IX

Ua Gobhann of Breffny O'Reilly, O'Gowan, McGowan, Smith, Smyth, Cv., IX, X

Ua hAimhirghin (Ó Beirgin, Ó Meirgin) of Tuath Géisille (q.v.), of Uí Failge, Oy., Bergen, (Berrigan, *O'Havergan, O'Hemergin*), IX

Ua hAinbhéith of Fir Bile (q.v.), O'Hanvey (Hanafy, Hanway) of Farbill, Wm., IX

Ua hAnradháin see *Ua hIonnradháin*

Ua hAodha of Eastern Tethba (q.v.), *O'Hay* (Hayes, Hughes), Lf-Wm., IX

Ua hAodha of Odba in Brega, *O'Hay* (Hayes, Hughes) Mth., IX

Ua hAodha of Uí Dega (q.v.), *O'Hay* (Hayes, Hughes) of Gorey Barony, Wx., IX

Ua hAonghusa of Clánn Colgan (q.v.), in Uí Failge, O'Hennessy (Hinchy, Ennis). Lower Phillipstown (about Croghan Hill), Oy., and (?) East Offaly, Kd., IX

Ua hAonghusa of Gailenga Becca (q.v.), O'Hennessy (Hinchy, Ennis), Du., IX

Ua hAonghusa of Uí Maic Uais Breg (q.v.), O'Hennessy (Hinchy, Ennis), Mth., IX

Ua hArtghaile of *Ferann na Cenél* (q.v.), Hartley of *Shel-*

U maliere Barony East (*q.v.*), Wx., IX; (see also *Síl Máeluidir, Uí Cheinnselaig*)

Ua hIonnradháin (Ua hIonráin, Ua hAnradháin) of Corco Roíde (*q.v.*), O'Heneran (Henrion, Hanrahan, Horgan, Horan, O'Hourigan), Wm., IX

Ua hIonráin, see *Ua hIonnradháin*

Ua hUrachán of Uí Fairchelláin (*q.v.*), in Osraige, Lx., IX

Ua Lachtnáin, O'Loughnane, (Loughrane, Lawton, Loftus), Wm., IX

Ua Leócháin of Gailenga Móra (*q.v.*), O'Loughan, Loghan, Mth., IX

Ua Lorcáin of Fotharta in Chairn (*q.v.*), Larkin (Lorkan, *O'Lurkaine*) of Forth, Wx., IX

Ua Maoil Challann of Delbna Bec (*q.v.*), *O'Mulchallan* (Mulholland, Holland), Mth-Wm., IX

Ua Maoil Chéin of Tuath dá Maige (*q.v.*), in Uí Failge, O'Mulkeen (Mulqueen, Mulquin), Oy., IX

Ua Maoil Lughdhach of Brug (?) na Bóinne, Mth., IX

Ua Maoil Mhuaidh, O'Molloy Oy., IX, X; (see also *Fir Cell*)

Ua Maoil Seachlainn, O'Melaghlin, Wm., IX, X; (see also *Clann Cholmáin*). Cf. *Mac Giolla Seachlainn*

Ua Mórdha of Lóigis of Mag Réta, O'More of Leix, IX, X

Ua Muirte of Cenél Aitheamhain (q.v.), Kd., IX

Ua Murchada of Uí Felmeda Thes (q.v.), O'Murroughe (Murphy, *O'Moroghoe*), Wx., IX, X, XV

Ua Murcháin of Fid nGaible (q.v.), in Uí Failge, Morrin (Moran, Morkan, Murchan, *O'Moraghan, O'Morghane*), Kd-Oy., IX

Ua Néill of Mag dá Chonn (q.v.), O'Neill of Moyacomb, Cw-Wk-Wx., IX, X

Ua Nualláin of Fotharta Fea (q.v.), O'Nolan of Fotheret Onolan (q.v.), Cw., IX, X. See also *Forth Barony*, Cw.

Ua Raghallaigh of Breifne O'Reilly, Cv., X

Ua Riáin of Uí Dróna (q.v.), O'Ryan, Cw., IX

Ua Rónáin of Cairpre Gabra (*q.v.*), O'Ronan (Ronayne), Lf., IX

Ua Ruairc of Breifne (q.v.), O'Rourke, Cv., IX, X

Ua Scolaidhe of Delbna Iarthair (*q.v.*), O'Scully, Wm., (?), IX

Ua Taidhg of Uí Máil (*q.v.*), *O'Teige* (Tighe, Teague, Tye) of Imaal, Kd-Wk., IX

Ua Tolairg of Cuircne (*q.v.*), Wm., IX

Ua Tuathail of Uí Muiredaig (*q.v.*), and earlier of Uí Dúnlainge, O'Toole (*O'Toughill,* Touhill, Toale) of *Omurethy* (*q.v.*), Kd-Wk., IX, X. In *Imaal* from late twelfth century, and also rulers of Fercullen (Powerscourt) and Upper Vartry from the mid-fourteenth until the seventeenth century. Wk., XI, XII

Uachtar Árd, Oughterard Hill, Kd., X, XII

Uachtar Fine, Kd., XI; (see also *Oughterany Barony*)

Uaithne, Lk., VIII

Uí Báetáin of Fothairt, at Maistiu (*q.v.*), XI

Uí Bairrche, Lx-Cw-Kk., II, IV-V, VIII, XI, XIII, XV, in Slievemargy and Carlow Baronies, at Cell Mo Lapóc (q.v.), and Gabrán (q.v.); see also *Mac Gormáin*

Uí Bairrche Tíre, Wx., II, IV-V, VIII, XVI; (see also *Bargy* and *Obarthy, Ferann Deisceartach, Síl Rossa, Ua Duibhginn, Uí Rónáin*)

Uí Bercháin of Osraige, Ibercon, formerly a barony occupying northern Ida (*q.v.*), Kk., (see also *Ua Caollaidhe*), XV

Uí Berraide of Uí Failge, Kd., XI

Uí Bráen Deilgni, of Uí Garrchon, Wk., XI

Uí Briúin Chualann, Du-Wk., VIII, XI; (see also *Obrun, Ua Cosgraigh*)

Uí Buide of Dál Cormaic (q.v.), Lx., VIII, XI, XIII, XV; (see also *Oboy, Ua Caollaidhe*)

Uí Cairpri Laigen, Kd., IV, VIII, XI; see also *Carbury Barony*

Uí Ceallaig Cualann, Kd-Wk., VIII, XI; (see also *Uí Máil*)

Uí Cellaig in Uí Failge, Lx-Oy., XIII

Uí Cheinnselaig, Cw-Wx., II, IV-V, VIII, XV; (see also *Cenél Cobthaig; Síl Cormaic, Síl Máeluidir, Síl Mella, Uí Dróna, Uí Dega, Uí Felmeda,* etc.)

Uí Chéithig, Kd., VIII, XI; (see also *Ikeathy Barony*)

Uí Colcan of Brega, Du., XI

Uí Crimthainn Áin, Lx., IV, VIII, XIII; (see also *Ua Duibh*)

Uí Cuain of Cell Deilge (q.v.), Mth., XI

Uí Cuilinn, Wx., XV

Uí Cúlduib of Fothairt Cille Dara, Kd., XI

Uí Cumain, Du., VIII, XI

Uí Dála of Corcu Adaim (q.v.), Wm., XIII

Uí Dega (Mór Laigen), Wx., IV, VIII, XV; (see also *Ua hAodha, Uí Cheinnselaig*)

Uí Dega Bic in Uí Failge (?), Oy., XIII

Uí Dega Tamhnaige in Osraige, Lx., XIII; of Ráth Tamhnaige (q.v.), in Osraige

Uí Diarmata of Fothairt, Kd., XI

Uí Domnaill of Bregmuine, Wm., XIII

Uí Dróna, (Idrone, *Odrone*), Cw-Kk., IV, VIII, X, XI, XV, Idrone Barony and Irarda (q.v.), Kk., also in Uí Dróna. (See also *Idrone Barony, Ua Riáin, Uí Cheinnselaig*)

Uí Duach, Kk-Lx., IV, VIII, XIII

Uí Dubáin, Wm., XIII

Uí Dúnchada, Du., IV, VIII, XI; (see also *Mac Gilla Mo-Cholmóg, Uí Dúnlainge*)

Uí Dúnlainge, Kd-Du., II, V; (see also *Uí Dúnchada, Uí Fáeláin* and *Uí Muiredaig*, VIII)

Uí Enechglaiss, Wk-Wx., IV, V, VIII, XI, XV; (see also *Ua Fiachrach, Uí Enechglaiss Maige, Uí Gobáin*)

Uí Enechglaiss Maige, Kd., XI

Uí Ercáin, of Fothairt, Kd., XI

Uí Fáeláin, Kd., IV, VIII, XI; (see also *Ua Broin, Uí Dúnlainge*)

Uí Failge, Oy-Kd., II, IV, V, VIII, XI, XIII; (see also *Ua Conchobhair, Ua Díomasaigh, Ua Duinn*). For earlier sub-divisions of the dynasty see *Clann Colgan, Clann Máel Chéin, Clann Máelugra, Clann Mugróin, U. Berraide, Uí Onchon, Uí Riacáin*. Later, Offaly (*Offalie*), O'Conor Faly, etc.

Uí Fairchelláin in Osraige, Offerlane, Lx., XIII; (see also *Ua hUrachán*)

Uí Felmeda Thes, *Offelimy,* Wx., IV, VIII, X, XV; (see also *Ua Murchada, Uí Cheinnselaig*)

Uí Felmeda Tuaid, Cw-Wk., IV, VIII, XI, XV; (see also *Ua Gairbith, Uí Cheinnselaig, Uí Onchon*)

Uí Fergusa, Du-Wk., VIII, XI; (see also *Tulach Fergusa*

U   and *Uí Dúnlainge*)

Uí Fionáin, Kd., XI

Uí Flainn in Fir Tulach (*q.v.*), Wm., XIII

Uí Gabla of Dál Cormaic, Kd-Oy., XI

Uí Garrchon, see *Dál Messin Corb;* see also *Uí Bráen Deilgni, Ua Ferghaile.*

Uí Gobáin (? of Uí Enechglaiss), Wk., XI

Uí Maic Uais (Breg), Mth., IV, VIII; (see also *Ua hAonghusa*)

Uí Maic Uais (Mide), Wm, VIII, XIII; (see also *Moygoish Barony, Ua Comhraidhe*)

Uí Máil, Kd-Wk., II, IV, V, VIII, XI; (see also *Imaal, Ua Taidhg, Uí Ceallaig Cualann, Uí Théig*)

Uí Mailifithrig of Cell Duma Glinn (*q.v.*), in Southern Brega., XI

Uí Maine of Connaught, Rc-G-Cl-Oy., XIII. Part of Uí Maine extended east of Shannon in Lusmag (*q.v.*), in Offaly.

Uí Muca of Cell Chúile (*q.v.*), Wm., XIII

Uí Muiredaig Kd., IV, VIII, XI; (see also *Ua Tuathail, Uí Dúnlainge, Omurethy*)

Uí Néill, see *Southern Uí Néill* (in *English-Irish Index*)

Uí nEirc of Osraige, Iverk Barony, Kk., VII; (see also *Ua Bruadair*)

Uí Onchon, Cw-Wk., XI, XV; sept of Uí Felmeda Tuaid (*q.v.*)

Uí Onchon of Uí Failge of Lége (*q.v.*), Lx., XIII

Uí Riacáin of Uí Failge, Iregan (Yregan), Lx., XIII; (see also *Ua Duinn*)

Uí Rónáin of Tech Mo-Sacro (*q.v.*), of Uí Bairrche Tíre, Wx., XV

Uí Shuanaig of Rathan (*q.v.*), Oy., XIII

Uí Théig, Kd-Wk., IV, VIII; (see also *Othee, Ua Ceallaigh, Ua Cuinneacháin, Ua Finnacáin, Uí Máil*)

Uí Tigernáin (Machaire Ua dTigernáin), Wm., XIII; (see also *Magheradernon Barony*)

Uí Tommaid of Tethba, Lf., XIII

Uisnech, Hill of Ushnagh, Wm., III, V, XIV

Urmuma (Air-Muma), Ormond, ('East Munster'), VIII, X; (see also *Mumu*)

General Index

See also Index to Historical Atlas (English-Irish and Irish-English)

A

Abban, St., of Camaross and Kill-abban, 59, 65
Abbeyleix, (Clon Kyne), Co. Leix, 72
Aberffraw, Anglesey, 27
Adomnán, St., of Iona, 63, 79, 94, 99, 118-21; see also *Life of Columba*
Áed, bishop of Sleaty, 19, 60, 123
Áed, ninth-century abbot of Clon-enagh and Terryglass, 91
Áed Allán, Uí Néill highking, 33, 89
Áed Dub, seventh-century bishop and abbot of Kildare, 28, 41 66, 103
Áed Find, seventh-century Uí Dún-lainge prince, 41, 103
Áed Findliath, Uí Néill highking, 11, 79
Áed mac Diarmata, Uí Dúnlainge king, 98
Áed mac Tomaltaigh, eighth-century Uí Failge prince, 76
Áed Oirdnide, Uí Néill highking, 92
Áed Rón, seventh-century king of Uí Failge, 68
Áed Sláine, Uí Néill highking, 36
Áed Ua Crimthainn, twelfth-century coarb of Terryglass, 102, 132
Áedán mac Gabráin, king of Scots, 79, 82
Áedán of Rahan, Céli Dé, 92
African kingship, 79, 129
Aghaboe, Co. Leix, 9, 32, 71, 94
Aghade, Co. Carlow, 20
Aghowle, Co. Wicklow, 26, 28, 131
agriculture, 30, 51, 108-9; see also *cattle, corn, fields, food, pastoralism, etc.*
Aidan, St., of Lindisfarne, 30
Ailech, Co. Donegal, 49
Ailerán and Wise, of Clonard, 94
Ailill Corrach, eighth-century king of Uí Failge, 78, 129
Ailill mac Áeda Róin, seventh-century king of Uí Failge, 68
Ailill mac Máta, legendary king of Cruachu, 18
Ailill Molt, Uí Néill king, 31
Áine, fourteenth-century queen of O'Kennedy of Ormond, 95
Airgialla, 7, 82

Airther Life, see *Liffey Plain*
alder, 25, 26
Aldfrith, king of Northumbria, 118-21
Aldhelm, abbot of Malmesbury, 119-20
ale, 41, 117
Alfred, king of Wessex, 104, 121
Allen, see *Bog of Allen*
Allen, Hill of, Co. Kildare, 26, 48-9, 117
Allen, Isle of, Cos. Kildare-Offaly, 48, 126
Almaith, Scottish princess, 82
altars, 132
Anatrim, Offerlane, Co. Leix, 91
anchorites, 29-30, 88
Andrews, Dr. J.H., 23, 86
angels, 73
Angevins, 4, 44, 109
Anglesey, Wales, 19, 27
Anglo-Normans, see *Normans*
Anglo-Saxon Chronicle, 104
Anglo-Saxons, 4, 8, 28, 32, 33, 45, 49, 76, 80, 94, 104, 119-22
annals, 95, 121; see also *Chronicum Scotorum, Four Masters, Three Fragments,* etc.
Annals of Clonmacnoise, 83, 96
Annals of Tigernach, 103
Annals of Ulster, 36, 45, 46, 83, 92, 111
apple trees, 26; see also *crab apple*
Ardamine, Co. Wexford, 34, 65
Ardristan, Co. Carlow, 34
Arklow (Inber Dee), Co. Wicklow, 3, 9, 16, 19, 24, 26, 44, 45, 46, 51, 52, 54, 65, 105, 107, 110, 111, 123, 127
Armagh, county, 4
Armagh, monastery, 46, 60, 71, 89, 95, 103, 115, 123; see also *Book of Armagh*
Armes Prydein, 8, 49
armour, 107; see also *weapons*
Art Mac Murrough Kavanagh, see *Mac Murrough Kavanagh*
Art Mes Delmann, legendary Leinster king, 18
arts, 33, 34-5; see also *crafts*
Ascaill Gall, 44
ash, 25, 26

Assemblies, (*Óenach, rígdal, synods,* etc.), 4; at Cloncurry, 10, 45, 89; Mag Lena, 89; Óenach Cholmáin, 34, 35; Rathcore, 45, 46; Rahugh, 89; Terry-glass, 33, 89; inter-tribal assemblies, 116; see also *Carman* and *Slige Dála*
Áth Cliath, see *Dublin city*
Áth Slabai, 66
Athgreany, Co. Wicklow, 3
athletics, 34-5
Athlone, Co. Westmeath, 29, 30
Athy, Co. Kildare, 66, 114
Atlantic ocean, 119
Augaire, see *Ugaire*
Augustinian order, 112
Avoca, river, 24, 51
Avonbeg, River, 24
Avonmore, river, 12, 24, 51, 52, 54

B

badgers, 38
Báetán, abbot of Clonmacnoise, 93
Bahana, Co. Wicklow, 26
Ballaghkeen, barony, Co. Wexford, 63
Ballaghmoon, Co. Kildare, (Belach Mugna), 11, 47, 83, 106
Ballaghmore, (Belach Mór), Co. Leix, 72, 96; see also *Slige Dála*
Ballinderry crannóg (no. 1), Co. Westmeath, 25, 29, 87
Ballinderry Lough, Cos. Offaly-Westmeath, 25
Ballintogher, Co. Offaly, 75
Ballinvarry Hills, Co. Kilkenny, 40
Ballybrittas, Co. Leix, 72, 76
Ballycowan, Co. Offaly, 114
Ballyedmonduff, Co. Dublin, 3
Ballykilleen Hill, Co. Offaly, 74
Ballynaboley, Co. Carlow, 36, 126
Ballynowlart, Co. Wicklow, 26
Ballynultagh, Co. Wicklow, 36
Ballyragget, Co. Kilkenny, 114
Ballyroan, Co. Leix, 72
Baltinglass, Co. Wicklow, 3
Bamborough, (Bamburgh), North-umberland, 30
Bangor, Caernarvonshire, Wales, 29
Bangor, Co. Down, 77, 94, 95

B

Bannbán, scholar of Kildare, 93-4
Bantry, barony, Co. Wexford, 63
Bargy, barony, Co. Wexford, 19, 60
barnacle geese, 36
baronies, 10, 70; boundaries and
    origins of, 85
Barrow, basin, 5, 11, 12, 39, 40,
    42, 105, 106, 112
Barrow, river, 7, 16, 21, 22, 25, 60,
    62-3, 67, 69, 71, 72, 74, 75,
    81, 108, 111, 114, 117
Barrow, valley, 3, 8, 9, 11, 16, 20,
    24, 26, 28, 30, 32, 40, 61,
    106, 108, 109, 113, 133
battles, monastic, 64; scale of, 5,
    82; see also *military service*
beards, 64, 76
beavers, 38
Bede, Anglo-Saxon scholar and
    writer, 99, 121
beehive cells, 53
bees, 76
Belach Mugna, see *Ballaghmoon*
Belderg Beg, Co. Mayo, 36
Bellingham, Sir Edward, 24, 39
bells, 97, 132
Benntraige, 34; see also *Bantry bar-
    ony*
Berminghams, the, see *de Berming-
    ham*
Bernicia, Anglo-Saxon kingdom, 30
Bile maicc Cruaich, 66; see *Narragh*
    and *Narraghmore*
birch, 25, 26
birds, game, 36; in metalwork, 64;
    of prey, 25; poultry, 76; wood-
    land, 76
Birr, Co. Offaly, 29, 86, 87, 88, 89,
    90, 92, 94, 95, 96
Blackstairs, mountains, 16, 40, 63
Blackwater, river, Co. Meath, 3, 26
Blaeu, J., seventeenth-century car-
    tographer, 125
Blat, Uí Bairrche prince, 9
Blessington, Co. Wicklow, 17, 44,
    56
Boazio, Baptista, sixteenth-century
    cartographer, 45, 63
Bobbio, Italy, 94
Bodleian Library, Oxford, 96
bog 'island', see *islands*
Bog of Allen, 3, 5, 10, 12, 31, 38,
    48, 68, 84, 107, 113, 116
Bogland Zone, 61, 76, 84-100, 102-
    5, 108, 109, 111-7, 118, 120
bogs, 23, 26-7; see also *swamps*
Boher, Co. Offaly, 76
Bohernabreena, Co. Dublin, 9, 11
Boley, Co. Leix, 36
Boley, Co. Wexford, 36, 126
184 Boleycarrigeen, Co. Wicklow, 36

Book of Armagh, 62, 95, 96
Book of Ballymote, 13, 18, 54
Book of Dimma, 88, 90, 96
Book of Durrow, 90, 96, 99, 118,
    120-2, 131
Book of Hymns, 32
Book of Invasions, (*Lebor Gabála*),
    8
Book of Kells, 97, 98
Book of Kildare (genealogical com-
    pilation), 104; see *Rawlinson
    B 502*
Book of Kildare, (illuminated gos-
    pels, now lost), 97, 98
Book of Lecan, 59
Book of Leinster, 18, 31, 50, 54,
    59, 61, 62, 65, 79, 84, 102-3,
    111, 132
Book of Lindisfarne, 97
Book of Mac Regol, 90, 96
Book of Moling, 62, 90, 100; see also
    Yellow Book of Moling
Book of Noghaval, (*Lebor na Núa-
    chongbála*), alias *Book of
    Leinster* (q.v.)
Book of Rights (*Lebor na Cert*), 13,
    30, 44, 59
Book of the Dun Cow (*Lebor na
    hUidre*), 36, 102, 103, 104, 132
Book of the O'Byrnes, (*Leabhar
    Branach*), 49
book shrines (and covers), 95, 96,
    132; see also *satchels*
books, 97, 99, 121; Mass books,
    113; see also *hymnals, satchels*
    and *shrines*; *Calendar of Óengus,
    Leabhar Breac, Leighlin,
    Martyrologies, Rawlinson
    B. 502, Stowe Missal* etc.
booley, (buaile), see *transhumance*
Booleyvannanan, Co. Carlow, 36
Borris, Co. Carlow, 24
Borris-in-Ossory, Co. Leix, 72
Boughna Bog, Co. Westmeath, 32
Boyne, river, 3, 10, 19, 26, 46, 81
bracken, 25
Bran Ardcenn, king of Leinster, 54,
    82, 124
Bran Mac Conaill, Uí Dúnlainge
    king of Leinster, 82
Brandon Hill, Co. Kilkenny, 40, 62
Brandub, abbot of Kildare, 103
Brandub mac Echach, king of
    Leinster, 34, 79, 81, 82,
    106
Brannixtown, Co. Kildare, 9, 28
Bray, Co. Wicklow, 44, 51
Brega, kingdom of, 3, 7, 9, 10, 18,
    22, 26, 28, 29, 31, 32, 34,
    42-3, 45, 46, 51, 54, 69, 81
    82, 89, 90, 98, 118, 119, 120,

126; see also *Descert Breg,
    Lóegaire Breg* and *Meath*
Breifne (Breifney, Breffny), 115
Brendán, St., of Birr, 94
Brendán, St., of Clonfert, 32
Bressal Bélach, proto-historical
    Leinster king, 16, 66, 67,
    124
Bressal Enechglass, ancestor of Uí
    Enechglaiss, 129
Brí Dam, 75, 82
Brian Boru (Brian Bóruma), Irish
    highking, 78, 95, 129, 130
Brian Ua Conchobair, see *Ua
    Conchobuir*
bridges, 113
bridles, 97; see also *horse harness*
Brigantes, Romano-British tribe, 9,
    19, 77
Brigit, St., of Kildare, 4, 19, 21, 31-
    2, 41, 66, 68, 91, 94, 98, 103
Brión Lethderg, ancestor of Uí
    Briúin Chualann, 14
Britain, 4, 9, 18-9, 20, 29, 76, 77,
    130; see also *Anglo-Saxons,
    England, Scotland* and *Wales*
Bronze Age, 3, 26; 36; cemeteries,
    3, 34; stone circles, 3, 36
bronze work (Early Christian), 64,
    76, 132
brooches, penannular, 43, 88
Brosna, river, 88
Bruidge, king of Uí Failge, 68
Brusselstown Ring, (Dún Bolg), Co.
    Wicklow, 52
buaile, (booley), see *transhumance*
buildings, fairy palace, 56; legendary
    iron hall, 7; mythical hostels,
    11; historical buildings, 99, 108;
    at Durrow, 94, 118-9; at
    Killeigh, 99, 112-3; bridges
    and churches in Uí Failge, 113;
    houses and gates in Carlow
    town, 105; see also *beehive
    cells, crannogs, round towers*,
    etc.
Bullford, Co. Wicklow, 36
Bunclody, Co. Wexford, 63
burials, see *Bronze Age, Cemeteries*,
    etc.
burnings, 54, 97, 99, 105; see also
    fires
Burren, river, Co. Carlow, 35, 59
Byrne, Professor F.J., 77, 123, 128
Byzantium, 34

C

Cadoc, St., of Llancarvan, 9
Cadwallon, Welsh king, 120
Caernarvonshire, Wales, 19
Caimín, St., of Holy Island, Lough
    Derg, 91

C

Cainnech, St., of Aghaboe, 9, 94
Caintigern, (Kentigern), St., of Loch Lomond, 82
Cairnech Móel, scribe of Seirkieran, 97
Cairpre, see also *Coirpre*
Cairpre Lifechar, legendary king of Tara, 17
Cairpre mac Laidhgnéin, king of Uí Cheinnselaig, 127
Cairpre Mac Néill, (Cairpre son of Niall of the Nine Hostages), 46
Cairpre Nia Fer, legendary Leinster king of Tara, 18, 21
Cairpre the Generous, of Glendalough, 53
Calary, Co. Wicklow, 58
Calendar of Óengus, (*Félire Óengusso*), 38, 52, 73, 84, 91, 92, 94, 97, 119, 127
Camaross, Co. Wexford, 65
Camross, Co. Leix, 25
candles, 117
Canterbury, Kent, 95
capercailzie, (capercaillie or wood-grouse), 36
Carbury, barony, Co. Kildare, 21, 46, 48
Carbury Hill, Co. Kildare, 31, 46
Carlow, county, 3, 11, 16, 19, 20, 21, 22, 24, 26, 36, 39, 40, 42, 55, 59-63, 64, 65, 66-7, 77, 80, 82, 90, 100, 105, 106, 108, 123, 124, 125, 128
Carlow, town, 35, 71, 105-6, 132
Carman, games and assembly of, (Óenach Carman), 33, 34-5, 117
Carmelite, convent, 24
Carnsore Point, Co. Wexford, 60
Carolingians, 28, 80, 98, 103
Carrick, Co. Westmeath, see *Dún na Cairrge*
Carrownaglogh, Co. Mayo, 36
Cartae Baronum, 4
Carthage, (Carthach), St., of Rahan and Lismore, 24; *alias* Mochuda (q.v.)
Cashel, Co. Tipperary, 35, 44, 82, 83, 95; see also *Eóganacht Chaisil, Munster*, etc.
Castle Lea, see *Lea*
Castledermot, Co. Kildare, 47
Castleruddery, Co. Wicklow, 3
castles, 41, 105; see also *forts*
Cath Ruis na Ríg, 126
Cathair Mór, ancestor-god of the Leinstermen, 13, 16, 19, 51, 65-6, 69, 77, 106, 113, 124
Cathal, king of Connacht, 129

Cathal, sixth-century king of Uí Failge, 68
Cathal mac Finguine, king of Munster, 82, 89, 129
Cathal mac Gerthide, king of Uí Briúin Chualann, 82
Catholic Epistles, Commentary on, 93
Catrige, (Cuthraige), 18, 123
cattle (cows, oxen, etc.), 30, 34-5, 45, 62, 96, 108-9, 126, 131, 133; cattle raids, 103, 108; horns of wild ox, 41; see also *food, pastoralism, transhumance*, etc.
Caulfield, Dr. S., 30, 36, 126
cavalry, 113; see also *horses, military tactics*, etc.
Cavan, county, 64
Celestine I, pope, 47
Céli Dé, 33, 84, 92-3, 96, 101; *Rule* of, 92
celibacy, 83
Cell Bicsige, 65
Cell Chuile Dumai, Co. Leix, 54, 82
Cell Rois, 66
Cellach Bairne, Uí Cheinnselaig ruler, 62
Cellach Cualann, Uí Máil king of Leinster, 66, 81, 82
Cellach mac Cennfáelad, Uí Dúnlainge ruler, 66
cemeteries, monastic, 28, 50, 53, 119; pagan, 3, 34, 35
Cenél Conaill, 8, 82
Cenél Fhiachach, (*Kinoliegh*) 31, 69, 85, 89, 114, 115
Cenél nEógain, 8
Cenél nUcha, 46
Cenn Fuait, 55
Cennselach mac Brain, eighth-century king of Uí Cheinnselaig, 65
Central Plain of Ireland, 17, 19; see also *Midlands*
Central Region of Leinster, 39-40, 42, 50, 51, 59-67
Cerball mac Dúnlainge, king of Osraige, 79
Cerball mac Muirecáin, king of Leinster, 83
chalices, 31, 132
Chapelizod, Co. Dublin, 45
chariots, 17, 77
Charles the Bald, Frankish ruler, 80, 98
charters, 32
Chichester, Sir Arthur, 63
chrism jars, 132
Chronicum Scotorum, 36
Ciannachta, 10

Ciarán, St., of Clonmacnoise, 104
Ciarán, St., of Seirkieran, 25, 87, 97
Ciarraige, 92
Cináed mac Írgalaigh, Southern Uí Néill highking, 130
Cináed mac Mugróin, king of Uí Failge, 75
Cináed mac Tuathail, king of Uí Enechglaiss, 55
circulating kingship, see *kingship*
Clanmaliere, (Clann Máel Ugra), 70, 76, 113; see also *Ua Díomasaigh* (O'Dempsey)
Clann Cholmáin, 82, 89, 115
Clann Colcan, 103, 124
Clann Colgan, (Colcan), i Liphi, 74, 75, 103, 124
Clann Fiachu meic Ailella, of Uí Cheinnselaig, 65
Clann Guaire, of Uí Cheinnselaig, 65
Clann Máel Ugra, see *Clanmaliere*
Clann Mugróin, of Uí Failge, 124, 128
Clann Rotaidi, 103, 124
clans, 108; see also *tribes*
Clifford, Sir Conyers, 114
climate, 113
Clíu, Co. Carlow, 20, 32, 123
Clon Kyne, see *Abbeyleix*
Clonard, Co. Meath, 9, 30, 33, 54, 85, 87, 89, 90, 91, 94, 95, 99, 131
Cloncurry (Cluain Conaire Tomáin), Co. Kildare, 10, 42, 45, 46, 89
Clondalkin, Co. Dublin, 43
Clonegall, Co. Carlow, 63
Clonenagh, Co. Leix, 29, 30, 71, 72, 73, 84, 91, 92, 94, 95, 100, 102, 111, 115
Clonfad, barony of Farbill, Co. Westmeath, 29, 30, 32
Clonfad, barony of Fartullagh, Co. Westmeath, 29, 30, 32, 85, 86
Clonfert, Co. Galway, 32
Clonfertmulloe, (Kyle, Cluain Ferta Molua), Co. Leix, 9, 28, 29, 30, 32, 72, 73, 84, 86, 87, 88, 92, 93, 96, 97
Clonkeen, Co. Leix, 115
Clonmacnoise, Co. Offaly, 3, 29, 30, 32, 89, 90, 92, 93, 94, 95, 96, 97, 99, 103, 104, 118
Clonmore, Co. Carlow, 28
Clontarf, Co. Dublin, 56, 129
Clonygowan, Co. Offaly, 21
Cloonowen (Clonown), Co. Roscommon, 30-1, 126
clothing, 35, 64, 76, 108, 112, 113
Clwyd, river, Flintshire, Wales, 29
Clyde, river, Scotland, 48

C

Cobthach Coel, legendary king of Brega, 7
Cóemán, St., of Anatrim, 91, 131
Cóemán's Testimony on Sinchell's School, 93
Cogadh Gaedhel, 97, 129, 130
Cogitosus, of Kildare, 94, 97, 98
Coirpre, see also *Cairpre*
Coirpre, legendary ancestor of Dál Cairpre Arad, 17
Coirpre Mór, sixth-century Uí Dúnlainge king, 67, 81
Colby, Sir T., 1
Colcu, Uí Cheinnselaig king of Árd Ladrann, 65
Colmán, (Colum), mac Cormaic Camsróin, king of Uí Cheinnselaig, 65, 128
Colmán, moccu Loígse, Leinster bishop, 94
Colmán, St., of Lynally, 38, 87
Colmán, St., of Noghaval, 132
Colmán moccu Telduib, abbot of Clonard, 93
Colmán Mór, king of Mide, 82
Colmán Mór, Uí Dúnlainge king of Leinster, 79, 81
Colmán Rímid, Northern Uí Néill highking, 120
Colum, St., of Holy Island, Lough Derg, and of Terryglass, 19, 33, 38, 91, 102, 131
Columba, see *Columcille*
Columbanus, St., of Bobbio, 94, 98
Columcille, (Columba), St., of Iona, 19, 20, 38, 47, 62, 64, 82, 94, 97, 98, 118, 119
Comgall, St., of Bangor, 77, 94
commons land, 36
Conaing, seventh-century king of Uí Failge, 68
Conaire, legendary Leinster king of Tara, 11
Conall Gulban, Northern Uí Néill king, 82
Conall mac Con-congalt, (Cú-congalt), king of Dál Messin Corb, 55
Conall mac Fáeláin, Uí Dúnlainge ruler, 81
Conandil, Uí Dúnlainge princess, 81
Conchenn, Uí Máil princess, 81
concubines, 78, 129; see also *marriage* and *women*
Congalach Cnogba, (Congalach of Knowth), Uí Néill highking, 35
Conláed, (Conleth), St., bishop of Kildare, 19, 38, 94, 99, 103
Conn Cétchathach, (Conn of the Hundred Battles), legendary ancestor of connachta and

Uí Néill, 90
Connaught, 7, 8, 9, 18, 29, 32, 63, 82, 86, 105, 113, 114, 123, 129
Connell, barony, Co. Kildare, 42
Constantius, 118
Coolbanagher, Co. Leix, 29, 72, 73, 92
Coolestown, barony, Co. Offaly, 74, 75
Corbmac, (Cormac), legendary ancestor of Dál Chormaic, 17
Corcu Duibne, 92
Corcu Oiche, 92
Corinth, 35
Cormac Camsrón, Uí Cheinnselaig king, 65
Cormac mac Airt, legendary king of Tara, 9, 17, 123
Cormac mac Cuilennáin, bishop-king of Munster, 11, 47, 83
Cormac mac Diarmata, king of Uí Bairrche, 65, 77, 128
Cormac Ua Liatháin, Columban monk, 38, 119
corn, 30, 87, 108-9; see also *agriculture, fields, food, pastoralism,* etc.
Cornwall, 9, 48
counties, origin of, 22
crab apples, 26
crafts and craftsmen, 82-3, 94, 95, 97, 121, 132; see also *gold-, silver-, bronze-work; patronage,* etc.
cranes, 36
crannógs, 25, 29, 68; see also *Ballinderry* and *Lagore*
Creton, Jean, French chronicler, 106-11
Crimthann, son of Énna Cennselach, king of Uí Cheinnselaig, 31, 65, 128
Croghan Hill, (Brí Éle), Co. Offaly, 31, 32, 68, 74; see also *Tuath Cruacháin*
Cromwell, Oliver, 101
Cronán, St., of Roscrea, 38
cross slabs, 53, 104; see also *high crosses*
crosses, see *high crosses* and *cross slabs*
croziers, 97, 104, 132
Cruachu (Cruachain, Rathcroghan), Co. Roscommon, 18, 49
crucifixes, 132
Cruithin, 76, 77; see also *Picts*
Crundmáel mac Rónáin, Uí Cheinnselaig king of Leinster, 81
Cuach, Uí Bairrche princess, 59, 80
Cualu, 41, 52, 98, 117; see also *Óe Chualann, Slige Cualann, Uí*

Briúin Chualann, Uí Chellaig Chualann, and *Wicklow Mountains*
Cú Corb, legendary Leinster king, 17, 18, 124
Cúilíne, seventh-century king of Uí Failge, 68
Cuircne, see *Machaire Cuircne*
Cullenmore, Co. Wicklow, 26
Cumaine, Uí Dúnlainge princess, 67
Cumbria, 76
cumdach, see *book shrines* under *shrines*
Cumméne, abbot of Iona, 119
Cummian of Mag Lena, 93
Cummine, princess of Déisi, 79, 81
Curragh, Co. Kildare, 3, 21, 22, 34, 41, 42, 49, 52, 75, 98, 103, 124
Curtis, Professor, E., 70, 74, 75, 111
Curtlestown, Co. Wicklow, 44
Cuthraige, see *Catrige*

D

Da Derga, Irish Celtic god, 11, 123
Dael, river, Co. Wicklow, 127
Dagda, Celtic god, 56
Daig mac Cairill, craftsman of Seirkieran, 97
Daig, progenitor of Uí Dega, 124
Daig, St., of Inishkeen, Co. Louth, 132
Daingean, (Dangan), formerly Philipstown and Fort Governor, Co. Offaly, 39, 74, 114, 115
Daingin Gabra see *Gabair Laigin*
Daire Barrach, legendary ancestor of Uí Bairrche, 129
Dál Cairpre Arad, 8, 123
Dál Chormaic, 17-8, 19, 20, 34, 46, 66-7, 91, 93, 123
Dál gCais, 34, 95
Dál Messin Corb, 5, 17, 18, 19, 20, 22, 34, 38-9, 51-6, 66, 77, 91, 112, 123, 127
Dál Riata of Scotland, 79, 81, 82
Dar-carthaind, Uí Dúnlainge princess, 67
Dargle, river, Wicklow, 54
Dasinchell, see *Sinchell, St., of Killeigh*
David, St., of St. David's, Wales, 9, 64
de Bermingham, 74, 105, 111, 116
de Clahull, 59
de Lacy, Hugo, 48, 88, 104, 114
deer, 38, 117; fallow deer, 115; see also *food* etc.
Deichtre mac Findig, of Uí Ercáin, 66
Déisi, Munster tribe, 79, 81
Delbna Ethra, (Delvin Mac Coghlan),

D 22, 88, 89, 93

Delbna Mór (Delvin barony, Westmeath), 115

Delgany, Co. Wicklow, 43, 53, 54

Delvin, see *Delbna Mór*

Derbforgaill, Uí Máil princess, 81

Dermot MacMurrough, see *Mac Murrough*

Derry Hills, Co. Leix, 25

Derry, monastery, 118

Derry, river, Cos. Wicklow, Wexford, Carlow, 26

Derry Water, river, Co. Wicklow, 26

Derryclure, Co. Offaly, 25

Derrycoffey, Co. Offaly, 25

Derrycon, Co. Leix, 25

Derrygarran, Co. Offaly, 25

Derrygawny, Co. Offaly, 25

Derrygreenagh, Co. Offaly 25

Derrygrogan, Co. Offaly, 25

Derrylemoge, Co. Leix, 25

Derrylesk, Co. Offaly, 25

Derrylough, Co. Leix, 25

Derrynaflan, Co. Tipperary, 30

Derryounce, Co. Offaly, 25

Derryrobinson, Co. Offaly, 25

Derryvilla, Co. Offaly, 25

Descert Breg, 46; see also *Brega*

Desgabair, see *Gabair* and *Laigin Desgabair*

Devon, 48

Dialogues of Pope Gregory, 118

Diarmait, St., of Castledermot, 47

Diarmait mac Máel na mBó, king of Leinster, 54

Dillon, Theobald, 115

Dinn Ríg, (Túaim Tenba), hill-fort, Co. Carlow, 7, 8, 9, 18, 34, 35, 61, 67, 106, 117

Dinn Senchus, 58

diocese, 10, 41-2, 44-6

Dísert Bethech, Co. Leix, 92

Dísert Garad, in northern Ossory, 97

Diummasach, Uí Failge ruler, 75-6

Djouce mountain, Co. Wicklow, 58

Dodder, river, 9, 43, 54, 117

Dodimóc, abbot of Clonard and Kildare, 90

Dolphin's Barn, Dublin, 43

Domesday Survey, 4

Domnainn, 48; see *Dumnonii* and *Fir Domnann*

Domnall Dub Ua Ferghaile, king of Fortuatha (+ 1095), 54

Domnall mac Donnchada, king of Uí Fáeláin, 55

Domnall mac Ferghaile, king of Fortuatha, 56

Domnall Mide, Southern Uí Néill highking, 82, 89

Domnall Ua Ferghaile, king of Fortuatha (+ 1043), 54-5

Dondgal mac Laidcnén, Uí Cheinnselaig king, 61-2, 124

Donegal, county, 92

Donnchad, see also *Dúnchadh*

Donnchad mac Gilla Pátraic, king of Osraige, 44

Donnchad Mide, son of Domnall Mide, Southern Uí Néill highking, 89, 116, 131

Donnchadh, son of Brian Boru, king of Dál gCais, 95, 129

Donnchad, son of Domnall Clóen, king of Leinster, 43, 55

Donnchadh, son of Flann Sinna, Uí Néill highking, 95, 96

Dowris, Co. Offaly, 3

drainage, 26, 60

Dresan, in south Co. Kildare or north Carlow, 66

dress, see *clothing*

Dricriu, king of Uí Garrchon, 20

Drón, legendary progenitor of Uí Dróna, (q.v.), 61, 124

Druim dá Maige, Co. Offaly, 74-5; see also *Tochar etar dá Mag*, and *Tuath dá Maige*

Druim Derge, battle of, 8, 91

Drumcooly, (Drumcowley), Co. Offaly, 74

Drumcullen, Co. Offaly, 25, 29, 87

Drumlane, Co. Cavan, 64

Dubcalgach, Uí Cheinnselaig king, 65

Dub Daire, Osraige queen, 79

Dubhcobhlaigh, queen of Brian Boru, 129

Dublin Castle, 68, 113, 115

Dublin, city (Áth Cliath), 3, 10, 27, 42, 43, 44, 45, 54, 58, 72, 83, 99, 105, 106, 109, 110, 116, 117

Dublin, county, 5, 14, 18, 22, 25, 26, 43, 45, 56, 73, 82, 92, 106

Dublin, diocese, 41, 44, 45, 53

Dublin Mountains, 3, 11, 26, 28, 30, 43, 52

Dublitir, St., of Finglas, 92

Dubthach, abbot of Durrow, 99

Dubthach Ua Lugair, Leinster poet, 31

Duleek, Co. Meath, 19

Dumnonii, British tribe, 9, 18, 19, 48, 77, 82, 125; see *Fir Domnann*

Dún Ailinne, see *Knockaulin hill-fort*

Dún Bolg, see *Brusselstown Ring*

Dún na Cairrge, (Carraic, Carrick), Co. Westmeath, 34, 85

Dún na Scíath, Co. Westmeath, 34

Dún nGáileóin, 18

Dunamase, Rock of, Co. Leix, 28, 34, 72, 91, 92, 101-3, 111

Dúnchad, see also *Donnchad*

Dúnchad mac Murchada, king of Leinster, ancestor of Uí Dúnchada, 79, 82, 129

Dúnchadh Ó Taccáin, eleventh-century craftsman of Clonmacnoise, 95

Dúnlaing, (Dúnlang), ancestor of Uí Dúnlainge, 14, 16, 80

Dunseverick, Co. Antrim, 82

Dunshaughlin, Co. Meath, 32

Durrow, Co. Offaly, castle of, 104; Columban monastery, 29, 38, 81, 86, 87, 88, 89, 92, 93, 94, 95, 96, 99, 103, 114, 118-22; see also *Book of Durrow*

Dursey Island, Co. Cork, 11

Dymmok, John, 114, 133

Dysart, (Dysartenos), Co. Leix, 28, 72, 92

E

eagles, 36

Easter controversy, 87, 89, 93; see also *Roman church organization*

Eastern Liffey, see *Liffey Plain*

Ecgfrith, king of Northumbria, 119, 120-1

Echtigern mac Guaire, king of Uí Cheinnselaig, 127

ecology, 84-117, 120; see also *landscape*

economy, 30, 36, 108-9; see also *agriculture, cattle, corn, food, fullers, iron working, pastoralism, patronage, urban development,* etc.

Eden, river, Cumbria, 76

Edward I, king of England, 105

eels, 36

Egloga de Moralibus Job, 93

Elair, anchorite of Loch Cré, 92

Éle (Éle Thuaiscirt), 22, 29, 31, 53, 86, 113, 116; see also *Ely O'Carol*

Elisians, 35

Elizabeth I, queen of England, (Elizabethan Age), 36, 45, 49, 56, 63, 68, 108, 114, 115

Ely O'Carol, 69, 104, 112, 113, 116; see also *Éle Thuaiscirt*

Emain Macha (Navan Fort), Co. Armagh, 4, 49

enamelling, 90

enclosures, see *fields*

England, 4, 5, 9, 27, 28, 32, 33, 43, 49, 90, 95, 105, 119-22; see also *Anglo-Saxon*

E English Place-name Society, 2
Énna Cennselach, ancestor of Uí
    Cheinnselaig, 61, 65, 124, 130
Eochu of Dunseverick, Ulster king,
    82
Eógan Cáech, son of Nath Í, king of
    Uí Cheinnselaig, 65
Eóghanacht Chaisil, 8
Eóghanacht Locha Léin, 8
Érainn, 123
Ernéne of Clonmacnoise, 93
Érrenchu, Mide princess, 81
Erris, Co. Mayo, 18
Eskers, 3, 29, 86, 89, 90
Esposito, M., 93
Essex, Earl of, 111, 113-5
estates, boundaries of, 31, 33; see
    also *fields*
Etarscél Mór, legendary king, 18
Ethelbald, king of Wessex, 80
Ethelwulf, king of Wessex, 80
Ethne, Déisi princess, 81
Ethne, (Eithne), Leinster queen, 54
Ethne, (Eithne), Uí Dúnlainge
    princess, 67
Ethne, Mide princess, 82
Ethne, mother of Columcille, 19
Ethne, Uí Bairrche princess, 82
Ethne, Uí Cheinnselaig princess, 81
Eusebian Canons, 94
Evagrius, 118
Expugnatio Hibernica, 105

F Fáelán mac Cholmáin, Uí Dúnlainge
    king of Leinster, 66, 67, 82,
    127, 130
Fáelán mac Murchada, king of
    Leinster, ancestor of Uí
    Fáeláin, 79-80, 82, 129
Fahan, Co. Donegal, 92
Failbe, abbot of Iona, 118, 119
Failbe mac Domnaill, Uí Bairrche
    king, 81
Failend, Déisi princess, 81
Failend, Uí Dúnlainge princess, 82
fairs, see *assemblies*
falcons, 36
Falls, C., 114
Farbill, barony, Co. Westmeath, 85
Farnees, Co. Wicklow, 26
Fartoulogh, see *Fartullagh* and *Fir
    Tulach*
Fartullagh, barony, Co. Westmeath,
    85
Fasaghreban, see *Reban*
Feary, see *Ua Fiachrach*
Fedelm, Uí Théig princess, 79, 81,
    82, 127
Fedelmid, Connaught king, 82
Fedelmid, (Feidlimid), mac Crim-
    thainn, king of Munster, 10,

35, 89
Fedelmid, king of Cenél Conaill, 82
Feidelm, Connaught princess, 82
Feidlimid, see *Fedelmid*
Feighcullen, Co. Kildare, 26
Félire Óengusso, see *Calendar of
    Óengus*
Ferann Clainne Diarmata, 70
Ferann na Cenél, 65
Ferann Uí Muircáin, 71; see also *Uí
    Muircáin*
Feranoprior, Co. Leix, 74
Fergal mac Ailella, king of Cenél
    nUcha, 46
Fergall, see *Fir Cell*
Fergus, ancestor of Uí Fergusa, 16
Ferical, see *Fir Cell*
Ferns, Co. Wexford, 9, 28, 34, 60,
    62, 64, 65, 71, 87, 91, 95, 128
Ferns, diocese, 41, 44
ferries, 63
fertility, 5, 35
Fiach, (Fiacc), St., of Sleaty, 19,
    20, 60
Fiachra, king of Fortuatha, 55
Fiachu Baicced, proto-historical
    Leinster ancestor king, 16
fiana, (hunting bands), 48-9; see
    also *hunting*
Fid Dorcha, Co. Westmeath, 26
Fid Dorcha, Co. Wexford, 63
Fid Elo, Co. Offaly, 25, 125
Fid Gaible, 75
fields, 30, 87; enclosing of land, 36,
    72; Gaelic fields in Offaly,
    109; summer pastures, 34-5
Figile, river, Cos. Kildare-Offaly,
    18, 75; see also *Fid Gaible*
Fína, mother of King Aldfrith, 120
Finán, anchorite of Durrow, 119
Finán, St., of Kinnity, 91
Find, see also *Finn*
Find File, legendary Leinster king,
    18, 125
Fine Gall, (Fingal), Co. Dublin, 44
Fingal, see *Fine Gall*
Fingal Rónáin, 52, 81, 82
Finglas, Co. Dublin, 92
Finian, (Finnian), St., of Clonard,
    9, 33, 64, 87, 91, 94, 99, 118,
    131
Finn, twelfth-century bishop of
    Kildare, 102
Finn mac Cumail, legendary hero,
    48-9
Finneran, see *Ua Finntighearn*
Fínsnechta Fledach, Southern Uí
    Néill (Brega) highking, 81, 118
Fintán, see also *Munnu*
Fintán, St., of Clonenagh, 24, 84,
    91, 94, 102, 131

Fir Bile, 29, 32, 85; see also *Farbill*
Fir Cell, (*Fergall, Ferical*), 22, 25,
    29, 69, 81, 85-9, 91, 96, 104,
    111, 112, 114-5, 116; see
    also *Midland Corridor*
Fir Domnann, 8, 9, 18, 19, 20, 48,
    77, 113, 125; see also
    Dumnonii
Fir Tulach, (*Fartoulogh*), 26, 29,
    31, 32, 34, 69, 85, 94, 97,
    114, 116, 130; see also
    Fartullagh
fires, ritual, 41; see also *burnings*
firewood, 36
fish, 36, 76
Fith, early Leinster bishop, 123; see
    Iserninus
Fitz Dermots, the, 44
Fitz Geralds, the, see *Kildare, Earls
    of,*
Fitz Henry, Meiler, 111
Flaithbertach, king of Munster, 37
Flann-dá-Congal, king of Uí Failge,
    78, 81, 129
Flann Fína, see *Aldfrith*
Flann Léna, ruler in southern Mide,
    81, 100
Flann Sinna, Southern Uí Néill high-
    king, 11, 79, 83, 95, 96, 99
Flower, Robin, 97-8
food, 35, 110, 113; see also *agri-
    culture, bees, birds, cattle,
    corn, deer, fish, hunting, oats,
    pastoralism,* etc.
food rents, 32; see also *tribute*
Forannán, Uí Dúnlainge prince, 81
forests, 23-6, 36, 39, 40, 45, 49, 50,
    54, 58, 60, 63, 68, 69, 71,
    72, 76, 107-11, 114-6, 133
Formorians, legendary tribe, 48
Fort Governor, Co. Offaly, 115; see
    also *Daingean*
Fort Protector, Co. Leix, 115; see
    also *Maryborough* and *Port
    Laoise*
Forth, barony, Co. Carlow, 19, 60
Forth, barony, Co. Wexford, 19, 60
forts, royal, 34, 77; viking, 43; late
    medieval Gaelic, 108; English
    plantation forts, 24, 115; see
    also *crannógs, castles, hill-
    forts, ring-forts*
Fortuatha, (Wicklow), 40, 54-6, 110,
    127; see also *Dál Messin Corb*
    and *Uí Enechglaiss*
fosterage, 82, 83
Fotharta, (Fothairt), 5, 13, 19, 35,
    40, 54, 60, 76, 77
Fotharta Fea, 19, 40, 60, 63, 82,
    105
Fotharta in Chairn, 19, 60, 63, 65

F

Fotharta in Uí Failge, 19, 28, 66, 82, 103
Four Masters, Annals of, 1, 36, 44, 46, 111, 115
Fox, (O'Caharney), of Muinnter Tadhgain, bordering on Fir Cell, 104
France, 28, 105, 110
Franciscan, order, 112
Franks, 80
fruit, (fruit trees), 117, 119; see also *apple trees,* etc.
fullers, 71
funerals, 35
furs, 108; availability of, 38

G

Gabair Laigen, 41-2, 43, 59-60, 66, 67, 80; see also *Laigin Desgabair* and *Laigin Tuathgabair*
Gaelic League, 2
Gaelic revival, (late medieval), 105-13
Gaelic society, (late medieval), 106-17
Gailenga Becca, 18
Gailenga Móra, 18
Gáileóin, 8, 18, 20
Gallen, Co. Offaly, 9
game, see *birds, hunting,* etc.
games, see *assemblies, Carman, Isthmian Games*
Gauls, 7, 9, 13, 20
Geashill, barony, Co. Offaly, 74, 75
Geashill, (Géisill), 21, 34, 73, 74-5, 109; see also *Mag Géisilli*
geese, see *barnacle geese*
gems, 95; see also *jewellery*
genealogies, 13-20, 38, 51, 59-67, 76, 78-83, 94, 103
genealogists, 117
Gerald of Wales, see *Giraldus Cambrensis*
Germany, 28
Gildas, *Lorica* of, 93
Gilla Comgaill mac Donnchuan, Uí Muiredaig ruler, 103
Gilla Comhgaill Ua Tuathail, Uí Muiredaig abbot of Glendalough, 127
Gilla Pátraic Ua Ferghaile, king of Fortuatha, 54
Gilla Ruadáin Ó Macáin, fourteenth-century coarb or Lorrha, 95
Gilltown, Co. Kildare, 28
Giraldus Cambrensis, 1, 26, 36-8, 41, 69, 71, 97, 98, 105, 109
Glamorgan, Wales, 9
glass, see *window glazing,* 117
Glassgorman, river, Co. Wexford, 44
Glen of Imaal, Co. Wicklow, 17, 51-2, 109
Glencree, Co. Wicklow, 26
Glencullen, Co. Dublin, 26
Glendalough, Co. Wicklow, 3, 19, 25, 28, 29, 30, 32, 36, 38, 50-5, 58, 60, 71, 82, 91, 125, 127, 128, 130
Glendalough, diocese, 41-2, 44
Glenealy, Co. Wicklow, 24
Glenmalire, Co. Leix, 76
Glenmalure, Co. Wicklow, 51, 109
Glenn Serraig, 117
Gloucester, Earl of, 107
Gloucestershire, 9
Glyn, Co. Carlow, 25
Goidels, 8
Gokstad ship, 43
gold, 111; cloth of, 112; gold-work, 97, 99, 132; gilt bronze-work, 64
goldsmiths, 97
Goody, Professor J., 129
Gormlaith, eleventh-century Leinster princess, 83, 129, 130
Gormlaith, tenth-century Uí Néill princess, 83
gospels, 90, 95, 97, 98; see *Book of Kells,* etc.
Gowran, Pass of, Co. Kilkenny, 11, 40, 59, 61, 62, 63, 88, 106, 123, 124
granite, 40, 60, 62
gravel ridges, see *eskers*
graves, 73; see also *cemeteries*
Greece, 35
Greek, 97
Green, Mrs Alice Stopford, 130
Green, Professor, D., 52
Gregory the Great, pope, 93, 118; *Moralia* of, 93; *Dialogues of,* 118
Grey, Lord Leonard, (Lord Deputy), 109, 112-3
Gwynllŵg, Wales, 29

H

hairstyles, 64, 76; see also *clothing*
hares, 38
Harington, Sir John, 114, 133
harps, 64
Harrogate, W.R. Yorks., 29
Hartley, see *Ua hArtghaile*
Harvard Archaeological Expedition, 25
hawks, 36, 108
hazel, 25, 26
Hebrews, 1
Hebrides, 119
hedgerows, 36; see also *fields*
Henry II, king of England, 45, 65, 104, 105, 127
Henry IV, king of England, 111
Henry VIII, king of England, 116
Herity, Professor, M., 36, 126
hermitages, 30
hermits, see *anchorites*
hides, 108
high crosses, 27, 33, 43, 47, 60, 62, 95, 99, 100, 104, 132
highkings, see *Uí Néill* and *Tara*
highland zone of Leinster, 107, 108
hill-forts, 3, 18, 34, 36, 48, 61, 67, 81; see also *forts* and *ring-forts*
historians, 97, 112, 116; see also *genealogists*
Hogan, Edmund, 42, 43, 51, 61, 65, 74, 75
holly, 25, 26
Hollywood, Co. Wicklow, 36
Holy Island, Lindisfarne, 125
Holy Island, Lough Derg, (Inis Celtra), 72, 73, 91
holy wells, 112
horses, 35, 108, 113; horse harness, 107; horse racing, 35; see also *bridles* and *cavalry*
hospitality, 108, 111-2
hounds, 108
Hughes, see *Ua hAodha*
hunting, 36, 49; see also *fiana*
hymnals, 94

I

Íarthar Life, see *Liffey Plain*
Iceland, 1, 83, 121
Idrone, barony, Co. Carlow, 59, 61, 65; seventeenth-century map of, 23, 125; see also *Uí Dróna*
Ikeathy, barony, Co. Kildare, 42
Imaal, 52, 105; see also *Glen of Imaal* and *Uí Máil*
Imirche Ciaráin, (Ciarán's Penitential Journey), 97, 131-2 (chapter IX, *n.*71)
Inber Dee, 51; see *Arklow*
Inber Domnann, see *Malahide Bay*
incest, 79-80
inheritance, laws of, 78, 80
Inis Celtra, see *Holy Island, Lough Derg*
Inishkeen, Co. Louth, 132
Inishowen, Co. Donegal, 92
Iogenán, Pictish priest, 94
Iona, 20, 47, 63, 82, 89, 93, 95, 118, 119, 121
Iregan, (Yregan), 70, 75, 113; see also *Uí Riacáin*
Ireland's Eye, Is., Co. Dublin, 130
Írgalach, king of Northern Brega, 81, 130
Irish Augustine, 93

189

I

Irish Sea, 82
Irishry, (Great Irishry), 113
Iron Age, 3-4, 34-5, 48; see also *hill-forts*
iron working, 45
Irrus Domnann, see *Erris*
Iserninus, Leinster missionary, 9, 18, 20, 32, 123
islands, in bogs, 10, 30-1, 37, 48; see also *limestone drift*
Isthmian Games, 35

J

James I, king of England, 22
Jarrow, Co. Durham, 95
Jewellery, 83, 108, 132; see also *brooches, crafts, gems*, etc.
John IV, pope, 93
Jonas of Bobbio, 94
Jones, Professor Glanville, 27
Judith, Frankish princess, 80
jurists, 97, 112

K

Karlsruhe, Germany, 93
Kavanaghs, 24; see *Mac Murrough-Kavanagh*
Keating, Geoffrey, seventeenth-century Gaelic writer and historian, 45, 86
Kellistown, Co. Carlow, 63
Kells, Co. Meath, 10
Kenney, J.F., 93
Kentigern, see *Caintigern*
Kerry, county, 92
Kevin, (Cóemgen), St., of Glendalough, 19, 50-3, 55, 82, 91, 130; see also *Glendalough* and *St. Kevin's Road*
Kilanane, parish, Co. Carlow, 36
Kilbeg, parish, Co. Wicklow, 36
Kilbeggan, Co. Westmeath, 3
Kilberry, Co. Kildare, 25
Kilbride, parish, Co. Westmeath, 32
Kilbride, see *Pass of Kilbride*
Kilclare, Co. Offaly, 25
Kilclonfert, Co. Offaly, 30, 31, 74, 76
Kilcock, Co. Kildare, 45, 46
Kilcommon, parish, Co. Wicklow, 36
Kilcoole, Co. Wicklow, 36, 52, 53, 54
Kildare, county, 3, 4, 10, 11, 12, 16, 17, 18, 19, 20, 21, 22, 25, 26, 27, 29, 31, 34, 36, 39, 42, 43, 45, 47, 48, 51, 52, 54, 66, 67, 68, 69, 74, 75, 80, 81, 82, 83, 98, 105, 106, 111, 112, 128
Kildare, diocese, 41-2, 46, 69, 85
Kildare, earls of, (Fitz Geralds), 25, 111, 116
190 Kildare, monastery and nunnery,

17, 19, 28, 36, 38, 54, 60, 66, 68, 69, 71, 72, 74, 75, 82, 90, 91, 93-4, 95, 97-8, 99, 102-4, 112, 113, 124, 131
Kildare, town, 41, 71, 83, 127
Kileencormac, Co. Kildare, 20, 28, 47, 51
Kilgory, Co. Leix, 28
Kilkea, barony, Co. Kildare, 42
Kilkenny, city, 106, 114, 133
Kilkenny, county, 5, 21, 22, 40, 60, 61, 62, 114
Kill, Co. Kildare, 28, 67
Kill St. Anne, see *St. Anne's*
Killashee, (Killossy), Co. Kildare, 20
Killaughey, see *Killeigh*
Killeigh, (Killaughy, Killaghy), Co. Offaly, 19, 39, 71, 84, 86, 90, 93, 95, 99, 112-3; *Rule* of, 93
Killeshin, Co. Leix, 28, 59, 60, 61, 132
Killossy, see *Killashee*
Killyon, Co. Offaly, 88
Kilmacahill, Co. Kilkenny, 61
Kilmainham, Dublin 43
Kilranelagh, Co. Wicklow, 28, 34, 36, 52
Kilroe, J.R., 51
Kilteel, Co. Kildare, 28
King's Council, (Anglo-Norman), 105, 106, 110
King's County, see *Offaly*
kingship, pagan, 4; late medieval, 106, 111; number of kings, 8; title of king, 46; strength in modest scale of kingship, 116-7; symbolism of kingship, 77; inauguration, 34, 66; client kings, 116; overlordship, 32-3; royal descent, 78; rotational kingship, 79-80; circulating kingship, 79-80; royal assemblies, 34-5; royal demesne, 44-5; king-lists, 50-1, 59, 103; see also *queens, taboos,* etc.
Kinnegad, Co. Westmeath, 87
Kinnity, Co. Offaly, 28, 29, 87, 91, 95
Kinoliegh, see *Cenél Fhiachach*
Kinsale, Co. Cork, 115
kites, 36
knights, (Plantagenet), 107
Knockaulin, hill-fort, Co. Kildare, (Dún Ailinne), 4, 9, 18, 20, 27, 34, 42, 48, 49, 113, 129
Knocknaboley, Co. Wicklow, 36
Knowth, Co. Meath, 28, 34, 81
Kyle, see *Clonfertmulloe*

L

Labraid Loingsech, legendary Leinster king, 7, 8, 13, 67
Lagore, crannóg, Co. Meath, 28, 34, 81
Laidcend mac Baíth-Bannaig, St., and scholar, of Clonfertmulloe, 73, 93
Laidcenn mac Bairceda, Leinster poet and genealogist, 124
Laigin, Leinstermen, origin of, 18-9, 123
Laigin Desgabair, 19, 42, 59-60; see also *Gabair Laigen*
Laigin Tuathgabair, 59-60; see also *Gabair Laigen*
Laígsi, see *Loígis*
Laisrén, (Lasrian), see *Mo-Laise*
lake dwellings, see *crannógs*
lamps, 53
land ownership, 49; endowments, 97; see also *property*
landscape, Dark Age and medieval, 21-40, 68-9, 77, 84-5, 105, 109, 113, 114-6; destruction of, by Tudors, 116-7; modern, 68-9, 84-5; see also *bogs, ecology, fields, forests, soils,* etc.
Lann, Osraige princess, 79
Lann, see *Lynn*
Lann Élo, see *Lynally*
Laragh, barony of Shillelagh, Co. Wicklow, 20, 123
Laraghbryan, Co. Kildare, 45
Larcom, Lieutenant Thomas, 1
Lasair, Airgialla princess, 82
Lassi, Uí Máil princess, 81
La Tène iron age, 3
Latin, 97
Laurence O'Toole, see *O'Toole*
laws, 30, 34, 36, 78; ecclesiastical laws, 89, 92
Lea, (Castle Lea, Leys), Co. Leix, 75, 111, 112; see also *Mag Lége*
Leabhar Branach, see *Book of the O'Byrnes*
Leabhar Breac, (*Speckled Book*), 92, 100, 123
learning, (learned classes), 32, 33, 34-5, 118, 119, 121
leather, see *hides* and *satchels*
Lebor Gabála, see *Book of Invasions*
Lebor na Cert, see *Book of Rights*
Lebor na hUidre, see *Book of the Dun Cow*
leeks, 76
Leighlin, Co. Carlow, 24, 67, 108; *Long Book of,* 61; see also *Leighlinbridge* and *Old Leighlin*
Leighlin, diocese, 41-2, 60, 61, 69

L Leighlinbridge, Co. Carlow, 7, 24, 109; see also *Leighlin* and *Old Leighlin*

Leix, (Laois), county, (formerly Queen's Co.), 5, 9, 16, 17, 19, 21, 22, 25, 33, 36, 39, 54, 59, 60, 69-77, 84, 87, 91, 92, 93, 101-3, 104-5, 106, 111, 112, 113, 114, 117, 132, 133; sixteenth-century map of, 21, 23, 25, 69-76, 105, 115, 125, frontispiece

Lemanaghan, Co. Offaly, 76

Leningrad, U.S.S.R., 93

Leth Chuinn, 17, 88, 90, 92, 99, 115

Leth Mugha, 90, 99, 115

Leverocke, Co. Wexford, 63

Leys, see *Lea*

libraries, (scriptoria, etc.), 95, 97, 119

Lichfield, Staffordshire, 95

Life of Abban of Camaross, 59, 65

Life of Brigit by Cogitosus, 94

Life of Brigit, (Old Irish), 31, 94

Life of Carthage, (Mochuda), of Lismore and Rahan, 23, 73, 87, 97, 100

Life of Ciarán of Clonmacnoise, 104

Life of Ciarán of Seirkieran, 87

Life of Colmán mac Lúacháin of Lynn, (Lann), 31, 97

Life of Colmán of Lynally, (Lann Élo), 25, 73, 87, 125

Life of Columba by Adomnán, 63, 79, 87, 94, 118-21

Life of Columbanus by Jonas, 94

Life of Comgall of Bangor, 77, 94

Life of Daig of Inishkeen, 132

Life of Finian of Clonard, 131

Life of Fintán of Clonenagh, 23, 131

Life of Fintán, (Munnu), of Taghmon, 23-4, 59, 65, 128

Life of Kevin of Glendalough, 25, 29, 35, 38, 50-1, 54, 59, 82, 109, 127

Life of Máedóc of Ferns, 59, 62

Life of Moling, 11, 24, 59, 62-3

Life of Patrick, see *Tripartite Life, Tirechán's Collections*, etc.

Liffey, basin, 5, 11, 12, 41-2, 105, 111, 113

Liffey Plain, (Mag Life), 3, 14, 16, 17, 20, 21, 26, 29, 30, 35, 38, 39, 42, 66, 74, 75, 86, 94, 108, 115, 128; Eastern Liffey (Airther Life), 36, 42, 52, 60; Western Liffey (Íarthar Life), 42, 75

Liffey, river, 10, 19, 43, 44, 45, 98

Liffey Valley, 10

Limerick, city, 11, 37, 97

Limerick, county, 17, 73, 92

Limerick Hill, Co. Wexford, 61

limestone drift, 31, 39, 40, 104; 'islands' of, 62-3

Lindisfarne, or Holy Island, Northumberland, 30, 95, 125; see also *Book of Lindisfarne*

Lismore, Co. Waterford, 23

livestock, 35; see also *cattle, horses,* etc.

Llancarvan, Glamorganshire, 9

Llandaff, Glamorganshire, Wales, 29

Llanynys, Denbighshire, Wales, 29, 31

Lleyn Peninsula, Caernarvonshire, Wales, 9, 19, 123

Loch Cré, 37, 92; see also *Monaincha* and *Roscrea*

Loch Lomond, Scotland, 82·

Lóegaire, son of Niall of the Nine Hostages, Uí Néill king of Tara, 20, 31, 46

Lóegaire Breg, 34, 46; see also *Brega*

Lóegaire Lorc, legendary Leinster king, 7, 21

Loígis, (Laígis, Loíches, Loíchsi, Laígsi), 13, 19, 22, 25, 29, 34, 35, 42, 54, 60, 69-77, 82, 84, 86, 91, 92, 93, 94, 101-3, 105, 106, 111, 112, 113, 114

Londonderry, see *Derry*

Longarad Coisfind, sixth-century hermit, 97, 132

Long Hill, Sugarloaf, Co. Wicklow, 58

Long Island, Co. Roscommon, 30

Lorrha, Co. Tipperary, 8, 33, 72, 73, 90, 91, 92, 95, 96, 99

Lorum, (Cell Molapóc), Co. Carlow, 59, 61

Lough Derg, Shannon river, 91

Lough Ennell, Co. Westmeath, 34, 85

Lough Ree, 30

Louth, county, 43, 132

lucky things, of Leinster kings, 117; see also *taboos*

Lug, Celtic god, 35

Lugaid, St., see *Molua*

Lugnaquillia, mountain, Co. Wicklow, 58

Lugnasa, Celtic festival, 35

Lullymore, Co. Kildare, 31, 84

Lusma, Co. Offaly, 86, 88

Lydney Park, Gloucestershire, 9

Lynally, (Lann Élo), Co. Offaly, 25, 29, 38, 73, 86, 87, 114

Lynn, (Lann), Co. Westmeath, 26, 31, 85, 97

Lyon's Hill, Co. Kildare, 34, 38, 43-4, 49; see also *Newcastle Lyons*

Lythe, Robert, sixteenth-century cartographer, 23

MacAlaister, R.A.S., 53

Mac Assida, king of Uí Gobla, 46

Mac Caille, St., of Croghan Hill, 68

Mac Cairthainn of Uí Enechglaiss, 19

McCracken, Mrs E., 23, 45

Mac Dátho, legendary Leinster saga hero, 108

Mac Domnann, 18

Mac Firbisigh, Dubhaltach, (Duald Macfirbis, Dudley Ferbisie), seventeenth-century Gaelic historian, 112

Mac Gilla Pátraic, of Osraige, 44

Mac Giolla Mo-Cholmóg, of Uí Dúnchada, 44

Mac Gormáin, (Mac Gorman, O'Gorman), 59

Mac Mahons, the, 116

Mac Murrough, Dermot, (Diarmait mac Murchada), twelfth-century king of Leinster, 11, 63, 64, 65, 106

Mac Murrough-Kavanagh, Art, fourteenth-century king of Leinster, 24, 105-11

Mac Murroughs, the, 63-5, 101, 111, 112, 116, 133

MacNeill, Eoin, 2, 38, 86

Mac Raith, eleventh-century king of Cashel, 95

Mac Regol, (Mac Riaghoil), abbot of Birr, 96

Mac Táil, St., of Old Kilcullen, 20, 48

Mac Torcaill, of Dublin, 44

Machaire Cuircne, Co. Westmeath, 115

Máedóc, St., of Ferns, 9, 64, 87, 91; shrine of, 64, 95

Máel Bresal son of Flann Lena, of Fir Cell, 100

Máel Dítruib, St., of Terryglass, 33, 92, 93, 131

Máel Fothartaig mac Rónáin, Uí Máil prince, 82

Máelaugrai mac Conchobuir, Uí Failge ruler, 76

Máeldúin, seventh-century king of Uí Failge, 68

Máelmorda mac Murchada, Uí Fáeláin king of Leinster, 83

Máelmuire, twelfth-century scribe of Clonmacnoise, 103

Máelodrán ua Dímmae Chróin, champion of Dál Messin Corb,

M

M

53

Máelruain, St., of Tallaght, 92, 96

Máelsechnaill I, Uí Néill highking, 11, 79, 89

Máelsechnaill II, Uí Néill highking, 83, 130

Máelumai mac Colmáin, Uí Dúnlainge ruler, 66

Mag Adair, Co. Clare, 34

Mag Ailbe, Cos. Kildare-Carlow, 3, 26, 39, 47, 63, 80

Mag Asail, Co. Westmeath, 26

Mag Breg, 26; see also *Brega*

Mag Fea, Co. Carlow, 60, 63, 66, 77, 82, 106

Mag Géisilli, 75; see also *Geashill, Tuath Géisilli*

Mag Lacha, 72

Mag Laigen, Cos. Kildare-Dublin, 38

Mag Lége, Co. Leix, 71, 75; see also *Lea*

Mag Lena, Co. Offaly, 81, 86, 88, 89, 93, 116

Mag Rechet, (Mag Réta), 72, 73, 76, 86, 92; see also *Maryborough, Great Heath of*; and *Morett*

Mag Réta, see *Mag Rechet*

Mag Tulach, in Fir Tulach (*q.v.*)

Magen Garbáin, see *Gabair Laigin*

Mageoghagan, Conall, seventeenth-century Gaelic historian, 96, 99, 131

Mageoghagans of Cenél Fhiachach, 104

Maine Mál, legendary ancestor of Uí Mail, 17

Maistiu, see *Mullaghmast*

Malahide Bay, (Inber Domnann), 18

Malmesbury, Wilts., 120, 121

mammals, 36, 38

Manchán, abbot of Mondrehid, 93

Manchán, St., of Lemanaghan, 76

Manchán's Wish, 76

manors, (Anglo-Norman), 111-2

manuring of fields, 109

maps, see *Idrone, Leix, Offaly, Scara-Walsh, Boazio, Lythe,* etc.

Margaret, fifteenth-century queen of Offaly, 112-3

markets, 34-5, 71; see also *traders*

marriages, 78-83, 129-30; see also *queens* and *women*

Marshals, the, 111

martins, 38

Martyrology of Donegal, 96

Martyrology of Óengus, see *Calendar of Óengus*

Martyrology of O'Gorman, 52

Martyrology of Tallaght, 92

192 Maryborough, see *Port Laoise*

Maryborough, Great Heath of, Co. Leix, 72, 76, 101, 114; see also *Mag Rechet*

Maulin, mountain, Co. Wicklow, 58

Maynooth, (Mag Nuadat), Co. Kildare, 9, 18, 43, 45

Mayo, county, 18, 36

meadows, 32, 77; see also *fields*

Meath, Anglo-Norman lordship of, 48, 88, 104, 112, 114

Meath, county, 3, 4, 5, 9, 10, 18, 22, 26, 45, 46, 126; see also *Brega*

Meath, diocese, 69, 88

Mel, St., of Tethba, 31-2

Menai Strait, Wales, 29

Mercator, Gerardus, sixteenth-century cartographer, 125

Merovingians, 32

Mes Delmann, (Telmann), Domnann, 18, 48

Mes Domnann, 18

Mess Corb, legendary Leinster king, 17

metalwork, 97; see also *bronze, shrines, silverwork,* etc.

Meyer, Kuno, 17, 49, 125

Mide, 3, 7, 10, 19, 25, 29, 31, 34, 45, 46, 68, 69, 81, 82, 86, 87, 88, 91, 97, 115, 118, 126; see also *Westmeath*

Midland Corridor, pass leading from Leth Chuinn (northern half of Ireland) into Leth Mugha (southern half), 29, 73, 85-90, 91, 93, 96, 97, 104, 113, 114-5

Midlands, 8, 10, 36, 49, 70, 86, 118, 120; see also *Central Plain* and *Midland Corridor*

military service, 5, 46; see also *battles* and *military tactics.*

military tactics, 109, 113-7; see also *battles, military service*

milk pails, 87

millefiori enamel, 90

Mo-Chóeme, St., of Terryglass, 91, 131

Mo-Chuille, St., of Dresan, 66

Mo-Laise, (Laisrén, Lasrian), St., of Old Leighlin, 61

Mo-Sacru mac Senáin, St., of Clonenagh and Saggart, 91

Mochuda, (Carthach, Carthage), St., of Rahan and Lismore, 73, 87; see also *Carthage*

Móin Coisse Blae, Co. Offaly, 89

Móin Mór, 53

moles, 38

Moling, St., of St. Mullins, 38, 62

Molua, (Lugaid), St., of Clonfertmulloe, 9, 32, 38, 73, 87, 92

Monaincha, (Móin Inse Cré), Co. Tipperary, 31, 37, 88, 99, 125; see also *Loch Cré* and *Roscrea*

Monasterboice, Co. Louth, 43, 103

Monasterevin, Co. Kildare, 21, 71, 72, 92

monasteries, distribution of, 26; see also *buildings, cemeteries, hermitages, learning, patronage,* etc.

Monasteroris, Co. Offaly, 74, 75; see also *Tuath Muighe Mainister Fheorais*

Mondrehid, (Mundrehid), Co. Leix, 29, 93, 96

money, 108

Moone, barony, Co. Kildare, 42

Moone, Co. Kildare, 28, 47, 106

Morett, (Muret), Co. Leix, 76; see also *Mag Rechet*

Moryson, Fynes, Seventeenth-century traveller and writer, 109, 115, 133

Mount Leinster, Cos. Carlow-Wexford, 28, 63

Mount Seskin, Co. Dublin, 3

Mountgarret, Viscount, 114

Mountjoy, Lord (Charles Blount), 109

Mountrath, Co. Leix, 29, 72, 115

Moyacomb, parish, Cos. Carlow-Wicklow, 26

Moycashel, barony, Co. Westmeath, 85, 89

Mug Nuadat, legendary Munster and Leinster king, 90; see also *Mag Nuadat* and *Nuadu*

Mugain, Uí Bairrche princess, 81

Mugrón mac Flainn, king of Uí Failge, 75, 78, 124

Muinter Tadgáin, 22

Muirchertach of the Leather Cloaks, Northern Uí Néill king, 11, 79

Muirchertach ua Chatháláin, 53

Muiredach, abbot of Kildare, 28

Muiredach mac Brain, Uí Muiredaig ruler, 82

Muiredach of Monasterboice, 43

Muirend, Uí Máil princess, 81, 130

Muirenn, abbess of Kildare, 103

Mullaghmast, (Maistiu), Co. Kildare, 18, 34, 35, 42, 43, 49, 98, 106, 117

Mullaghreelion, Co. Kildare, 66, 82, 98

Mullingar, Co. Westmeath, 3

Mundrehid, see *Mondrehid*

Munnu, (Fintán), St., of Taghmon, 24-5, 63, 94

Munster, 7, 8, 10, 11, 17, 25, 29,

M 31, 33, 35, 37, 47, 53, 64, 66, 69, 72, 76, 78, 79, 81, 82, 83, 86, 87, 88, 89, 90, 91, 96, 97, 101, 104, 113, 116, 129

Murchad mac Brain Muit, Uí Dúnlainge king of Leinster, 81

Murchad mac Dúnlaing, Uí Muiredaig king of Leinster, 44

Murchad mac Dúnlaing, Uí Muiredaig ruler, 104

Murchad Mide, son of Diarmait, king of Mide, 81

Murchad ua Ferghaile, king of Fortuatha, 54

Muret, see *Morett*

Murphy, (*O'Murroughe*), see *Ua Murchadha*

music, 35; harp, 64; organ, 112

N Naas, Co. Kildare, 28, 34, 42, 43, 49, 51, 66, 67

Naas, barony, Co. Kildare, 42-3

Nadcáem, St., of Holy Island, Lough Derg, and of Terryglass, 91

Narragh, (Norragh), barony, Co. Kildare, 42, 106

Narraghmore, Co. Kildare, 66, 106; see also *Narragh*

Nath Í mac Crimthainn, king of Uí Cheinnselaig, 65

Navan Fort, see *Emain Macha*

Neolithic, cemetery, 34

Nethertoumuy, Co. Offaly, 70-1, 74

New Ross, Co. Wexford, 24

Newcastle, Co. Wicklow, 52, 56, 106, 110

Newcastle Lyons, Co. Dublin, 45; see also *Lyon's Hill*

Newrath, Co. Wicklow, 26

Nia Corb, legendary Leinster king, 17

Niall Caille, Northern Uí Néill highking, 10, 35, 89

Niall Glúndub, Northern Uí Néill highking, 79, 83

Niall of the Nine Hostages, (Niall Noígiallach), ancestor of the Uí Néill, 20, 31, 46, 79

Nicholls, Dr. K., 111

Njáls saga, 83

Nodens, Celtic god, 9, 18

Noghaval, (Oughaval), Co. Leix, 84, 102; see also *Book of Leinster*

Nore, basin, 69

Nore, river, 11, 88, 92, 114

Normans, in England, 4; Anglo-Normans in Ireland, 10, 11, 14, 16, 17, 27, 32, 36, 41, 43, 44-5, 48, 49, 51, 52, 56, 58, 59, 62, 64, 65, 69, 71, 74, 101, 104-13, 115, 116, 124, 127

Norragh, see *Narragh*

North Sea, 8

North-Eastern Region of Leinster, 40, 42, 50-8, 105-11

North-Western Region of Leinster, 40, 41, 42, 48, 50, 63, 68-77, 84-100, 105, 109, 111-6

Northern Region of Leinster, 39, 41-9, 50, 51, 53

Northumbria, 76, 96, 119-21

Nuadu Necht, legendary Leinster ancestor-king, 9, 18

nuns, 112

nutrition, 5

nuts, (mast, fruit), 36, 117

O O' Irish patronymic

O'Briens, the, see *Ua Briain*

O'Byrnes of Wicklow, see *Ua Broin*

O'Carroll, see *Ely O'Carol*

O'Clerys, (*The Four Masters*), 96

O'Cnigon, see *Ua Finnacáin*

O'Connor, Rory, (Ruaidhri Ua Conchobhair), Connacht highking, 63

O'Conor, Brian, (Brian Ua Conchobhuir, Brian O'Conor Faly), sixteenth-century king of Offaly, 70, 109, 113

O'Conor, Calvagh, (Calbach Ua Conchobuir), fifteenth-century king of Offaly, 112-3, 116

O'Conor Faly, see *Ua Conchobuir Failghe*

Ó Corráin, Professor D., 19

O'Curry, Eugene, 1, 31, 69

O'Donovan, John, 1, 2, 42, 69, 70

O'Dooley, see *Ua Dubhlaoich*

O'Dunne, see *Ua Duinn*

O'Farrell, see *Ua Ferghaile*

O'Farrelly, see *Ua Ferghaile*

O'Fieghraie, see *Ua Fiachrach*

O'Flaherty, Roderic, seventeenth-century Gaelic historian, 96

O'Garvey, see *Ua Gairbíth*

O'Gorman, see *Mac Gormáin*

O'Hanlon, Canon John, 68, 112

Ó hAodha, Dr. D., 95

O'Hay, (Hughes), see *Ua hAodha*

O'Kelly, see *Ua Ceallaigh*

O'Kennedy, Philip, fourteenth-century king of Ormond, 95

O'Kindghan, see *Ua Finnacáin*

O'Larkin, see *Ua Lorcáin*

Ó Lochlainn, C., 22, 52, 72

O'Molloy, see *Ua Maoil Mhuaidh*

O'More, Owen, (Owny O'More, Uaitne Ó Mórdha), sixteenth-century king of Loígis, 72, 114

O'More, Rory, (Ruaidhri Ó Mórdha), sixteenth-century king of Loígis, 102

O'Mores, the, see *Ua Mórdha*

O'Murroughe, (Murphy), see *Ua Murchadha*

O'Neill, Hugh, Northern Uí Néill king, Earl of Tyrone, 113-6

O'Nolan, see *Ua Nualláin*

O'Rahilly, T.F., 17, 18, 19, 49, 51, 52, 59, 60, 77, 123, 127

O'Ryan, see *Ua Riain*

O'Sullivan, Mr. W., 132

O'Teige, see *Ua Taidhg*

O'Toole, Laurence (Lorcáin Ua Tuathail), archbishop of Dublin, 98, 127

O'Tooles of Wicklow, see *Ua Tuathail*

oak, 25, 26, 39, 87, 95, 133

oats, 109, oat cakes, 109; see also *corn*

Oboy, 105; see also *Uí Buide*

Ocha, Co. Meath, 31

Odba, Co. Meath, 54

Óe Cualann, 56; see also *Sugar Loaf*

Óenach, see *assemblies*

Óenach Cholmáin, 34, 35; see also *assemblies, Carman*

Óengus, abbot of Kildare, 66

Óengus, St., and Céli Dé, of Clonenagh, 73, 84, 92, 98, 100, 131; see also *Calendar of Óengus*

Óengus mac Mugróin, eighth-century king of Uí Failge, 76

Offalie, 22; see also *Offaly*

Offaly, barony (East and West Offaly), Co. Kildare, 17, 69

Offaly, county, (formerly King's County), 5, 10, 11, 14, 19, 21, 22, 25, 29, 39, 58, 68-77, 81, 85, 87, 88, 93; 104, 108, 109, 111-5, 117, 133; forest of, 21, 25, 115; map of, sixteenth-century, 21, 23, 25, 69-76, 115, 125, frontispiece

ogham inscriptions, 19, 47

Oghil, Co. Wicklow, 26

Olaf Cuaran Sitricsson, tenth-century king of Dublin and York, 83, 130

Olaf Gothfrithsson, tenth-century king of Dublin and York, 27

Olaf the White, ninth-century king of Dublin 43

Old Kilcullen, Co. Kildare, 20, 27, 48

Old Leighlin, Co. Carlow, 28, 61, 124; see also *Leighlin* and

O *Leighlinbridge*
Old Ross, see *Ross*
Omorthy, (*Omurethy*), Co. Kildare, 42, 105; see also *Uí Muiredaig*
open countryside, 71, 72, 74-5, 76, 77
Ordnance Survey of Ireland, 1, 71
Orgain Denda Ríg, 9; see also *Dinn Ríg*
organs, 112
Orkneys, 56
Ormond, 69, 95
orphans, 113
Oskamp, Dr. H.P.A., 103, 132
Osraige, (*Ossory*), 7, 9, 11, 12, 16, 22, 30, 33, 40, 44, 59, 63, 66, 67, 69, 72, 76, 79, 86, 87, 88, 89, 93, 94, 96, 97, 99, 113, 114
Ossory, diocese, 69
Ossory, kingdom of, see *Osraige*
Ostmen, 44-5; see also *Vikings*
Oswiu, king of Northumbria, 120
Othee, 52; see also *Uí Théig*
Ottonian Germany, 28
Otway-Ruthven, Professor A.J., 111
Oughaval, see *Noghaval*
Oughterany, barony, Co. Kildare, 42
Oughterard, Co. Kildare, 28
outlaws, 25, 49
Owenduff, Co. Wexford, 36
Oxford, 96, 102, 103

P pagan rites, 35, 41, 110, 117
pails, 87
Palladius, Roman missionary, 9, 20, 47, 123
Paris, 110
partridges, 38
Pass of Kilbride, Co. Westmeath, 85
Pass of the Plumes, Co. Leix, 72, 114
pastoralism, 30, 34-5, 108-9
patens, 31, 132
Patrick, St., 9, 10, 19, 46, 123
patronage of arts and crafts, 32, 97, 111, 112-3
Pembrokeshire, Wales, 9
Petrie, George, 1, 2, 53
Philipstown, see *Daingean*
Philipstown, barony, (Lower and Upper), Co. Offaly, 70, 74, 76
philology, 2
Picts, 76, 77, 82; Pictish priest, 94; see also *Cruithin*
pigs, (domestic and wild), 38, 108
pilgrimage, 85, 112
Pilgrims' Road, Co. Offaly, 29
placenames, 2, 25-6, 30-2, 36, 39, 44, 52, 55, 74-5, 76, 114, 123

plague, 105, 131
Plantagenets, 106, 107, 109
plantation and transplantation, 23, 115, 116-7
poets, 97, 112, 116
Poitiers, France, 110
polygamy, 78, 129; see also *marriage* and *women*
poplar, 25
population, of Leinster tribes, 4-5, 56-7, 63, 83, 85; of Anglo-Norman colony at Carlow, 105-6; of medieval Gaelic society, 107-12, 115; movement of people, 116; see also *settlement*
pork, 108
Port Laoise (formerly Maryborough, and earlier *Fort Protector*), Co. Leix, 114, 115; see also *Maryborough, Great Heath of*
Portarlington, Co. Leix, 75
Portnahinch, barony, Co. Leix, 69
pottery, 30
poultry, 76
Powerscourt, Co. Wicklow, 44
Price, Liam, 44, 52, 65
property, 78, 80, 97, 129
Protecto(u)r, fort, see *Port Laoise*
pyxes, 132

Q quails, 36
Queen's County, see *Leix*
queens, ritual status of, 129-30; 'rotation' of, 79-80, 83; see also *marriages* and *women*
querns, 30

R Raghnall mac Torcaill, high-steward of Dublin, 44
Rahan, Co. Offaly, 73, 86, 87, 89, 92, 97, 100, 114
Rahugh, Co. Westmeath, 29, 86, 89, 90
rain, 113
ransom, 37
Ráth Branduib, (Rathbran), Co. Wicklow, 34
Ráth Falascich, 123
Ráth Inber, 127; see *Arklow*
Rath Turtle, Co. Wicklow, 44
Rathangan, Co. Kildare, 21, 34, 68, 69, 74, 75, 103, 112, 128
Rathaspik, Co. Leix, 28
Rathcoran hill-fort, Co. Wicklow, 3
Rathcore, Co. Meath, 45, 46
Rathcroghan, see *Cruachu*
Rathdown, Co. Wicklow, 44
Rathedan, Co. Carlow, 34
Rathgall, hill-fort, Co. Wicklow, 81
Rathleague, Co. Leix, 72

Rathmore, Co. Carlow, 128
Rathnagree hill-fort, Co. Wicklow, 4
Rathvilly, Co. Carlow, 34, 62, 63, 65, 128
ravens, 36
Rawlinson B 502 (MS), (*Book of Kildare*), 38, 102-4
Reban, (*Rheban*), barony, Co. Kildare, 42; *Fasaghreban*, Cos. Leix-Kildare, 114
Reefert Church, Glendalough, Co. Wicklow, 53
relics, 95, 97; see also *shrines*
Rheban, see *Reban*
Rheged, British kingdom, 76
Rhodán, St., of Lorrha, 33, 93
Riacán, Uí Failge ruler, 75
Rián, ancestor of Ua Riain (*q.v.*), 61, 124
Richard II, king of England, 106-11, 116, 133
Richards, Professor M., 29
ring-forts, 58; see also *hill-forts*
ritual, see *assemblies, fires, kingship, queens, relics,* etc.
roads, (trackways, passes, etc.), 29, 31-2, 71-4, 85, 86-8, 106, 109, 113, 114-5, 116; see also, *Midland Corridor, Slige Cualann, Slige Dála, Slige Mór*
Roman ecclesiastical organization, 61, 112; see also *Easter controversy*
Roman period, 4, 32
Romanesque, art and architecture, 37, 53, 60, 88
Rome, 20, 34, 89, 93
Rónán, magnate of Uí Maine, branch of Uí Dunlainge, 82
Rónán, seventh-century Uí Dúnlainge ruler, 66
Rónán mac Áeda, king of Uí Máil, 81
Ros mBroc, Co. Carlow, 61; see *St. Mullins*
Rosbercon, Co. Kilkenny, 24
Roscommon, county, 30
Roscore, wood, Co. Offaly, 25, 125
Roscrea, Co. tipperary, 29, 30, 37, 72, 73, 86, 87, 88, 90, 92, 96, 115, 125
Rosenallis, Co. Leix, 25, 28
Ross, Old Ross, forest of, Co. Wexford, 63; see *New Ross*
Ross Ruad, prehistoric Leinster king, 14
Rossnagad, Co. Leix, 25
rotational kingship, see *kingship*
Rouen, France, 93
round towers, 41, 43, 50, 62
Roundwood, Co. Wicklow, 58

194

R rowan trees, 26
Ruaidhrí mac Fáeláin, Uí Fáeláin king of Leinster, 124
Rus Failge, legendary ancestor of Uí Failge, 13, 129
Ryan, Rev. John, 2, 18, 54, 70
Rye Water, river, Co. Kildare, 10, 45-6, 126

S Saggart, Co. Dublin 28, 92
St. Anne's, (Kill St. Anne), Co. Dublin, 9, 11, 28
St. Asaph, Flintshire, Wales, 29
St. David's, Pembrokeshire, Wales, 9, 29, 95
St. Joseph, J.K.S., 28
St. Kevin's Bed, Glendalough, Co. Wicklow, 125
St. Kevin's Road, Co. Wicklow, 29, 52
St. Mullins, Co. Carlow, 11, 24, 25, 28, 29, 32, 61, 62-4, 71, 90, 100, 106, 128
Sally Gap, Co. Wicklow, 52, 53
salmon, 36, 76
Salt, barony, (North and South), Co. Kildare, 42, 45, 46
Samain, Celtic festival, 46
Sanctán, St., of St. Anne's, Bohernabreena, 9, 11
sandals, 87
Sandwich, Kent, 49
Sarán, St., of Tisaran, 93
Sarnat, princess of Fothairt, 82
satchels, 87, 95, 97, 132
Scarawalsh, barony, Co. Wexford, seventeenth-century map of, 23, 63, 125, Pl. C
Scattery Island, Co. Clare, 91
schools, 94, 118-21; see also *libraries*
Scotland, 43, 48, 76, 79, 81, 82, 95, 96, 119, 121
scribes, 97, 132
scriptoria, see *libraries* and *schools*
Scullogue Gap, Cos. Carlow-Wexford, 63
sculpture, 97, 99; see *high crosses*
Sedulius, Irish Carolingian scholar, 98, 103
Ségéne, abbot of Armagh, 123
Ségéne, abbot of Iona, 93, 119
Seirkieran, Co. Offaly, 25, 29, 87, 88, 89, 95, 97
Senach, St., of Loígis, 132
Senán, St., of Scattery Island, 91
Senchán, abbot of Killeigh and Birr, 90
Senghennydd, Wales, 29
Sétna Sithbacc, legendary Leinster king, 13, 14, 18, 21, 48
settlement, 2, 3, 4, 26, 27-38, 52-8,

63, 85; Irish tenants, 70; individual settlements, 78; southern aspect of, 76; see also *landscape, population,* etc.
Shanahoe, Co. Leix, 72
Shankill, Co. Kilkenny, 28
Shannon, basin, 72, 91, 97
Shannon, river, 8, 29, 30, 33, 86, 88, 91, 94, 99, 104
Shean, (Shian), Co. Leix, 72, 76
Shelmalier, barony, Co. Wexford, 65
shepherds, 38
shielings, see *transhumance*
Shilellagh, barony, Co. Wicklow, 20, 26, 63, 81
ships, 44
shrines, 97, 99, 132; of Conláed of Kildare, 99; of Finian of Clonard, 99; of Máedóc of Ferns, 64, 95; of Manchán of Lemanaghan, 76; book shrines, of *Book of Armagh,* 96; *Book of Durrow,* 96; Stowe Missal, 95
Sigurd the Stout, earl of Orkney, 56
Síl Alténi, 124
Síl Chormaic, 65, 124
Síl Máeluidir, 65
Síl Mella, 65
Silvermines, mountains, Co. Tipperary, 72
silverwork, 95, 96, 97, 99, 132
Sinchell, St., of Killeigh, (Sinchell the Younger, Sinchell the Older), 19, 93, 112
Sitric, grandson of Ivar, king of York and Dublin, 55, 83
Sitric Silkenbeard, king of Dublin, 43, 54, 83, 130
Skerries, Co. Dublin, 44
Slane, Co. Meath, 28
Slaney, basin, 40, 41-2, 65, 105, 111
Slaney, river, 59, 66, 128
Slaney, valley, 3, 4, 16, 19, 26, 63, 65, 66
slaves, 27
Sleaty, Co. Leix, 9, 59, 60, 123
Slieve Bloom, mountains, 11, 25, 28, 69, 72, 75, 84, 91, 94, 111, 113, 116
Slievemargy Hills, 11, 25, 28, 36, 40, 59, 60, 69, 105, 123
Slige Chualann, ('Cualu Road'), 52
Slige Dála ('Road of the Assemblies'), 29, 72-3, 76, 84, 114, 115
Slige Mór, ('Great Way'), 29, 85, 114
smiths, 97, 132
snipe, 36
Sodelb, Uí Dúnlainge princess, 67

soils, (land usage, etc.), 51, 52, 60, 62-3, 65, 69, 104, 111
Somerset, duke of, (Edward Seymour), Protector, in the reign of Edward VI of England, 115
Southern Region of Leinster, 40, 42, 50, 59-67
Speed, John, seventeenth-century cartographer, 23
Stenton, Sir Francis, 121
stoats, 38
stone circles, 3, 36
stone walls, enclosing fields, 36
Stowe Missal, 33, 90, 95, 96
Stradbally, Co. Leix, 102
streets, in towns, 71
Strongbow, (Richard fitz Gilbert, earl of Pembroke), 8, 16, 41, 44, 48, 54, 56, 59, 65, 71, 106, 111, 114, 116, 127
Stuart government, 117
Sugar Loaf, Co. Wicklow, 56, 58
Suibhne mac Máelumai, ninth-century scribe of Clonmacnoise, 104
Suibne, son of Colman Mór, king of Mide, 82
Sulpicius Severus, 118
swamps, 109, 110, 113; see also *bogs*
Swan, Mr. L., 28
swans, 36, 38

T taboos, of Leinster kings, 110, 117
Taff, river, Glamorgan, Wales, 29
Taghmon, Co. Wexford, 63, 64, 65, 82
Táin Bó Cuailgne, ('Cattle Raid of Cooley'), 103
Tallaght, Co. Dublin, 73, 92, 93, 96; *Customs of,* 33, 92-3
Tara, Co. Meath, 4, 9, 17, 18, 20, 34, 49, 62, 72
Tech Conán, Co. Westmeath, 97
Temple na Skellig, (Teampall na sceillige), Glendalough, Co. Wicklow, 125
Templerainy, Co. Wicklow, 127
Templeshanbo, Co. Wexford, 28
Terryglass, Co. Tipperary, 8, 19, 33, 38, 72, 89, 90, 91, 92, 93, 94, 95, 96, 102, 131
Testament of Cathair Mór, 13, 59, 66
Tethba, Cos. Longford-Westmeath, 91
Tethmoy, Co. Offaly, 105; see also *Tuath dá Maige*
Thomond, 34
Three Fragments of Annals, 71, 79, 118, 123

195

T Tighe, see *Ua Taidhg*
Tihilly, Co. Offaly, 29, 87
Timahoe, Co. Leix, 28, 72, 74
Timolin, Co. Kildare, 28
Tinnahinch, barony, Co. Leix, 69, 75
Tipperary, county, 17, 31, 33, 36, 95
Tipperkevin, Co. Kildare, 51
Tírechan's Collections, (Additions to Tírechan, etc.), 32, 123, 128
Tiree, Scotland, 119
Tisaran, Co. Offaly, 93
Tochar-etar-dá-mag, 74-5; see also *Tuath-dá-maige*
Togail Bruidna Da Derga, 123
Togher, The, Co. Leix, 72
toghers, 21, 72, 75; see also *roads*
Toi Cuile, 20, 32, 123
Topographia Hiberniae, 69, 98; see also *Giraldus Cambrensis*
towns, 71; see *urban centres*
traders, 35, 82, 109; see also *markets*
transhumance, 35-6
Trevet, Co. Meath, 28
tribes, (*tuatha*), and tribalism, extent of, 5, 10, 38, 70, 85; population of, 5, 85; ancestral populations, 117; influence of geography on, 6; Free Tribes of Leinster, 16, 17, 19, 69, 77, 81, 106, 113; tribal society, 31-2; tribal patronage of arts, 32; tribal trees, 66; expulsion from tribes, 49; tribal lore (*senchus*), 34; see also *assemblies, Carman, kingship, queens, taboos, genealogies*, etc.
tribute, (black rents, etc.), 30, 32, 62, 106, 109, 112
Trim, Co. Meath, 46, 133
Tripartite Life of Patrick, 20, 46, 62, 123, 128
Trooperstown, Co. Wicklow, 54
trout, 36
Túaim Tenba, see *Dinn Ríg*
Tualaith, (Tuathlaithe), Munster princess, 79-80, 82, 129-30
Tuath Cruacháin, 71, 74; see also *Croghan Hill*
Tuath dá Maige, 74-5, 105, 112, 116; see also *Druim dá Maige, Tethmoy*, and *Tochar-etar-dá-mag*
Tuath Fhidga, 77
Tuath Géisilli, 70-1, 74-5; see also *Mag Géisilli*, and *Geashill*
Tuath Muighe Cloinne Cholgain, 71, 74; see also *Clann Colcan*
Tuath Muighe Mainister Fheorais, 71, 74; see also *Monasteroris*

Tuath na Cille, 71, 74
Tuath Rátha Droma, 70-1, 74
tuatha, see *tribes*
Tuathal Techtmar, legendary king of Tara and Ushnagh, 46
Tudor wars and conquest of Ireland, 23, 109, 112-7
Tulach meic Comgaill, see *Noghaval*
Tullamore, Co. Offaly, 39
Tullow, Co. Carlow, 34, 63, 66, 67
Tullyard, Co. Meath, 34, 46
Tyne, river, Northumberland, 121
Tyrrells, the, 114, 116
Tyrrellspass, Co. Westmeath, 85, 86, 114

U Ua Briain, (O'Briens of Thomond), 34, 64, 101
Ua Broin, O'Byrne, formerly Uí Fáeláin, 22, 49, 105, 111, 112
Ua Ceallaigh, (O'Kelly), 56
Ua Conchobhuir, see *O'Conor Faly, Brian; Calvagh*, etc.
Ua Conchobhuir Failghe, (O'Conor Faly), kings of Offaly, 22, 49, 69, 70, 74, 104, 111, 112, 115, 116
Ua Cuinneacháin, see *Ua Finnacáin*
Ua Díomasaigh (Ua Diummasaigh), O'Dempsey of Clanmaliere, 49, 70, 75-6, 104, 111, 113
Ua Dubhlaoich, (O'Dooley), of Fir Tulach, 114, 130
Ua Duinn of Uí Riacáin, (O'Dunne of Yregan), 49, 75, 112, 113
Ua Ferghaile, (O'Farrell, O'Farrelly), 54-6
Ua Fiachrach, (*O'Fieghraie*, Feary), 54-6
Ua Finnacáin, Ua Cuinneacháin, (O'Kindghan, O'Cnigon), 56
Ua Finntighearn, (Finneran), 65
Ua Gairbíth, (O'Garvey), 63
Ua hAodha, (O'Hay, Hughes), 65
Ua hArtghaile, (Hartley), 65
Ua Lorcáin, (O'Larkin), 60
Ua Maoil Mhuaidh, (O'Molloy), of Fir Cell, 104
Ua Mórdha, kings of Loígis, (O'Mores of Leix), 25, 49, 70, 76, 84, 101-2, 104, 106, 111, 112, 115; see also *O'More, Owen*, etc.
Ua Murchadha, (O'Murroughe, Murphy), 63-5
Ua Nualláin, (O'Nolan), 60, 105
Ua Riain, (O'Ryan), 61, 124
Ua Taidhg, (O'Teige, Tighe), 56
Ua Tuathail, (O'Toole), formerly Uí Muiredaig, 22, 49, 54-6, 105, 111, 112, 127

Uachtar Fine, 42
Uasal, princess of Mide, 82
Ugaire, (Augaire), mac Dúnlainge, Uí Muiredaig king of Leinster, 54
Uí Báeth, 124
Uí Bairrche, 9, 16, 17, 19, 20, 34, 35, 40, 51, 59-61, 63, 65, 66, 69, 77, 80, 81, 82, 105, 106, 112, 123, 128, 129
Uí Bráen Deilgni, 53
Uí Briúin, of Connaught, 8
Uí Briúin Chualann, 14, 16, 34, 44, 52-3, 56, 82
Uí Buide, 17, 105, 106, 112; see also *Oboy*
Uí Cairpri Laigin, 31, 46-8
Uí Cellaig, of Uí Failge, 75
Uí Cellaig Chualann, 17, 51-2
Uí Cheinnselaig, 9, 14, 16, 17, 18, 19, 20, 28, 30, 34, 35, 40, 44, 46, 51, 59-67, 69, 79, 80, 81, 82, 88, 91, 106, 108, 123, 124, 127, 128
Uí Chéithig, 16, 42
Uí Colcan ó Tech Cainén, 103
Uí Crimthainn, of Airgialla, 82
Uí Crimthainn Áin, 5, 16, 34, 91, 101-2, 112
Uí Dega, 16, 25, 60-2, 65, 124
Uí Dróna, 16, 20, 32, 34, 60-2, 123, 124
Uí Duach, 22, 69
Uí Dúnchada, 14, 42, 43-5, 55-6, 79, 91
Uí Dúnlainge, 5, 14, 16, 17, 18, 19, 20, 28, 35, 39, 40, 41-9, 50, 52, 53, 54-6, 59, 62, 65-7, 69, 79, 80, 81, 82, 97, 98, 103, 112, 113, 124, 127
Uí Enechglaiss, 16, 17, 19, 22, 34, 35, 51-2, 54-6, 69, 76-7, 112, 127, 129
Uí Enechglaiss Maige, 19
Uí Ercáin, 66
Uí Fáeláin, 5, 22, 42, 43, 46, 49, 55, 56, 66, 79, 83, 90, 105, 124
Uí Failge, 5, 13, 16, 17, 19, 22, 25, 28, 29, 31, 34, 35, 38, 40, 41, 42, 46, 50, 51, 65, 66, 68-77, 78, 81, 82, 86, 90, 92, 93, 94, 97, 99, 103, 105, 111-5, 124, 128, 129; see also *Offaly, Ua Conchobhuir Failghe*, etc.
Uí Failge Iarmotha, 103, 124
Uí Felmeda Thes, 63
Uí Felmeda Tuaid, 63, 67
Uí Fergusa, 14, 16
Uí Fergusa, of Wexford, 65
Uí Fogartaig, 53

UWY

Uí Gabla, (Uí Gobla), 18, 46, 66
Uí Garrchon, 20, 46, 51, 65, 123;
    see also *Dál Messin Corb*
Uí Luascán, 16
Uí Máelceithirnaich, 124
Uí Máeltopair, 124
Uí Máil, 3, 4, 17, 28, 34, 42, 51-3,
    56, 66, 79, 80, 81, 82, 106,
    127; see also *Imaal*
Uí Maine, of Connaught, 8, 86
Uí Maine, of Uí Dúnlainge, 81, 82
Uí Maine, of Uí Failge, 124
Uí Meic Cruaich, 66
Uí Muiredaig, 22, 42, 43-4, 49, 56,
    67, 82, 98, 103, 105, 106,
    124, 127; see also *Omorthy*
Uí Muiricáin, 75; see also *Ferann Uí
    Muircáin*
Uí Náir, 91
Uí Néill, 8, 9, 10, 17, 19, 20, 27, 33,
    34, 45-6, 48, 54, 62, 92, 96,
    123, 131; Northern Uí Néill,
    8, 79, 83, 116, 120, 121;
    Southern Uí Néill, 7, 22, 29,
    31, 34, 46, 68, 69, 79, 81,
    82, 86, 88, 89, 90, 97, 98,
    118, 120, 121
Uí Onchon, of Uí Failge, 75
Uí Riacáin, of Uí Failge, 75, 103,
    124; see also *Ua Duinn*
Uí Suanaigh, (Ua Suanaigh), of
    Rahan, 92, 100, 125
Uí Théig, 10, 17, 51-3, 56, 79, 81,
    82
Uí Timmíne, 124
Ullard, Co. Kilkenny, 60
Ulster, (Ulaid), 6, 7, 10, 77, 82,
    105, 109, 113, 115, 126
uninhabited areas, 26, 52-8, 114;
    see also *population* and
    settlement

Uppertoumuy, Co. Offaly, 74
urban centres, 4, 30, 36, 64, 71, 77,
    99, 100, 106, 116
Ushnagh, Hill of, Co. Westmeath, 8,
    16, 19, 85, 86, 91, 130

Vartry, river, Co. Wicklow, 24, 52,
    54
Veele, Elizabeth, queen of Art Mac
    Murrough Kavanagh, 106
Verona, Italy, 93
vessels, see *pails, pottery, wood*
Vestfold, Norway, 43
Victoria County History, 2
Vienna, Austria, 93
Vikings, 8, 10, 27, 29, 30, 35, 37,
    38, 43, 44, 45, 51, 54-6, 60,
    64, 83, 89, 90-1, 92, 97, 98,
    99, 101, 104, 106
villages, Gaelic, 108
Virgil, 69

Wales, 9, 19, 27, 28-9, 31, 32, 49,
    64, 95, 105, 123; see also
    Welsh
Walsh, Rev. Paul, 42, 70, 85
Warrenstown, barony, Co. Offaly,
    74
waste land, 36, 49, 76
water supply, 28, 76
Waterford, county, 81, 109
Waterford, town, 106
weapons, 108; see also *armour*
Welsh, language, 9
Welsh, people, 8, 11, 20, 120
Wessex, 80, 104
Western Liffey, see *Liffey Plain*
Westmeath, county, 3, 5, 9, 11, 16,
    25, 26, 29, 32, 69, 70, 86, 87,
    89, 113, 115, 116, 126

Wexford, county, 3, 4, 5, 16, 19,
    21, 22, 24, 25, 26, 28, 30,
    36, 44, 45, 60, 61, 62, 63-5,
    82, 105, 106, 109, 111, 113,
    124, 125, 128
Wexford, town, 60, 106
Whitby, N.R. Yorks., 90
Wicklow, county, 5, 18, 19, 21, 22,
    26, 28, 34, 35, 36, 43, 44,
    47, 50-8, 60, 81, 82, 105-11,
    109, 111, 131
Wicklow Gap, 52
Wicklow Mountains, 3, 12, 14, 16,
    17, 22, 25, 28, 29, 30, 39,
    40, 42, 50-8, 63, 105-11, 113,
    117, 133
Wicklow, town, 24, 44, 51, 52, 53,
    54, 105, 110, 111, 127
Wilde, Sir William, 1
William of Malmesbury, 120, 121
willow, 25, 87
window glazing, 112
Windsor, House of, 49
wine, 108; wine strainer, 31
Wolfhill, Co. Leix, 114
wolves, 25, 38
women, 35, 112-3, 129-30; see also
    marriage and *queens*
wood, implements, 36; vessels, 25,
    26, 87; for industries, 23
woodlands, see *forest*
wool, 108
writing, 32-3

Yellow Book of Lecan, 102
Yellow Book of Moling, 61; see also
    Book of Moling
yew, 25, 26
York, 27, 83, 95
Yregan, see *Iregan*

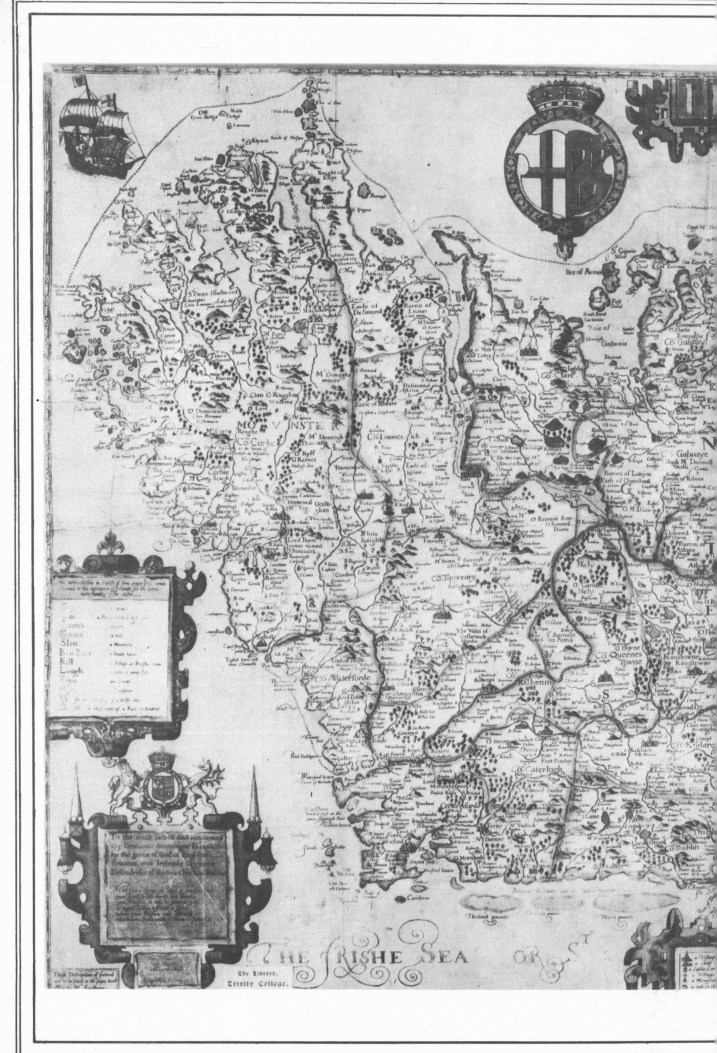